D1592029

Big Data and Learning Analytics in Higher Education

Ben Kei Daniel
Editor

Big Data and Learning Analytics in Higher Education

Current Theory and Practice

Editor
Ben Kei Daniel
University of Otago
Dunedin, New Zealand

ISBN 978-3-319-06519-9 ISBN 978-3-319-06520-5 (eBook)
DOI 10.1007/978-3-319-06520-5

Library of Congress Control Number: 2016947402

Printed on acid-free paper

This Springer imprint is published by Springer Nature
The registered company is Springer International Publishing AG Switzerland

This book is dedicated to one of my brothers, Mr. Lowo Joseph Daniel, who is thrilled with the idea of big data and analytics. I hope this book will inspire you Lowo to follow your dreams along this route.

Foreword

Educational data science (EDS) is an emergent interdisciplinary field of inquiry, which brings together computer science, education, statistics, and other social sciences to examine and understand social and technical phenomena. EDS researchers and practitioners utilize various sets of procedures and techniques to gather, organize, manipulate, and interpret rich educational data sources. EDS also presents techniques for merging voluminous and diverse data sources together, ensuring consistency of these data sets, and creating unified visualizations to aid in understanding of complex data. Further, in this field, educational data scientists build mathematical models and use them to communicate insights/findings to other educational specialists and scientists in their team and if required to nonexpert stakeholders.

As a subdiscipline of data science, EDS originated from discussions held during several workshops between years 2000 and 2007, mainly from the Educational Data Mining (EDM) Conference in 2008. EDM itself as a field of research is concerned with developing methods for exploring increasingly large-scale educational data, to better understand students and the settings in which they learn.

In the last years, other two international conferences were held, focusing on EDS themes. Learning and Knowledge Analytics (LAK2011) was the first conference, followed by Learning at Scale (L@S) in 2014. Lately, conferences in this area focus discourse on exploring the impact of big data and learning analytics in fostering learning and teaching and in engaging the growing community of researchers, practitioners, and learners within higher education to build tools, procedures, and techniques to explore and solve complex learning problems.

This book introduces the reader to two current topics in EDS, big data and learning analytics. Learning analytics examines the challenges of collecting, analyzing, and reporting data with the specific intent of improving student learning. Big data (BD), on the other hand, offers the potential to tackle a wide range of issues that appear when collecting and working with a large volume, variety, and velocity of data. Specifically, applying BD in education or learning at scale enables researchers to work with large numbers of students, where "large" is preferably thousands of students but can also apply to hundreds in in-person settings.

This book contains 15 chapters written by 32 international authors. It is organized into two parts: big data and learning analytics. Chapters cover both introduction, theory, limitations, methods, techniques, ethical considerations, recent trends, future research, case studies, and examples. They provide a comprehensive and full understanding of the current state of big data and learning analytics within higher education. The book is written in a simple style, making it accessible to undergraduate students and to other readers who might be interested in learning about big data and learning analytics within the realm of higher education. Because of the simplicity of presentation and illustrative nature of the issues presented, the book can serve both as an introductory text and as an advanced text for students, policymakers, and researchers interested in exploring issues related to these two current hot topics of EDS.

University of Cordoba
Córdoba, Spain

Cristóbal Romero

Acknowledgments

My research is funded by the Department of Higher Education Development Centre (HEDC), University of Otago, through the Performance-Based Research Fund (PBRF). I want to thank the university and the government of New Zealand for funding my research. I want to thank all contributors for sharing their research. Thanks go to my colleague, Russell Butson, for contributing early ideas that led to the development and maturity of the book. I want to express my sincere appreciation to the members of the Springer technical and editorial team, especially to Ms. Anitha Chellamuthu and Lakshmi Narayanan R of SPi Technologies for overseeing the project, as well as to the anonymous reviewers for their constructive insights that have significantly helped in improving the quality of work presented in this book. Thanks go to my wife Michelle Daniel, family, and friends for their continuous support while working on the book. Finally, to all who have contributed or inspired me in one way or another, while working on the project, I thank you!

Educational Technology
Higher Education Development Centre (HEDC)
University of Otago
Dunedin, New Zealand

Ben Kei Daniel

Acknowledgements

[illegible]

[illegible]

Contents

List of Contributors

About the Editor

Ben Kei Daniel is a senior lecturer in higher education and heads the Educational Technology Group at the University of Otago, New Zealand. Previously, Dr. Daniel was a lecturer and a senior health research and innovation analyst with the Office of the Associate Vice President Research-Health (University of Saskatchewan)/Vice President Research and Innovation (Saskatoon Health Region)—Saskatoon, Canada. For over a decade, Dr. Daniel taught undergraduate and postgraduate students, academic staff, and senior corporate executives on research methodologies, program evaluation and logic modeling, quality improvement, statistics and biostatistics, as well as advanced learning technologies. He has also widely published and consulted internationally on these subjects. His current research is focused generally on exploring the value of big data and learning analytics in influencing learning, teaching, and research in the context of higher education. He is also investigating theories and praxis of teaching research methodologies in higher education and the corporate sector.

Contributors

Russell Butson is a senior lecturer in higher education/educational technology at the University of Otago, New Zealand. His research is focused on the learning that takes place within the university setting. He is currently leading a research program that incorporates innovative topics and methods to explore, understand, and change our conceptions and approaches to academic learning. He is a pioneer in the use of digital devices and sensors to capture naturally occurring behavioral data (reality mining). His current research is focused on the role of information and communications technologies (ICT) in the academic development of faculty and students.

Vanessa Chang is director of learning design in Perth, Australia. Vanessa's research activities and interests in information systems are focused in the areas of leadership and governance in ICT and the use of systems, applications, and data in organizations. In addition to her information systems research, she is an active researcher in immersive learning in 3D virtual world environment, mobile learning, e-learning ecosystems, and learning analytics. She has also worked on a number of experiments in 3D virtual worlds in Second Life, OpenSim, OpenWonderland, and Unity. She has also collaborated with international researchers in teaching ERP/ SAP enterprise systems business process in a globalized context using 3D virtual worlds. She developed the Web-Based Learning Environment Instrument (WEBLEI), and this instrument is active in use and adopted by researchers and institutions around the world to assess the use and effectiveness of the online learning environments. She has published in ranked international journals and conference proceedings.

Mohamed Amine Chatti received the diploma degree in computer science from the University of Kaiserslautern, Germany, in 2004 and the Ph.D. degree in computer science from the RWTH Aachen University, Germany, in 2010. He is an assistant professor of computer science in the Learning Technologies Group (Informatik 9) at the RWTH Aachen University, Germany. His research focuses on web information systems, technology-enhanced learning, knowledge management, and data science.

Lei Chen received his Ph.D. in electrical and computer engineering from Purdue University, West Lafayette. He worked as an intern in the Palo Alto Research Center (PARC) during the summer of 2007. He is a senior research scientist in the R&D division at the Educational Testing Service (ETS) in Princeton, NJ. Before joining ETS, his research focused on using nonverbal communication cues, such as gestures and eye gazes, to support language processing. He has been involved in the NSF KDI project and DARPA ARDA VACE project to investigate multimodal signals, including speech, gestures, and eye gazes, used in human-to-human conversations. In the 2009 International Conference on Multimodal Interfaces (ICMI), he has won the Outstanding Paper Award sponsored by Google. After joining in ETS, he has been focusing on the automated assessment of spoken language by using speech recognition, natural language processing, and machine learning technologies. Since 2013, he has been working on utilizing a new generation of multimodal sensors, e.g., Microsoft's Kinect depth sensors, on learning and assessment tasks.

Simon Cross is lecturer at the Institute of Educational Technology at the Open University UK. His work is focused on several areas including assessment and badges, learning design, issues associated with adaptive and visualized learning, and open online learning. He is currently involved in several projects related to the OU's institutional assessment program. These range from review of institutional assessment practice to research into collaborative learning and student experiences of assessment. There are clear synergies here with learning design and learning analytics as is indicated by his research on the pedagogic uses of digital badges.

David C. Gibson is director of learning engagement at Curtin University in Perth, Australia. He works as a thought leader, educational researcher, learning scientist, professor, and innovator. With funding from the Australian Office for Learning and Teaching, National Science Foundation, US Department of Education, MacArthur Foundation, EDUCAUSE, and others, Gibson's research focuses on games and simulations in education, learning analytics, complex systems analysis, and the use of technology to personalize learning via cognitive modeling, design, and implementation. He has published ten books, 15 chapters, and over 60 articles and presentations on these topics. He is the creator of simSchool, a classroom flight simulator for preparing educators, and eFolio, an online performance-based assessment system, and provides vision and sponsorship for Curtin University's Challenge, a mobile, game-based learning platform.

Jiangang Hao is a research scientist at the Center for Advanced Psychometrics at ETS. He obtained both his Ph.D. in physics and M.A. in statistics from the University of Michigan. Prior to joining ETS, he has been working on modeling and mining terabyte-scale data in physics at the Fermi National Accelerator Laboratory. He works extensively on data mining and machine learning, statistical modeling and inference, data standardization, and data model schema design for big data. Jiangang published over 40 papers in peer-reviewed journals with over 2100 total citations. His work has been reported by leading technology media, such as Wired and MIT Technology Review. He created several widely used packages in Python and C++ for astronomical digital image analysis, measurement-error-corrected Gaussian mixture model, and probabilistic clustering analysis. Jiangang's current research centers on collaborative problem solving, game- and simulation-based assessment, educational data mining, and log file structuring and analysis. He is also applying natural language processing techniques to analyze the conversations in collaboration to develop an intelligent (adaptive) facilitating mechanism.

Tony Harland is a professor of higher education at the Higher Education Development Centre, University of Otago, New Zealand. Professor Harland studies the purposes of the contemporary university. Recent projects have examined the ways in which higher education is valued, how teaching values form an important part of a student's education, what critical theory has to offer to our thinking about university work and its relationship to society, and how students learn through doing research. He teaches qualitative research methods and other topics such as learning theory, leadership, and peer review.

Ángel Hernández-García holds an M.Sc. in telecommunications engineering, a master degree in SAP integrated information systems, and a Ph.D. in information systems from the Universidad Politécnica de Madrid. Ángel is assistant professor at the UPM's School of Telecommunications Engineering. Currently, Ángel's research lines cover information systems' acceptance and educational technologies, with special focus on learning analytics and educational data mining methods and applications. Ángel has been guest editor of and published research papers in international journals. He has also participated as chair in several international conferences and is member of the editorial board and reviewer for leading journals in the fields of technology-enhanced learning, information systems, and business.

Dirk Ifenthaler is a professor of instructional design and technology at the University of Mannheim, Germany, and adjunct professor at Deakin University and Curtin University, Australia. Professor Ifenthaler's previous roles include professor and director at the Centre for Research in Digital Learning at Deakin University, Australia, manager of applied research and learning analytics at Open Universities Australia, and professor for education and interim department chair at the University of Mannheim, Germany. He was a 2012 Fulbright scholar-in-residence at the Jeannine Rainbolt College of Education, at the University of Oklahoma, USA. Dirk's research outcomes include numerous coauthored books, book series, book chapters, journal articles, and international conference papers, as well as successful grant funding in Australia, Germany, and the USA. He is the editor-in-chief of the Springer journal *Technology, Knowledge and Learning*.

Kinshuk holds the NSERC/iCORE/Xerox/Markin research chair for adaptivity and personalization in informatics. He is also full professor in the School of Computing and Information Systems and associate dean of the Faculty of Science and Technology at Athabasca University, Canada. Areas of his research interests include learning analytics; learning technologies; mobile, ubiquitous, and location-aware learning systems; cognitive profiling; and interactive technologies.

Vivekanandan Kumar is associate professor in the School of Computing and Information Systems at Athabasca University. His research interests are in applications of causal modeling in big data and learning analytics, artificial intelligence in education, self-regulated learning, co-regulated learning, and mixed-initiative interactions using anthropomorphic pedagogical agents.

Jay Liebowitz is the distinguished chair of applied business and finance at Harrisburg University of Science and Technology. He previously was the Orkand endowed chair of management and technology in the graduate school at the University of Maryland University College (UMUC). He served as a professor in the Carey Business School at John Hopkins University. He was ranked #1 of the top ten knowledge management researchers/practitioners out of 11,000 worldwide and was ranked #2 in KM strategy worldwide according to the January 2010 *Journal of Knowledge Management*. At John Hopkins University, he was the founding program director for the graduate certificate in competitive intelligence and the capstone director of the MS-Information and Telecommunications Systems for Business Program. Prior to joining Hopkins, he was the first knowledge management officer at the NASA Goddard Space Flight Center. Professor Liebowitz is the founding editor-in-chief of *Expert Systems with Applications: An International Journal* (published by Elsevier).

Alexandra List is an assistant professor in the Department of Educational Psychology at Ball State University. Her research focuses on how learners use, integrate, and evaluate multiple textual sources, the impact of learner and task features on multiple source use, and process measures of online learning. She received her Ph.D. in educational psychology from the University of Maryland, College Park.

Lei Liu is a research scientist from the Learning Sciences Group at the Educational Testing Service. She is leading multiple projects focusing on the design of innovative and technology-rich science assessments that are competency based and NGSS aligned. Her research has drawn heavily on cognitive and socio-constructivist learning theories. Her research interest is on the role of technology in learning and assessing. She has developed simulation-based learning environment and assessments, learning progression-based assessments, conversation-based assessments, and collaborative problem-solving assessments. She has published numerous journal articles and book chapters in the field of assessment of complex scientific competencies, learning about complex systems, computer-supported collaborative learning, and learning sciences. She earned her Ph.D. from Rutgers University, and her dissertation won the Best Doctoral Research Award by the National Association of Research in Science Teaching.

Arham Muslim is a research assistant of computer science in the Learning Technologies Group (Informatik 9) at the RWTH Aachen University, Germany. He got his bachelor degree in software engineering from the University of Engineering and Technology, Taxila, Pakistan, in 2006 and a master degree in software systems engineering from the RWTH Aachen University, Germany, in 2011. His research focuses mainly on technology-enhanced learning, learning management systems, educational data mining, and learning analytics.

Denise Nadasen is the associate vice provost for institutional research at the University of Maryland University College (UMUC). For 3 years, she led a team of researchers who conducted data mining research at UMUC with a $1.2 million grant from the Kresge Foundation. She is currently working on her dissertation on student success in online learning. She received her master degree in measurement, statistics, and evaluation from the University of Maryland, College Park.

Shastri L. Nimmagadda has been an expert with the Schlumberger Company in Moscow, Russia, with more than 25 years of oilfield experience. Shastri, as a senior seismic interpreter, was involved with several exploration and field development onshore and offshore projects worldwide. Currently, Shastri is a research fellow with the big data group, School of Information Systems, Curtin Business School, Curtin University, Australia. He worked for several petroleum companies in India, Australia, Uganda, Kuwait, the UAE, Egypt, Malaysia, Indonesia, Colombia, and

Russia. His current research interests are multidimensional data modeling, data warehousing and mining, and data visualization and interpretation. He published and presented more than 80 research and technical papers, relevant to oil and gas exploration and information systems, in various international journals and conference proceedings. He successfully organized IEEE international conference tracks in Istanbul, Turkey, Dubai, the UAE, and Porto Alegre, Brazil. Shastri is a professional member of AIS, AAPG, SEG, SPE, IEEE, ASEG, IGU, and EAGE.

Geetha Paulmani is a freelancing researcher, interested in improving learning experience and learning outcomes of different kinds. She is currently associated with the OpenACRE (http://www.openacre.org) project as its Lean & Agile coach.

Vivek Perumal is a professional practical fellow in clinical anatomy in the Department of Anatomy at the Otago School of Medical Sciences, University of Otago, New Zealand. Previously, he worked at Manipal University, India, in a twinning program with the American University of Antigua. Vivek is an award-winning teacher recognized for his innovation in the use of learning technologies to enhance student learning in medical education. His current research interests are focused on clinical anatomy and medical education. He is currently pursuing a Ph.D. in clinical anatomy at the University of Otago.

Colin Pinnell is a student researcher at Athabasca University. His areas of research interests include artificial intelligence techniques and their correlation to neuroanatomy, augmented reality and its application in human–computer interfaces, self-regulated learning, co-regulated learning, and pattern detection in big data.

Paul Prinsloo is a research professor in open distance and e-learning at the University of South Africa (Unisa). An overview of his research outputs indicates a wide interest with as leitmotif an interest in student success and retention in distribution learning environments whether relating to curriculum development, the use of technology, different disciplinary contexts, or conceptual modeling. Since 2012, his research focuses mainly on learning analytics and postgraduate supervision. He has published widely and presented at numerous international conferences. He holds a range of academic qualifications including theology, art history, business management, online learning, and religious studies.

Bart Rienties is a reader in learning analytics at the Institute of Educational Technology at the Open University UK. He is program director of learning analytics within IET and chair of the Analytics4Action project, which focuses on evidence-based research on intervention on OU modules to enhance student experience. As educational psychologist, he conducts multidisciplinary research on work-based and collaborative learning environments and focuses on the role of social interaction in learning, which is published in leading academic journals and books. His primary research interests are focused on learning analytics, computer-supported collaborative learning, and the role of motivation in learning.

Lynne D. Roberts is the director of higher education research in the Faculty of Health Sciences at Curtin University in Perth, Australia. Lynne's interest in the ethical issues associated with learning analytics builds on previous research on techno-ethics and online research ethics.

Amit Rudra is a lecturer in the School of Information Systems at the Curtin Business School. Amit has extensive experience in tertiary education and in software development including database management systems and computer-aided learning (CAL) systems. As part of his role as an academic, he has collaborated with overseas (Norway, Japan) academics which resulted in several publications in international journal and high-level conferences. As part of his research portfolio, he has published a research book based on his research studies in decision support systems including data warehousing, data mining, and parallel processing. Currently, he is in the process of coauthoring a research book on business intelligence including business analytics and big data.

Ulrik Schroeder is a professor of computer science at the RWTH Aachen University. He heads the Learning Technologies Group. He is also the head of the Center for Innovative Learning Technology (CiL) and the director of the school laboratory for computer science (InfoSphere) at the RWTH Aachen University. His research interests include assessment and intelligent feedback, mobile learning, gender mainstreaming in education, and computer science teacher education.

Sharon Slade is a senior lecturer in the Faculty of Business and Law at the Open University. Her research interests encompass ethical issues in learning analytics. She has recently led work to develop a university-wide student support framework to improve retention and progression and a tool which identifies students based on characteristics and study behaviors and triggers relevant and targeted interventions. In addition, she has led the development of a new policy around the ethical use of learning analytics at the Open University and is an academic lead for the analytics project. Recent research includes papers and chapters establishing an ethical framework for the use of learning analytics within higher education, examining the concept of educational triage and broader issues around an ethics of care.

Ignacio Suárez-Navas holds an M.Sc. in telecommunications engineering from the Universidad Politécnica de Madrid. His master's thesis covered the study and development of Moodle web services for the analysis of social interactions in online courses. Ignacio currently works as a programmer at Scotland's National Tourism Organization. His main interests include the development and deployment of web services and applications. Ignacio is also involved in innovative personal projects focused on mobile applications and services.

Alina A. von Davier is a senior research director and leader of the Center for Advanced Psychometrics at ETS. She also is an adjunct professor at Fordham University. At ETS, von Davier is responsible for developing a team of experts and a psychometric research agenda in support of a next generation of assessments. Computational psychometrics, which include machine learning and data mining techniques, Bayesian inference methods, stochastic processes, and psychometric models, are the main set of tools employed in her current work. She also works with psychometric models applied to educational testing: test score equating methods, item response theory models, and adaptive testing. She published several books, authored or edited; she also published numerous papers in peer-reviewed journals.

Diego Zapata-Rivera is a senior research scientist in the Cognitive Science Research Group at the Educational Testing Service. He earned a Ph.D. in computer science (with a focus on artificial intelligence in education) from the University of Saskatchewan in 2003. His research focuses on innovations in score reporting and technology-enhanced assessment, including work on assessment-based learning environments and game-based assessments. His research interests also include evidence-centered design, Bayesian student modeling, open student models, conversation-based assessments, virtual communities, and authoring tools. He has published numerous articles and has been a committee member and organizer of international conferences and workshops in his research areas. He is a member of the editorial board of the *User Modeling and User-Adapted Interaction* journal and an associate editor of the *IEEE Transactions on Learning Technologies* journal. Most recently, Dr. Zapata-Rivera has been invited to contribute his expertise to projects sponsored by the National Research Council, the National Science Foundation, the Army Research Laboratory, and NASA.

Zdenek Zdrahal is professor of knowledge engineering at the Knowledge Media Institute at the Open University UK. His research interests include the application of AI in design, case-based reasoning, information extraction, predictive modeling, machine learning, and knowledge sharing. He is the founder of one of the leading analytics tools at the Open University UK, OU Analyse.

Chapter 1
Overview of Big Data and Analytics in Higher Education

Ben Kei Daniel

Overview

Our interactions with digital technologies in various spaces and time continue to generate a large amount of data. Big Data describes the significant growth in volume and variety of data that is no longer possible to manage using traditional databases. With the help of analytics, these seemingly disparate and heterogeneous quantities of data can be processed for patterns, which can in turn engender useful insights critical for decision-making. Business organisations are starting to systematically understand and explore how to process and analyse these vast array of data to improve decision-making.

Big Data might not be a new phenomenon in many fields, after many scientists notably those at the European Organization for Nuclear Research (CERN) [http://home.cern/] have worked with a large amount of data for a longer period of time even prior to the invention of the World Wide Web in 1989. The major difference between the forms of data in the past and those we know today is the increased availability and access. In addition, the growing forms of unstructured data, generated by social media and mobile and ubiquitous computing devices, can be combined with other forms of structured data to reveal useful insights. Further, in the business sector, there is an increasing emphasis on data as a form of currency and competitive advantage.

Although Big Data and analytics are sometimes treated as one integral concept, analytics generally refers to a set of software tools, machine-learning techniques and algorithms used for capturing, processing, indexing, storing, analysing and visualising data. According to Norris, Baer, and Offerman (2009), analytics enables

B.K. Daniel (✉)
Educational Technology, Higher Education Development Centre,
University of Otago, Dunedin, New Zealand
e-mail: ben.daniel@otago.ac.nz

B. Kei Daniel (ed.), *Big Data and Learning Analytics in Higher Education*,
DOI 10.1007/978-3-319-06520-5_1

us to engage in a process of data assessment and measurement and is aimed at improving the performance of individuals or institutions. Mayer (2009) noted that the increase in attention to analytics is also driven by advances in computation.

Data-Driven Decision-Making

Decision-making has always been one of the most important roles in the higher education sector. However, in an atmosphere of internal and external pressures on higher education, it has become imperative that decisions be based on evidence instead of intuition or experience alone. The epoch of grounding decisions on evidence is a key determinant of successful and sustainable performance. Additionally, with rapid advances in technologies, the large part of making decision involves extracting information from a variety of data sources.

The deployment of Big Data techniques in higher education can be transformative, altering the existing processes of administration, teaching, learning and academic work (Baer & Campbell, 2011; Ellaway, Pusic, Galbraith, & Cameron, 2014; Eynon, 2013; Long & Siemen, 2011); contributing to policy and practice outcomes, and helping institutions address contemporary challenges (Atif, Richards, Bilgin, & Marrone, 2013; Daniel & Butson, 2014). With large volumes of student information, including enrolment, academic and disciplinary records, institutions of higher education have the data sets needed to benefit from targeted analytics that can reveal useful for decision-making. However, the biggest challenge is no longer whether or not institutions use data but how data is captured, processed, stored, presented and used to make better decisions and how decisions made today are likely to affect tomorrow's outcomes.

The contributions of Big Data and analytics to the landscape of higher education can be understood at fundamentally three—micro, meso and macro levels. At micro level, Big Data and analytics will help institutions improve the quality of learning and teaching while streamlining processes and reducing administrative workload. Furthermore, analytics can be applied to understand learning at student behaviours level. For instance, when students interact with learning technologies, they leave behind data trails which can reveal their sentiments, social connections, intentions and goals. Researchers can use such data to examine patterns of student performance over time—from one semester to another or from one year to another—and develop rigorous data modelling and analysis to reveal the obstacles to student access and usability and to evaluate any attempts at intervention.

On the meso level, matters relating to efficacy of programme performance such as improvement in graduate rates and graduate satisfaction can be addressed. Further, with mounting pressure on institutions to constantly report to multiple stakeholders (government, public and others) on key performance indicators (KPIs), Big Data techniques can be used to harness available data to provide a broad macro [scopic] view of institutional performances and accountability and identify areas that need particular attention.

While the benefits of Big Data and analytics might appear obvious, the added value will come from the ability to develop and deploy robust models that can adequately capture and assess the present state of performance, as well as accurately predict future outcomes. Daniel (2015) broadly categorised models that can be developed from Big Data into descriptive, predictive and prescriptive.

Descriptive models are grounded in the analysis of transactional and interactional data about teaching or learning. They can be used to identify trends such as student enrolment, graduation rates and patterns likely to trigger important dialogue on improving student learning. The presentation of descriptive models alone is inadequate. Institutions need to be able to examine their present performances and be able to predict future outcomes.

Predictive models provide institutions with the ability to uncover hidden relationships in data and predict future outcomes with a certain degree of accuracy. For instance, they enable institutions to identify students who are exhibiting risky behaviours during their academic programme.

Prescriptive models are actionable tools built based on insights gained from both descriptive and predictive models. They are intended to help institutions to accurately assess their current situation and make informed choices on alternative course of events based on valid and consistent predictions.

Since data inherent in Big Data is highly heterogeneous, ability to control access and usage will become a major concern. Issues of governance, privacy, security and ethics of user-generated data are what concerns many researchers in higher education. Moreover, Big Data, as a set of data presented in the form of text, graphics, audio and visual content, is often incomplete and unstructured, which poses additional challenges in extracting useful insights from it. Research on Big Data and learning analytics in higher education is at its infancy. This book brings together early work in the area. The chapters presented in the book cover both breadth and depth of issues related to this growing area of inquiry.

Book Audience

This book is primarily intended for researchers, technology professionals and policymakers in higher education. The book can also be used in postgraduate programmes in Educational Technology, Education, Computer Science, Information Sciences and related subjects. Since this is the first research book in the area, it hopes to advance thinking in the area and help researchers to think about issues that need further analysis as Big Data and analytics continue to permeate into the landscape of higher education.

Organisation of the Book

The book contains 15 chapters organised into two parts. Part I (Big Data) consists of seven chapters focused on analysis of current trends, theory, opportunities and challenges associated with Big Data. In Chap. 2, trends and future research perspectives on Big Data in higher education are discussed. Chapter 3 examines the conceptual foundations of Big Data as a field of inquiry in higher education. In Chap. 4, authors propose new methods and techniques on research methodology education to tackle the challenges of Big Data. Chapter 5 provides an example of a large-scale implementation and management of embedded digital ecosystem and discusses its relevance to higher education context. Chapter 6 presents the contemporary landscape of the research university and describes how new digital technologies have influenced research, teaching and learning and caution additional challenges Big Data might bring to the research university's environment. These concerns are further echoed in Chap. 7, where ethical considerations in collection and use of data are discussed, and Chap. 8 extends the discussions to include ethics of care and justice.

In Part II (Learning Analytics) eight chapters on different aspects of learning analytics research are presented. Starting with Chap. 9, an overview of learning analytics within the Big Data paradigm is presented. Chapter 10 reports on a framework guiding the implementation of learning analytics. Chapter 11 presents a web service application for learning analytics in Moodle. Chapter 12 discusses a research project on open learning analytics. In Chap. 13, authors provide an example of a large-scale implementation of a learning analytics project that utilises predictive modelling on student success in a degree programme. Chapter 14 provides a case on the use of learning analytics in the assessment of science skills within an immersive learning environment. Chapter 15 concludes the book with a presentation of an ongoing research into the use of learning analytics in an informal learning environment.

References

Atif, A., Richards, D., Bilgin, A., & Marrone, M. (2013). Learning analytics in higher education: A summary of tools and approaches. Retrieved October 13, from http://www.ascilite.org/conferences/sydney13/program/papers/Atif.pdf.

Baer, L., & Campbell, J. (2011). *Game changers*. EDUCAUSE. Retrieved March 24, 2014, from http://net.educause.edu/ir/library/pdf/pub72034.pdf.

Daniel, B. (2015). Big data and analytics in higher education: Opportunities and challenges. *British Journal of Educational Technology, 46*, 904–920. doi:10.1111/bjet.12230.

Daniel, B., & Butson, R. (2014, September). *Foundations of big data and analytics in higher education*. In International conference on analytics driven solutions: ICAS2014 (p. 39). Academic Conferences Limited.

Ellaway, R. H., Pusic, M. V., Galbraith, R. M., & Cameron, T. (2014). Developing the role of big data and analytics in health professional education. *Medical Teacher, 36*(3), 216–222.

Eynon, R. (2013). The rise of Big Data: What does it mean for education, technology, and media research? *Learning, Media and Technology, 38*(3), 237–240.

Long, P., & Siemen, G. (2011). Penetrating the fog: Analytics in learning and education. *EDUCAUSE Review, 46*(5), 30–40.

Mayer, M. (2009). Innovation at Google: The physics of data [PARC forum]. Retrieved 11 August, 2009, from http://www.slideshare.net/PARCInc/innovation-at-google-the-physics-of-data.

Norris, D., Baer, L., & Offerman, M. (2009). A national agenda for action analytics. In: National Symposium on Action Analytics, St. Paul, MN. Retrieved September 2009, from http://lindabaer.efoliomn.com/uploads/settinganationalagendaforactionanalytics101509.pdf.

Part I
BIG DATA

Chapter 2
Thoughts on Recent Trends and Future Research Perspectives in Big Data and Analytics in Higher Education

Jay Liebowitz

Abstract In many sectors, including education, the growth of data has been increasing dramatically over the years. In order to make sense of this data and improve decision-making, analytics and intuition-based decision-making should be key components in this "Big Data" era. Educational data mining and learning analytics are becoming the lingua franca for those institutions who seek to improve their strategic and operational decision-making abilities. This chapter highlights some thoughts in these areas.

Keywords Learning analytics • Big Data • Educational data mining • Intuition • Decision-making

Big Data Ahead

Many sectors are facing the onslaught of massive amounts, speeds, and varieties of data for organizational consumption. Jagadish et al. (2014) states that:

> We have entered an era of Big Data. Many sectors of our economy are now moving to a data-driven decision making model where the core business relies on analysis of large and diverse volumes of data that are continually being produced. (p. 86)

Data growth in some sectors like healthcare, education, and others are growing as much as 35 % a year (Liebowitz, 2013, 2014a, 2014b). The SAS Institute predicts that there will be a 240 % growth by 2017 for employees needed to handle Big Data tasks. Gartner predicts that by 2017, cloud-empowered chief marketing officers

J. Liebowitz (✉)
Harrisburg University of Science and Technology, 326 Market Street, Harrisburg, PA 17101, USA
e-mail: jliebowitz@harrisburgu.edu

B. Kei Daniel (ed.), *Big Data and Learning Analytics in Higher Education*, DOI 10.1007/978-3-319-06520-5_2

(CMOs) will spend more on IT than chief information officers (CIOs) do (Gorenberg, 2014).

We are already seeing a variety of analytics applications targeting the CMO such as optimizing cross-channel influences between online and offline marketing (e.g., OptiMine) and increasing mobile app users' loyalty and conversion rate tied to corporate customer relationship management (e.g., FollowAnalytics) (Gorenberg, 2014). According to the 2014 Big Data in Retail Study, commissioned by 1010 data, 96 % of the respondents, all of them executives in retailing, think Big Data is important in keeping retailers competitive.

No matter where you turn, Big Data will have an impact. The education sector is no different. Lane (2014) points this out in his edited book about how to build a smarter university through Big Data, Analytics, and Innovation. Whether looking at student success measures, student retention, learning outcomes, or other educational metrics, the use of analytics and predictive modeling can be an asset to navigate through these Big Data waters. The Aberdeen Research Group, in their 2014 business intelligence (BI) in Retail Industry survey of over 200 retail companies, showed that to move from Industry Average to Best-in-Class, the following actions are recommended: (1) implement data integration and cleansing tools, (2) aggregate and clean your data, (3) institute BI application development procedures, and (4) create a continued education training program for BI users (in fact, many organizations have a BI competency center (BICC) for this purpose).

In the same research study, in order to improve as a best-in-class company, the following should be done: (1) improve exception reporting, (2) adopt scorecards to measure and track performance, and (3) update all data, dashboards, and reports in real-time across all channels. In many ways, universities and colleges can apply these suggestions in their own "business." In the following paragraphs, we will identify some important Big Data and Analytics techniques, trends, and research issues as related to the education sector. Hopefully, this will provide a platform for further investigation into these areas.

BI/Analytics Conceptual Framework

Before delving into some targeted areas for future development, it may be helpful to develop a BI/analytics conceptual framework to allow students and faculty to further test and validate. To date, there have been very few, if any, conceptual frameworks in the BI/analytics area—no matter what sector is explored. Liebowitz (2014c), based on his research and best practices in the BI/Analytics area, proposes the following conceptual framework as shown in Fig. 2.1 for further testing and enhancement.

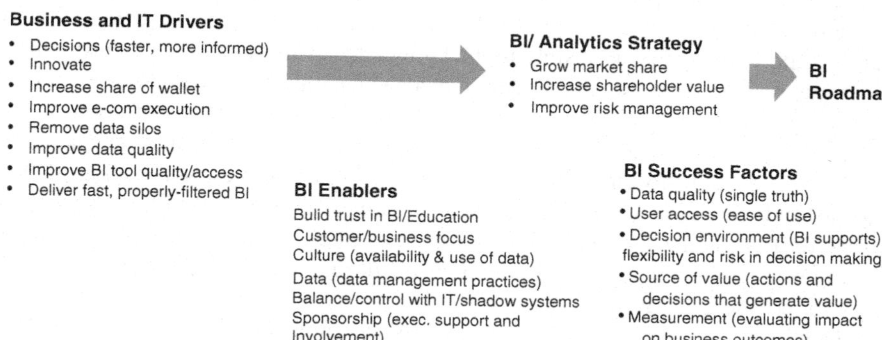

Fig. 2.1 BI/analytics conceptual framework (Liebowitz, 2014c)

The framework shows that there are business and IT drivers that influence the BI/analytics strategy of the organization. There are also BI enablers that impact how successful is the BI/Analytics strategy. As part of the framework, there are BI Success Factors that can be used to derive value from the BI/Analytics strategy. Last, a BI road map (typically 3 years) is built based upon the strategy. This conceptual framework is fairly generic across industries, although there may be some different factors in each area.

Adaptive Learning/Courseware and Educational Data Mining

Adaptive learning/courseware and educational data mining are interesting areas that continue to evolve over the recent years (Chen, Chiang, & Storey, 2012; Siemens & Baker, 2012). Adaptive learning is often equated with personalized e-learning, adaptive courseware, and intelligent tutoring systems. Grubisic (2013) presents a fairly recent review of the literature in these areas. In reviewing the literature, adaptive learning as pertains to e-learning often involves the WHERE-WHY-WHAT-HOW for adaptation—that is, the adaptive system (WHERE), adapting goals (WHY), focus of adaptation (WHAT), and adaptation methods and techniques (HOW). Grubisic (2013) found 5924 papers that relate to either adaptive e-learning systems, intelligent tutoring systems, courseware generation, courseware sequencing, automatic courseware, dynamic courseware, adaptive courseware, or automatic generation of courseware. Twenty-one percent (21 %) of the papers are related to adaptive e-learning systems. For adaptive e-learning systems, two main approaches are used to achieve adaptability (macro- and micro-adaptation). The macro-adaptation occurs before the learning and teaching process, whereby data about a student's cognitive abilities are collected, and then this information drives the type of learning environment and instruction that will best suit those decisions (Grubisic, 2013).

Micro-adaptation occurs during the learning and teaching process, whereby the learning approaches vary according to the knowledge of the student user during the e-learning session. This latter approach may also be called "personalized learning." According to Garrido and Onaindia (2013), some of the challenges of e-learning include selecting the proper learning objects, defining their relationships, and adapting their sequencing to the student's specific needs, objectives, and background. Garrido and Onaindia (2013) developed an approach for assembling learning objects for personalized learning through artificial intelligence (AI) planning. They apply metadata labeling and an AI planning/scheduling technical mapping methodology for course generation.

Educational data mining is related to adaptive learning and is focused on uncovering hidden patterns and relationships to drive student learning outcomes (Romero, Ventura, Pechenizkiy, & Baker, 2011). For example, the University of Maryland University College (UMUC), Kresge Foundation grant applies data mining to identify the critical "at-risk" transfer students in the first or second semester of their UMUC programs in order to provide the necessary support services to help them succeed toward graduation, as explained shortly. Pena-Ayala (2013) performed a recent review of the educational data mining (EDM) field by examining 240 EDM papers from 2010 through the first quarter of 2013.

Usually, descriptive or predictive approaches are applied to EDM. In terms of future trends, EDM modules may become more integrated within the typical architecture of an educational system. Also, the educational environment must continue to advance the notion of data-based decision-making, which highlights the importance of Big Data and Analytics in an educational environment. Last, from a technology viewpoint, EDM will be enhanced by advances in social networks, web and text mining, virtual 3-D environments, spatial mining, semantic mining, collaborative learning, Big Data architectures, and other technology areas (Pena-Ayala, 2013).

Example: Data Mining and Data Integration: A Community College and University Partnership to Improve Transfer Student Success Funded by the Kresge Foundation (Nadasen, 2013)

An interesting 3-year, $1.2 million Kresge educational data mining grant was pursued at the University of Maryland University College (UMUC). The UMUC, Prince George's Community College, and Montgomery College collaborated to build an integrated database to make data-driven decisions on how to improve student success. The students are working adults who enrolled at a community college, then transferred to UMUC. Data mining techniques and statistical analyses were used to analyze the integrated data to identify relationships among variables.

The research objectives were:

- Prepare an integrated database with collaborative community college partners.
- Identify success and failure factors using data mining techniques.
- Build predictive models using statistical analysis and results from data mining.
- Build student profiles and implement models for decision-making.
- Track the impact on retention and graduation.

UMUC is an online institution that enrolls over 90,000 students each year worldwide. The Prince George's Community College (PGCC) is located within 2 miles of UMUC's Academic Center and transfers over 37,000 students. The Montgomery College (MC) is located within 10 miles of UMUC's largest regional center and enrolls over 35,000 students. Through the collaborative data-sharing process, the integrated database contains information on over 11,000 students who transferred from PGCC to UMUC and over 10,000 students transferred from MC. The Data Exchange was set up as follows:

- A memorandum of understanding (MOU) governed the data-sharing agreement and the protection of individual student data. The data were restricted to four researchers who were funded by the Kresge Foundation and UMUC.
- Historic course information on students identified as UMUC transfer students were provided by the community colleges using a secured transfer process.
- Data were stored in a UMUC database located on an Oracle Exadata machine.
- The database contains millions of records on student demographics, courses, and online classroom activities.

Figures 2.2, 2.3, and 2.4 show the tools used in this educational data mining application, as well as the interactions and datasets used.

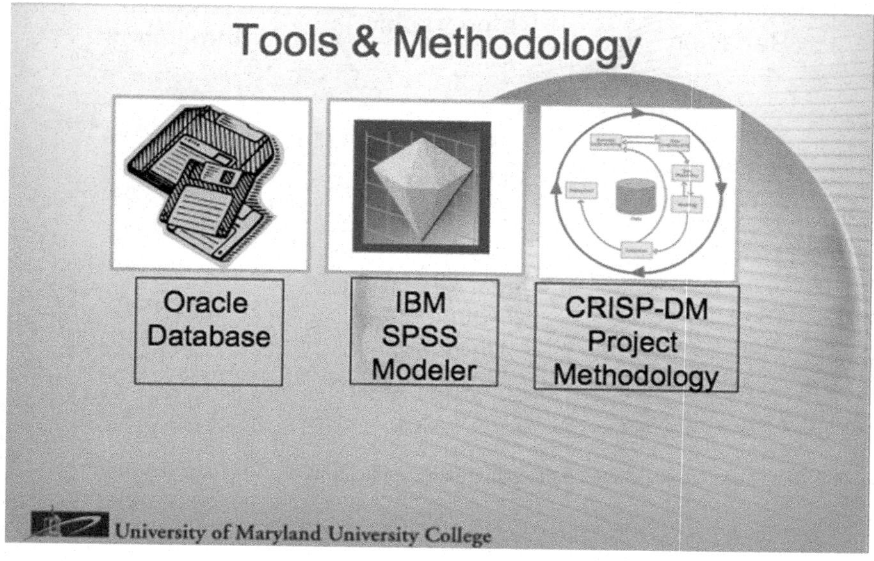

Fig. 2.2 Tools and methodology

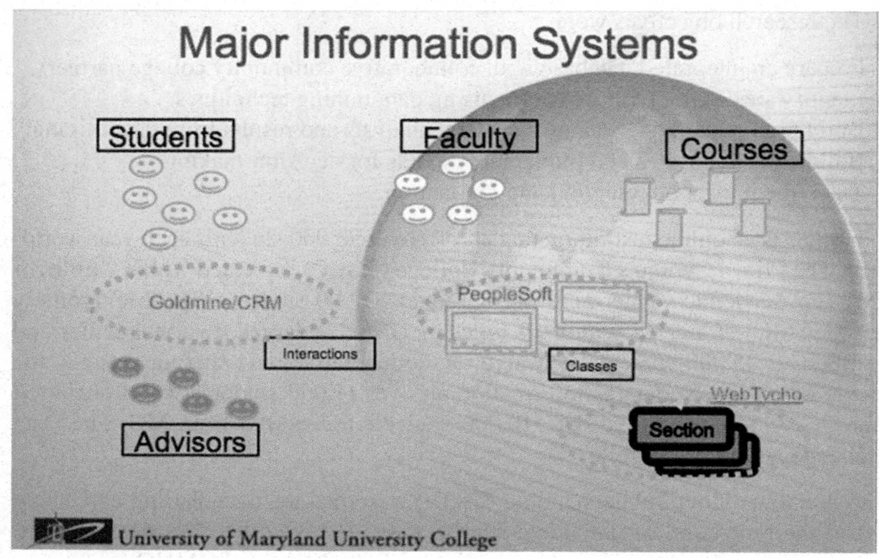

Fig. 2.3 Major information systems used (note: WebTycho was our learning management system (LMS))

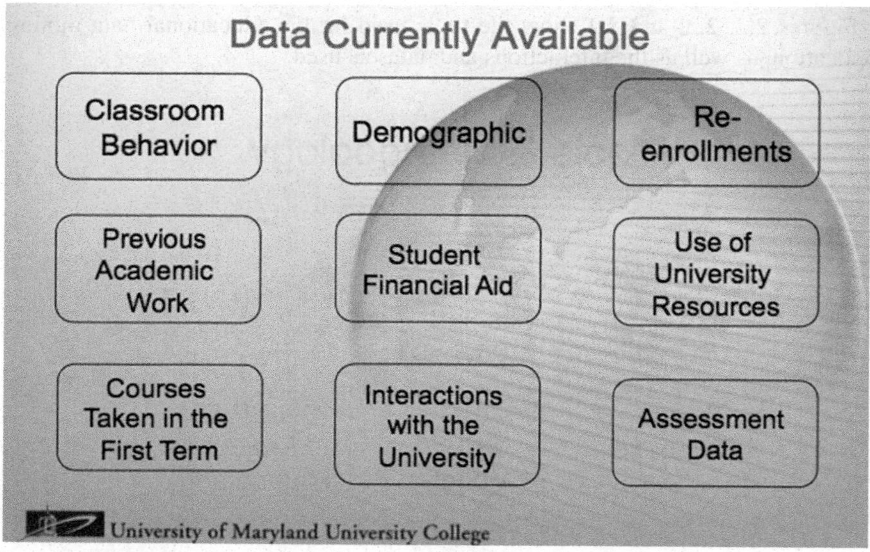

Fig. 2.4 Data currently available in the data mining application

Selected results from this data mining application showed that course-taking behavior prior to transfer influences success at the subsequent institution. Also, online classroom activity prior to the first day of class can predict course success.

Faculty engagement is critical for course/student success. A Civitas pilot, with our data, predicted with 85 % confidence how successful a transfer student would be in their UMUC program within 8 days of starting their program (Nadasen, 2013).

Data Visualization and Visual Analytics

The old adage still holds true—a picture is worth a thousand words. Especially, for C-level executives, data visualization is paramount for understandability and a quick grasp of the analytics/Big Data results. No matter whether it's a CEO of a company or a university president, the analytics results must be displayed in a manner that is easy to understand. Executive dashboards (such as through the popular Tableau Software) are one way to apply data visualization on the analytics results.

One of the key areas of growth in the educational Big Data/analytics field is the use of visual analytics. SAS, probably the leading tool vendor for analytics on the market worldwide, has SAS Visual Analytics as a fairly new feature within its software toolset. Figure 2.5 shows an example of a student analysis using SAS Visual Analytics (of course, there is an interactive component which is hard to see from this static figure).

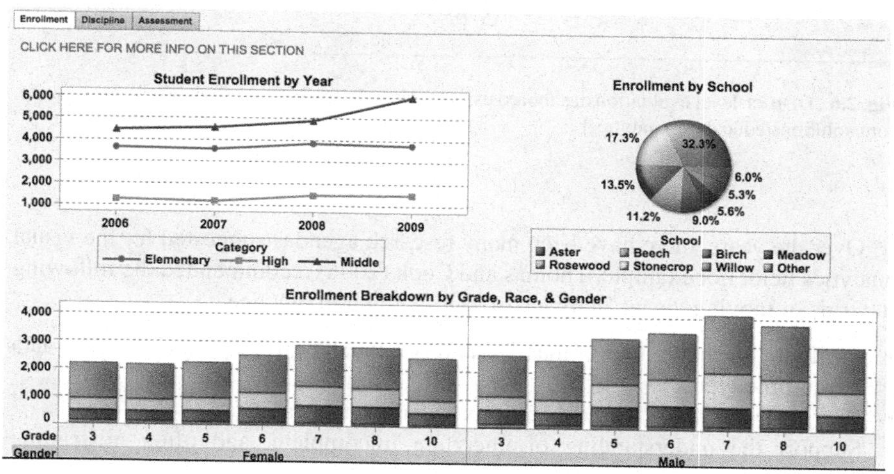

Fig. 2.5 K-12 student analysis using SAS Visual Analytics [http://www.sas.com/software/visual-analytics/demos/k12-student-analysis.html]

Figure 2.6 shows an example using Tableau Software (www.tableau.com) in terms of a district-level evaluation dashboard comparing student scores with meal plans over time.

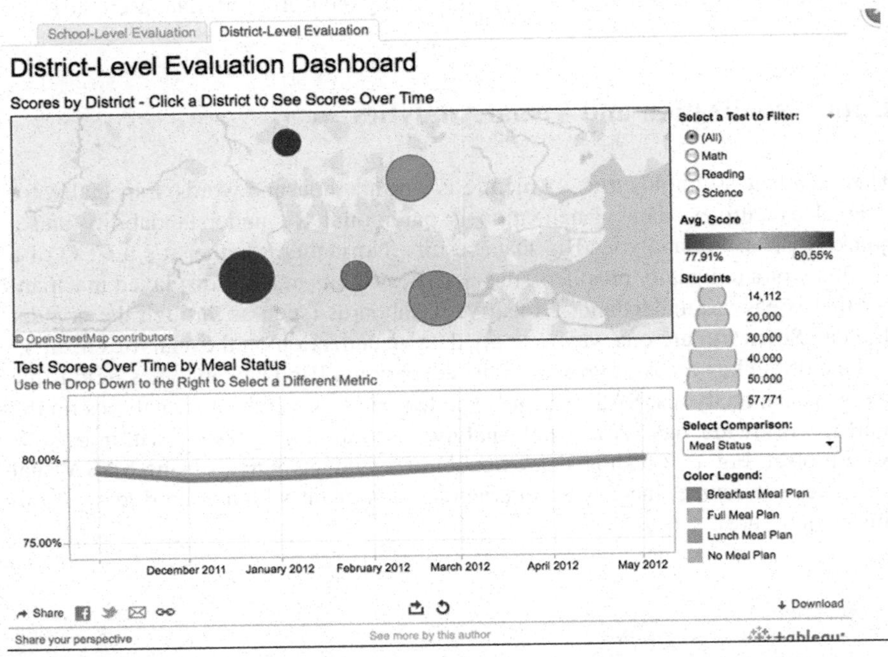

Fig. 2.6 District-level evaluation dashboard using Tableau Software [http://www.tableausoftware.com/solutions/education-analytics]

Over the years, there have been many research agendas suggested for the visual analytics field. For example, Thomas and Cook (2006) recommended the following in terms of moving visual analytics from research into practice:

- Facilitate understanding of massive and continually growing collections of data of multiple types.
- Provide frameworks for analyzing spatial and temporal data.
- Support the understanding of uncertain, incomplete, and often misleading information.
- Provide user- and task-adaptable guided representations that enable full situation awareness while supporting development of detailed actions.
- Support multiple levels of data and information abstraction, including integration of different types of information into a single representation.

- To accelerate the transition of research into analytical practice, the R&D community must:
  - Develop an infrastructure to facilitate evaluation of new visual analytics technologies.
  - Create and use a common security and privacy infrastructure, incorporating privacy-supporting technologies such as data minimization and data anonymization.
  - Use a component-based software development approach for visual analytics software to facilitate evaluation of research results in integrated prototypes and deployment of promising components in diverse operational environments.
  - Identify and publicize the best practices for inserting visual analytics technologies into operational environments.

Many organizations, such as the Educause and the Knowledge Media Institute (UK), are looking at how visual analytics can be improved in the education environment. For example, Educause's Learning Analytics Initiative has been looking partly at how visual analytics play a key role in education [http://simon.buckinghamshum.net/2012/04/educause-learning-analytics-talk/]. The Catalyst project at the Knowledge Media Institute augments existing social media platforms with web-based annotation tools, recommenders to help users prioritize attention, online creativity triggers, interactive visualizations, and social network and deliberation analytics [http://kmi.open.ac.uk/projects/name/catalyst]. Certainly, in the years ahead, data visualization and visual analytics will continue to evolve and further allow the decision-maker to analyze data in immersive environments and interactive gaming scenarios.

Knowledge Management in Education

Another important area that we will see increased attention deals with knowledge management issues in education, especially as Big Data and analytics continue to evolve. Knowledge management (KM) refers to how best to leverage knowledge internally and externally in an organization (Liebowitz, 2012a, 2012b). More specifically, it deals with knowledge retention and transfer issues, and organizations are applying knowledge management to increase innovation, build the institutional memory of the organization, allow for adaptability and agility, and improve organizational internal and external effectiveness.

In the education field, there are organizations like the Institute for the Study of Knowledge Management in Education (http://www.iskme.org/) whose mission is to improve the practice of continuous learning, collaboration, and change in the education sector. At the Vanderbilt University Medical Center, their Knowledge Management Informatics Center provides high-level data and knowledge organization skills to optimize the enterprise clinical, research, and educational initiatives [http://www.mc.vanderbilt.edu/km/]. The Notre Dame of Maryland University has a new Master of Science in Analytics in Knowledge Management to look at the synergies between knowledge management and analytics [http://www.ndm.edu/academics/school-of-arts-and-sciences/programs/ms-in-knowledge-management/]. We are also seeing a variety of applications of applying knowledge management with e-learning (Liebowitz & Frank, 2010). There is even a relatively new journal from the Faculty of Education in the University of Hong Kong titled *Knowledge Management & E-Learning* [http://www.kmel-journal.org/ojs/].

The 2014 Horizon Report reports short-, mid-, and long-term trends in higher education. One of the six key trends cited is the "Rise of Data-Driven Learning and Assessment," as a midrange trend in driving changes in higher education within 3–5 years [http://cdn.nmc.org/media/2014-nmc-horizon-report-he-EN-SC.pdf]. Here again, the synergy between Big Data, analytics, and knowledge management becomes apparent. For example, the confluence of these areas may produce a strategy to identify "at-risk" students through assessment of critical knowledge areas and competencies via looking at hidden patterns and relationships in large masses of student data and other databases. Coupled with this data-driven approach should be the application of intuition-based decision-making (Liebowitz, 2014b), formed through experiential learning.

Summary

The years ahead look bright for the application of Big Data and analytics in higher education. Certainly, adaptive/personalized learning, educational data mining, data visualization, visual analytics, knowledge management, and blended/e-learning will continue to play growing roles to better inform higher education officials and teachers. And of course, analytics plus intuition should equal success as decision-makers apply "rational intuition" in their education challenges and opportunities.

References

Chen, H. Chiang, R. H. L., & Storey, V. C. (Eds.). (2012, December). Special issue on "business intelligence and analytics: from big data to big impact". *MIS Quarterly, 36*(4).

Garrido, A., & Onaindia, E. (2013). Assembling learning objects for personalized learning: An AI planning perspective. *IEEE Intelligent Systems., 28*, 64–73.

Gorenberg, M. (2014). Investing in analytics: Optimizing the data economy. IEEE Computer.

Grubisic, A. (2013). Adaptive courseware: A literature review. *Journal of Universal Computer Science, 21*(9), 1168–1209.

Jagadish, H., Gehrke, J., Labrinidis, A., Papakonstantinou, Y., Patel, J., Ramakrishnan, R., et al. (2014). Big data and its technical challenges. *Communications of the ACM, 57*(7), 86–94.

Lane, J. (Ed.). (2014). *Building a smarter university: Big data, innovation, and analytics*. Albany, NY: SUNY Press.

Liebowitz, J. (Ed.). (2012a). *Knowledge management handbook: Collaboration and social networking* (2nd ed.). Boca Raton, FL: CRC Press.

Liebowitz, J. (Ed.). (2012b). *Beyond knowledge management: What every leader should know*. New York: Taylor & Francis.

Liebowitz, J. (Ed.). (2013). *Big data and business analytics*. New York: Taylor & Francis.

Liebowitz, J. (Ed.). (2014a). *Business analytics: An introduction*. New York: Taylor & Francis.

Liebowitz, J. (Ed.). (2014b). *Bursting the big data bubble: The case for intuition-based decision making*. New York: Taylor & Francis.

Liebowitz, J. (2014c). *"Editorial: A conceptual framework for business intelligence/analytics", submitted to INFORMS Analytics*.

Liebowitz, J., & Frank, M. (Eds.). (2010). *Knowledge management and E-learning*. New York: Taylor & Francis.

Nadasen, D. (2013). *"Data mining and data integration: A community college and university partnership to improve transfer student success" summary slides*. Adelphi, MD: University of Maryland University College, Office of Institutional Research.

Pena-Ayala, A. (2013). Educational data mining: A review of recent works and a data mining-based analysis of the state-of-the-art, Expert Systems With Applications: An Int. Journal, Elsevier.

Romero, C., Ventura, S., Pechenizkiy, M., & Baker, R. (Eds.). (2011). *Handbook on educational data mining*. Boca Raton, FL: CRC Press.

Siemens, G., & Baker, R. (2012). Learning analytics and educational data mining: towards communication and collaboration. In *Proceedings of the 2nd Int. Conference on Learning Analytics and Knowledge, Association for Computing Machinery (ACM)*.

Thomas, J., & Cook, K. (2006). A visual analytics agenda. *IEEE Computer Graphics and Applications, 26*(1), 10–13.

Chapter 3
Big Data in Higher Education: The Big Picture

Ben K. Daniel

Abstract Globally, the landscape of higher education sector is under increasing pressure to transform its operational and governing structure; to accommodate new economic, social and cultural agendas; relevant to regional, national and international demands. As a result, universities are constantly searching for actionable insights from data, to generate strategies they can use to meet these new demands. Big Data and analytics have the potential to enable institutions to thoroughly examine their present challenges, identify ways to address them as well as predict possible future outcomes. However, because Big Data is a new phenomenon in higher education, its conceptual relevance, as well as the opportunities and limitations it might bring, is still unknown. This chapter describes the conceptual underpinning of Big Data research and presents possible opportunities as well as limitations associated with unlocking the value of Big Data in higher education.

Keywords Big Data • Learning analytics • Higher education

Introduction

Globally, the landscape of higher education sector is under increasing pressure to transform its operational and governing structure; to accommodate new economic, social and cultural agendas; relevant to regional, national and international demands. As a result, universities are constantly searching for actionable insights from their data, to generate strategies they can use to meet these new demands. Among many others, the pressure to implement new far-reaching changes in higher education is triggered by individual and combined forces of globalisation. The direct influence of globalisation in higher education can be seen in the neoliberal reform initiatives at universities, including increase in the number of students, massification and marketisation of higher education, continuous reduction in funding to support

B.K. Daniel (✉)
Educational Technology Group, Higher Education Development Centre, University of Otago, Dunedin, New Zealand
e-mail: ben.daniel@otago.ac.nz

B. Kei Daniel (ed.), *Big Data and Learning Analytics in Higher Education*,
DOI 10.1007/978-3-319-06520-5_3

operations and management of higher education sector, increasing privatisation, the growing need for internationalisation (student mobility) and regional integration.

In addition, it is undeniable that over the last decade the higher education sector has been witnessing a pervasive growth in the number of learning technologies in almost all areas of learning and teaching, creating both excitement and concerns among faculty. The prevalence of emergent forms of technology enhanced learning environments such as Massive Open Online Courses (MOOCs) (Rodriguez, 2012; Yuan, Powell, & CETIS, 2013), for example, seen by many as a form of disruptive innovation into learning technology, challenging beliefs about teaching effectiveness using student-teacher ratio. Furthermore, the rising adoption of various forms of mobile and ubiquitous technologies by students, which provide greater flexibility in their studies and more timely access to learning materials, contests with traditional lecture style of teaching and the way learning is assessed. In response to some of these developments, new pedagogies, such as flipped classroom which encourages the use of Open Educational Resources (OERs), videos, audios, and PowerPoint slides and the transformation of classroom lecture experience into a tutorial experience, are being explored.

For many decades, higher education has always practised data-driven decision-making, but such practice has rarely been systematically investigated (Menon, Terkla, & Gibbs, 2014; Terkla, Sharkness, Conoscenti, & Butler, 2014). As demands for accountability from diverse stakeholders increases, so are the challenges associated with the choice of the right alternative measures to achieve desirable outcomes. With limited resources and continuous pressure to achieve more with less, institutions are obliged to make informed decisions based on thorough examination of alternative outcomes and minimise risks using available data.

Conceptual Foundation of Big Data

Decision-making theory strongly advocates for the use of systematic research prior to actual decision-making. The increasing number of challenges facing higher education has inevitably resulted in institutions collecting and utilising more data to drive their decisions (Menon et al., 2014). The intensification of data harvesting for decision-making in higher education has been mostly linked to the availability of data from social media, online data repositories, educational digital libraries (Borgman et al., 2008; Choudhury, Hobbs, & Lorie, 2002; Sin & Muthu, 2015; Xu & Recker, 2012), growth in the volume of data from Gigabytes (1000^3), Exabyte (1000^5) and Zettabytes (1000^6), drop in the cost of storage and the availability of technologies to facilitate easy access and analytics. As Wagner and Ice (2012) noted, technological developments served as catalysts for growth of analytics in higher education. In recent years, Big Data has been proposed as the dominant paradigm to examine and address challenges in higher education (Prinsloo, Archer, Barnes, Chetty, & Van Zyl, 2015; West, 2012); it is regarded as a concept with the power to transform management decision-making theory (Kudyba, 2014).

Big Data is regarded as term that describes an incredible growth in volume, structure and speed in which data is being generated. Douglas (2001) provides a summary of what constitutes Big Data in what has commonly come to be known as the "three Vs" (volume, velocity and variety) as a way of understanding the structural features of what can regarded as Big Data. Generally, the literature extends from the three-core features and presents the following as key characteristics associated with the notion of Big Data (Daniel, 2015):

- *Volume*—used to describe a large amount of information that is often challenging to store, process, transfer, analyse and present.
- *Velocity*—term associated with increasing rate at which information flows within an organisation—(e.g. institutions dealing with financial information and relating that to human resources and productivity).
- *Veracity*—refers to the biases, noise and abnormality in data generated from various sources within an organisation. Veracity also covers questions of trust and uncertainty associated with the collection, processing and utilisation of data.
- *Variety*—referring to data presented in diverse format both structured and unstructured.
- *Verification*—refers to data corroboration and security.
- *Value*—refers to the ability of data in generating useful insights, benefits, business processes, etc., within an institution.

There are also other important features of Big Data (see Fig. 3.1) such as data validity, which refers to accuracy of data, and data volatility, a concept associated with the longevity of data and their relevance to the outcomes of the analytics. It also refers to the length and time required to store data in a useful form for further appropriate value-added analysis.

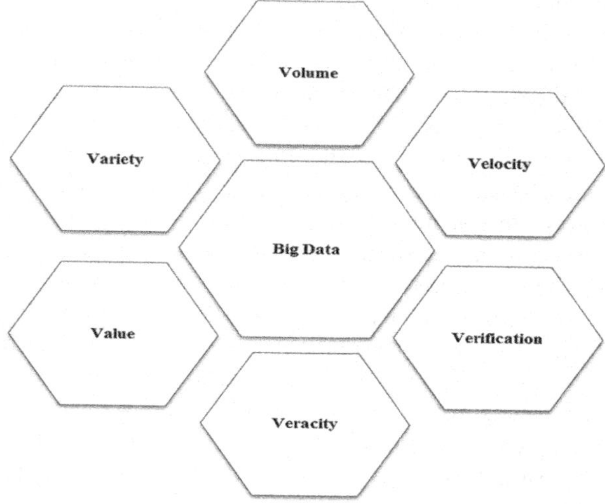

Fig. 3.1 Key characteristics of Big Data

Big Data and Analytics in Higher Education

Big Data is a fast-growing phenomenon which has already become pervasive across a number of sectors—health, business and government. As a new field of inquiry in higher education, it incorporates research areas such as Educational Data Mining (EDM) and learning analytics. EDM is concerned with the development of computational tools for discovering patterns in educational data, while learning analytics is focused on understanding individual student and their performance in a particular learning environment (Luan, 2002; Romero & Ventura, 2010). Viewed as a theory, Big Data in education describes voluminous didactic amounts of data, be it in physical or digital format, stored in diverse repositories, ranging from tangible account bookkeeping records of an educational institution to class test or examination records to alumni records (Sagiroglu & Sinanc, 2013).

A successful deployment of Big Data solutions in higher education requires a proper interpretation and an understanding of a wide range of administrative and operational data that helps in assessing performance and progress and identifying potential issues related to academic programmes, research, teaching and learning (see, e.g. Hrabowski III, Suess, & Fritz, 2011; Picciano, 2012; Siemens & Long, 2011; Siemens, 2011). In an attempt to conceptualise Big Data in the context of higher education, Daniel and Butson (2013) proposed a conceptual framework that described Big Data along four dimensions (institutional analytics, information technology analytics, learning analytics and academic analytics).

Institutional analytics describe operational data that can be analysed to help with effective decisions about making improvements at the institutional level, which include policy analytics, instructional analytics and structural analytics. Outcomes of institutional analytics are captured and stored in data warehouses and business intelligence enterprise systems. When processed, they are presented in the form of data dashboards. The use of institutional analytics provides an institution with the capability to make timely data-driven decisions across all departments and divisions. Institutional analytics combine large data sets from various sources (surveys, databases, systems logs, etc.) and provide data that administrators can use to support the strategic decision-making.

Information technology (IT) analytics cover usage and performance data relating to institutional use of technology services, developing data standards, tools, processes, organisational synergies and policies. Information technology analytics largely aims at integrating data from a variety of systems—student information, learning management system and alumni systems—to garner a holistic view of services consumptions.

Academic analytics refer to analytics at academic programme levels which cover all the activities affecting administration, resource allocation and management of programmes (Tulasi, 2013). Academic analytics provide overall information about what is happening in a specific programme and how to address performance challenges.

Academic analytics can be used to address matters of retention, attrition and early warning systems (see, e.g. Charlton, Mavrikis, & Katsifli, 2013; West, 2012).

Examples of current implementation include experimentations with early detection systems (EDS) (Dawson, Bakharia, & Heathcote, 2010; Siemens, 2013); using the information provided by an EDS, faculty can learn about students and their learning environments and provide needed targeted interventions.

Learning analytics is concerned with the measurement, collection and analysis and reporting of data about learners and their contexts, for purposes of understanding and optimising learning and the environments in which it occurs (Siemens & Long, 2011). Learning analytics is undertaken more at the teaching and learning level of an institution and is largely concerned with improving learner success (Jones, 2012). For instance, learning analytics can be used to understand students' behaviours in learning management systems.

The widespread introduction of learning management systems (LMS) such as Blackboard and Moodle resulted into increasingly large sets of data. Each day, LMS accumulate increasing amounts of students' interaction data, personal data, systems information and academic information (Romero et al., 2008). LMS keep record of students' key actions. Student data in LMS could also include more detailed information on the content of students' postings or other writing, their choices and progress through a specific interactive unit or assignment or their particular preferences and habits as manifested over a range of tasks and interactions or semester (Friesen, 2013). Using learning analytics, this information can be used to understand student behaviour, the learning environment, teaching effectiveness as well as the environment in which teaching is performed.

Opportunities and Limitations

The use of Big Data can inform the next innovation in higher education (Siemens (2011) and advance educational research. For a number of years, researchers in higher education have worked with relatively small amounts of data to research their disciplines. This is because the tools for collecting, organising, analysing and presenting data are limited. They have also relied on methods such as perception-based data gathered through surveys or interviews that have relatively limited interpretative power and latency validity.

In conventional research design, researchers depend on probability and non-probability sampling techniques to guide them in capturing data, which can be costly and limiting in interpretation (Mayer-Schönberger & Cukier, 2013). Big Data methodologies enable researchers to work with a large set of data, removing the barriers of sampling inadequacy, increasing generalisability confidence and enhancing validity rigour. In addition, by working with large amount of data, researchers can use advanced statistical clustering techniques to investigate in more details a particular subgroups within a population without necessarily relaying on expensive probabilistic techniques.

Additionally, when used effectively, Big Data can help institutions enhance learning experience and improve student performance across the board, reduce dropout rates and increase graduation numbers (Dringus, 2012). More specifically, the Big Data approach can help researchers collect information in real time on students and their activities through the use of automated systems, tracking their interactions with the learning environment, peers and instructors, and provide other information that might be relevant to understand how a particular population of students or subgroup of students are performing in their academic programme. This information might also serve as basis for providing academic support to students who need it.

Theoretically, the meaning underlying the term Big Data is contestable. Many researchers still limit their understanding of the term based on the volume, velocity and variety but rarely agree on the granularity of each of these features. Some still focus on size alone as the main determinant of what constitutes Big Data. Yang (2013) pointed out the definition of Big Data has little to do with the data itself, since the analysis of large quantities of data is not new, but rather Big Data includes emergent suit of technologies that can process massive volumes of data of various types at faster speeds than ever before.

Crawford, Gray and Miltner (2014)) critiqued Big Data from lack of pluralistic epistemic grounds. They suggested that to advance our understanding of the theory driving the use of Big Data, researchers from a range of disciplines need to engage in a dialogue on how Big Data shapes our understanding of society.

Big Data and analytics is a new research phenomenon in higher education. A number of institutions are not thoroughly familiar with the terms and conditions in which these technologies can work effectively. Although the number of institutions embracing Big Data and analytics in higher education for the first time is growing, most of these are still in explorative and experimentation stages. Even those with experience in data warehousing, reporting, online analytic processing (OLAP) and business intelligence will quickly realise that the deployment of Big Data and analytics in higher education will require a number of technical requirements and institutional regiments of data scientists and data wranglers to navigate this new landscape of Big Data to achieve desirable outcomes. In addition, most of institutional data systems are not interoperable, so aggregating various forms of data to extract meaning can be a challenge (Daniel & Butson, 2013). Further, since there is a large amount of data coming in both structured and unstructured forms (blogs, tweets, websites content, etc.), the frequency in which this data needs to be validated and verified is more likely to present additional challenge.

For the higher education sector to fully embrace Big Data technologies, it needs to adopt a culture of data-driven decision-making. It needs to overcome organisational and individual cultural barriers and resistance to share personal or proprietary data. It also need to clear any suspicion associated with the use of data at all levels of the institution. Most of these would depend on the establishment of clear Big Data and analytics institutional strategy, which include data governing structures and more progressive policies data utilisation (Dringus, 2012; Dyckhoff, Zielke, Bültmann, Chatti & Schroeder, 2012; Wagner & Ice, 2012).

Other barriers to overcome are technical in nature. They are related to the choice of Big Data platforms and analytics, which include ease of use, scalability and ability to support different forms of privacy and data security. It is also worth noting that presently the field of Big Data and analytics is dominated almost entirely by technology professionals, many of whom have limited pedagogical knowledge needed to effectively support learning. This might change in the future with the establishment of Data Science programmes that provide learning technologies as areas of specialisations.

The collection of educational data raises issues on ethics associated with data ownership, privacy, security and ethics of use (Jones, 2012; Prinsloo et al., 2015). There are also matters of accountability associated with the use of student data for predictive modelling. For instance, Eynon (2013) noted that the more we know about student challenges during their education, it is likely that the social implications of decisions to support learning will become more complex. For instance, it becomes difficult to make a decision on what to do when we know that a student is more likely to drop out of their programmes.

Further, research driven by Big Data is by large limited to correlational models and predictive analytics. In others words, through the use of data mining techniques, researchers search through an ocean of data but only answer questions of "what" rather than "why". Outcome of educational research is often needed to address learning problems; while asking "what" questions are necessary, it is not sufficient to provide necessary advice to support educational outcomes. Additionally, the utilisation of Big Data has hidden biases inherent in both the collection, analysis and reporting. Reliance on the results of Big Data alone without other sources of evidence, such as experience, can be misleading and likely to disadvantage some individuals or subgroup of people in an institution.

Conclusion and Future Research

The reliance on data-driven decision-making will become a central approach in many research- and teaching-intensive institutions in higher education. Big Data and analytics are more likely to effectively transform the way higher education operates and governed itself through the use of various technologies to capture, process, analyse, present and use data to generate actionable insights to drive their decisions.

Key drivers of the implementation of Big Data and analytics in higher education can be linked to increasing pressure to base evidence on data rather than intuition or experience. Other factors include increased accountability demanded by stakeholders, which in turn, necessitates the collection of different forms of data for the purpose of generating reports for internal and external regulations. The increasing use of various information technologies by students, faculty and other staff generates a vast amount of data that can be mined for useful information. The emergence of unstructured forms of new data often associated with social media technologies (images, tweets, videos, audios and web pages) and the value that might accrue from processing this data (Sagiroglu & Sinanc, 2013) in higher education is an additional reason for exploring data to gain useful information.

There is also falling costs associated with data storage and emergent business processes to outsource information technology services—adoption of cloud computing, which encourages higher consumption of information technology services. For instance, over the last decade a number of higher education institutions have increased outsourcing use of software as services (SaaS), platform as a service (PaaS) and soon Big Data as a service (BDaaS [1]).

As Big Data and analytics become mainstream in higher education, more research is needed to understand and measure the value add of these technologies and address challenges of implementation as well as matters relating to privacy security and data governance. While research is on the way, both theoretical and empirical research are needed to explore both breadth and depth of issues underpinning our understanding of these technologies in the milieu of educational research.

References

Ali, L., Adasi, M., Gasevic, D., Jovanovic, J., & Hatala, M. (2013). Factors influencing beliefs for adoption of a learning analytics tool: An empirical Study. *Computers & Education, 62*, 130–148.

Baer, L., & Campbell, J. (2011). *Game changers*. Louisville, CO: EDUCAUSE.

Base, A. (2013, March/April). Five pillars of prescriptive analytics success. *Analytics*, 8–12. http://www.analytics-magazine.org/

Borgman, C. L., Abelson, H., Dirks, L., Johnson, R., Koedinger, K. R., Linn, M. C., et al. (2008). *Fostering learning in the networked world: The Cyberlearning opportunity and challenge. A 21st century agenda for the National Science Foundation* (Report of the NSF Task Force on Cyberlearning. Office of Cyberinfrastructure and Directorate for Education and Human Resources). National Science Foundation. Retrieved July 12, 2015 from http://www.nsf.gov/publications/pub_summ.jsp?ods_key=nsf08204

Charlton, P., Mavrikis, M., & Katsifli, D. (2013). The potential of learning analytics and big data. *Ariadne, 71*.

Chen, M., Mao, S., & Liu, Y. (2014). Big data: A survey. *Mobile Networks and Applications, 19*(2), 171–209.

Choudhury, S., Hobbs, B., & Lorie, M. (2002). A framework for evaluating digital library services. *D-Lib Magazine*, 8. Retrieved July 12, 2014 from http://www.dlib.org/dlib/july02/choudhury/07choudhury.html

Crawford, K., Gray, M. L., & Miltner, K. (2014). Big Datal critiquing Big Data: Politics, ethics, epistemologyl special section introduction. *International Journal of Communication, 8*, 10.

Daniel, B. (2015). Big Data and analytics in higher education: Opportunities and challenges. *British Journal of Educational Technology, 46*(5), 904–920.

Daniel, B. K., & Butson, R. (2013). Technology Enhanced Analytics (TEA) in Higher Education. *Proceedings of the International Conference on Educational Technologies* (pp. 89–96.), 29 Novemebr–1 December, 2013, Kuala Lumpur, Malaysia.

Dawson, S., Bakharia, A., & Heathcote, E. (2010, May). SNAPP: Realising the affordances of real-time SNA within networked learning environments. In *Proceedings of the 7th International Conference on Networked Learning* (pp. 125–133). Denmark, Aalborg.

[1] BDaaS is a new terminology that describes the processes of outsourcing various Big Data activities to the cloud. It may include supply of data, renting analytical tools from third-party companies.

Dean, J., & Ghemawat, S. (2010). MapReduce: A flexible data processing tool. *Communications of the ACM, 53*(1), 72–77.

Douglas, L (2001). *3D data management: Controlling data volume, velocity and variety* (Gartner Report). Retrieved October 24, 2015 from http://blogs.gartner.com/doug-laney/files/2012/01/ad949-3D-Data-Management-Controlling-Data-Volume-Velocity-and-Variety.pdf.

Dringus, L. (2012). Learning analytics considered harmful. *Journal of Asynchronous Learning Networks, 16*(3), 87–100.

Dyckhoff, A. L., Zielke, D., Bültmann, M., Chatti, M. A., & Schroeder, U. (2012). Design and implementation of a learning analytics toolkit for teachers. *Educational Technology & Society, 15*(3), 58–76.

EDUCAUSE (2011). Learning initiative, "7 things you should know about first-generation learning analytics." December 2011. Retrieved October 24, 2015 from http://www.deloitte.com/assets/DcomIreland/Local%20Assets/Documents/Public%20sector/IE_PS_making%20the%20grade_IRL_0411_WEB.pdf.

Eynon, R. (2013). The rise of big data: What does it mean for education, technology, and media research? *Learning, Media and Technology, 38*(3), 237–240.

Friesen, N. (2013). Learning analytics: Readiness and rewards. *Canadian Journal of Learning Technology, 39*(4). Retrieved from http://www.cjlt.ca/index.php/cjlt/article/view/774.

Hilbert, M. (2013, January 15). Big Data for development: From information- to knowledge societies. Available at SSRN: http://ssrn.com/abstract=2205145 or http://dx.doi.org/10.2139/ssrn.2205145.

Hrabowski, III, F.A., Suess, J., & Fritz, J. (2011, September/October). Assessment and analytics in institutional transformation. *EDUCAUSE Review, 46*(5). Retrieved October 24, 2015 from http://www.educause.edu/ero/article/assessment-and-analytics-institutional-transformation.

IBM What is Big Data?—Bringing Big Data to the enterprise. Retrieved from https://www-01.ibm.com/

Jones, S. (2012). Technology review: The possibilities of learning analytics to improve learner-centered decision-making. *Community College Enterprise, 18*(1), 89–92.

Kudyba, S. (2014). *Big Data, mining, and analytics: Components of strategic decision making*. New York: CRC Press.

Luan, J. (2002). Data mining and its applications in higher education. In A. Serban & J. Luan (Eds.), *Knowledge management: Building a competitive advantage in higher education* (pp. 17–36). San Francisco, CA: Josey-Bass.

Macfadyen, L. P., & Dawson, S. (2010). Mining LMS data to develop an "early warning system" for educators: A proof of concept. *Computers & Education, 54*, 588–599.

Macfadyen, L. P., & Dawson, S. (2012). Numbers are not enough. Why e-learning analytics failed to inform an institutional strategic plan. *Educational Technology & Society, 15*(3), 149–163.

Manyika, J., Chui, M., Brown, B., Bughin, J., Dobbs, R., Roxburgh, C., et al. (2011). *Big Data: The next frontier for innovation, competition, and productivity*. McKinsey Global Institute. Retrieved July 14, 2014 from http://www.mckinsey.com/Insights/MGI/Research/Technology_and_Innovation/Big_data_The_next_frontier_for_innovation.

Mayer, M. (2009). The physics of Big Data. Retrieved October 24, 2015 from http://www.parc.com/event/936/innovation-atgoogle.html.

Mayer-Schönberger, V., & Cukier, K. (2013). *Big data: A revolution that will transform how we live, work, and think*. Boston, MA: Houghton Mifflin Harcourt.

Menon, M. E., Terkla, D. G., & Gibbs, P. (Eds.). (2014). *Using data to improve higher education: Research, policy and practice*. London: Springer.

Picciano, A. G. (2012). The evolution of Big Data and learning analytics in American higher education. *Journal of Asynchronous Learning Networks, 16*(3), 9–20.

Prinsloo, P., Archer, E., Barnes, G., Chetty, Y., & Van Zyl, D. (2015). Big (ger) data as better data in open distance learning. *The International Review of Research in Open and Distributed Learning, 16*(1).

Rodriguez, C. O. (2012). MOOCs and the AI-Stanford Like courses: Two successful and distinct course formats for massive open online courses. *Education XPress, 2012*(7), 1–1.

Romero, C. R., & Ventura, S. (2010). Educational data mining: A review of the state of the art. *IEEE Transactions on Systems, Man, and Cybernetics Part C: Applications and Reviews, 40*(6), 601–618.

Romero, C., Ventura, S., & García, E. (2008). Data mining in course management systems: Moodle case study and tutorial. *Computers & Education, 51*(1), 368–384.

Sagiroglu, S., & Sinanc, D. (2013, May). *Big data: A review. In Collaboration Technologies and Systems (CTS)*, 2013 International Conference on (pp. 42–47). IEEE. Date: 20–24 May 2013.

Schleicher, A. (2013). Big Data and PISA. Retrieved October 24, 2015 from http://oecdeducation-today.blogspot.co.nz/2013/07/big-data-and-pisa.html?m=1.

Schroeck, M., Shockley, R., Smart, J., Romero-Morales, D., & Tufano, P. (2012). *Analytics: The real-world use of Big Data. How innovative enterprises extract value from uncertain data* (Research report: IBM Institute for business value). Retrieved July 12, 2014 from http://www.ibm.com/smarterplanet/global/files/se__sv_se__intelligence__Analytics_-_The_real-world_use_of_big_data.pdf.

Siemens, G. (2011, July). How data and analytics can improve education. Retrieved August 8 from http://radar.oreilly.com/2011/07/education-data-analytics-learning.html.

Siemens, G. (2013). Learning analytics: The emergence of a discipline. *American Behavioral Scientist, 57*(10), 1380–1400. doi:10.1177/0002764213498851.

Siemens, G., & Long, P. (2011). Penetrating the Fog: Analytics in learning and education. *EDUCAUSE Review, 46*(5), 30.

Sin, K., & Muthu, L. (2015). Application of Big Data in education data mining and learning analytics. A literature review. Retrieved August 22, 2015 from http://ictactjournals.in/paper/IJSC_Paper_6_pp_1035_1049.pdf.

Terkla, D. G., Sharkness, J., Conoscenti, L. M., & Butler, C. (2014). Using data to inform institutional decision-making at Tufts University. In M. E. Menon, D. G. Terkla, & P. Gibbs (Eds.), *Using data to improve higher education* (pp. 39–63). Rotterdam: Sense Publishers. doi:10.1007/978-94-6209-794-0_4.

Tulasi, B. (2013). Significance of Big Data and analytics in higher education. *International Journal of Computer Applications, 68*(14), 23–25.

U.S. Department of Education, Office of Educational Technology (2012). *Enhancing teaching and learning through educational data mining and learning analytics: An Issue Brief.* Author: Washington, DC.

Wagner, E., & Ice, P. (2012). Data changes everything: Delivering on the promise of learning analytics in higher education. *EDUCAUSE Review, 2012*, 33–42.

West, D. M. (2012). Big data for education: Data mining, data analytics, and web dashboards. *Governance Studies at Brookings*, 1–10

Xu, B., & Recker, M. (2012). Teaching analytics: A clustering and triangulation study of digital library user data. *Educational Technology & Society, 15*(3), 103–115.

Yang, L. (2013). Big Data analytics: What is the big deal? Retrieved October 24, 2015 from http://knowledge.ckgsb.edu.cn/2013/12/30/technology/big-data-analytics-whats-big-deal/

Yuan, L., Powell, S., & CETIS, J. (2013). MOOCs and open education: Implications for higher education. Retrieved October 26, 2015 from http://publications.cetis.org.uk/wp-content/uploads/2013/03/MOOCs-and-Open-Education.pdf.

Chapter 4
Preparing the Next Generation of Education Researchers for Big Data in Higher Education

David C. Gibson and Dirk Ifenthaler

Abstract Research in social science, education, psychology, and humanities is still dominated by research methodologies that primarily divide the world into either *qualitative* or *quantitative* approaches. This relatively small toolkit for understanding complex phenomena in the world limits the next generation of education researchers when they are faced with the increased availability of big data. In this chapter, we are calling attention to data mining, model-based methods, machine learning, and data science in general as a new toolkit for the next generation of education researchers and for the inclusion of these topics in researcher preparation programs. A review of the state of the art in research methodology courses and units shows that most follow a traditional approach focusing on quantitative and/or qualitative research methodologies. Therefore, this chapter makes a case for a new data science foundation for education research methodology. Finally, benefits and limitations of computationally intensive modeling approaches are critically reviewed.

Keywords Learning analytics • Big data • Research methodology • Machine learning • Higher education research • Computational modeling

Introduction

Given the increasing availability of data from vast interconnected and loosely coupled systems of administrative, academic, and personal information flowing within and across organizations and businesses, the challenge of data management, analysis, visualization, and interpretation, which is integral to advancing knowledge and understanding in the arts and sciences, is constantly evolving. The situation highlights two concepts at the heart of our argument, *complexity* and the *role of large amounts of dynamic evolving data* in scientific modeling and theory formation. We argue that the current tools and processes for the preparation of researchers in many fields are inadequate for facing both complexity and big data, and we propose a new

D.C. Gibson (✉) • D. Ifenthaler
Curtin University, Bentley, WA, Australia
e-mail: david.c.gibson@curtin.edu.au

B. Kei Daniel (ed.), *Big Data and Learning Analytics in Higher Education*,
DOI 10.1007/978-3-319-06520-5_4

conceptual foundation for research preparation and support courses and units in higher education.

Concerning complexity, the phenomena studied in all fields are often complicated as well as highly varied, with many overlapping elements and parts interconnected in a variety of ways. The phenomena are often set inside of other systems or are themselves made of many subsystems, with numerous relationships. As important as being *complicated*, both the systems and their environments are *dynamically evolving* in time, often with many self-referential influences and flows that can lead to chaotic and surprising behavior such as self-organizing and adaptive capabilities in natural and living systems (Bar-Yam, 1997; Holland, 1995; Liu, Slotine, & Barabási, 2011; Rockler, 1991).

In relation to the challenges brought on by dynamic data in knowledge creation, the large amount of data now available for social scientists, for example, is far too complex for conventional database software to store, manage, and process. In addition to the huge volume of data, the data accumulates in real time, with a requisite need to analyze and use the information to make timely decisions. Finally, the source and nature of this enormous and quickly accumulating data is highly diverse (Gibson & Webb, 2015; Ifenthaler, Bellin-Mularski, & Mah, 2015). Hence the next generation of researchers across all fields of arts and sciences face new challenges for identifying valuable information from big data and understanding multilayered interactions of complex phenomena.

But research in social science, education, psychology, and humanities is still dominated by research methodologies that primarily divide the world into either *qualitative* or *quantitative* approaches (see Creswell, n.d. for a 40-year history retrospective shaped by Sage Publications). For the most part, the two approaches are treated as philosophically and operationally disconnected and capable of being bridged only by "mixing" the methods. This has led to a simplistic view of research that is hampering understanding of complex phenomena in many fields. We believe that there is a new "third way" to approach research and this article outlines its main features as part of a call for higher education research preparation programs to invest in up-skilling faculty and redesigning research methodologies units and courses. In this article, we concentrate the examples on the social sciences, education, humanities, and arts, but the same argument holds as well for many of the sciences.

To illustrate the problem of the traditional divide and the lack of resolution of the twentieth-century debates (see, e.g., Caporaso, 1995; Onwuegbuzie & Leech, 2005; Rihoux & Grimm, 2006; Shah & Corley, 2006; Tarrow, 2010) that are now frozen into the research preparation programs in higher education, we offer a brief example. On the *quantitative* side of research preparation, null hypothesis significance testing (NHST) is the dominant analytical strategy taught to each successive generation of researchers. However, NHST is a limited way to interpret data because it refers primarily to the question of whether there is a *significant effect* or not (Cumming, 2012) and whether to support or discredit a priori speculations about some aspect of a population (Kachigan, 1991). This approach, a mainstay of doctoral dissertations, leaves unaddressed the questions of in what ways data are related, within what structures, and with what specific predictable (or approximately predictable) bounded as well as changing sequences and sets of relationships. Currently, higher education research preparation courses and processes are educating the next generation of researchers without an adequate toolkit for understanding complex models and enabling them to participate in the benefits of a computational mindset to theory and knowledge building.

By "computational mindset" we mean to differentiate a capacity for research conceptualization that differs from applying a specific set of skills, such as whether one can program a computer, solve an equation, or build an operational model of a mechanism. We refer instead to a capacity of "awareness plus literacy" (where all those specific skills are highly welcomed on the team!) concerning the role of algorithms in transforming the nature of scientific inquiry in the late twentieth century (Chaitin, 2003). The next generation of researchers needs to understand this change and its implications for significance in new research and embrace a "third way" of thinking about the integration and new empowerment of both qualitative and quantitative perspectives of a research program through computationally intensive modeling, visualization, and exploratory data analytic methods.

Therefore, in this chapter, we are calling attention to data mining, model-based methods, machine learning, and data science in general as part of a new toolkit needed in higher education research. The next section provides a discipline-based example that focuses on new challenges for education researchers. The third section reviews the state of the art in higher education unit and course-based research methodology offerings in order to note the absence of knowledge about big data analytics. The fourth section proposes key elements of a framework for preparing the next generation of researchers for the era of big data analytics. The chapter concludes by asking for integrating alternative analytics methodologies into existing curricula, which will better enable a new generation of researchers to participate in big data research.

Challenges for a New Era of Education Researchers

One of the promises of big data in educational settings is to enable a new level of evidence-based research into learning and instruction and make it possible to gain highly detailed insight into student performance and their learning trajectories as required for personalizing and adapting curriculum and assessment (Shum & Ferguson 2011). Being accountable for student success, higher education institutions that analyze and create new interventions and actions based on data analytics in their contexts may enhance their institutional effectiveness. Furthermore, if developed as an organizational capacity, the ongoing analysis of big data can provide insights into the design of learning environments and inform decisions about how to manage educational resources on all levels (Ifenthaler et al., 2015).

Educational data mining (EDM) describes techniques and tools to analyze all kinds of data on different hierarchical levels in educational settings (Berland, Baker, & Berland, Baker, & Bilkstein, 2014; Romero, Ventura, Pechenizkiy, & Romero, Ventura, Pechenizkiy, & Baker, 2011). In addition to the nested hierarchical character of much educational data (e.g., answer level, session level, student level, teacher and institutional level), the performance time, sequence of actions, and evolving elements of the learning context are also important features of relevant data in educational settings. EDM is interdisciplinary and draws on machine learning, artificial intelligence, computer science, and classical test statistics to analyze data collected during learning and teaching. Although closely related to learning analytics, which focuses on improving learning and performance with feedback loops to the learner and instructor (Ferguson, 2012; Ifenthaler, 2015; Long & Siemens, 2011), EDM focuses on exploring new patterns in data and on developing new models at all levels of an educational system. Some of the common goals of current EDM practices are (1) predicting academic performance and student success for recruitment, retention, and work readiness, (2) evaluating student learning within course management systems and improving instructional sequences, as well as (3) evaluating different kinds of adaptive and personalized support. Additionally, EDM is advancing research about modeling student, domain, and software characteristics.

EDM involves five methods: (1) prediction, (2) clustering, (3) relationship mining, (4) distillation of data for human judgment, and (5) discovery via models. Prediction includes models about academic performance of students, for example, by analyzing their behavior in an online learning environment. Clustering methods can be used to group students according to specific characteristics, e.g., preference or performance patterns to recommend actions and resources to similar users. Relationship mining, which is perhaps the most often applied method in EDM, refers to identifying relationships among variables, like classroom activities, student interaction or student performance, and pedagogical strategies. The fourth technique, distillation of data for human judgment, aims to depict data in a way that enables researchers to quickly identify structures in the data. The last method, discovery via models, uses a preexisting model that is then applied to other data and used as a component in further analysis.

Accordingly, the next generation of education researchers need to be equipped with a new set of fundamental competencies that encompass areas needed for such computationally intensive research (e.g., data-management techniques for big data, working with interdisciplinary teams who understand programming languages, as well as cognitive, behavioral, social, and emotional perspectives on learning) and the fundamental principles of the computational mindset, by which we mean a bedrock of professional knowledge (including heuristics) that inclines a researcher toward computational modeling when tackling complex research problems.

State of the Art in Research Methods Units and Courses

Since the nineteenth century, debates among education researchers have focused on the differences between *quantitative* and *qualitative* approaches to research (Gage, 1989). However, the two methodologies entail more than different ways of gathering data; they also express different, often opposing and conflicting, assumptions about the purpose of research and phenomena in the world (Bryman, 1988). An in-depth analysis of research literature reveals several common dichotomies, such as qualitative–quantitative, subjective–objective, inductive–deductive, hermeneutics–positivism, understanding–explanation, and descriptive–predictive (McLaughlin, 1991). Only recently, this dichotomous view on education research has faded as more and more research studies combine qualitative and quantitative features of inquiry through the "mixed methods" approach (Creswell, 2008). The mixed methods approach primarily alternates between the two methods, places them in sequences, or interleaves the various perspectives. In the approach we are advocating here, there is a tighter connection that operationalizes the qualitative aspects of both content and process via algorithmic integration with computational resources as a coadjutant (mutually assisting cocreator) in theory formation. For example, active visualization is not viewed as a representation of what is known or an illustration of what has been found in data but is instead used to explore, discover, and in multiple ways present the possible relationships among data points, assisting in the search for patterns rather than performing a role as a display of knowledge. The proposed stance we are introducing and discussing here is thus an active, interactive coproducer of knowledge, with algorithms and algorithmic agents working alongside human thought and action.

The current state of the art in preparing education researchers for the future is the research dissertation project, often supported by a research methodology course. Differences exist across the world as well as across the university in terms of the specificity of that preparation, for example, preparation for research in physics is quite different from that in education or psychology. Numerous textbooks have been published to support research methodology courses, mostly focusing on classical research practices including (1) linear steps in the process of conducting research, (2) restricted number of possible research designs, and (3) limited number of accepted analytics strategies (e.g., Bortz & Döring, 1995; Cohen, Manion, & Morrison, 2011; Creswell, 2008; Denzin & Lincoln, 2000).

Only recently, researchers in education have started to bridge between standard research practices in the humanities-oriented educational, social, and psychological research fields and the scientifically oriented cognitive science, computer science, and artificial intelligence fields. However, most research preparation courses in higher education still follow a traditional approach focusing on quantitative, qualitative, or mixed methods research designs. The following four examples provide evidence for the absence of alternative computationally intensive modeling methodologies required for the analysis of big data in educational settings.

Example 1: Short Certificate Course on Research Methods

A 3-month online course created by a consortium of partners of the Alexis Foundation aims at preparing researchers to develop the most appropriate methodology for their research studies. The short certificate course includes four modules. The first module deals with types of research and the research process. The second module focuses primarily on hypothesis-driven research (identifying a hypothesis, gathering and making sense of data that test it, and interpreting the data). The third module explores alternative models of research but with much less weight as alternatives to hypothesis testing. The fourth module supports the "write-up" with a range of scholarly reports and mentions ethics fairly close to the advice on footnoting and citations (http://www.ccrm.in/syllabus.html).

Example 2: Research Methods in a Faculty of Education

An introductory research methods course in education at the University of Freiburg, Germany, is taught over two semesters (32 weeks) and has a strong emphasis on quantitative analytical strategies including descriptive and inferential statistics. The course uses a research-based learning approach (Freeman, Collier, Staniforth, & Smith, 2008; Healey, 2005) by integrating a research project conducted by the students as the driver of the overall course experience. The lecturer introduces a current research problem (e.g., teacher's perception of school development) at the beginning of a semester, and students are asked to form small research groups (approximately four students per group). After a self-guided in-depth literature review, students are asked to identify research problems within the larger context of the research project (e.g., what factors hinder teachers from active participation in school development?). In the next step, students develop the research methodology including instruments and procedures. Depending on the status of the overall research project, instruments are provided by the lecturer or are developed as pilot instruments by the students. The lecturer and teaching assistants help in organizing the sample for the data collection (including necessary permissions, etc.). The data analysis is performed within groups in the tutorials, while problems and outcomes are addressed in the lectures to enable students to develop a broader understanding of the issues emerging across all the projects. As a final outcome of the course, students produce a research project report following scientific guidelines (Ifenthaler & Gosper, 2014).

Example 3: Research Methods in a Faculty of Information

A research methods course in the faculty of information at the University of Toronto has an emphasis on qualitative methods. First, the course offers an overview of different approaches, considerations, and challenges involved in social research. Second, the course reviews core human research methods such as interviews, ethnographies, surveys, and experiments. Third, it explores methods used in critical analysis of texts and technologies (discourse/content/design analysis, historical case studies), with an emphasis on digital information (e.g., virtual worlds, videogames, and online ethnographies). Fourth, it also discusses mixed methods approaches, case studies, participatory and user-centered research, as well as research involving minors (http://current.ischool.utoronto.ca/course-descriptions/inf1240h).

Example 4: Research Methods in a Faculty of Business Education

The last example stems from a postgraduate fully online course with a duration of 13 weeks that is provided by the Australian Catholic University through Open Universities Australia (www.open.edu.au). The course includes a range of concepts and techniques associated with both qualitative and quantitative methods of research that are applicable for business and/or information systems. The syllabus includes sessions focusing on (1) types of research, (2) design, (3) defining the research question, (4) search and reviewing the literature, (5) methods and instrument in quantitative research, (6) methods and instruments in qualitative research, (7) sampling and data collection, (8) presenting and describing quantitative data, (9) inference for quantitative data, (10) qualitative data analysis, (11) mixed methods (quantitative and qualitative), and (12) writing a research report (http://www.open.edu.au/courses/business/australian-catholic-university-research-methods--mgmt617-2015).

Summary of Current State of Research Preparation

These four examples are emblematic of the current state in higher education research preparation courses and offer evidence of the absence of awareness of the transformation of the leading edge of research and practice driven by computational science methods. In spite of the rise of "computational" as a prefix to new fields in biology, chemistry, political science, modeling, architecture, neuroscience, and elsewhere, the basic research preparation experiences in the arts, humanities, and social sciences have, for the most part, remained rooted in late-nineteenth- and early-twentieth-century epistemology. In the next section, we outline why the current state of research preparation is inadequate for the era of big data and some of the key ideas central to the third way which deeply integrates the traditions to better advance knowledge as well as research practice via computational science approaches to understanding complex systems.

Preparing the Next Generation of Education Researchers for the Era of Big Data

A new foundation for research methodology in multidisciplinary research extends the traditional quantitative and qualitative approaches with complex systems understandings that entail and require new data-management and analysis techniques for big data. Big data in higher education is driven and enabled primarily by interactive technologies such as user tracking on web sites, user actions and products in highly interactive digital learning and assessment platforms, and large-scale data collection in projects at increasing scale sizes and complexity (diversity of data sources) as well as resolutions (data records per user). Therefore, the next generation of researchers must be able to demonstrate competencies in the fast-changing technological field of big data analytics and be able to apply new tools, algorithms, and analytic platforms to various scenarios in education, social sciences, humanities, business, health systems, leadership, policy, and many other areas of application.

Limitations of Regression Models for Big Data

A major analytic strategy in education and other social science research is regression modeling or prediction analysis (Kachigan, 1991). In this section, we provide a simple example that illustrates a linear regression, with one or multiple criteria and predictors. However, linear regression algorithms are limited for application in big data analytics because they assume that rules and data are independent. Specifically, there are three assumptions about the population of data that must be met in order for linear regression to be an adequate model of the phenomenon under study: (1) there needs to be a probability distribution of *independent* values of each criterion, (2) the variances of all the distributions have to be *equal* to one another, and (3) the means of the distributions must all *fall on the regression line*. But in a complex data environment with dynamic interdependencies, these assumptions are almost never met. Worse still, to make research-based predictions and discuss findings as though these conditions *have* been met when they are often unstated and assumed and that the phenomenon under study *is therefore reasonably represented* as linear, independent, and well behaved creates inaccurate models and understandings. The emergent qualitative traditions that matured in the late twentieth century noticed and reacted to this shortcoming (e.g., Guba, 1985; Lincoln, Guba, Lincoln, & Guba, 1985) but did not extend the computational toolkit. Instead a whole new branch of methods and traditions arose which did not depend upon or take advantage of computational resources. Data science methods now emerging have reintroduced the possibility of a scienfitically defensible bridge between the two worlds of qualitative and quantitative methods for those who wish to unify the divide by discovering and modeling nonlinear and complex relationships.

For example, to identify nonlinear and complex parameter relationships in data, one successful approach uses support vector machines (Cortes & Vapnik, 1995). A support vector machine (SVM) is a binary classification technique based on supervised machine learning in the broad area of artificial intelligence (Drucker, Burges, Kaufman, Smola, & Vapnik, 1997). The basic SVM takes a set of input data and predicts, for each given input, which of two possible classes forms the output, making the SVM a non-probabilistic binary linear classifier. Given a set of training examples, each marked as belonging to one of two categories, an SVM training algorithm builds a model that assigns new examples into one category or the other. An SVM model is a representation of the examples as points in space, mapped so that the examples of the separate categories are divided by a clear gap that is as wide as possible. New examples are then mapped into that same space and predicted to belong to a category based on which side of the gap they fall on. SVMs can efficiently perform a nonlinear classification using what is called the kernel trick, implicitly mapping their inputs into high-dimensional feature spaces. This example illustrates how an alternative analysis method can help overcome one of the limitations that students trained in a traditional research methodologies course will be confronted with when they are requested to approach a research problem in big data.

Big Data

Big data is often referred to with three "v" aspects: volume, variety, and velocity (Romero et al., 2011). There are usually a large number of records representing by "orders of magnitude" more information than in past research practices. The data typically streams in from a wide network of sources at varying timescales, resolutions, and levels of semantic import. Finally, the data builds up in near real time and must be analyzed rapidly if timely decisions are to be made, so new forms of filtering, patterning, and saving aggregate information on the fly are needed to assist in the rapid analysis and decision-making process (Ifenthaler & Widanapathirana, 2014). A complex adaptive education system, in comparison, has a large number of possible state-spaces (volume), systems, and subsystems that are actively contributing to the system's evolution while remaining open to an ever-changing outside environment (variety) and multiple time scales that depend on the fastest subsystem (velocity).

Both data science and complex adaptive systems are unique fields and are evolving separate terms, tools, practices, and communities, but there is a remarkable alignment, as we might well expect, since our knowledge of systems is often created by sensor networks that feed our best-fit and ever-changing models in the form of computational representations. That is, the computer-based models that are now the common architecture of the sciences (e.g., astronomy, chemistry, biology, medicine, physics, sustainable ecosystem models) are both a result of and a creator of big data. As a result, a new worldview has emerged in which data science integrated with a conception of evolutionary algorithms is now the applied mathematics of empirical science. This change in worldview has been chronicled by writers from many fields: political and economic (Beinhocker, 2006; Friedman, 2005; Radzicki, 2003), philosophical and practical (Manning, 1995; Newman, 1996; Putnam, 1992; Tetenbaum, 1998), scientific and mathematical (Holland, 1995; Prigogine, 1996), and historical and sociological (Diamond, 2005; McNeill, 1998; Wicks, 1998).

Six Key Ideas for a New Conception

We hold that research preparation in many fields needs to catch up to the rest of science and move quickly to incorporate complexity and data science ideas into research methods courses in all fields. A rebalancing is needed to shift practice from its roots

Table 4.1 Six key ideas for a new conception of a research methodology course

Complex system concept	Definition
Nonlinearity	A nonlinear system is one in which the output is not directly proportional to its input; the cause of some response by the system is not the simple sum of the stimuli, as it is in linear systems
Feedback loops	Information is recycled, connecting the current state to past states of the system
Openness	The system accepts "inputs from" and "outputs to" a larger external environment
Memory	Impacts on the current state of the system are carried forward into future states of the system
Nested relationships	Components of the system may themselves be complex systems
Emergent properties	Properties of the whole system depend upon the nonlinear nested relationships of the components and often need a new level of analysis and representation from that of the components

and current practices and into innovative exploratory new arenas. Table 4.1 shows six key ideas which were outlined in Gibson and Knezek (2011) and could form the backbone of a new conception of a research methodology course to begin the process of acquainting researchers with complexity ideas. These are not offered as an exhaustive list but as a set of key ideas underpinning the new analysis methods.

The concepts presented in Table 4.1 imply the use of new computational, representational, and epistemological tools and methods that help connect complex systems knowledge with the knowledge created via traditional qualitative and quantitative methods.

The comfort zone of researchers starts with the tools and processes they already know and must add to that knowledge base incrementally when the need arises. If a research team sees that there is nobody on the team with the knowledge and skills to deal with the above in both a qualitative and quantitative sense, then the team needs to expand its capacity to include a trained data scientist who can help fill the gaps.

Big Data Analytics in Education

A new foundation for research methodology in education research needs to provide people with practical hands-on experience on the fundamental platforms and analysis tools for linked big data, introduce several data storage methods and how to distribute and process them, introduce possible ways of handling analytics algorithms on different platforms, and highlight visualization techniques for big data analytics. Additional competencies include large-scale machine learning methods as foundations for human–computer interaction, artificial intelligence, and cognitive networks.

An example of key topics for a course focusing on big data analytics in education can be found at Columbia University (http://www.ee.columbia.edu/~cylin/course/bigdata). An introductory unit could focus on big data analytics, platforms, data storage, and data processing. A second unit could introduce different big data analytics algorithms, such as recommender, clustering, and classification. A final unit could introduce key concepts of data visualization and graph computing.

In addition to the abovementioned course content, the following elements could be integrated into a course focusing on big data analytics in education:

- Distributed and cloud-based data management, data cleaning, and data integration
- Using metadata
- Harvesting and extraction of unstructured data
- Probabilistic and predictive modeling
- Pattern recognition
- Data, text, and image mining
- Network analyses (social relationships, structural implications, information flows)
- Semantic web and ontologies
- Sentiment analysis

Conclusion

The key idea here is that we are comparing how knowledge emerges from exploratory analytics versus from hypothesis testing. Both approaches can lead to a model, but the first approach invents the model where the second approach validates it.

What we are advocating is a balancing of the creative impulse with external validation, both with increased global professional community engagement and the establishment of research that is more open, transparent, and amenable to scientific scrutiny, meeting the criteria of reproducibility and generalizability.

We may be criticized that some science cannot be made reproducible or generalizable and that insisting on these criteria might lose something. So we reply that what we are proposing does not have to replace current methods that are subjective, opaque, and incommensurable; we only need to allow the new methods and knowledge to take their place among the current practices as quickly as possible so that a new generation of scientists in all fields will have the option of participating in big data research and analysis.

Benefits include:

- Open data (anonymous data sets that form a new benchmark community)
- Open data transformation processes (no black box data transformations)
- Open algorithms and algo-sequences (fully transparent processing)
- Reproducible results (might lead to new forms of "meta-analysis" where the concerns are NOT commensurability and confidence in ES)

- Generalizable results (might lead to actual models in the scientific sense of the word)

Limitations include:

- Key teaching and learning information may not be captured (this applies to all methodologies, not just computational approach).
- Difficulties in translating computational models developed into actions to improve teaching and learning (especially where relationships are not linear/curvilinear).
- Variables identified within models may be indicators rather than the causal variables (e.g., the number of books borrowed from library is an indicator; causal variable may be amount of time spent reading. The act of taking books out of the library does not in itself promote learning and teaching). Without a theory driving the analysis, it is difficult to distinguish between the two.

Researching big data is a new and fast-growing field with numerous career opportunities for people with the curiosity, knowledge, and skill to collaborate on teams that solve complex problems with computational methods. Researching big data is most often a collaborative process, because the problems and attendant solutions are complex, entailing overlapping fields of expertise. Solutions often call for computational and discipline knowledge including mathematics, systems thinking, and educational, psychological, and organizational theory. Therefore, a new data science foundation for education research methodology and preparing the next generation of education researchers for big data in higher education is inevitable.

References

Bar-Yam, Y. (1997). *Dynamics of complex systems*. Reading, MA: Addison-Wesley.

Beinhocker, E. (2006). *The origin of wealth: Evolution, complexity and the radical remaking of economics*. Boston, MA: Harvard Business School Press.

Berland, M., Baker, R. S., & Bilkstein, P. (2014). Educational data mining and learning analytics: Applications to constructionist research. *Technology, Knowledge and Learning, 19*(1-2), 205–220. doi:10.1007/s10758-014-9223-7.

Bortz, J., & Döring, N. (1995). *Forschungsmethoden und Evaluation*. Berlin: Springer.

Bryman, A. (1988). *Quantity and quality in social research*. London: Unwin Hyman.

Caporaso, J. A. (1995). Research design, falsification, and the qualitative-quantitative divide. *American Political Science Review, 89*(2), 457–460. doi:10.2307/2082441.

Chaitin, G. (2003). *Algorithmic Information Theory Third Printing*. Computer.

Cohen, L., Manion, L., & Morrison, K. (2011). *Research methods in education* (7th ed.). New York: Routledge.

Cortes, C., & Vapnik, V. (1995). Support-vector networks. *Machine Learning, 20*(3), 273–297. doi:10.1007/bf00994018.

Creswell, J. W. (2008). *Educational research. Planning, conducting, and evaluating quantitative and qualitative research*. Upper Saddle River, NJ: Pearson.

Creswell, J. (n.d.). How Sage has shaped research methods: A forty year history.

Cumming, G. (2012). *Understanding the new statistics. Effect sizes, confidence intervals, and meta-analysis*. New York: Taylor & Francis Group.

Denzin, N. K., & Lincoln, Y. S. (2000). *Handbook of qualitative research*. Thousand Oaks: Sage.

Diamond, J. (2005). *Collapse: How societies choose to fail or succeed*. New York: Viking Penguin.

Drucker, H., Burges, C. J. C., Kaufman, L., Smola, A., & Vapnik, V. (1997). Support vector regression machines. In M. C. Mozer, M. I. Jordan, & T. Petsche (Eds.), *Advances in neural information processing systems 9* (pp. 155–161). Cambridge, MA: MIT Press.

Ferguson, R. (2012). Learning analytics: drivers, developments and challenges. *International Journal of Technology Enhanced Learning, 4*(5/6), 304–317. doi:10.1504/IJTEL.2012.051816.

Freeman, J. V., Collier, S., Staniforth, D., & Smith, K. J. (2008). Innovations in curriculum design: A multi-disciplinary approach to teaching statistics to undergraduate medical students. *BMC Medical Education, 8*, 28. doi:10.1186/1472-6920-8-28.

Friedman, T. (2005). *The world is flat: A brief history of the twenty-first century*. New York: Farrar, Straus & Giroux.

Gage, N. L. (1989). The paradigm wars and their aftermath: A "historical" sketch of research on teaching since 1989. *Educational Researcher, 18*(7), 4–10.

Gibson, D., & Knezek, G. (2011). Game changers for teacher education. In P. Mishra & M. Koehler (Eds.), *Proceedings of Society for Information Technology & Teacher Education International Conference 2011* (pp. 929–942). Chesapeake, VA: AACE.

Gibson, D., & Webb, M. (2015). Data science in educational assessment. *Education and Information Technologies, 20*(4), 697–713.

Guba, E. G. (1985). The context of emergent paradigm research. In Y. S. Lincoln (Ed.), *Organizational theory and inquiry* (pp. 79–104). Newbury Park, CA: Sage.

Healey, M. (2005). Linking research and teaching exploring disciplinary spaces and the role of inquiry-based learning. In R. Barnett (Ed.), *Reshaping the university: New relationships between research, scholarship and teaching* (pp. 30–42). Maidenhead, UK: McGraw-Hill International.

Holland, J. (1995). *Hidden order: How adaptation builds complexity*. Cambridge, MA: Perseus Books.

Ifenthaler, D. (2015). Learning analytics. In J. M. Spector (Ed.), *Encyclopedia of educational technology*. Thousand Oaks, CA: Sage.

Ifenthaler, D., Bellin-Mularski, N., & Mah, D.-K. (2015). Internet: Its impact and its potential for learning and instruction. In J. M. Spector (Ed.), *Encyclopedia of educational technology*. Thousand Oaks, CA: Sage.

Ifenthaler, D., & Gosper, M. (2014). Research-based learning: Connecting research and instruction. In M. Gosper & D. Ifenthaler (Eds.), *Curriculum models for the 21st Century. Using learning technologies in higher education* (pp. 73–90). New York: Springer.

Ifenthaler, D., & Widanapathirana, C. (2014). Development and validation of a learning analytics framework: Two case studies using support vector machines. *Technology, Knowledge and Learning, 19*(1-2), 221–240. doi:10.1007/s10758-014-9226-4.

Kachigan, S. K. (1991). *Multivariate statistical analysis: A conceptual introduction*. New York: Radius Press.

Lincoln, Y. S., Guba, E. G., Lincoln, E., & Guba, Y. (1985). *Naturalistic inquiry*. Newbury Park, CA: Sage.

Liu, Y.-Y., Slotine, J.-J., & Barabási, A.-L. (2011). Controllability of complex networks. *Nature, 473*(7346), 167–173. doi:10.1038/nature10011.

Long, P. D., & Siemens, G. (2011). Penetrating the fog: Analytics in learning and education. *EDUCAUSE Review, 46*(5), 31–40.

Manning, P. K. (1995). The challenges of postmodernism. In J. Van Maanen (Ed.), *Representation in ethnography*. Thousand Oaks, CA: Sage.

McLaughlin, E. (1991). Oppositional poverty: The quantitative/qualitative divide and other dichotomies. *Sociological Review, 39*(2), 292–308.

McNeill, W. (1998). History and the scientific worldview. *Hisotry and Theory, 37*(1), 1–13.

Newman, D. V. (1996). Emergence and strange attractors. *Philosophy of Science, 63*(2), 245–261.

Onwuegbuzie, A. J., & Leech, N. L. (2005). Taking the "q" out of research: Teaching research methodology courses without the divide between quantitative and qualitative paradigms. *Quality and Quantity, 39*(3), 267–296. doi:10.1007/s11135-004-1670-0.

Prigogine, I. (1996). *The end of certainty: Time, chaos, and the new laws of nature.*

Putnam, H. (1992). *Renewing philosophy*. Cambridge, MA: Harvard University Press.

Radzicki, M. J. (2003). Mr. Hamilton, Mr. Forrester, and a Foundation for Evolutionary Economics. *Journal of Economic Issues, 37*(1), 133–173.

Rihoux, B., & Grimm, H. (2006). Innovative comparative methods for policy analysis: Beyond the quantitative-qualitative divide. *Innovative Comparative Methods for Policy Analysis: Beyond the Quantitative-Qualitative Divide*. doi:10.1007/0-387-28829-5

Rockler, M. J. (1991). Thinking about chaos: Non-quantitative approaches to teacher education. *Action in Teacher Education, 12*(4), 56–62.

Romero, C., Ventura, S., Pechenizkiy, M., & Baker, R. S. J. D. (Eds.). (2011). *Handbook of educational data mining*. Boca Raton, FL: CRC Press.

Shah, S. K., & Corley, K. G. (2006). Building Better Theory by Bridging the Quantitative – Qualitative Divide. *Journal of Management Studies, 43*(8), 1821–1835. doi:10.1111/j.1467-6486.2006.00662.x.

Shum, S. B., & Ferguson, R. (2011). *Social learning analytics* (pp. 1–26). Knowledge Media Institute & Institute of Educational Technology. doi:10.1145/2330601.2330616.

Tarrow, S. (2010). Bridging the quantitative-qualitative divide. *Rethinking Social Inquiry* (pp. 101–110). Retrieved from http://books.google.com/books?hl=en&lr=&id=1VQK7EGohB4C&oi=fnd&pg=PA171&dq=Bridging+the+Quantitative-+Qualitative+Divide&ots=Z7fT2VDyFr&sig=Sg2h7poL6RrbxUkVcJGNwNuFtKs

Tetenbaum, T. J. (1998). Shifting paradigms: from Newton to chaos. *Organizational Dynamics, 26*(4), 21–32.

Wicks, D. (1998). Organizational structures as recursively constructed systems of agency and constraint: compliance and resistance in the context of structural conditions. *The Canadian Review of Sociology and Anthropology, 35*(3), 369–390.

Chapter 5
Managing the Embedded Digital Ecosystems (EDE) Using Big Data Paradigm

Shastri L. Nimmagadda and Amit Rudra

Abstract Big data sources and their mining from multitude of ecosystems have been the focus of many researchers in both commercial and research organizations. The authors in the current research have focused on embedded ecosystems with big data motivation. Embedded systems hold volumes and a variety of heterogeneous, multidimensional data, and their sources complicate their organization, accessibility, presentation, and interpretation. Objectives of the current research are to provide improved understanding of ecosystems and their inherent connectivity by integrating multiple ecosystems' big data sources in a data warehouse environment and their analysis with multivariate attribute instances and magnitudes. Domain ontologies are described for connectivity, effective data integration, and mining of embedded ecosystems. The authors attempt to exploit the impacts of disease and environment ecosystems on human ecosystems. To this extent, data patterns, trends, and correlations hidden among big data sources of embedded ecosystems are analyzed for domain knowledge. Data structures and implementation models deduced in the current work can guide the researchers of health care, welfare, and environment for forecasting of resources and managing information systems that involve with big data. Analyzing embedded ecosystems with robust methodologies facilitates the researchers to explore scope and new opportunities in the domain research.

Keywords Big data paradigm • Embedded digital ecosystems • Domain ontologies • Systems connectivity • Human-disease-environment ecosystems • Learning analytics and higher education

Introduction

The ecosystems involving humans, the environment in which they live in, and diseases that exist have connections. They are linked and influenced by one another. For example, when the environment is pristine, humans are more likely to be

---

S.L. Nimmagadda (✉) • A. Rudra
School of Information Systems, Curtin Business School,
Curtin University, Perth, WA, Australia
e-mail: shastri.nimmagadda@curtin.edu.au

B. Kei Daniel (ed.), *Big Data and Learning Analytics in Higher Education*,
DOI 10.1007/978-3-319-06520-5_5

healthier and less disease prone. As humans alter the purity of the environment, the diseases, in turn, get influenced. Thus, we can say that their underlying ecosystems are connected. In other words, they are embedded. Using constructs, models, and methodologies, the authors attempt to connect multiple ecosystems. Neuman (2000) and Vaishnavi & Kuechler (2004) describe articulation of constructs, models, and methods in the information systems' development. These constructs and models are added tools in the integration process of ecosystems as well. For the purpose of connecting the ecosystems, *human-disease-environment* and understating its connectivity, the big data are considered from multiple data sources. The authors choose multiple domains from multiple ecosystems, to analyze an inherent interconnectivity in which each domain appears to have dependence on the other and agreeing to the concepts of inheritance and polymorphism (Coronel et al., 2011; Vaishnavi & Kuechler, 2004). A domain model thus verified is expected to validate the problem domains of our research. For example, a domain model created for *human-disease-environment* inherits from multiple domains, in which either entities or dimensions associated with their common attributes explore the connectivity. The domain model represents vocabularies and key concepts of the problem domain among embedded ecosystems. The authors choose domain models that identify and describe the relationships among all the dimensions of *human-disease-environment* structure, with constraints and set of business rules. The scope of big data, needed for connecting multiple domains, is exploited within the context of problem definition. Several plot and map views computed from warehoused metadata are presented for new knowledge interpretation. Several conclusions, recommendations, and future scopes are made at the end of the paper.

Domain Description

Human existence deserves an understanding of embedded ecosystems (Gruber, 2007) and how best each and individual ecosystem is embedded with one another. Ecosystem modeling and its analysis typically involves associated data dimensions (Hoffer et al., 2005; Pratt & Adamski, 2000), their connection with dimensions of other ecosystems. Keeping in view the dynamicity, ecosystems have undergone turbulent situations (Kemp, 2004) since the last several decades, especially to perceive how they affect geographically and periodically with varying human, disease, and other ecological dimensions and their attributes. Modeling and mapping processes involving acquisition of big data and interpretation of the processed data for comprehensible embedded ecosystem model and its evaluation are needed. Understanding integrity and connectivity of ecosystems is crucial for analyzing broader view of ecological system, under varied process-engineering situations (Kemp, 2004). Mapping of an embedded ecosystem is always challenging, including implementation of models and embedded metadata.

Environment ecosystems of industrially developed and populated countries, often high pollution levels, pose poor visibility and discomfort, chemical radiations, and rain affecting the river systems. Fog and smog are carrier ways, polluting the human ecosystems (Nimmagadda et al., 2010). Acid rains caused by industry emissions of sulfur dioxide and nitrogen oxides into the atmosphere negatively affect freshwater lakes, vegetation, and even man-made structures. Anthropogenic pollutants are responsible for reducing the air quality and visibility, which affect the human and disease ecosystems. The effects of inadvertent alterations over long period of time pose serious threats to ecosystems, natural resources, food and fiber production, and ultimately economic and human development. These pollutants cause serious damage to disease ecosystems (Hadzic & Chang, 2005), causing respiratory illnesses such as asthma, tuberculosis (TB), and other chronic and communicable diseases. Toxic radiations too affect the environment, human, and disease ecosystems. Agriculture industry piles up large amounts of radiations affecting human and environment ecosystems. Currently, man-made pollutions made in manufacturing, energy, chemical, and transport industries are significantly affecting human, environment, and disease ecosystems and the breakdown of their connectivity.

Environment and disease ecosystems have direct impact on human ecosystems that consist of mass populations in industrial and populated countries. Emission of greenhouse gases (Nimmagadda & Dreher, 2009) into the atmosphere disturbs human ecology in many countries and is causative to frequent occurrence of extreme weather events, such as drought, extreme temperatures, heavy flooding, high winds, and severe storms. All these events on a larger scale affect the climate change and global warming, causative to even natural calamities. Recent wars in many countries have affected the human life significantly. Great devastation on the environment and unexploded ordinances make human life dangerous and fatal in many countries. Recent Ebola cases and deaths in West Africa are alarming, affecting the human ecosystems at faster rates. These alarming situations are good case studies and learning experiences to domain researchers. Domain experts and researchers identify and document all digital data associated with these ecosystems.

Problems and Issues

Human ecosystem has undergone turbulent and volatile periods for its existence especially during last century (Nimmagadda et al., 2008, 2010) due to rapid increase of populations; spread of viral, infectious, and chronic diseases; global warming; and natural disasters such as tornados, cyclones, and earthquakes. The authors contend that these events are interconnected in the form of cause and effect, through phenomena of an embedded ecosystem. World economic challenges and geopolitical instabilities are causative to human ecosystem impacts. These embedded ecosystems possess volumes of heterogeneous and multidimensional data. These big data are either poorly organized or unstructured, complicating the understanding of integrity and coexistence of ecosystems. Data integration including managing interactive ecosystems across multiple geographic and distributed environments is complex, and periodic understanding of embedded system is challenging. Historical big data pertaining to multiple ecosystems (spatial dimension) archived for many decades (periodic dimension) are good data sources for embedded ecosystems' analysis. The historical data, in general, fluctuate with period and modeling of time-varying ecosystems that involve big data. Warehousing big data in an integrated database environment is a much needed task. Warehoused ecosystems' metadata need effective mining and visualization schemes, through which inheritance and connectivity can be explored and exploited by domain experts and researchers.

Understanding of embedded ecosystems in different periodic intervals is a significant problem. Data integration and sharing of processed data among several geographically located operation units (in a country or time span) are a challenging issue. In order to understand disease and environments on human impacts, the authors propose integration of big data sources among several lateral and longitudinal data dimensions. So far, little attention is given in integrating and organizing these historical ecosystems' data sources. To date, there has been limited systematic investigation done using these data volumes from multiple domains and dimensions. The authors contend that unorganized and unstructured volumes of massive stores of ecosystems' data hide undiscovered scientific and technical knowledge or intelligence. Further limitations of organizing heterogeneous and multidimensional ecosystems with the existing information systems are described in the following sections.

Limitations of the Current Information Systems (IS) Development Methodologies

Current IS development methodology has inherent limitations (Indulska & Recker, 2008; O'Brien & Marakas, 2009; Pratt & Adamski, 2000; Rainer & Turban, 2009) in managing application domains associated with heterogeneous and multidimensional embedded systems. This limitation is constrained by type and size of heterogeneous data including process of IS research. Existing IS methodologies in complex application domains pose widening gaps in terms of their development and implementation. The prevailing IS methodology cannot handle multiple application domains, such as *human-disease-environment* with historical periodic and geographic dimensions *such as country*, *culture*, *size*, and *local environments*. Generalization may not be done especially for applications of dynamic and progressive environments in which big data play key roles. Prevailing IS practice is not compatible and user-friendly within progressive business, government, and social network systems. Complex embedded systems at times are difficult to manage because of heterogeneity and multidimensionality, thus posing problems in extracting new knowledge and adding value to the problem solutions. Such is an example, *human*, *disease*, *and environment* ecosystems, knowing that they are inherently embedded and their data volumes are difficult to manage. The authors propose new approaches for managing these embedded systems in this research.

From the problem descriptions, *human-disease-environment* dimensions are closely connected. If a dimension gets disturbed, other dimensions closely associated to it also get affected. This implies that all the dimensions described here are inherently interconnected. The authors conceptually describe entities as dimensions in the current heterogeneous and multidimensional ecosystems' scenarios.

Significance of the Research Work

1. Domain experts and researchers involved in big data projects can make use of the robust methodologies in the research institutes.
2. Big data information systems for heterogeneous and multidimensional data sources.
3. Domain ontologies (Nimmagadda & Dreher, 2011; Sidhu et al., 2009) and data models possess flexibility in the warehousing environment—accommodating future changes in complex embedded ecosystems.
4. Ecosystems' data analytics considered here are of both technical and business nature—focused on building new knowledge, under different geographic and spatial dimensions, with an intention minimizing the risk of interpretation of multiple embedded ecosystems' knowledge.
5. For accessing the data views, faster operational and user-response times—minimizing operational costs in warehousing, mining, visualization, and interpretation, adding value to the new knowledge.
6. Trend- and pattern-based scenarios in ecosystems' big data science management.

Related Work

Volumes and a variety of multiple dimensions, attributes, and instances considered from big data sources are described in the current research work. Existing literature and models, described by various researchers, are given. Shanks et al. (2004) describe numerous composite attributes in conceptual modeling requirement analysis. Keller (2005) provides detailed description of statistical analysis in the management and economic domains. Nimmagadda et al. (2010) and Nimmagadda & Dreher (2007) narrate human ecosystems and modeling of human anatomy. Nimmagadda & Dreher (2009) describe robust and comprehensive methodologies for managing CO_2 emission ecosystems' heterogeneous data sources in both geographic and time-period dimensions. Nimmagadda & Dreher (2011) describe new emerging concepts of digital ecosystems in petroleum domain application, demonstrating design, development, and implementation of models. Nimmagadda & Dreher (2011) demonstrate robust methodologies for diabetic disease big data organization and its management among mass populations worldwide. Baker (2010) and Ali (2013) consider various data mining procedures and algorithms for education purposes. Siemens & Baker (2012) and Romero & Ventura (2007, 2010) provide the significance of data mining in the educational sector for which big data and their attributes are taken for higher education research. Hoffer et al. (2005) and Pujari (2002) describe various data modeling techniques with business constraints. Pujari (2002) narrates several algorithms of data mining schemes. Big data analytic concepts and tools are given in Cleary et al. (2012). Multidimensional modeling approach, with schema architectures used in petroleum industries, is described in Nimmagadda & Dreher (2014). Big data and business information systems, their impacts in various application domains, have been discussed in Dhar et al. (2014). Big data in technology perspective and as an interdisciplinary opportunity for information systems research are demonstrated in Schermann et al. (2014). Big data skills and intelligence interpreted with data science and analytic perspectives are compared in Debortoli et al. (2014).

Description of Proposed Research Approach

Our proposed IS development methodologies are generalized version, handling heterogeneous big data that can support two or more systems or their merge in the integration process. These methodologies handle generalization, specialization, and contextualization issues. In other words, generalization and specialization, feasible and applicable in IS research and practice, are conceptualized and contextualized in multiple data structures and problem domains. Data structuring describes fine-grained data schemas (Rudra & Nimmagadda, 2005) in multiple domains and integration of domain ontologies. The multidimensional big data structuring process supports heterogeneity, multidimensionality, and granularity, among multiple data sources and domains. These approaches are needed to address the current IS problem domain and solution development in different geographic and periodic dimensions. Proposed IS methodology and practice in heterogeneous big data arena can address human ecosystems broadly with *population scale*, *country-range*, *sizes*, and *cultures* attributes, including their *value chains* (Nimmagadda & Dreher, 2014) extended to disease and environments of each country under study.

Concept of Big Data Information Systems and Its Development

Either structured or unstructured volumes of a variety of data that move at faster rates in big companies at global scale are characterized by heterogeneity, multidimensionality, and granularity (Dhar et al., 2014; Schermann et al., 2014). In big data paradigm, sets of components associated with data collection, storage, and processing are integrated for developing information systems that can deliver quality of information, knowledge, and digital products. Integration, in our context, is a process of connecting data from multiple sources (even from multiple problem domains), providing users with a unified view of metadata that enable us to interpret domain knowledge for quality decision-making. *Human-disease-environment* domains possess big data sources, with each other having inherent connectivity problems. The authors enunciate systems dealing with big data in multiple problem domains, articulating heterogeneous data types in the multidimensional structuring process. Spatial-temporal big data on global scale need new IS research paradigms. Presently, the authors intend to analyze an integrated framework in the context of developing and implementing an embedded ecosystem. Description of domain, data modeling, data mining, visualization, and interpretation are artifacts discussed in the following sections for evaluating the integrated framework.

Computational methodologies and procedures used to analyze the computed data are elaborated. The authors interpret and analyze data views for new information and knowledge, which have value to sustain and add values to embedded systems that deal with big data.

Data Sources Considered in the Study

Enormous spatial-temporal big data are available in different unstructured data sources. Data sources from human, disease, and environment ecosystems are considered. Hundreds of data attributes and their instances are used. Around 150 countries' geographic and 53 years of periodic data (1960–2013) dimensions are considered. But the authors focus on 16 countries' "geographic and periodic" data dimensions, comprising of developed countries, developing countries, and war-torn, disease-prone, and environmentally sensitive countries, in order to test and evaluate the phenomena human-disease-environment and their ecosystems' inheritance and connectivity. Modeling and mapping data sources from these countries may outline the connectivity among human ecosystems affected by disease and environment ecosystems.

Though ecosystems are interconnected (Kemp, 2004), often they are either interpreted in isolation or misinterpreted, when human ecosystem is to be narrated in its totality. These periodic data are represented for each country, for populations of different ages and genders, including types of viral, chronic, infectious, and hereditary data sources of disease ecosystems. *CO_2 emissions* and *air pollutions* (particulate matter, PM 10 and PM 2.5) are other data sources considered in the environment ecosystems' domain. The World Health Organization (WHO) has volumes of big data and information on geographical locations, intensities of storms, tropical cyclones, and official warnings made to the mass populations including short- and long-term forecasts.

Keeping in view the significance of integration process and the connectivity among multiple ecosystems, a framework is designed in which acquisition of heterogeneous data is made. Different schemas used for organizing each and individual ecosystem data sources are described. Data sources of multiple ecosystems are documented keeping in view the multidimensional data, their attributes from multiple domains, and for data warehouse purpose.

Description of an Integrated Framework

Domain, data modeling, schema, warehouse, mining, visualization, and interpretation schemes are typical components of an integrated framework (Nimmagadda & Dreher, 2012). They are put together to store, integrate, and process data sources. Several ecosystems that appear to have digital interconnection are described in the following sections.

Human ecosystems: Population, *age*, and *gender* along with the living and working conditions are parts of human species and human ecosystem description. Human anatomy is an integrated structural pattern of the human body system (Nimmagadda et al., 2008). Physiological, psychological, and emotional data patterns (Nimmagadda et al., 2010) are observed and interpreted to narrate the human system integrity and its connectivity with its closely associated disease and environmental ecosystems.

Disease ecosystems: The chronic, respiratory, viral, infectious, and hereditary illnesses are considered with disease ecosystems (Hadzic & Chang, 2005; Nimmagadda et al., 2008). This ecosystem explores connections from human and environmental ecosystems. All the data patterns acquired are processed in presentable form and interpreted them for knowledge mapping.

Environmental ecosystems: CO_2 emissions and *air pollutions*, *particulate matter* (PM 10 and PM 2.5) data sources observed in each and every *country*, are geographically interconnected (Nimmagadda & Dreher, 2009), and in the present context, they are said to be inherently associated, affecting human and disease ecosystems.

The authors address the issues associated with embedded systems including applicability and feasibility of integrated framework. Health-care industry that involves human, disease, and environment ecosystems produces volumes of time-varying data (Nimmagadda et al., 2011; Nimmagadda & Dreher, 2011). The authors document and organize historical data sources of human, disease, and environmental ecosystems for warehousing, mining, visualization, and ultimately pattern interpretation and analysis at different geographic locations and periodic intervals. For this purpose, multiple dimensions from different domains are conceptualized (Agarwal et al., 1996; Nimmagadda & Dreher, 2006) in the integrated framework. The proposed integrated framework narrates domain ontologies, structuring multidimensional data models, mining schemes, visualization, and interpretation of metadata procedures. Several such components considered in the current framework are briefly described in the following sections.

Domain Modeling

Description of entities associated with knowledge base structure human-disease-environment and building their relationships are highlights of the domain modeling. As demonstrated in Fig. 5.1, multiple domains, their dimensions, their attributes, and their instances are identified. Dimensions identified from data sources from human, disease, and environment ecosystems are considered in the modeling process. In environment ecosystems, air pollution and CO_2 emissions are typical attributes. Injurious smoke, emitted by cars, buses, trucks, trains, and factories, are other attributes of environment ecosystems. Sulfur dioxide, carbon monoxide, and nitrogen oxide are most common forms of harmful emissions. Smoke released from burning leaves and cigarettes are dangerous to human and environment. Lung cancer, asthma, allergies, and various other breathing entities are most common dimensions that damage to flora and fauna. Even birds and animal kingdom is also affected by severe air pollutions. These attributes that affect the disease ecosystems are connected to both environment and human ecosystems through data modeling and warehouse. Figure 5.1 demonstrates modeling of multiple domains through connections of attribute relations among ecosystems.

As shown in Fig. 5.1, data sources and their anomalies from human, disease, and environment domains are described, with depiction of multiple dimensions in each domain. Relational, hierarchical, and networking multidimensional data modeling studies are carried out (Nimmagadda et al., 2011; Nimmagadda & Dreher, 2011), using simple and explicit *comparison*-based ontology. The *comparison* is performed on relationally and hierarchically structured data dimensions. These models are

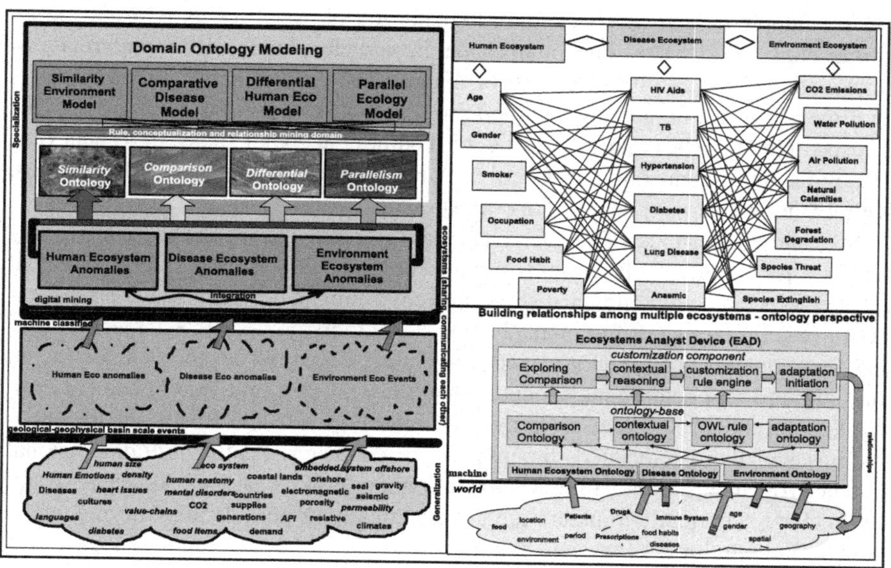

Fig. 5.1 Domain modeling for exploring connectivity among attributes of multiple ecosystems

compatible to data warehousing and data mining. This methodology is adopted to understand the connectivity among human, disease, and environment ecosystems. Several human behavioral, social disorders, emotional data sources can be added (beyond the scope of current study), under category of human ecosystems. Similarly, disease and clinical related, such as physiological and psychological data sources, under category of disease ecosystems are considered. Environmental data sources considered from climatologically described geographies of different countries affected by human and disease ecosystems are used. For example, a *comparison* may be made among human ecosystems, which could be between *male* and *female*, *fat* and *skinny*, *disabled* and *normal* and abnormal (psychologically disturbed) persons, *smokers* and *non-smokers*, and among different *age* group domains. There are different hierarchies among which different super-type dimensions are conceptualized into several subtype dimensions. Domain ontologies built based on the known-knowledge mining and thus unknown data relationships evolved through conceptualization and contextualization are modeled. These relationships are mere occurrence of series of events in multiple ecosystems and their integration in an integrated framework.

Data Modeling

Several dimensions and their attributes are described for modeling human, disease, and environment data sources. Different dimensions identified for logical and physical modeling are documented along with their facts. The authors narrate type and size of data to consider in the data modeling approach. Three levels of data modeling are adopted, such as conceptual, logical, and physical levels (Gornik, 2000; Hoffer et al., 2005). The conceptual model investigates highest level data relationships, either among entities, objects, or dimensions. In this analysis, more focus is on dimensions, for organizing and modeling multiple dimensions of heterogeneous datasets. No attributes and keys are described at conceptual stage. In logical data modeling, the dimensions are described with more details on data relationships, without any concern on physical organization.

Star, snowflake, and constellation schemas (Nimmagadda & Dreher, 2006, 2011) are used for building relationships among multiple dimensions, described for all entities associated with human, disease, and environment domains. Several schemas exist in the literature (Hoffer et al., 2005). The authors propose the star, snowflake, and fact constellation schemas, since they are compatible to accommodating in multidimensional heterogeneous data structuring process in a warehouse environment. Several such schemas are provided in the Figs. 5.2 and 5.3. Embedded ecosystems and their associated dimensions are characteristically multidimensional and heterogeneous. For example, spatial-temporal dimensions (Khatri & Ram, 2004) characteristically in nature are geographically or periodically varying, especially among multiple ecosystem situations.

Big data being unstructured, heterogeneous, and multidimensional from variety and volumes of data sources, research organizations get benefited from studies of

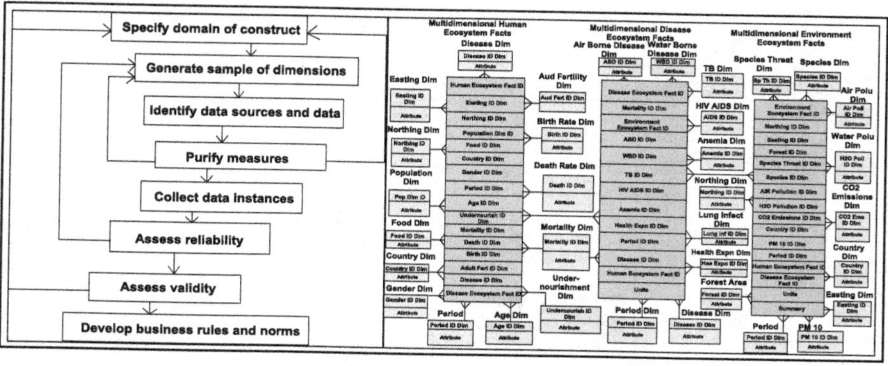

Fig. 5.2 Multidimensional data acquisition workflow and schemas for ecosystems

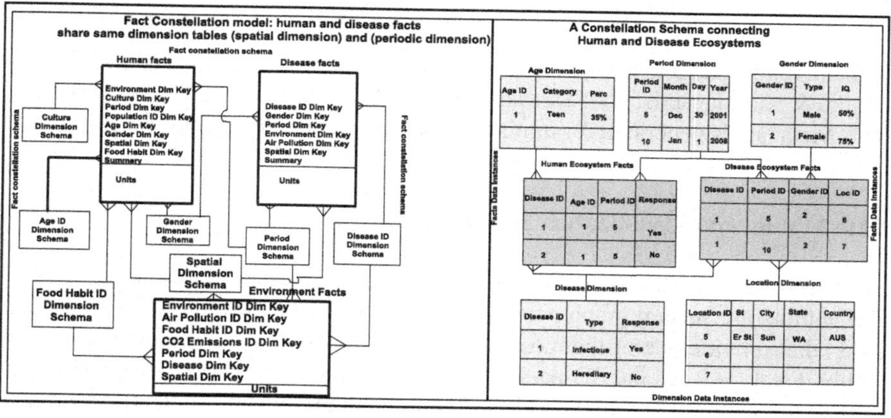

Fig. 5.3 Design of fact constellation schemas, connecting spatial and periodic dimensions

embedded digital ecosystems that can generate large amount of learning analytic information. Clustering, classification, outlier, association, patterns' matching, and text mining are different mining techniques used for analyzing the big data metadata views. These approaches can even be incorporated in curriculum of educational systems. This can help use, interact, participate, and communicate between student and research communities and among educational institutes.

Warehouse Modeling

Multidimensional models designed and developed for various ecosystems are accommodated in the warehouse modeling for storage, integration, and processing for metadata, mining, and visualization purposes as demonstrated in Fig. 5.4.

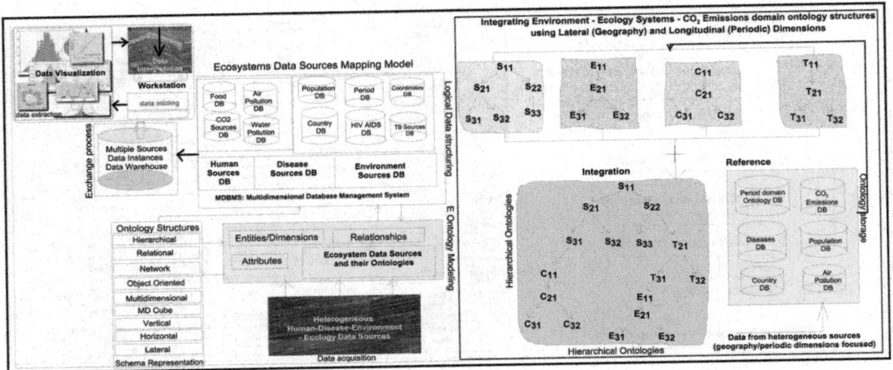

Fig. 5.4 An integrated framework, narrating integration process of embedded systems using data warehousing, mining, visualization, and interpretation entities

Domain ontologies and fine-grained denormalized multidimensional data structures (Rudra & Nimmagadda, 2005) are accommodated in the integrated framework (Fig. 5.4). Metadata is generated for mining, visualization, and interpretation purposes.

Data Mining and Visualization Schemes

Baker (2010) and Ali (2013) use data mining techniques for education purposes. The authors use several graphic tools (Cleary et al., 2012; Nimmagadda & Dreher, 2011) that provide one of the most effective means of communication, because of highly developed 2D and 3D pattern-recognition capabilities, perceiving and processing the pictorial and high-quality digital data rapidly and efficiently. Mattison (1996) discusses several case studies, narrating applications to data visualization technique. Data views are extracted from warehoused metadata and presented for visualization and interpretation. By using visualization, data are summarized and the trends are highlighted. Unknown phenomena are uncovered through various kinds of graphical representation. Several visualization techniques are used to analyze spatial-temporal multidimensional datasets of human, disease, and environment ecosystems.

Brief description of data mining methods is given, for which data correlations, trends, and patterns among embedded ecosystems' data attributes are interpreted. The plot and map views are made good use of interpreting data mining patterns. The scientific goals (Neuman, 2000) of data mining are:

1) *Explanatory*—explain observed events or conditions (such as why *aging population* is increased in a particular period of time and space)
2) *Confirmatory*—confirm a hypothesis (such as whether a particular *age* or *gender* can create similar symptoms of diseases, or different *age* groups may have same *disease*)

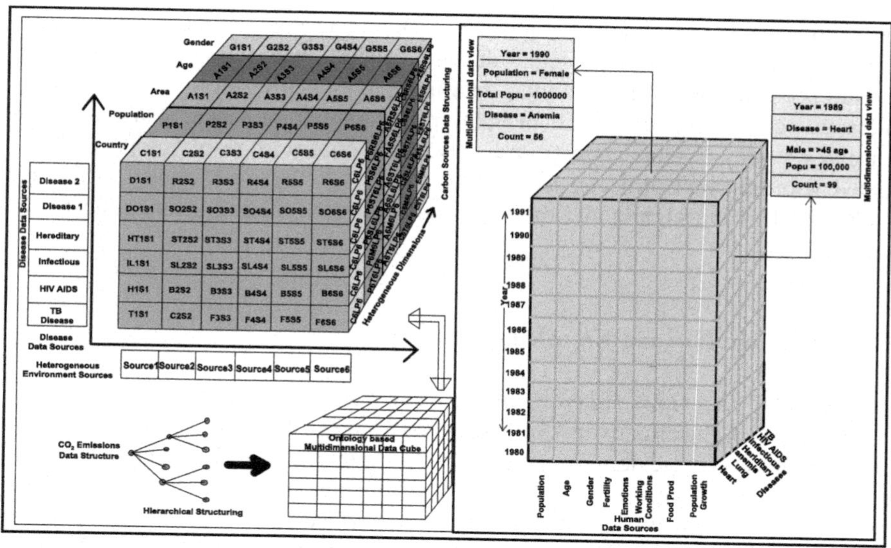

Fig. 5.5 Mining and visualization of the data views from big data cubes

3) *Exploratory*—to analyze data for new or unexpected relationships (such as what health expenditure patterns are likely to appear in a particular *period* of time, and what *CO_2 emissions* and *air pollution* levels affect certain populated countries and population categories including *endangered species*)

Periodic dimensions are included among *population* data sources of different countries in the integration process. Data views extracted with reference to the *period* dimension are used for interpreting the new knowledge and information. In other words, data mining of *population, disease, and CO_2 emissions*' data volumes, characterizing multidimensional visualization, perceives an interpretable knowledge in multiple domains. Metadata in the form of several cubes are generated for mining and visualization, and one of such cube is narrated in Fig. 5.5.

Forecasting focuses on the decomposition (Miller & Han, 2001; Moody & Kortink, 2003) of data attributes into different periodic components, estimating each pattern separately and then combining the projected impact of each component into the future to produce the final forecast. For instance, determining a drop either in human *population* patterns or increase in *disease* patterns, due to seasonal, random, or trend variations (or how much can be attributed to each) may be vitally significant in evaluating current policies and indicating the corrective action required in the evaluation process.

Researchers involved in the big data mining, visualization, and adding values to the projects of digital ecosystems have immense scope of extending their knowledge and learning experience in the educational institutions. In higher education systems, educational institutes can do undertake domain research relevant to data integration, ontology modeling connecting different academic dimensions and educators, interacting various systems' development projects through their learning experience. Large amount of digital data is accumulated in the educational institutes, though they are sensitive data and information, but for academic and research purposes, it may be challenging to use these data sources for resolving issues associated with research projects. Siemens & Baker (2012) and Romero & Ventura (2007, 2010) have highlighted the significance of data mining in the educational sector.

Data Interpretation and Knowledge Discovery

The extracted data views are interpreted for new knowledge, thus for evaluating the implementation and effectiveness of integrated framework and data models designed in different knowledge domains (Fig. 5.6). Data interpretation is crucial, which can test the validity of the data models, data warehousing, and mining including effectiveness of visualization. Qualitatively, the trends, patterns, and correlations observed among data events are interpreted for understanding knowledge enhancements in the new knowledge. In addition, relevance, effectiveness, efficiency, impacts, and sustainability criteria are described. Extent and duration of usage of data models and integrated framework including implementation of contextual, short- and long-term research outcomes between easting and northing dimensions are other interpretation objectives.

Data analysis and interpretation are meant for transforming the data collected or processed into meaningful new knowledge and its interpretation. Interpretation outcomes ensure effective evaluation of data organization and descriptive analysis. Data interpretation is expected to confirm the measure, consistency, and effectiveness of multidimensional and heterogeneous data organization, modeling, mapping, and data mining including effectiveness of data visualization. Interpretation may be qualitative and quantitative and the data patterns, trends, and correlations interpreted that lead to discovery of knowledge are implementable for new knowledge.

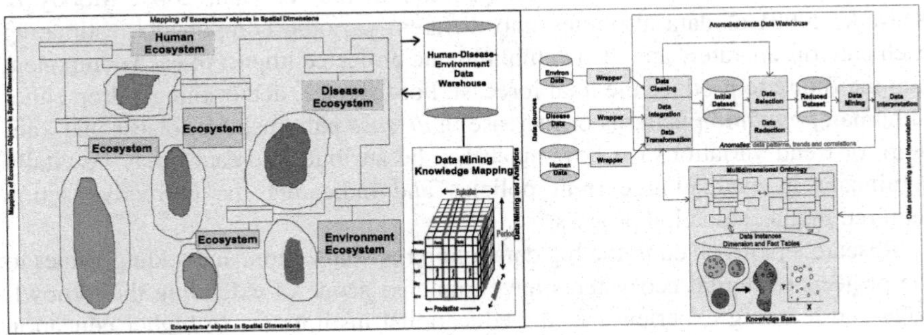

Fig. 5.6 Knowledge-based workflows for ecosystems' metadata

Implementation of an Integrated Framework—New Knowledge Representation

Data mining methods are used to extract multiple data views from the warehoused embedded ecosystems' data. The data views that contain several patterns, correlations, and trends are successfully interpreted into valuable business data knowledge. Several statistical data models are deduced for the benefit of the managers engaged in the ecosystems' analysis. The computed models forecast and provide inputs to corporate health-care management, based on human and environment conditions. Technological changes are challenging in addition to economic situations, predicting human health care and survival in different countries. This robust methodology provides definite clues for understanding ecosystem of ecosystems and their connectivity.

The following recommendations are made based on the periodically varying ecosystems' big data analysis and interpretation:

- Statistical models computed in the present paper are useful to guide managers involved in the ecosystems and health-care management.
- Some of the actual data presented may contain noise, but not necessarily random, which could be due to ecosystems and their conflicts of connectivity. However a good statistical trend is estimated and helps in understanding of the attribute variation.

Data mining approaches, as described in Pujari (2002), are tried in understanding the correlations, trends, and patterns in the ecosystems' data, since all the multidisciplinary data sources are in the form of an integrated metadata.

In the present studies, data sources considered are from the period 1960 to 2013 (periodic dimension) for 150 countries (geographic dimension). These long-term tendencies are known as trends. For particular time periods, the observed values are dipping below the trend curve. They are representing the peaks of their respective business cycles. Any observed data that do not follow the smooth-fitted trend curve modified by the aforementioned cyclical movements are indicative of turbulence or the irregular or random factors of influence. When data are recorded monthly rather than annually, an additional factor has influence on the time series data, which could be due to the seasonal component. At certain periods of time, the trends appear to be irregular or random and seasonal at other periods of time.

As shown in Fig. 5.7, several bubble plot views are extracted from metadata for interpreting the trends and patterns. Exploring and interpreting several patterns, correlations, and trends are the goals of current research from data sources that have *geographic coordinates*, *forest-added and lost areas*, *HIV/AIDS*, and *mortality* and *population birth rate* attributes. Similar bubble plots are used with patterns of time series data that can detect spatial-temporal variations among embedded ecosystems for new knowledge. Current human-disease-environment, an embedded ecosystem, in which enormous amount of time-varying heterogeneous data and instances

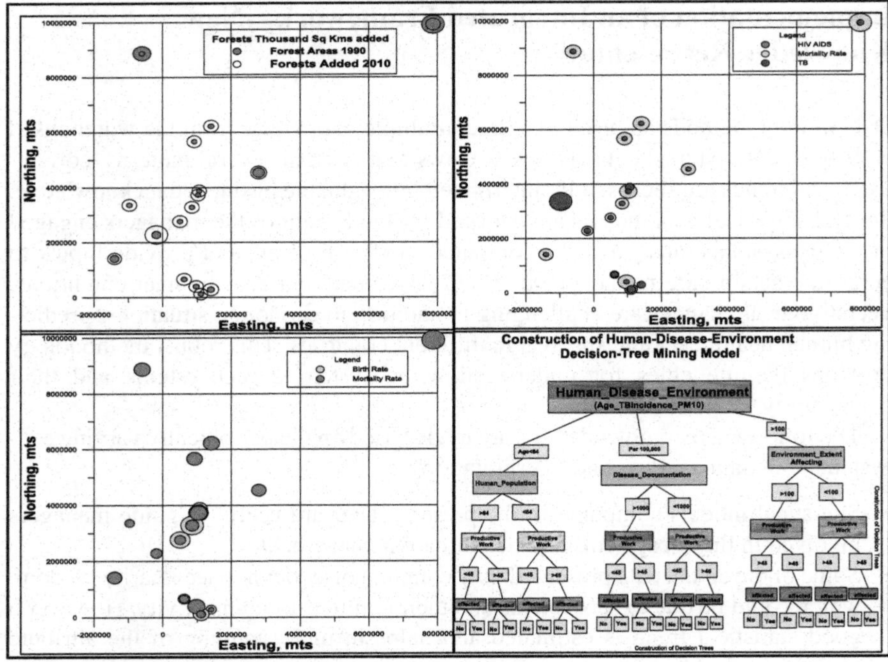

Fig. 5.7 Bubble plot views of multidimensional data attributes among multiple ecosystems

acquired, is used for analyzing the phenomena. Statistical mining approaches (Keller, 2005) are used for interpreting time series patterns. The computed data presented in Figs. 5.8 and 5.9 are examined for data correlations, trends, and patterns and thus for interpretation of human-disease-environment structure at geographically varying and temporal dimensions. Visualization of the characteristics of time series data plots of human disease patterns has shown a tendency to increase in proportion with period of 53 years.

Different types of trends are distinguished from human-disease-environment ecosystems' data viewpoint. Brief interpretation of these bubble plots and their description is given in the following sections.

Interpretation of Multidimensional Bubble Plots

Yearly (from 1960 to 2013), *population growth*, *food production*, *CO_2 emissions*, and *mortality (male/female)* attribute trends are plotted in individual plot views as displayed in Figs. 5.8 and 5.9. As shown in Fig. 5.8, a total of 17 geographic locations are analyzed. Attributes such as *population growth* vs. *food production*, *female population* vs. *total population*, *food production* vs. *total population*, and CO_2

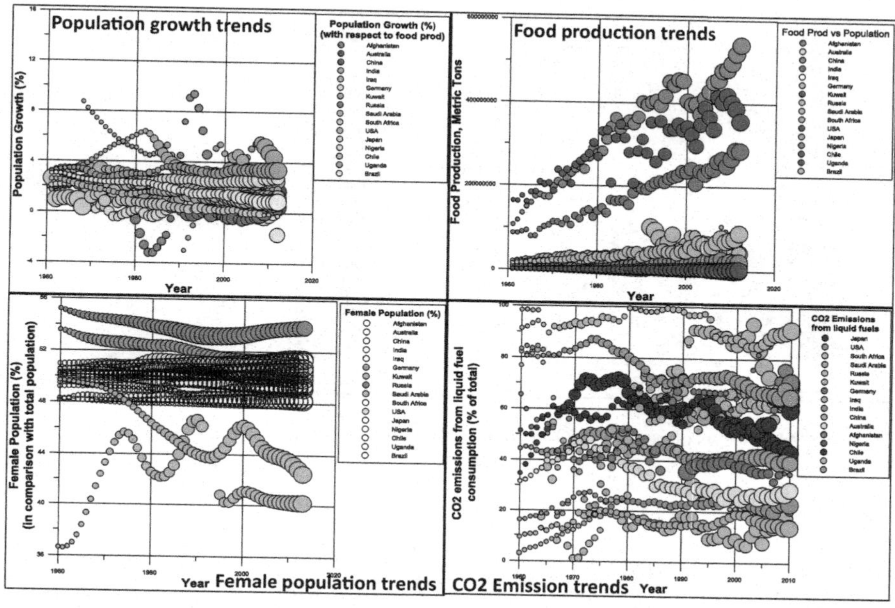

Fig. 5.8 Bubble plot views among multidimensional attributes for interpreting data trends and patterns among male and female population growth and CO_2 emission patterns

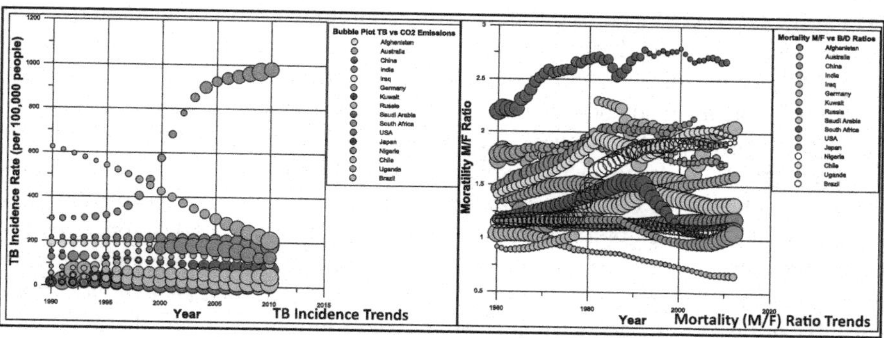

Fig. 5.9 Bubble plot views among multidimensional attributes for interpreting data trends and patterns of mortality rates due to tuberculosis

emissions (due to liquid fuel consumption) and total *CO_2 emissions* are considered. Overall *population growth* varies in range 0–4 % among 17 geographic locations from developed, populated, disease-prone, environmentally sensitive countries. Increasing in bubble size with periodic time dimension suggests population increase with every *year.* *Population growth* in China, India, and the USA is under control, whereas countries such as Saudi Arabia, Kuwait, and Afghanistan have uneven

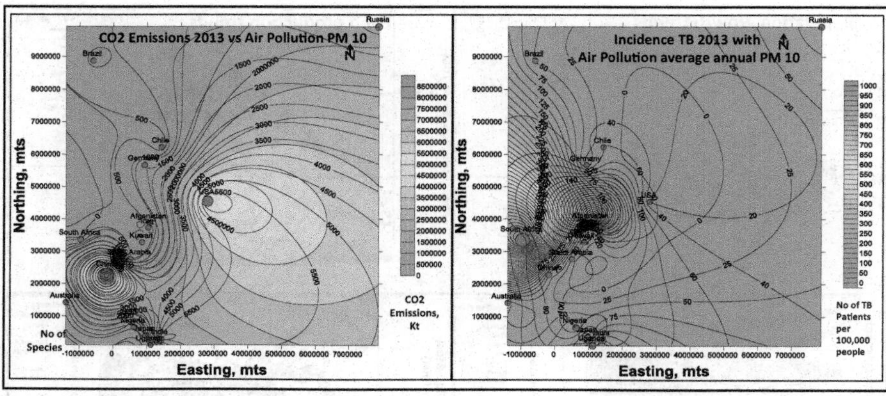

Fig. 5.10 Map views of periodic CO_2 *emissions* in correlation with *air pollutions*

population growth, especially in between 1980 and 2000 years, compared with other countries, in which a steady *population growth* with *period* is interpreted.

Female population attribute with respect to *overall population*, though, is steadily decreasing with period, but interestingly with an increase in bubble size, suggesting *female population* growth, is much better in the industrially developed countries, such as the USA, Germany, and Russia. Attributes plotted between *food production* and *population* suggest that *food production* in populated countries such as China, the USA, and India is much better compared with other countries.

Bubble plots are made between overall CO_2 *emissions* and CO_2 *emissions due to liquid fuel consumption* attributes, though they lead in the industrially developed countries, but their dominance is worst in the Middle Eastern countries. It is the percentage change of CO_2 *emissions* from liquid fuel consumption to total CO_2 *emissions*, and it varies in a large range of 4–98 % among these developed, populated, war-torn, and disease-prone countries. These emissions are minimum in between years 1980 and 1990. Bubble plots drawn between *incidence of tuberculosis* (TB) and *mortality rate* attributes, as shown in Fig. 5.9, suggest that mortality rate is higher in African countries compared with other countries in Asia and America. This attribute is also badly affected in Russia.

Several map views are extracted from metadata and they are represented in Figs. 5.10, 5.11, 5.12, 5.13, 5.14, and 5.15 in multidimensional attributes with varying *easting* and *northing* coordinate dimensions. The maps views are drawn with equal attribute instance values on different *contours*. The color bar is representative of high and less attribute strengths. The description of contour interpretations on map views is given in the following sections.

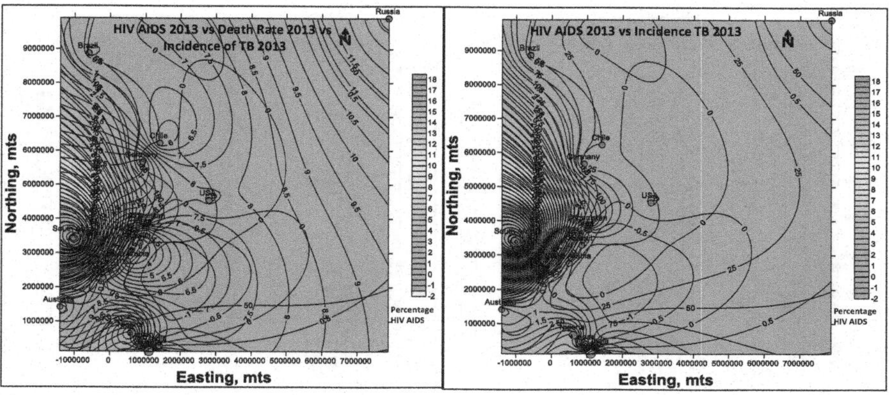

Fig. 5.11 Map views, showing HIV/AIDS vs. *death rate* vs. *incidence of TB* cases (all contours superimposed in each map view)

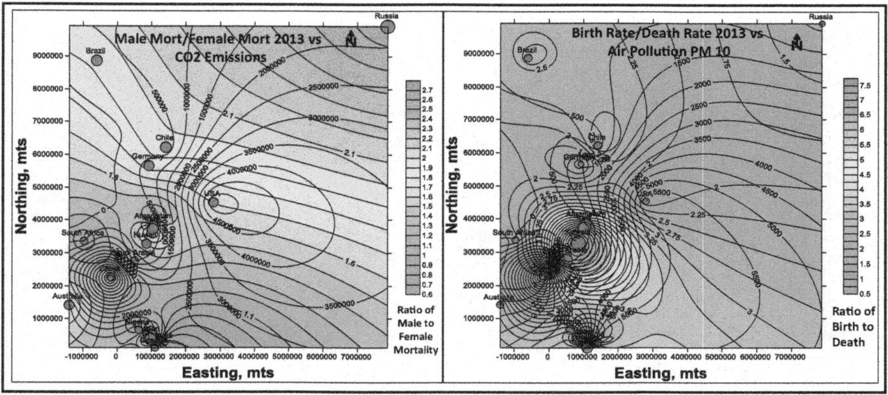

Fig. 5.12 Map views of human mortalities with respect to periodic *CO_2 emissions* and *air pollutions*

Interpretation of Multidimensional Map Views

Map views as shown in Fig. 5.10 narrate distributions of *CO_2 emissions* vs. *air pollutions (PM 10)* with respect to geographic *easting* and *northing* dimensions. These are dominant in the industrially developed and populated countries. A scale bar is shown ranging from red to green color, red color indicating dense emissions and pollutions. Right-hand map view narrates *prevalence of tuberculosis (TB) disease* attribute in the southern parts of Africa and its attribute strength increases toward Russia. Distribution of air pollutions is also observed wherever the tuberculosis attribute is prevalent. Similar observations are made with dense *HIV/AIDS*

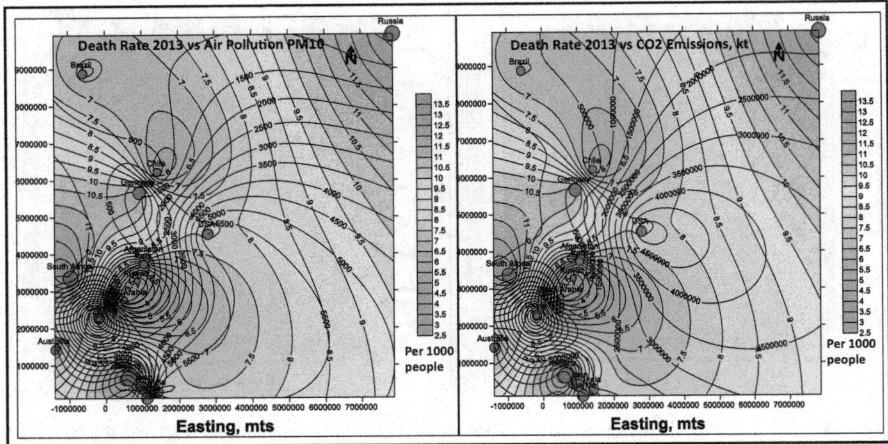

Fig. 5.13 Map views showing periodic *death* rates vs. *air pollutions* and CO_2 *emissions*

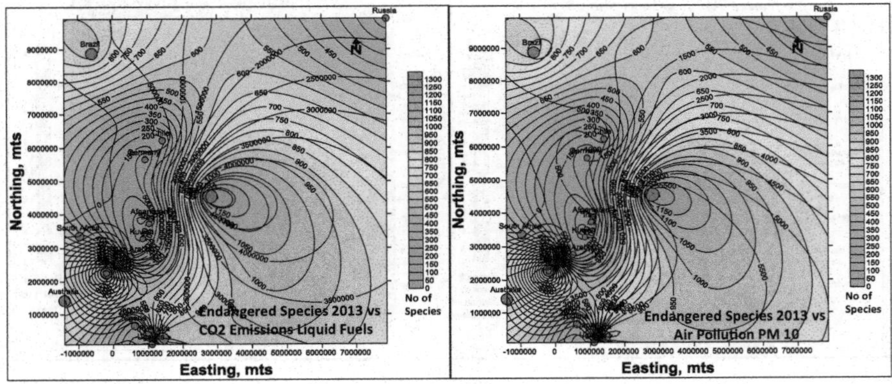

Fig. 5.14 Map views showing endangered species with CO_2 *emissions* and *air pollutions*

attributes in the Eastern, Southern, and sub-Saharan African countries, wherever TB attribute cases are reported as shown in Figs. 5.11 and 5.12.

As shown in Figs. 5.13 and 5.14, increase in *mortality rate* (*male to female ratio*) is also observed around Middle Eastern Africa including Russia where dense CO_2 *emissions* attribute is prevalent. *Birth to death ratio* attribute (shown in right-hand map view of Figs. 5.13 and 5.14) is prevalent in the Middle East and Asia countries including African countries. Color scale is interpreted to have a range of red color to green color, respectively, dense air pollutions to less-dense pollution areas. Similar observations are made with increase of death rates wherever the dense air pollutions are prevalent as interpreted in map views of Fig. 5.15. *Species endangered* attribute correlates well with the spread and distributions of CO_2 *emissions* and other air pollutions as shown in Fig. 5.15, especially for countries the USA,

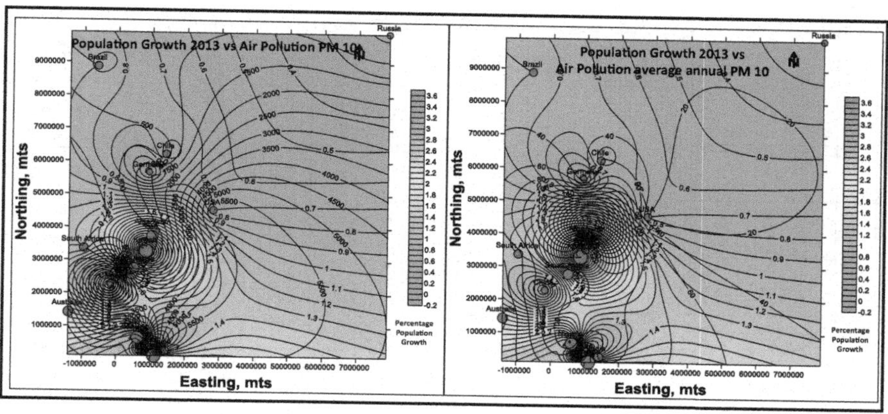

Fig. 5.15 Map views showing periodic population growth with air pollutions

China, India, Australia, and Brazil. This affect is less in the Middle Eastern, African, and Russian countries.

Population growth attributes get affected with dense *air pollution* attributes, PM 10 and PM 2.5, in the Asian and Middle Eastern regions as demonstrated in Figs. 5.10–5.15. *Air pollutions* in the form of particulate matter (PM) refer to fine-suspended particulates less than 10 μm in diameter, capable of penetrating deep into the respiratory tract, causing health damage. *CO_2 emissions* and *air pollutions* are causative to drop in *population growth* including *female fertility rates*. As demonstrated in Figs. 5.12, 5.13, 5.14, and 5.15, *mortality* and *death rate* attributes are higher in countries in Africa including Asian countries. *Air pollutions* and *CO_2 emissions* characterize similar attribute trends in the Guinea, Liberia, and Sierra Leone regions. Instances of recent *Ebola cases* and *deaths* reported are less in comparison with big data sources of worldwide populations and diseases. However, the authors attempt to deduce trends of *Ebola cases* and *Ebola deaths* with *periodic* dimension as described in Fig. 5.16 with bubble and scatter plot views. The increasing size of the bubble is interpreted to be associated with increasing number of *Ebola cases and Ebola deaths*.

Map views are drawn (Fig. 5.17) for interpreting the trends of attributes, *HIV/AIDS*, *air pollution*, *CO_2 emissions*, and *population growth* that added to *Ebola cases* and *Ebola deaths* of West African nations. *Ebola cases* and *Ebola deaths* attributes are in increasing trend in the Liberia and Sierra Leone countries, suggesting an increase in patterns in the northwesterly direction. Increasing in *CO_2 emissions* and *air pollution* rates have definite impact on *endangered species attribute* in the populated areas, affecting population growth. These map views do not show any impact on *HIV/AIDS* attribute dimension, including *TB incidence attribute*. But in comparison, *HIV/AIDS* and *TB incidence* attributes have positive correlation.

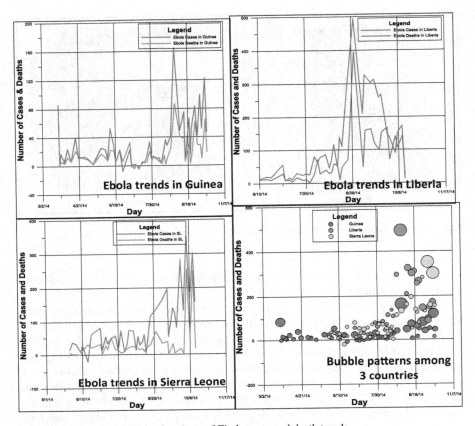

Fig. 5.16 Scatter and bubble plot views of Ebola cases and death trends

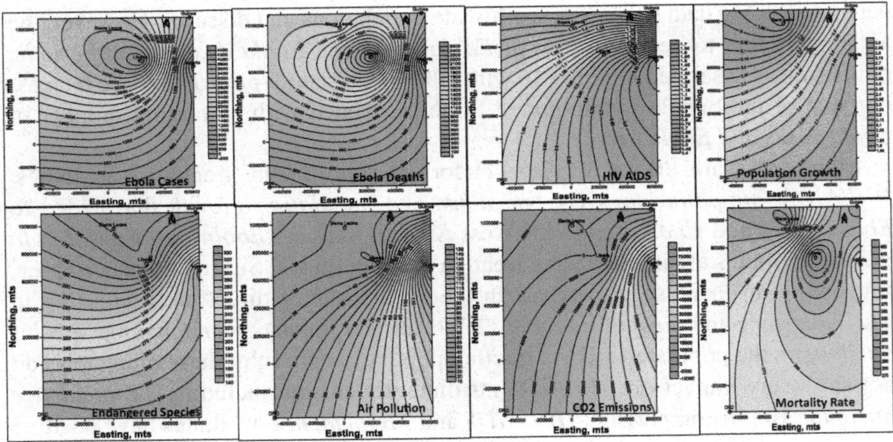

Fig. 5.17 Population, disease, and CO_2 emissions patterns in Ebola affected areas of West Africa (colors interpreted on the scale bar narrate attribute strengths)

Results and Discussions

The robust methodologies associated with embedded ecosystems and big data are novel ideas. Big data collected from various sources are analyzed for ecosystems' connectivity. Data models are ontology-based representation, meant for identifying and building relationships among ecosystems. Data warehousing is used for integrating various ecosystems embedded in nature. Multidimensional domain ontologies are integrated in a warehouse to generate a metadata; thus, data cubes and data views are generated for interpretation and knowledge discovery for value extraction from big data sources. Typically data acquired from war-torn, most populated, most industrialized, most energy-dominated, most disease-prone countries are compared through data mining views for interpreting data patterns for new knowledge.

Human ecosystem is a group of individuals, commonly of the same species occupied in a specific area. Human species occupy the entire Earth; as per the data analysis suggests, their distribution is uneven. Based on existing environmental ecosystems and their conditions, some regions remain largely unpopulated. Population tends to fluctuate based on the environment and with which situations of human ecosystems are surviving. Natural disasters, terrorist activities, and diseases try to imbalance the human ecosystem and its associated embedded ecosystems. *HIV/AIDS* epidemic killed in Africa 2.4 million people in 2002. Equal number existing now is surviving worldwide. Because of *HIV/AIDS*, 20 million people lost lives since it was discovered in 1981; an estimated 42 million people are still living with *HIV/AIDS*. 85 % of these victims are from developing world such as Asia, Africa, and Latin America. To this extent, average life expectancy has drastically reduced to 50 below in recent years. Other diseases, such as influenza, pneumonia, tuberculosis, malaria, and Ebola, are in increasing trends in more populated African countries affecting the imbalance among human, disease, and environment ecosystems. In addition, there are many other socioeconomic issues affecting these ecosystems.

The earthquakes (Nimmagadda & Dreher, 2007) are severely affecting human and environment ecosystems creating pandemic situations for human existence. Small-scale disasters involving disease, drought, famine, typhoons, and hurricanes have significant effects on the balance of human ecosystems. Famine associated with climatic variability in Northern Europe during 1960 brought about loss of 20 % population of Finland and perhaps 10 % of population of Scotland. More recently, between 1958 and 1961, as many as 20 million people lost their lives in a combination of situations such as famine and mismanagement of agriculture systems in China. Drought and famine caused the deaths of hundreds of thousands of people in sub-Saharan Africa in the past decades affecting the balance of human ecosystem on this planet. In addition to wars, millions of people lost their lives because of avoidable human activity. The authors opinionate that environmentally sensitive mining and oil- and gas-producing industries come within the purview of human-disease-environment ecosystem scenarios. Mining of radioactive minerals and emissions of sulfur dioxide (SO_2) and carbon dioxide (CO_2) from the producing oil and gas fields severally affect the environment, human associated with these environments creating chronic and communicable diseases, in particular TB, asthma, and lung cancer diseases.

Vehicles that emit burnt gases are real culprits of environmental pollutions. In populated countries, such as China and India, air pollution levels are increasingly concerning, the grey-white "haze" that covers dense populated city areas, at times which appear to be smog, may have linked to the rapid rise in particulate matter (PM 10 and PM 2.5) and nitrogen dioxide levels. They may be highly toxic and poisonous gases. This demonstrates how human activity causing environment a serious damage that leads to different kinds of diseases such as respiratory- and lung-related problems. An ecosystem that encompasses this connectivity among human-disease-environment entities has significance in terms of system design, development, and implementation. Keeping in view these mere phenomena, the proposed research addresses description of various constructs and models.

The relationship among human, disease, and environment ecosystems is hard to simplify. Exponential growth of human ecosystem and advances in technology that facilitate increase in demand for resources has radically changed the relationships between these systems over the last three centuries. Severe damage occurring to environment by natural calamities is an added dimension to the existing man-made activities.

Practical Views of Information Systems (IS) That Involved with Big Data

Growing pressures of business, technology, and fast-changing societies make information technology, information systems' solutions with more demanding commercial research and competitive markets. In addition, global competition, customer-centric, and other technical challenges are forced to review and renovate the existing IS development methodologies. Globalization, IT, and logistics environment are intrinsically connected as driving dimensions and committed each other in their operations for transformation and change. In recent years, there is shift in IS research paradigm in analyzing multiple dimensions of various application domains in which the dimensionality is impacting the organization of information ecosystems. The authors are of the view that dimensionality makes more attractive for IS research development and transformation of globalization through its effective implementation. Type of data and information use in multiple domains demand a rigor on IS design, development, and implementation procedures. As an example, *human*, *disease*, and *environment* ecosystems though are different in different domains but they are inherently interconnected. In this context, each ecosystem is an information system, which handles big data and information from different domains, but process and workflow, how each system functions and operates, are inherently the same.

Policies, strategies, and solutions also impact the motivation and selection of a particular dimension or composited dimension; the mechanism of each dimension is designed, developed, and implemented under what changes. Driving dimensions, if they are inherently interconnected, would have definitely impacted on each other's information systems (ecosystem) design approach. Here, the authors introduce *value chain* (Nimmagadda et al., 2010), knowing the emerging conceptualization and contextualization (of multiple dimensions and attributes) that add value to an ecosystem design and its connectivity, from which an inheritance is described. Local systems facilitate the connectivity process and help characterizing and shaping the global system. For example, having understood the systems independently, like *human, disease*, and *environment* locally, alignments of global impacts are understood through value-added *chains* (Nimmagadda et al., 2011).

Having understood the systems, connectivity, local issues, and value chains (if the connectivity concept is truly related to "*value chain*"), multinational teams and domain experts evaluate and deliver embedded ecosystems better. Categorically, one-shop (stop) mechanism can help understand *human, disease*, and *environment* ecosystems' connectivity among big data. For example, integration of multiple dimensions from multiple domains can minimize the ambiguity involved in the organizational alignment and conflicts/frictions taken place, if any, during integration process. In this context, different systems in different domains, such as *human, disease*, and *environment*, if integrated, the solution delivered from IS development has better understanding of its implementation. Voluminous, heterogeneous, and multidimensional big data in multiple domains have an effective role in data modeling, data warehousing, mining, visualization, and interpretation aspects.

IS innovation in a big data-integrated interactive approach has definite benefit to sustainable development as well. For example, different ecosystems as narrated from *human, disease*, and *environment* entities and/or dimensions, though embedded in nature, the phenomena are evaluated in terms of their sustainability, relating to the benefits to each system and their integration to offer broadly to embedded systems. Organizations involved in the IS design and development projects must address the issues associated with set of integrated inputs of collection, storage, and processes that affect the IS implementation solutions. Organizations are equipped to address these changes that enable to maintain the IS solutions as well. Design and development of embedded ecosystems (especially in the context, *human-disease-environment*) are environmentally sensitive but complex in nature and inherently intricate their conceptualization and contextualization descriptions.

Impact of Methodologies in Organizations Dealing with Big Data

Big data IS research is expected to create business alliances with vendors and managing outsourcing projects in mega scale. IS in big data organizations connects external organizations, such as vendors, business partners, consultants, research institutions, and universities. Big data IS sets standards for hardware and software purchases, including information security. Impact of new systems approach is holistic. Its cyclic life is long. The new big data IS practices and strategies can change business as well as scientific environment. Maintenance is easy and flexible as per changes demanded within an ecosystem or its associated ecosystem.

The impact of IS on organization, business, and scientific goal is enormous, and it is measured by effective and efficient data mining, visualization, and interpretation strategies. The combined integrated strategies can facilitate knowledge discovery from large volumes of data and information hidden among embedded ecosystems. IS research methodology in big data paradigm is evaluated based on the measure of the impact on the organization. IS research involved with big data, its impact, and evaluation are coherently, consistently reported and documented for each system and coexistent embedded ecosystem.

Projects involved in the data modeling and data warehousing in the areas of big data associated with embedded digital ecosystems can provide new knowledge to the researchers in the educational institutes. In other words, various data mining, visualization, and interpretation techniques described in the current research are useful for the researchers involved in the projects associated with embedded digital ecosystems. In addition, student records, markings, and new innovations can as well be documented and integrated using these robust methodologies in educational institutes. Periodic and geographic information of students' records and researchers' innovative ideas can be included in the current research approaches.

Impact of IS in Organizations Dealing with Big Data

IS is likely to create business alliances with vendors and managing outsourcing projects. IS in an organization closely works with external organizations, such as vendors, business partners, consultants, research institutions, and universities. IS sets standards for hardware and software purchases, including information security. Current IS practice is not compatible and user-friendly within business, government, and other social network systems. More complex systems such as embedded systems, comprising of human resources, accounting, finance, marketing and operations, are inherently embedded within a larger organization. They are at times difficult to integrate and manage their data and information resources. In another example, human, disease, and environment are ecosystems inherently embedded but difficult to manage data and information resources. New approaches are described in the current research work to manage data and information among multiple embedded systems. Impact of new systems approach is huge and enormous. Its cyclic life is long. The new IS practices and strategies can change business as well as scientific environment. Maintaining new approaches is easier and flexible as per changes needed within an ecosystem or its associated ecosystem, if added to the existing integrated system.

The impact affecting the organization or a scientific concept is enormous, and it is measured by data mining, visualization, and interpretation strategies (Nimmagadda & Dreher, 2011). The combined or integrated strategies facilitate knowledge discovery hidden under large volumes of data and information within these embedded systems. Reporting of IS research is coherently and consistently documented for each system and associated embedded systems. IS action research approach (Indulska & Recker, 2008; Neuman, 2000; Vaishnavi & Kuechler, 2004) may be encouraged to collaborate with the proposed new IS methodologies in the organizations and universities.

Conclusions and Recommendations

The methodological approach is robust and flexible for analyzing heterogeneous and multidimensional data sources of embedded ecosystems. Models built based on the existing data sources have further scope of extending them to other interrelated systems, keeping in view the dynamics of Earth's ecosystem. Applicability and feasibility of integrating multiple ecosystems' data in a warehousing environment, with combined application of data mining and visualization including interpretation, has tremendous impact on ecosystems' new knowledge discovery that can change mere understanding and perception of embedded ecosystems. Fine-grained multidimensional data structuring approach proposed can assist an effective data mining, visualization, and interpretation. Human ecosystems play significant role in embedment of disease and environmental ecosystems.

Understanding of human ecosystem is significant because it has inherent effect and impact on other ecosystems. Multiple ecosystems ultimately appear to be influencing the human existence. The connectivity among ecosystems continues to be explicitly undisputable phenomenon and topic of interest. There are varying multidisciplinary and heterogeneous data sources impacting these phenomena on large scale in big data. The authors recommend sharing of knowledge and learning experience attained through new innovative ideas, tools, and technologies periodically with researchers and student communities involved in IT/IS projects.

Future Trends and Scope

Researchers involved in IT/IS research projects on embedded digital ecosystems have an opportunity and scope connecting and interacting various academicians and educators of educational systems. The new knowledge established from the big data paradigm must be shared among researcher communities. The authors contend that the new ideas and tools described in the current research have opportunity and scope in many domains of research. In spite of major breakthroughs and advances in ecosystems and technologies, identification and precise description of mining and embedded ecosystems that narrate human ecosystems that impact other ecosystems remains unresolved. Issues associated disease ecosystems and the environment with which these systems are surviving are explored. Even without additional resources and inputs, many other ecosystems can be explored and/or discovered by data mining of warehoused data patterns of embedded ecosystems. Ontology-based warehouse modeling combined with data mining has future technological edge and economic opportunities, especially when incorporated with health-care industries are enormous. For example, the authors believe that they have a wide scope in analyzing the other associated ecosystems data and predicting them through sophisticated and robust IT remedies. These have wide implications on understanding human ecosystems impacted by diseases and environment, saving enormous human life on this planet. Analysis of climatic changes with respect to increasing carbon levels in the atmosphere is a much needed research, and our proposed technologies have wide scope of extracting knowledge and resolving issues of global warming and carbon emissions (Nimmagadda & Dreher, 2009; Orr, 2004) that affect human and disease ecosystems. Several data sources associated with open-cast mining and oil and gas exploitation have a further scope integrating them to environments affecting human and disease ecosystems. Work is in progress, adding more spatial and temporal data sources from more geographic and periodic dimensions in the modeling and mapping process.

References

Agarwal, S., Agrawal, R., Deshpande, P., Gupta, A., Naughton, J., Ramakrishnan, R., et al. (1996). On the computation of multidimensional aggregates, in the *Proceedings of the Very Large Data Bases Conference* (pp. 506–521), 3–6 September 1996, Bombay. San-Francisco: Morgan Kaufmann.

Ali, M. M. (2013). Role of data mining in education sector. *International Journal of Computer Science and Mobile Computing, 2*(4), 374–383.

Baker, R. S. J. D. (2010). Data mining for education. *International Encyclopedia of Education, 7*, 112–118.

Cleary, L., Freed, B., & Elke, P. (2012). *Big data analytics guide*. Rosemead, CA: SAP.

Coronel, C., Morris, S., & Rob, P. (2011). *Database systems, design, implementation and management, course technology*. Boston, MA: Cengage Learning.

Debortoli, S., Muller, O., & Brocke, J. V. (2014). Comparing business intelligence and big data skills. *Business & Information Systems Eigineering, 6*(5), 289–300. doi:10.1007/s12599-014-0344-2.

Dhar, V., Jarke, M., & Laartz, J. (2014). Big Data. *WIRTSCHAFTSINFORMATIK, 56*(5), 277–279. doi:10.1007/s11576-014-0428-0.

Gornik, D. (2000). *Data modelling for data warehouses*. A rational software white paper. Lexington, MA: Rational E-Development.

Gruber, T. (2007). Collective knowledge systems: Where the social web meets the semantic web. *Web Semantics: Science, Services and Agents on the World Wide Web, 6*(1), 4–13. doi:10.1016/j.websem.2007.11.011; http://tomgruber.org/

Hadzic, M., & Chang, E. (2005). Ontology-based support for human disease study, *published in the Proceedings of the 38th Hawaii International Conference on System Sciences*, Hawaii, USA.

Hoffer, J. A., Presscot, M. B., & McFadden, F. R. (2005). *Modern database management* (6th ed.). Upper Saddle River, NJ: Prentice Hall.

Indulska, M., & Recker, J. C. (2008). Design science in IS research: A literature analysis. In G. Shirely, & H. Susanna (Eds.) *Proceedings 4th Biennial ANU Workshop on Information Systems Foundations*, Canberra, Australia.

Keller, G. (2005). *Statistics for management and economics* (7th ed.). Belmont, CA: Thomson Brookes/Cole.

Kemp, D. D. (2004). *Exploring environmental issues—An integrated approach* (pp. 1–406). London: Routledge.

Khatri, V., & Ram, S. (2004). Augmenting a conceptual model with geo-spatio-temporal annotations. *IEEE Transactions on Knowledge and Data Engineering, 16*(11), 1324–1338.

Mattison, R. (1996). *Data warehousing strategies, technologies and techniques* (100–450p). New York, NY: Mc-Graw Hill.

Miller, H. J., & Han, J. (Eds.) (2001). Fundamentals of spatial data warehousing for geographic knowledge discovery. In: *Geographic data mining and knowledge discovery* (pp. 51–72). London: Taylor & Francis.

Moody, L. D., & Kortink, M. A. R. (2003). From ER models to dimensional models: Bridging the gap between OLTP and OLAP Design, Part 1 and Part 2. *Business Journal Intelligence*, Summer Fall editions, *8*(3). http://www.tdwi.org.

Neuman, W. L. (2000). *Social research methods, qualitative and quantitative approaches* (4th ed.). Boston, MA: Allyn & Bacon, USA.

Nimmagadda, S. L., & Dreher, H. (2006). Ontology-base data warehousing and mining approaches in petroleum industries. In H. O. Negro, S. G., Cisaro, & D. Xodo (Eds.), *Data mining with ontologies: Implementation, findings and framework.* Calgary, AB: Idea Group. Retrieved from http://www.exa.unicen.edu.au/dmontolo/

Nimmagadda, S. L., & Dreher, H. (2007). Ontology based data warehouse modelling and mining of earthquake data: Prediction analysis along Eurasian-Australian continental plates. In *International Conference of IEEE in Industry Informatics Forum*, Vienna, Austria.

Nimmagadda, S. L., & Dreher, H. (2009). Ontology based data warehouse modelling for managing carbon emissions in safe and secure geological storages. In Paper presented in the international SEGJ symposium—*Imaging and Interpretation*, in a forum “Science and Technology for Sustainable Development”, October, Sapparo, Japan; published in the digital library of Society of Exploration Geophysicists (SEG), USA.

Nimmagadda, S. L., & Dreher, H. (2011). Data warehousing and mining technologies for adaptability in turbulent resources business environments. *International Journal of Business Intelligence and Data Mining, 6*(2), 113–153.

Nimmagadda, S. L., & Dreher, H. (2012). On new emerging concepts of Petroleum Digital Ecosystem (PDE). *Journal Wiley Interdisciplinary Reviews Data Mining Knowledge Discovery, 2*, 457–475. doi:10.1002/widm.1070.

Nimmagadda, S. L., & Dreher, H. (2014). On robust methodologies for managing public health care systems. *International Journal of Environmental Research and Public Health, 11*, 1106–1140. doi:10.3390/ijerph110101106.

Nimmagadda, S. L., Nimmagadda, S. K., & Dreher, H. (2008, February). Ontology based data warehouse modelling and managing ecology of human body for disease and drug prescription management. In Proceedings of the *International Conference of IEEE-DEST*, Bangkok, Thailand.

Nimmagadda, S. L., Nimmagadda, S. K., & Dreher, H. (2010, April). Multidimensional ontology modelling of human digital ecosystems affected by social behavioural patterns. In Proceedings of the *IEEE-DEST-2010*, Dubai, UAE.

Nimmagadda, S. L., Nimmagadda, S. K., & Dreher, H. (2011, July). *Multidimensional data warehousing and mining of diabetes & food-domain ontologies for e-health management.* In Proceedings of the *IEEE-INDIN-2011*, Lisbon, Portugal.

O’Brien, J. A., & Marakas, G. M. (2009). *Management information systems* (9th ed.). Boston, MA: McGraw-Hill.

Orr, F. M., Jr. (2004). Storage of carbon dioxide in geologic formations. *Journal of Petroleum Technology, 56*(9), 90.

Pratt, J. P., & Adamski, J. J. (2000). Concepts of database management (3rd ed.). In *Excellence in information systems* (pp. 253–275): Cambridge, MA: Mass Course Technology.

Pujari, A. K. (2002). *Hyderabad.* India: University Press (India). Data mining techniques.

Rainer, K. R., & Turban, E. (2009). *Introduction to information systems* (2nd ed.). Hoboken, NJ: Wiley.

Romero, C., & Ventura, S. (2007). Educational data mining: A survey from 1995 to 2005. *Expert Systems with Applications, 33*(1), 135–146.

Romero, C., & Ventura, S. (2010). IEEE educational data mining: A review of the state of the art. *IEEE Transactions on Systems, Man, and Cybernetics–Part C: Applications and Reviews, 40*(6), 601–618.

Rudra, A., & Nimmagadda, S. L. (2005). Roles of multidimensionality and granularity in data mining of warehoused Australian resources data. *Proceedings of the 38th Hawaii International Conference on Information System Sciences*, Hawaii, USA.

Schermann, M., Hemsen, H., Buchmüller, C., Bitter, T., Krcmar, H., & Markl, V. (2014). Big Data, an interdisciplinary opportunity for information systems research. *Business & Information Systems Engineering, 6*(5), 261–266. doi:10.1007/s12599-014-0345-1.

Shanks, G., Tansley, E., & Weber, R. (2004). Representing composites in conceptual modeling. *Communications of the ACM, 47*(7), 77–80.

Sidhu, A. S., Dhillon, T. S., & Chang, E. (2009). Data integration through protein ontology, a book chapter published under a title: Knowledge discovery practices and emerging applications of data mining: Trends and new domains. Retrieved from http://www.igi-global.com/

Siemens, G., & Baker, R. S. D. (2012). Learning analytics and educational data mining: towards communication and collaboration. In *Proceedings of the 2nd international conference on learning analytics and knowledge* (pp. 252–254). New York, NY: ACM.

Vaishnavi, V., & Kuechler, W. (2004). Design research in information systems. Retrieved July 27 from http://www.isworld.org/Researchdesign/drisISworld.htm.

Chapter 6
The Contemporary Research University and the Contest for Deliberative Space

Tony Harland

Abstract In this chapter, I will argue that responses to neo-liberalism and new digital technologies have changed how research, teaching and learning are experienced. Realignment of work tasks has reduced the time and space required for achieving some important knowledge objectives that the academic community and society value. These include enlightenment ideas of seeking truth, reason, criticality and emancipation. I will lay the foundations for my analysis by starting with a consideration of these values, in terms of the purposes of a university education. In particular, I will introduce the concept of 'worthwhile knowledge'. I will then explore neo-liberalism and how this ideology has transformed higher education and continues to exert influence and control over much of what is possible and permissible. Finally, I will make some observations about digital technology in the context of contemporary academic work and examine how technology not only changes the knowledge project but also influences neo-liberal reform. I will conclude with some thoughts on the idea of resistance and subversion to attain spaces for deliberative thinking.

Keywords Neo-liberalism • Teaching and learning • Big data • University education

Introduction

The fundamental objectives for the contemporary research university have remained unchanged for the last 200 years: academics are expected to produce advanced knowledge through research and then use what they have learned for teaching and ultimately, for the well-being of society. In this view, the university is understood as a site of knowledge production and knowledge dissemination.

What constantly changes, however, is the context in which these activities are carried out, with shifting practice environments directly affecting the quality of research, teaching and learning. It is therefore important to understand the circumstances in which academics work and how current situations enhance or degrade

T. Harland (✉)
University of Otago, Dunedin, New Zealand
e-mail: tony.harland@otago.ac.nz

B. Kei Daniel (ed.), *Big Data and Learning Analytics in Higher Education*, DOI 10.1007/978-3-319-06520-5_6

this quality. The last 30 years or so have been marked by the contemporary period of globalisation, and the university has had to make major adjustments in response to the neo-liberal political and economic rationalisation of society and the digital revolution that saw the onset of a new information age. These two developments, one essentially political and the other technological, have acted independently and in concert to change the university in a variety of ways, some positive and others negative. Both, however, have had a profound bearing on the experiences of academics and students and the contributions that university education makes to society. If the modern research university is to maintain its core objectives and realise its potential, then the academic community ought to understand the consequences of how the integration of neo-liberal and digital technologies has modified what can now be achieved.

In this chapter, I will argue that responses to neo-liberalism and new digital technologies have changed how research, teaching and learning are experienced. Realignment of work tasks has reduced the time and space required for achieving some important knowledge objectives that the academic community and society value. These include enlightenment ideas of seeking truth, reason, criticality and emancipation. I will lay the foundations for my analysis by starting with a consideration of these values, in terms of the purposes of a university education. In particular, I will introduce the concept of 'worthwhile knowledge'. I will then explore neo-liberalism and how this ideology has transformed higher education and continues to exert influence and control over much of what is possible and permissible. Finally, I will make some observations about digital technology in the context of contemporary academic work and examine how technology not only changes the knowledge project but also influences neo-liberal reform. I will conclude with some thoughts on the idea of resistance and subversion to attain spaces for deliberative thinking.

The Purposes of a University

The modern public research university exists for many purposes, but its principal responsibility is the creation of knowledge (Barnett, 1997). This activity is usually done in an international scholarly community of learners that comprise academic staff, students and all those who support this work. In this sense, individuals and institutions make a worldwide contribution to knowledge and learning and are the source of highly educated and well-rounded students who will take their place in work and broader society. Society expects these future citizens to graduate with certain skills and capacities that make the enterprise a worthwhile investment. From such an epistemological foundation comes a vast assortment of functions, including teaching advanced subjects and inculcating values. Society's expectations for a university education are broad and range from educating a section of the future workforce to assisting in the preservation of democracy.

What the university stands for and how it achieves its educational objectives has occupied academics and politicians in considerable debate. However, there are certain values that the community tends to agree upon as foundational, and in the following sections, I will argue that these have been modified by the neo-liberal and digital revolutions (Harland & Pickering, 2011). This value structure has stood the test of time, and it is generally accepted that it falls within the broad domain of 'being critical' or 'scholarly'. Included are the key concepts of developing critical thinking and evaluative judgement as a precursor to the discovery of new knowledge. Being critical is essential in the search for truth and foundational to how the university can provide a service for society.

Even though such fundamental ideas will be realised in different ways in each subject and discipline, the general concept of criticality has widespread acknowledgement and support from the academic community. Critical social engagement is, however, more controversial and often perceived as characteristic of the liberal arts and humanities subjects. Engagement includes learning to be 'critic and conscience of society' and, at least in New Zealand, is enshrined in law as one of the conditions for a university education (Education Act, 1989). Even though all New Zealand academics and students are charged with acting as critic and conscience of society, for some, this will be seen (if considered at all) as peripheral to the core tasks of creating and disseminating high-quality subject knowledge. Such an obligation, however, allows all universities to make a distinctive contribution to society, both locally and globally, and, at least for institutions that operate within the Western liberal tradition, provide a disinterested public critique that helps to influence and maintain democratic structures.

In addition, knowing lots of things (typically advanced subject knowledge) is not the same as creating knowledge, and although this is a conception of university learning that is concerned with the types and qualities of knowledge, it is quite clear that knowledge creation is a scholarly activity that requires careful reflection and deliberation. One of the key conditions for researching, reasoning or learning to be critic and conscience of society is that these activities take time. They require the careful and thoughtful creation and maintenance of particular spaces in both the curriculum and in academic work. In the contemporary university, academics are very busy, and time for creative and innovative tasks is becoming harder to find as academic life speeds up (Parkins, 2004).

Parkins (2004) argues that scholarship calls for detachment, calm and care and that such spaces for thinking deliberatively cannot be accelerated. There are no shortcuts and academics need time for achieving 'worthwhile things' (Reisch, 2001). What is 'worthwhile' should be given much thought. My personal view is that it starts within the critical domain and an education concerned with developing 'powerful knowledge' (Beck, 2013; Wheelahan, 2007; Young & Muller, 2013). Powerful knowledge is a complex idea that has certain qualities that distinguish it from other forms of knowledge (Harland, 2016). For the student learner, I consider that it has the following characteristics:

1. Being skilled in producing one's own knowledge
2. Being able to evaluate knowledge claims
3. Being able to apply the skills of production and evaluation to different knowledge contexts over time
4. Being prepared to use knowledge wisely for the good of oneself and others

In principal, these are the same qualities academics seek in their research, but power is also derived from the esoteric nature of the subject (Beck, 2013). Even so, power from advanced subject knowledge is limited, and academics and students need more than this in order for their learning to operate in everyday situations and influence what will later become common sense knowledge. It is the generative principles of disciplinary knowledge that provide such an outcome, and one method of achieving this is to educate students as authentic researchers (Jenkins, Healey, & Zetter, 2007). Such a knowledge-creating experience gives students the best chance of learning different ways of thinking and being that allows them to enter new conversations in society (Wheelahan, 2007). In addition, if learning through research is done from the first day at a university, it then provides something useful and 'powerful' for every single student because it allows them all to be involved in sustained knowledge production over time. I contrast this experience with the older elitist curricula types that are predicated on developing the next generation of academics and so typically reserve the research experience for the last year of a degree programme. If students from elite programmes are not going to work in their field of study after university, they are soon likely to forget most of the subject information they have been taught (Custers, 2010).

If it is accepted that the critical nature of a university education is (a) fundamental to the educative project, (b) has the potential to provide powerful knowledge for all students and (c) is also what the sector and society requires and values, then any changes that impact on these need to be identified and thoroughly understood. In the next section, I want to examine the two major changes for the sector and how these have altered the knowledge project, primarily by redirecting academic work towards compliance, accountability and administration, activities that have marginalised time and space for the critical project of higher education.

Neo-liberalism and the 'Privatisation' of the Public University

The first change started to impact in the late 1970s. Societies across the world began to experience the full force of neo-liberal economic and political reform that heralded what has been called the contemporary period of globalisation (Steger, 2013). Governments throughout the world, regardless of political persuasion, began to understand their roles and responsibilities in different ways, and the free market became a dominant ideology to guide thinking. Prior to the rise of neo-liberalism, governments tended to have a much larger role in overseeing both the commercial and social aspects of society. When free market ideas became the overriding principle for this project, there was a dramatic rationalisation in government function and the social contract changed. Neo-liberalism was largely experienced as a shift from the public to the private sector and from the collective to a new emphasis on the individual as a competitive economic actor.

When it came to reform and privatisation of public sector organisations, neo-liberalism had limits with respect to particular services, and it was too difficult to fully privatise some of the institutions governments managed on behalf of society. These included educational institutions such as the public universities (Marginson, 2007). Nevertheless, there was still an expectation that these institutions would mirror the private sector and behave in an efficient businesslike way in order to enhance economic performance. To do this required the creation of competitive environments through setting standards and introducing a variety of compliance measures. These were designed to drive up performance and provide more control over educational services that were viewed as strategically important for each nation's economic future (Olsen & Peters, 2005).

At the same time, universities were encouraged to promote academic capitalism and engage in 'third mission' commercial enterprise activities to generate additional private income (Leisyte & Dee, 2012). Central governments had the ability to exercise financial compression though reduced funding while increasing their influence through legislation and policy (Neave, 1988). The outcome of forcing public universities to operate more like private businesses in a global free market has been to fundamentally change the educational enterprise. Institutions are managed differently, there has been a move to mass higher education and differentiation of university types, the academic workforce is now more casualised (Schuster & Finkelstein, 2006), there are changes in what can be taught, and a raft of compliance measures ensures universities are more accountable to the government and the taxpayer.

An example of accountability and compliance is the research assessment exercises that now impact on academics in research universities in several Western countries. Governments measure the quantity and quality of research for the purposes of reallocating limited funding. Assessment brings individual reward (or punishment) and institutional prestige through local and world ranking exercises, and so research becomes valued above other academic activities such as teaching (Elton, 2000). Once this effect was identified, the neo-liberal response was to introduce new quality assurance measures to hold researchers accountable for the quality of their teaching and so raise and protect standards and restore balance (Cheng, 2011). At present, however, in the situation across those sectors in which both research and teaching are measured, research still tends to be valued above teaching. The reasons behind this difference are complex but can partly be attributed to the quantitative measurement of research (numbers of publications, impact factors of journals and so on) and the lack of precision in attempts to measure teaching quality.

Furthermore, in the research-intensive universities, academics are trained only in research before they enter the profession and may have few skills in all the activities they are expected to perform, including teaching. Such a situation can create a different value base for each component of academic work, and there is evidence to show that the relationship between research and teaching has radically changed in the neo-liberal university (Elton, 2000). What is not known is whether or not research, when measured by quality of thought and knowledge, has genuinely improved across the sector, stayed the same or declined and similarly if current student experiences and learning are better or worse.

The technology of compliance is not just imposed on universities but is embraced by them. Institutions have adopted the same tools for performance management in order to drive up productivity (Harley, 2002). Adoption has created a new type of academic workforce that has less freedom to decide on appropriate work activities, less collegiality and a seemingly continuous increase in bureaucratic tasks. At the same time, academics have been complicit in accepting and adopting neo-liberal reform and have recreated themselves as neo-liberal subjects (see Ball, 2012). For example, tightening fiscal constraints on research tends to require a shift to more entrepreneurial activities that often places academics in a competitive relationship with colleagues. With external and internal performance management to control scarce resources, there will always be winners and losers. Some in the university are empowered while others subordinated. The work done by academics then changes to meet the required criteria for success, and so values gradually shift and align themselves to the new standards set by others.

A second illustration of neo-liberal reform is the move to mass higher education. Greater student access can be viewed positively from an inclusion perspective, even though the increase in numbers is principally accounted for by a larger diaspora of society's middle class (Marcenaro-Gutierrez, Galindo-Rueda, & Vignoles, 2007). It can also be seen positively in terms of economies of scale and the best use of infrastructure and resources. However, teaching large classes of more diverse students creates a number of problems for teachers, and what was possible in the older elite system now poses huge challenges. A simple illustration from my own experience of teaching Ecology is taking a class of 20 first-year students on a 7-day field course in the late 80s and finding this unthinkable with the 150 that I am faced with today. Students in this subject now have a different educational experience. Data on changes to staff and student numbers from my own research-led institution illustrate many of these observations:

Figure 6.1 shows student numbers increasing at a faster rate than lecturers with fairly steady numbers of research-only staff. The largest increase has been in the

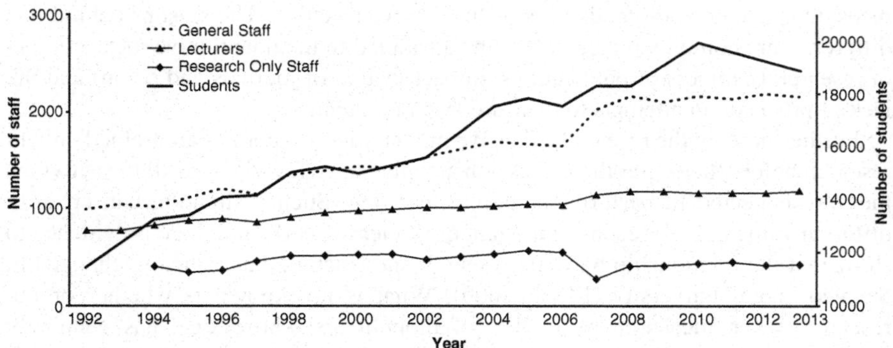

Fig. 6.1 Lecturing, general administrative and research staff with total students (1992–2012) at the University of Otago. *Source*: University of Otago Annual Reports, http://www.otago.ac.nz/

administrative and managerial category now required for dealing with new business activities and compliance measures. With regard to research productivity at the University of Otago (measured by numbers of publications), between 2004 and 2014, research outputs increased by about 50 %. It is not known how representative this situation is for other institutions, but it is likely that such changes are mirrored across the whole sector because universities tend to respond similarly to the pressures of globalisation. What is important to note, however, is that the administrative work of academics in many Western countries has also increased.

All these changes have occurred when the total weekly working hours of an academic has been constant over time. Analyses by Tight (2010) and Staniforth and Harland (1999) have shown that since the end of the 1960s, and spanning the introduction of neo-liberal reforms, the average working week for a university lecturer remains around 50 h. In this limited period, more research and teaching are now required, while increasing time is spent on administration (Ball, 2012; Menzies & Newson, 2007; Staniforth & Harland, 1999; Tight, 2010). Menzies and Newson (2007) describe the new bureaucratic work as 'self-serve administration' (p. 93). So if student numbers have increased to put pressure on teaching, and there is more administration for academics (despite the huge increases in administrative support staff), then there must also be pressure on research in a finite week resulting in work intensification (see Hartman & Darab, 2012). Tight (2010) also draws attention to the paradox that increasing amounts of compliance activities threaten the quality of teaching and research: the very activities they are meant to protect. Stephen Ball (2012) makes a similar observation:

> [ ] we are required to spend increasing amounts of our time in making ourselves accountable, reporting on what we do rather than doing it.
> (Ball, 2012, p. 19)

Yet whether or not we are 'at work' is a moot point for academics as the boundaries between public and private life tend to blur and time spent thinking about a research problem, for example, is unlikely to be accounted for. Barnett (2011) has proposed that academics occupy practical, virtual and imagined space. Practical is characterised by the work diary and documented activities, virtual is the non-documented activities such as writing at home, and imagined is the mind working in an expanded ontological space.

Furthermore, similar issues impact on students who now experience 'study intensification' and a different type of education. I will provide a case study example that illustrates what I mean by this. In response to neo-liberal pressures, my university changed its teaching practices and moved from degree programmes and reliance on a final examination to a structure of semesters and modules with internal summative assessment and frequent exams (Harland, McLean, Wass, Miller, & Sim, 2015). Students became more like consumers of education as they were offered more choice in what to study. They could access a wide range of modules and to a large extent construct their own degree pathways. However, because each module was largely independent of others, student learning had to be assessed and graded more often. A culture of frequent summative assessment of short pieces of work in modules and submodules gradually evolved and altered the learning experience.

The new system marginalised higher-order tasks that take time to develop, and students had very little opportunity to mature as autonomous independent learners. The study showed that they became obsessed with their grades that were the main objective for study. Teachers knew that students would work for such reward and used grading liberally, but this pedagogical move was also student driven as students wanted to accumulate small grades that could be combined for a final mark (rather than sit an exam at some distant point). Many in the study were assessed and graded more than once a week for the whole of their 3-year degree. The frequency of grading also meant that most students reported that they were living in a continual state of mild stress (I doubt anyone really likes to be assessed, and if this is happening constantly, then university life must be less enjoyable than it could be).

Over-assessed students were no longer seen as the independent learners characteristic of earlier times, and very few in the study read anything outside of their subject or prescribed tasks. In this sense, there was little space for the critical project of learning. The end result was a curriculum managed in small chunks, with much information learned, forgotten and never revisited again. May (see May 2001 in Cribb & Gerwitz, 2013) introduced the idea of the 'miniaturisation of knowledge', and I would suggest the students experienced study intensification through frequent grading and the 'miniaturisation of learning'. However, one academic who took part in the study pointed out that a continual state of compliance for the reward of a grade produced good neo-liberal subjects who were likely to fit in and be successful in a work environment characterised by individual competition and reward. If the problems illustrated by this case study are more widespread across the sector, then the challenge will be to ensure that teaching and curriculum experiences genuinely align with the core values that each university stands for.

Taken as a whole, the main neo-liberal-driven changes have converted a portion of an academic's daily life into new administrative tasks for compliance with increased pressure on performance. There is simply less time available to carry out activities, and this situation is compounded by mass higher education and its associated challenges. What is clear is that academics would like more time for their core work of research and teaching. What is not clear, however, is whether or not academics across disciplines attach similar importance to their civic and democratic roles as critic and conscience of society (Harland & Pickering, 2011; Macfarlane, 2005). In the present day, to get by in research and teaching may be sufficient in itself:

> As society is defined through the culture and values of neoliberalism, the relationship between critical education, public morality, and civic responsibility as conditions for creating thoughtful and engaged citizens are sacrificed all too willingly to the interest of financial capital and the logic of profit making.
>
> (Giroux, 2002, p. 427)

One neo-liberal solution for concerns about increasing pressures on different academic activities has been the unbundling of traditional research, teaching and service roles and the rise of the para-academic who specialises in selected tasks (Macfarlane, 2011). A second is the casualisation of academic jobs with increasing part-time and fixed-term contracts (e.g. Ryan, Burgess, Connell, & Egbert, 2013). However, both strategies offer limited solutions and also have implications for the critical project of the research university.

The Promise of Big Data

The contemporary period of globalisation has also seen the digital revolution characterised by rapid advances in information and communications technology (ICT) that have now become a motif for living in modern-day society. Much has been written about the remarkable advances of ICT and the impact it has had on knowledge and education, and I would like to make some observations about digital technology, its connection to neo-liberal reform and its impact on academic work and the university's critical project. The assertion I would like to explore is that despite much greater efficiencies in communication and information flows, there is little evidence that the quality of the knowledge project, in terms of research and teaching, has improved. There is no doubt that technology has enhanced access to and dissemination of certain forms of knowledge and, for many, that these opportunities are available instantly. However, more and faster does not necessarily mean better. Furthermore, I will suggest that the possibility of technology helping to liberate academic labour and so enhance spaces for reflection and deliberation has not materialised. In fact the reverse may be true as ICT has made possible the neo-liberal technologies of control that impact on all areas of academic life. Without advances in ICT, very little compliance would be possible as the economic cost to the individual, institutions and society would be too high.

Despite continuing technological advances and the new opportunities that these open for the university, ICT developments have also aided an increasingly compliant sector move into a low-trust environment that has changed traditional notions of academic freedom. The university lecturer has gone from having a vocation to becoming a knowledge worker in a regulated commercially oriented industry. Yet without a certain measure of trust and freedom, it is difficult to see how academics can fully discharge their roles and responsibilities towards knowledge, students and society's democratic project. In this sense, technology has helped diminish the core of academic work, while it has changed the way we understand and talk about education. ICT has also enabled a previously unthinkable industrial language to become widespread across the sector (e.g. for profit, knowledge producer, service provider, student as customer).

Advances in technology have led to the speeding up of information flows that make many university activities faster and more efficient. It would be hard to dispute the benefits this brings. For example, knowledge can now be accessed remarkably quickly and shared efficiently with anyone with an uncensored network connection (at least in the elite universities). This communication can be seen as part of the democratisation of education, and much knowledge is no longer the privilege of the university but open to all. It can also be argued that technology per se does no harm and that is how individuals and communities adopt it that make a difference. Technology that enables the gathering of data for academic research may be positive, while using the same technology for gathering data for meaningless compliance is certainly negative. Similarly, ICT specifically designed for teaching (e.g. a learning management system) can be used well or poorly.

Modern technology does not seem to free up time but increases the number of tasks possible and that soon become required. As such it speeds up academic life. One clear impact of the advances in ICT is that various technologies have ensured that academics are always available for work (Parkins, 2004), a situation that blurs the distinction between employment and leisure and between measured activity and ontological spaces for thinking. Towers, Duxbury, Higgins and Thomas (2006) talk about the 'third space' (p. 597), which has been enabled by mobile technologies. It is no longer helpful to distinguish between work and home life because academics can be at work wherever they are. Parkins (2004) suggests that because we are expected to respond quickly to the immediate demands of others, time for reflection becomes difficult to find. In a study of Canadian academics, 69 % said they did not thrive in the new technological environment because of time pressure and the fast pace of academic work (Menzies & Newson, 2007). The time used for the production and dissemination of knowledge has now been labelled 'network time' (Hassan, 2003).

There is additional pressure because academic work is seldom done in isolation but in a broader academic community. The idea of the lone scholar working in seclusion has long been a myth, and knowledge is typically constructed in social communities. ICT has enabled connectivity between individuals and communities and opened up new possibilities for collaboration. However, Stephen Ball (2012) argues the more time we spend adapting to performativity through accountability that 'social structures and social relations are replaced by information structures' (p. 19). There are now more short meaningless exchanges between academics, and quantity has replaced quality in communication (Menzies & Newson, 2007). If we take this idea further by arguing that in the information age, information structures themselves are becoming more efficient and impersonal, then the spaces for both the social and the critical are in danger of erosion.

Using digital information in the form of big data and analytics is relatively new and has been made possible by advances in computing and analytical procedures. I will not say much about the concept of big data in the university beyond the idea that it is about our ability to harness massive and dissimilar data sets that offer predictive potential for managing institutions and academic work. However, I would like to raise some issues because the potential of big data is unknown. Although there seems to be some optimism that it will be beneficial, this has yet to be demonstrated. I have two concerns about possible detrimental effects:

1. That big data will be used to accelerate the neo-liberal reform of higher education
2. That big data will result in more work for academics outside of the core tasks of research and teaching

It is inevitable that the neo-liberal project will make very good use of big data to ensure that its ideological objectives continue to be met and evolve. As such it will be interesting to see how data is interpreted and managed and for what ultimate purposes it will be put to use. Who actually owns the information on which decisions rest will need careful consideration, and because of this, there will be ethical concerns around 'mining' massive and disparate data sets, often without an a priori question. Depending on what is discovered, those commissioning such work might be tempted to use the information for meddling in academic affairs. Such a situation may seem reasonable if the outcome is, for example, the ability for management to make more accurate predictions and forecasts. However, given society's fixation with numerical and measurable data as a determinant rather than contributing factor to decision-making, certain values that the university represents may become less visible and so more vulnerable.

Vulnerability concerns derive from the track record of ICT when viewed as a technology that supports compliance, increases administrative tasks and compresses academic life. In this interpretation, ICT has already damaged the core functions of the university with respect to time available for research and teaching. Why should big data be any different? Like ICT it has the potential to do both good and harm, but I doubt, despite the best efforts of the data experts, that it will ultimately free up the spaces required for enhancing the knowledge project. This single measure of quality should be the judge of whether or not big data will be worthwhile for the university sector.

Resistance for Deliberative Space and Worthwhile Things

How can an academic preserve, recreate or reinvent working practices commensurate with the university's knowledge project? The neo-liberal university is unlikely assisted with this challenge, judging by the relentless reform agenda that continues to redirect academic work towards compliance and the market. Similarly, the digital revolution is a powerful driver of speed and complexity, and so it seems inevitable that research and teaching will have to continue under both pressures. There is of course a bottom line to change and reforms must have limits. These will be reached when the profession is no longer attractive to high-quality staff or when the quality of knowledge production and teaching falls below an acceptable standard. The question will be who decides what these standards are: is it the public, the politicians, the free market or the academy? If university academics are included in decision-making, then they must take responsibility for ensuring the kind of academic life that is conducive to high-quality knowledge and learning.

Space for scholarly activity may require a subversion of time. It has been claimed that busy academics do not want more free time but struggle to gain enough time for what they value (Reisch, 2001). Questions need to be asked about accountability, compliance and administrative loads. What difference do these really make? Compliance in all forms should be put to the test with the same rules of evidence that these technologies demand of those being measured. Does any policy or quality assurance exercise genuinely improve the quality of research, teaching or student learning? If it does, and gains seem worthwhile, then there may be a rationale for keeping it. I suspect that no compliance activities have ever been put to such a test, and because compliance technology changes the distribution of power, those who now hold that power will not easily relinquish it through opening up these processes to scrutiny.

It is also unclear if academics see the need to resist neo-liberalism (see Harland, Tidswell, Everett, Hale, & Pickering, 2010). Many of those working today have only lived as neo-liberal subjects or taken up a university post after 1979, and it is possible to be very successful knowledge workers under neo-liberalism, solely focused on research and teaching. Furthermore, the scholar lives on in the life of the mind and so resists reform and, in this sense, limits it. As such the scholar can still achieve a measure of slow scholarship and deliberative spaces for thinking and learning. It is debatable, however, whether or not the university as a whole can live up to its full potential with respect to the knowledge project and wider society. Successful researchers and teachers once had many different associations with society, and this powerful group, gradually weakened by successive governments, has withdrawn and retracted many of its previous services and responsibilities. There is a decline in political literacy through the erosion of academic self-governance (Macfarlane, 2005), and it seems to be enough to research and teach a subject and be content within a narrow version of academic work.

When it comes to technology, any resistance is likely to have less success. When PowerPoint became the favoured visual aid for communication in lecturers, it swept the world and shaped our consciousness. Yet it was accepted without empirical research to ascertain the impact on teaching and learning, despite the fact that it radically changed communication. Similarly, email, social media and mobile technologies enable us to remain connected and be at work and on call on a permanent basis. One could argue that academics are free to decide their use of ICT, but it is often presented with little choice. Individuals may not be free in an institutional or broader global context. As examples, I am required to use my university's learning management system, and if my vice chancellor wants to communicate with me by email, it is unlikely that I will pick up my fountain pen and post a handwritten response. Once we get used to speed in communication, it makes it harder to return to other methods characteristic of a more contemplative academic life.

Hassan (2003) argues that critical reasoning works on different epistemological assumptions to instrumental reasoning, and the former usually cannot be done in order to comply with the often short-term demands of performativity and accountability. In addition, I argue that critical reasoning also has a practical use because it allows us to subject all forms of knowledge to critical and reflexive evaluation. To do this constitutes a powerful action. However, although academics have traditionally studied every subject imaginable, they are reluctant to be critical of themselves, the institutions in which they work and the manner in which they are governed. Until they redirect some of their considerable intellect towards this task, governments and the free market will progressively determine the purposes of the university. Academics will be recast as subservient knowledge workers (Leisyte & Dee, 2012), and critique will be left to a few interested sociologists and those who study higher education. Neo-liberal ideology with its concomitant reliance on ICT and the promises of big data require critical debate by the entire scholarly community and wider society because the changes they bring impact on everyone associated with the university project.

References

Ball, S. (2012). Performativity, commodification and commitment: An I-Spy guide to the neoliberal university. *British Journal of Educational Studies, 60*(1), 17–28.

Barnett, R. (1997). *Higher education: A critical business*. Buckingham: Open University Press and Society for Research into Higher Education.

Barnett, R. (2011). *Being a university*. London: Routledge.

Beck, J. (2013). Powerful knowledge, esoteric knowledge, curriculum knowledge. *Cambridge Journal of Education, 43*(2), 177–193.

Cheng, M. (2011). The perceived impact of quality audit on the work of academics. *Higher Education Research and Development, 30*(2), 179–191.

Cribb, A., & Gerwitz, S. (2013). The hollowed-out university? A critical analysis of changing institutional and academic norms in UK higher education. *Discourse: Studies in the Cultural Politics of Education, 34*(3), 338–350.

Custers, E. J. F. M. (2010). Long-term retention of basic science knowledge: A review study. *Advances in Health Sciences Education, 15*, 109–128.

Education Act. (1989). Part 14 Establishment and disestablishment of tertiary institutions, S162, 4(a)(v), New Zealand Government.

Elton, L. (2000). The UK research assessment exercise: Unintended consequences. *Higher Education Quarterly, 54*(3), 274–283.

Giroux, H. A. (2002). Neoliberalism, corporate culture, and the promise of higher education: The university as a democratic public sphere. *Harvard Educational Review, 72*(4), 425–463.

Harland, T. (2016). Deliberate subversion of time: Slow scholarship and learning through research. In F. Trede & C. McEwen (Eds.), *Educating the deliberative professional: Preparing practitioners for emergent futures*. New York: Springer.

Harland, T., McLean, A., Wass, R., Miller, E., & Sim, K. N. (2015). An assessment arms race and its fallout: High-stakes grading and the case for slow scholarship. *Assessment & Evaluation in Higher Education, 40*(4), 528–541.

Harland, T., & Pickering, N. (2011). *Values in higher education teaching*. London: Routledge.

Harland, T., Tidswell, T., Everett, D., Hale, L., & Pickering, N. (2010). Neoliberalism and the academic as critic and conscience of society. *Teaching in Higher Education, 15*(1), 85–96.

Harley, S. (2002). The impact of research selectivity on academic work and identity in UK universities. *Studies in Higher Education, 27*(2), 187–204.

Hartman, Y., & Darab, S. (2012). A call for slow scholarship: A case study on the intensification of academic life and its implications for pedagogy. *Review of Education, Pedagogy, and Cultural Studies, 34*, 49–60.

Hassan, R. (2003). Network time and the new knowledge epoch. *Time & Society, 12*(2/3), 225–241.

Jenkins, A., Healey, M., & Zetter, R. (2007). *Linking teaching and research in disciplines and departments*. York: The Higher Education Academy.

Leisyte, L., & Dee, J. R. (2012). Understanding academic work in a changing academic environment. Faculty autonomy, productivity, and identity in Europe and the United States. In J. C. Smart & M. B. Pulsen (Eds.), *Higher education: Handbook of theory and research* (Vol. 27, pp. 123–206). Dordrecht: Springer.

Macfarlane, B. (2005). The disengaged academic: Retreat from citizenship. *Higher Education Quarterly, 59*(4), 296–312.

Macfarlane, B. (2011). The morphing of academic practice: Unbundling and the rise of the para-academic. *Higher Education Quarterly, 65*(1), 59–73.

Marcenaro-Gutierrez, O., Galindo-Rueda, F., & Vignoles, A. (2007). Who actually goes to university? *Empirical Economics, 32*(2), 33–357 (special issue "The Economics of Education and Training").

Marginson, S. (2007). The public/private divide in higher education: A global synthesis. *Higher Education, 53*, 307–333.

Menzies, H., & Newson, J. (2007). No time to think. Academics' life in the globally wired university. *Time & Society, 16*(1), 83–98.

Neave, G. (1988). On the cultivation of quality, efficiency and enterprise: an overview of recent trends in higher education in Western Europe, 1986–1988. *European Journal of Education, 23*(1/2), 7–23.

Olsen, M., & Peters, M. A. (2005). Neoliberalism, higher education and the knowledge economy: From the free market to knowledge capitalism. *Journal of Education Policy, 20*(3), 313–345.

Parkins, W. (2004). Out of time. Fast subjects and slow living. *Time & Society, 13*(2/3), 363–382.

Reisch, L. A. (2001). Time and wealth. The role of time and temporalities for sustainable patterns of consumption. *Time & Society, 10*(2/3), 367–385.

Ryan, S., Burgess, J., Connell, J., & Egbert, G. (2013). Casual academic staff in an Australian University: Marginalised and excluded. *Tertiary Education and Management, 19*(2), 161–175.

Schuster, J. H., & Finkelstein, M. J. (2006). *The American faculty: The restructuring of academic work and careers*. Baltimore: Johns Hopkins University Press.

Staniforth, D., & Harland, T. (1999). The work of an academic: Jack of all trades or master of one? *International Journal for Academic Development, 4*(2), 142–149.

Steger, M. B. (2013). *Globalisation: A very short introduction*. Oxford: Oxford University Press.

Tight, M. (2010). Are academic workloads increasing? The post-war survey evidence in the UK. *Higher Education Quarterly, 64*(2), 200–215.

Towers, I., Duxbury, L., Higgins, C., & Thomas, J. (2006). Time thieves and space invaders: Technology, work and the organization. *Journal of Organizational Change Management, 19*(5), 593–618.

Wheelahan, L. (2007). How competency-based training locks the working class out of powerful knowledge: A modified Bernsteinian analysis. *British Journal of Sociology of Education, 28*(5), 637–651.

Young, M., & Muller, J. (2013). On the powers of powerful knowledge. *Review of Education, 1*(3), 229–250.

Part II
LEARNING ANALYTICS

Chapter 7
Ethical Considerations in Adopting a University- and System-Wide Approach to Data and Learning Analytics

Lynne D. Roberts, Vanessa Chang, and David Gibson

Abstract The rapid adoption of learning analytics in the higher education sector has not been matched by ethical considerations surrounding their use, with ethical issues now slated as one of the major concerns facing learning analytics. Further, adoption of learning analytics within universities has typically involved small-scale projects rather than university- or system-wide approaches, and missing from the research literature is consideration of learning analytics from a 'big systems' point of view. We begin to address these gaps through providing an introduction to ethical considerations in adopting a university- and system-wide approach to learning analytics. Drawing on the existing literature on ethical considerations associated with learning analytics, we identify key questions that require consideration during the process of introducing learning analytics within a university. We then map these questions onto layers of systems and roles within universities, detailing how these ethical considerations may affect learning analytics decisions at differing levels of the university.

Keywords Learning analytics • Ethical considerations • Big data • Privacy • Student agency • Consent • Data governance

Introduction

Learning analytics, 'the measurement, collection, analysis, and reporting of data about learners and their contexts, for the purposes of understanding and optimizing learning and the environments in which it occurs' (Siemens, 2013, p. 1382), is a new but rapidly growing field. The *NMC Horizon Report—2015 Higher Education Edition* (New Media Consortium, 2015) identified learning analytics as part of the 'midterm horizon' for higher education, with a growing focus on measuring learning over the next 3–5 years. Indeed, most universities are currently exploring or using learning analytics, albeit in limited ways (Siemens, Dawson, & Lynch, 2013).

L.D. Roberts (✉) • V. Chang • D. Gibson
Curtin University, Perth, WA, Australia
e-mail: Lynne.Roberts@curtin.edu.au

B. Kei Daniel (ed.), *Big Data and Learning Analytics in Higher Education*,
DOI 10.1007/978-3-319-06520-5_7

The rapid increase in adoption of learning analytics in the higher education sector has not been matched by ethical considerations surrounding their use (Slade & Prinsloo, 2013; Swenson, 2014), with ethical issues now slated as one of the major concerns facing learning analytics (Siemens, 2013). Further, adoption of learning analytics within universities has typically involved small-scale projects rather than university- or system-wide approaches (Siemens et al., 2013), and missing from the research literature is consideration of learning analytics from a 'big systems' point of view (Macfadyen, Dawson, Pardo, & Gaševic, 2014). In this chapter, we begin to address these gaps through providing an introduction to ethical considerations in adopting a university- and system-wide approach to learning analytics. First, drawing on the existing literature on ethical considerations associated with learning analytics, we identify key questions that require consideration prior to introducing learning analytics within a university. Next, we provide a broad outline of data governance in universities, with a focus on structures, processes and relational communications. We then map ethical considerations onto layers of systems and roles within universities, providing a meso-level (Buckingham Shum, 2012) overview of how these ethical considerations may affect learning analytics decisions at differing levels of the university.

Ethical Considerations

The systematic consideration of ethical issues has failed to keep pace with the rapid development and implementation of learning analytics in higher education (Slade & Prinsloo, 2013). There is debate over whether learning analytics should be considered research and whether it requires approval by institutional ethics review committees (Graf, Ives, Lockyer, Hobson, & Clow, 2012) or the development of institutional codes of conduct (Slade & Prinsloo, 2013). Only recently have codes of practice for learning analytics begun to emerge. Prominent among these are the Open University (2014) *Policy on Ethical Use of Student Data for Learning Analytics* (http://www.open.ac.uk/students/charter/essential-documents/ethical-use-student-data-learning-analytics-policy) and the *JISC Code of Practice for Learning Analytics 2015* (Sclater & Bailey, 2015). Whether the focus is on learning analytics as research or as core business requiring only a code of practice, there are a number of key considerations that universities need to grapple with when developing policies and practices relating to the use of learning analytics. In this section, we present a series of questions that can guide ethical considerations prior to introducing or further developing learning analytics within a university.

Who Benefits from Learning Analytics?

Slade and Prinsloo (2013) identify a key ethical consideration for higher education institutions as who benefits from learning analytics and under what conditions (p. 1521). Results from a survey of teachers, researchers and learning designers with an interest in learning analytics indicate that the perceived key beneficiaries are learners, teachers and then institutions (Drachsler & Greller, 2012). Posited benefits for students and faculty include identification of at-risk students, providing insight into learning habits, making recommendations for improvement, leveraging the potential for early intervention and providing personalised learning experiences (Greller & Drachsler, 2012; Long & Siemens, 2011; Pardo & Siemens, 2014). The posited benefits of learning analytics for higher education institutions are data-driven decision-making (Dietz-Uhler & Hurn, 2013); improved shared understanding, administrative decision-making and resource allocation with the potential for innovation and transformation; and increased organisational productivity and effectiveness (Long & Siemens, 2011). Overall, learning analytics promise competitive advantage:

> It is envisaged that education systems that do make the transition towards data-informed planning, decision making, and teaching and learning will hold significant competitive and quality advantages over those that do not. (Siemens et al., 2013, p. 2)

However, while impressive claims have been made for the potential of learning analytics, and support by some institutions has been described as 'unreservedly enthusiastic and uncritical' (Griffiths, 2013, p. 4), the field lacks maturity (Siemens, 2013; Siemens et al., 2013), and apart from isolated reports of increased retention rates (e.g. Arnold & Pistilli, 2012), the promised results have yet to materialise. The development of research tools is continuing but current research tools don't enable system-level integration or institutional support (Siemens, 2013). Despite higher education institutions' partnerships with government departments, corporations and software agencies, Siemens and colleagues (2013) note that to date 'the outcomes of this research and productivity has largely failed to be translated into teaching and learning' (p. 10), a sentiment echoed by MacNeill, Campbell, and Hawksey (2014).

Who Is at Risk of Potential Harm from Learning Analytics?

In addition to considering the beneficiaries of learning analytics, it is important to identify who may be at risk of potential harm from learning analytics, to enable the weighing of risks and benefits. Within higher education institutions, stakeholders in learning analytics include students, teachers and managerial/administrative staff (Pardo & Siemens, 2014). If not managed carefully, learning analytics poses some risk of harm for teaching staff and students.

Staff

With regulators and managers initiating the adoption of learning analytics and determining the questions guiding their use, typically without input from teaching staff or students, Griffiths (2013) argues the use of learning analytics may exert greater managerial control over teaching with a focus on accountability. Griffiths foresees a danger in focussing on student retention and completion at the expense of other pedagogic issues, with a marginalisation of professional practice.

Faculty engagement is critical to ensure successful implementation of learning analytics applications (Campbell, DeBlois, & Oblinger, 2007). Focus groups conducted at one Australian university indicated that while academics are interested in the opportunities learning analytics may provide to support student performance and engagement, they remain sceptical about the utility of learning analytics (Corrin, Kennedy, & Mulder, 2013). Teaching staff have reported mixed experiences with learning analytics dashboards. Arnold and Pistilli (2012) report that prior to implementation of a learning analytics dashboard, staff reported concerns about coping with increased student demand for assistance, increased student dependency and lack of information on best practices. However, following implementation, while there was an increase in emails from concerned students, staff reported the system enabled earlier feedback to struggling students and promoted earlier engagement in assessment activities (Arnold & Pistilli, 2012).

Students

Learning analytics applications have generally been received positively but not universally by students. Arnold and Pistilli (2012) reported that 89 % of first-year students surveyed at Purdue University viewed their experience with 'Course Signals' (a learning analytics-based traffic light system accompanied by emails to students) as positive, with over half (58 %) supporting its use in other courses. Emails generated by the system were generally viewed by students as personal communications from teaching staff. However, students who are not doing well may have different reactions. For example, Arnold and Pistilli (2012) noted that two students reported 'becoming demoralized by the "constant barrage" of negative messages from their instructor' (p. 269). There is also concern that messages indicating the need for improved performance may act as self-fulfilling prophecies, with students giving up (Dietz-Uhler & Hurn, 2013; Willis & Pistilli, 2014). Further research is required to determine the approaches that are effective with at-risk students.

Results from learning analytics can also be used as a basis for educational triage, with additional resources provided to at-risk students (Prinsloo & Slade, 2014). However, Prinsloo and Slade warn that the implementation of educational triage in universities has occurred without sufficient conceptual and theoretical development or consideration of the moral cost. Further, where demographic and previous education are entered as predictors in learning analytics modelling, there is the potential for stereotyping, bias and discrimination based on group characteristics (Slade & Prinsloo, 2013).

Who Makes the Decisions?

A third key ethical consideration is who makes the decisions about learning analytics within an institution. This includes decision-making about the questions to be asked; the data to be collected, analysed and visualised; and who will have access to what data (Buckingham Shum, 2012; Campbell et al., 2007; Clarke & Nelson, 2013). Misuse of data was a large or major concern of more than a third of EDUCAUSE members surveyed (EDUCAUSE, 2012). Kay, Korn, and Oppenheim (2012) recommend a principle of clarity: 'open definition of purpose, scope and boundaries, even if that is broad and in some respects open-ended' (p. 6). *The JISC Code of Practice for Learning Analytics* 2015 (Sclater & Bailey, 2015) recommends that staff and student representatives be consulted as part of the decision-making process.

What Data Is Used in Learning Analytics?

With the increasing use of e-learning in tertiary institutions, there is a vast array of possible data for inclusion in learning analytics. The potential for error increases with the matching of data across databases (Cumbley & Church, 2013), and inaccurate data was found to be a large or major concern of almost a quarter of EDUCAUSE members surveyed (EDUCAUSE, 2012). In addition to data collected within the institution, there is potential to match data from external systems such as social networking sites (Kay et al., 2012), raising further concerns relating to authentication of student identity, lack of control over external sites policies and the need to obtain student consent for data harvesting (Slade & Prinsloo, 2013). Dringus (2012) outlines how the utility of learning analytics is reliant on obtaining the right data, the use of good algorithms, transparency, responsible assessment and use, with the results used to inform process and practice. Without each of these components, learning analytics may be harmful rather than helpful.

Who Needs to be Informed About Learning Analytics and What Do They Need to Know?

Questions have been raised in the literature as to whether institutions have an obligation to advise staff and students that their behaviour is being tracked (Campbell et al., 2007). Despite the growing awareness of data mining, students are not necessarily aware of the use of learning analytics within their own institutions (Slade & Prinsloo, 2013). Calls have been made in the literature for greater transparency, with all stakeholders advised of the types of data collected; methods of data collection, storage and analysis; and possible uses (Pardo & Siemens, 2014; Willis & Pistilli, 2014). Pardo and Siemens (2014) further advocate for institutions to develop terms of use for student data.

To What Extent Do Privacy Provisions Apply?

Privacy, defined by Pardo and Siemens (2014) in the context of learning analytics as 'the regulation of how personal digital information is being observed by the self or distributed to other observers' (p. 438), is a contentious issue. Questions arise over what data is collected, who can view analytics relating to individual students (e.g. other faculty not directly involved in teaching the unit? other institutions? future employers?) and how long the data should remain accessible (Rubel & Jones, 2016; Siemens, 2013). Pardo and Siemens (2014) note the absence of a comprehensive definition of right to privacy in learning analytics research, rejecting the need for absolute privacy on the grounds that use of historical student data advances research with potential benefits for future students. However, limited attention has been given to privacy in learning analytics from the student perspective, and best practice in this field has yet to be determined (Drachsler et al., 2015).

Do Students Need to Consent to the Use of Their Data, and if so, How?

More than just advising staff and students of data tracking, questions have been raised in the literature as to whether it should be a requirement for students to consent to the use of their data (Campbell et al., 2007), and if so, under what circumstances and with what frequency (Prinsloo & Slade, 2015; Slade & Prinsloo, 2013). Kay et al. (2012) outlined three possible strategies for obtaining consent:

- Initial opt in at start of course/year with further opt-in consent when policy or materials collected change.
- Initial opt in at start of course/year with further opt-out consent when policy or materials collected change.
- Initial opt out at start of course/year with further opt-out consent when policy or materials collected change.

Slade and Prinsloo (2013) suggested that the need for consent should be based on the type of learning analytics, supporting opt-out consent for personalised learning analytics but not for institutional reporting, on the basis that the benefit for the majority was greater than the right of the individual.

Students may be 'consenting' to the use of their data for data analytics purposes upon enrolment without being aware they have done so. Fisher, Valenzuela and Whale (2014) reported that none of the nine students they interviewed about their learning analytics experience recalled consenting to university use of student-generated data in learning management systems. Calls have been made for the establishment of a 'Charter of Learner Data Rights' to provide a basis for future learning analytics developments that do not cross the 'creepy line' (Connolly, 2014) of surveillance (Beattie, Woodley, & Souter, 2014).

Should Student Data Be De-identified, and if so, Is This Sufficient to Protect Anonymity?

Data used in academic analytics can easily be de-identified. However, as data sets increase in size and content and are combined to produce 'big data', the reidentification of individuals from anonymised data becomes easier (Cumbley & Church, 2013). To address these issues, one university has put in place a two-stage process of de-identification of data coupled with restricted access to data sets (de Freitas et al., 2014). However, learning analytics data used for personalised learning applications cannot be de-identified while in use. Current recommendations in the literature include de-identification of data after the period specified in regulatory frameworks (Slade & Prinsloo, 2013) or upon the student leaving the institution (Pardo & Siemens, 2014).

Who Is Responsible for the Stewardship and Protection of Learning Analytics Data?

Once data from learning analytics has been harvested, whether from institutional or external sources, questions relate to who has responsibility for the preservation, securing and sharing of the data (Campbell et al., 2007; Clarke & Nelson, 2013). The *JISC Code of Practice for Learning Analytics 2015* (Sclater & Bailey, 2015) recommends that institutions allocate responsibility to specific areas within the university for data collection, data anonymisation, analytical processes and the retention and stewardship of data.

Who Owns Learning Analytics Data and What Are the Implications for Intellectual Property Rights and Licensing for Reuse?

The legal position on who owns learning analytics data and the outputs from this data (the student, the university or educational product companies) is currently unclear (Pardo & Siemens, 2014; Siemens et al., 2013), raising further questions regarding intellectual property rights and licensing of data for reuse. Trust may be enhanced where institutions prohibit the further sharing of data outside of the institution (Pardo & Siemens, 2014).

Is There an Obligation to Act on the Findings from Learning Analytics?

Learning analytics hold out the promise of personalised learning resulting in increased student success. As such, what obligations are there on institutions to implement learning analytics applications once learning analytics techniques have been used to determine predictors of success (Campbell et al., 2007; Willis, Campbell, & Pistilli, 2013)? Slade and Prinsloo (2013) noted that the financial cost of implementation is a growing concern and argued that where the benefits accruing from implementation are likely to be minor, resources may be better allocated elsewhere.

How Can Student Agency Be Recognised and Supported?

Concerns have been raised that learning analytics applications may infantilise students, failing to treat them as autonomous adults responsible for their own learning (Willis & Pistilli, 2014) and potentially intruding upon their privacy (Graf et al., 2012). Further research is required to determine optimal methods of providing feedback to students that support learning (Corrin et al., 2013). Of particular concern is the need to ensure that students are not obligated to act in accordance with recommendations initiated from learning analytics (Slade & Prinsloo, 2013).

What Opportunities Are There for Redress?

A further consideration is the opportunity to seek redress. Kay et al. (2012) recommend a principle of 'consequence and complaint' (p. 6) in recognition that learning analytics may result in unforeseen consequences for students.

University Governance Structures, Systems and Roles

The ethical considerations in the previous section highlight the need for each university to develop governance plans to guide the implementation and practice of learning analytics. With the prevalence of the use of data and learning analytics at higher education institutions, information and data analytics governance has emerged as a fundamental business imperative because it is key to achieve business purpose and value (Peterson, 2004a, 2004b). While to date learning analytics initiatives have largely focused on predicting retention of undergraduate students (de Freitas et al., 2014), as the demand for data and learning analytics increases, more and more academics, administrators and university executives are requesting data about students and their learning behaviour and activities to help universities improve business and teaching processes in order to provide meaningful support to students. The effective use of data and learning analytics for the benefits of students will undoubtedly require changes to university policies, procedures and guidelines. With tighter regulations and compliance that require better control over data, the creation of a data and learning analytics governance framework needs to be embraced by every university. Good data governance mechanisms can help universities achieve their strategic objectives and gain competitive advantage.

Good data governance mechanisms can enable access to the multiple sources and systems where data can be located, from student enrolment data (e.g. demographics, pre-university education, socio-economic status, and others) to learning data (e.g. access to learning management systems, learning activities, assessment activities and grades). Regardless of the types of data required, intervention may be applied based on the intelligence from the collection of data and its associated usage and behaviour. The conundrum is that while this should provide benefits to both students and the university, there are risks associated with how the data are used and applied which may result in both positive benefits and adverse impacts on students. In this section, we first outline university data governance in relation to learning analytics. The decision to implement a data and learning analytics governance framework for universities is imminent especially where some universities have existed over a very long period of time with a vast amount of data collected and stored. Tighter management of data resulting in the creation of a data and learning analytics governance framework is vital for every university. We then consider how robust data and learning analytics governance is able to address the ethical considerations for universities in expanding learning analytics capacity.

University Data Governance Applied to Learning Analytics

With the rise and growing interest of big data analytics and data mining, it is imperative and strategic for institutions to ensure there is good information and data governance as part of the university's ethical use of big data to improve learning, teaching and its business processes. In general, governance is defined as 'the exercise of authority, direction and control of an organization in order to ensure its purpose is achieved' (Gill, 2005, p. 15). Gill asserts that governance has four key components of accountability, transparency, predictability and participation. These components advance healthy mechanisms for governance as they endorse transparency and trust of the stakeholders. Issues such as data quality, interpretability and analytics, ethics and privacy, trust and security need to be understood and addressed to draw valid and reliable inferences (Graf et al., 2012). Within this broader governance framework, data governance comprises the process of storing, monitoring, securing and managing data (Bloor Research, 2014). Whether the analysis and usage of data are applied at the macro-, meso- or micro-levels of the university (e.g. at the system, faculty, school, classroom and learning activity levels), the use of academic and learning data affects all stakeholders, from the vice chancellor to potential students. Universities must be confident with the validity, resilience, storage and management of data and analytics that they are responsible for and have trust in the information that is disseminated.

In order to address data quality issues, Friedman (2006, p. 4) recommends that organisations adopt 'a holistic approach, focusing on people, process and technology'. Tools and people shape the data and tell it where to go, and in this regard, data governance is the governance of 'people and technology' (Thomas, 2006, p. 77). Thomas (2006, p. 92) explains that 'data governance refers to the organisational bodies, rules, decision rights and accountabilities of people and information systems as they perform information-related processes'. Thomas further adds that the data governance programme should be driven by the business (or university) as the business uses the data to make decisions. Therefore, the business should define and control the data and have access to the data and the context in which the data will be and should be used (Thomas, 2006).

A critical part of information and data governance is the context in which data analytics are presented and manipulated. The data must be validated, and justification of data integrity follows on from data cleansing, data deduplication, data de-anonymisation and data reformatting (Bloor Research, 2014). Data governance is mission critical and institutions must ensure data are not misused or leaked. Importantly, as data analytics are gaining prominence across universities and businesses, it is essential that the usage and access to the data are monitored and controlled. While universities may own the entire data across multiple applications, systems and platforms, there is a need for executive leadership to drive data governance process (Cohen, 2006). Marinos (2004) identifies ten critical success factors of data governance. They are as follows:

- *Strategic accountability*. The need to define roles and responsibilities for people in the organisations who are involved in the data governance process.
- *Standards*. Definition of data standards is important as corporate data needs to be defined and made sure that it is 'fit for purpose'.
- *Managerial 'blind spot'*. There is a need for the alignment of data-specific technology, process and organisation bodies with business objectives.
- *Embracing complexity*. The data stakeholder management is complex as data could be collected, enriched, distributed, consumed and maintained by different data stakeholders.
- *Cross-divisional issues*. The data governance structure must be designed in such a way that it includes participation from all levels of the organisation to reconcile priorities, expedite conflict resolution and encourage the support of data quality.
- *Metrics*. Definition of outcome-specific data quality metrics is important for measuring data governance success.

- *Partnership*. When an organisation shares data with other organisations, there is a requirement for its partner to be held accountable for its data quality so that the data management efforts of both organisations are not undermined.
- *Choosing strategic points of control*. Controls need to be put in place to determine where and when quality of the data is to be assessed and addressed.
- *Compliance monitoring*. Data management policies and procedures need to be assessed periodically in order to ensure that the policies and procedures are being followed.
- *Training and awareness*. Data stakeholders need to be aware of the value of data governance. The importance of data quality and the benefits of quality data need to be communicated to all data stakeholders in order to raise their awareness.

Structures, Processes and Relational Communications

Effective information and data governance are influenced by the way structures, policies and communication processes are organised and implemented. Questions concerning ethics, transparency, trust and use of data in learning analytics have increasingly reverberated across higher education academic circles. Universities across the globe are contending with the need to assess the benefits of big data and having to explain to academics and students what data they are collecting and utilising. Adhering to data privacy is a legal and compliance obligation which must be upheld, a responsibility that can sometimes challenge the complex 'ethics and consent' process. While informed consent is warranted for data and learning analytics, a relational and sharing model should be employed to explain the purposes and intentions of data-based decision-making to key stakeholders. At all times, personal and sensitive data must be anonymised and protected to mitigate risks and trust must be assured that the data will be de-identified and difficult to reidentify. To address risks and ensure data validity and resilience require security and the overall management of data and a formal data governance framework comprising structures, processes and relational communications.

Based on the work by Peterson (2004a, 2004b) and De Haes and Van Grembergen (2004) in the effort to improve information technology governance (ITG) in the corporate world, an ITG framework was set up using the elements involving *structures*, *processes* and *relational communications*. Similarly, these elements can be applied for a data and learning analytics governance framework (see Table 7.1). These elements are also well aligned with Marinos' critical success factors of data governance. Contextualising to this governance framework, structures involve the existence of responsible functions, roles and responsibilities held by senior executives and committees. Marinos conceived *structures* as 'strategic accountability' which is critical to define various organisational roles and responsibilities. The second element, processes, refers to strategic decision-making, implementation and operational monitoring. To do this well, standards and metrics are required to ensure that data are managed effectively. According to Marinos, standards and metrics are

Table 7.1 A framework for implementing data and learning analytics governance

Structures	Processes	Communications
Roles and responsibilities	– Strategic decision-making	– Active participation by key stakeholders
– University council, academic board and university committees (e.g. courses, learning and teaching, academic services, admissions)	– Data definition and standards	– Collaboration among key stakeholders
– Senior executives	– Metadata management	– Strategic dialogue
– Senior management	– Metadata repository	– Shared learning/communities of practice
– Data custodianship	– Metrics development and monitoring	– Transparency and education
– IT strategy/steering committees	– Data profiling	– Shared understanding of business objectives
– Project steering committees	– Data cleansing	– Ethical clearance for reporting purposes
– Data stewardship	– Data remediation	
– User groups/roles (e.g. academic staff and sessionals, administrators)	– Privacy, trust and security protocol	
	– Ethics 'notice and consent'	
	– Legal compliance	
	– Third-party service-level agreements	
	– Risks mitigation plan	
	– Information security strategy and plan	

critical factors for data governance. Marinos argues that extracting the correct data is highly dependent on the alignment of technology, process and the organisation's business objectives. The final and third element of relational communications refers to stakeholder participation, collaboration and shared learning. According to Marinos, as 'data stakeholder management is complex', data must be designed with participation across the institution. As various stakeholders may have different needs, requirements and objectives, 'cross-divisional' issues and priorities may also be addressed upfront. Working together through a shared partnership will ensure that data governance and management is the main focus of all affected parties.

The elements of structures, processes and relational communications are deemed to be relevant and applicable to guide universities to govern and oversee the enrichment, consumption, dissemination, sharing, reporting and maintenance of elements and integration of data for business improvement, teaching and learning practices and research activities. These elements also address the critical success factors as highlighted by Marinos. The holistic approach of this framework acknowledges that the data and learning analytics governance is complex in that data that are stored in the university's systems are interlinked and dynamic in nature with interdependencies between systems and subsystems.

University Structures

Embedded within university structures are roles and responsibilities. The effectiveness of data and learning analytics governance is only partially dependent on the chief information officer or the deputy vice chancellor—academic.[1] This new challenge and development should be viewed as a shared responsibility and university-wide commitment towards ensuring a sustainable framework and processes are implemented. The responsibility should be shared across all levels of the universities. At the university's highest level, the university or academic council is responsible for approving policies; engaging the council at the strategic level; strategically aligning business, initiatives and innovations; and reviewing budget plans. This group has the overall accountability of the management of asset data and the use and dissemination of data including learning analytics. The members of this council, which consists of university executives and external high-profile representatives, should keep abreast with an up-to-date knowledge of the current business and strategic activities and the potential risks and benefits associated with the operation of the university business. In particular, with today's contemporary view of student retention strategy and student learning behaviour with the use of learning analytics data, the council or board level can ask the right questions in relation to learning activities and intelligence, along with the potential risks and benefits associated with the availability, application and use of learning analytics data. University committees such as courses committee, learning and teaching committee and research committee could take responsibility relating with the use of learning data while committees such as admission and academic and support services could take responsibility over student retention data. Together, these committees work in close partnership with the university council to endorse the use of learning analytics data, review and agree with intervention strategies that align with the university's goals and values.

In addition to the roles and responsibilities, the establishment of a data and learning analytics governance can help to support the university committees' work and oversee the requirements to access students and learning data in order to achieve the university's goals of providing the best learning experience and support for students. Given the criticality of student and learning data, IT and learning management systems also should be managed in the same way, with a steering committee having specific responsibility for overseeing and managing strategic projects.

---

[1] Position and committee names used in this chapter are common across Australian universities. We recognise that nomenclature and structure may vary across countries and hope to have provided sufficient information to allow for 'translation'.

Other key stakeholders who share responsibility are the senior executives (e.g. deputy vice chancellors, pro-vice-chancellors, deans of learning and teaching, heads of school/department), academic staff (course directors, unit coordinators and sessional staff) and administrative staff who collect the data, process and report off the data. These data users are responsible for reporting any data-related issues, requesting functionality that would help them collect data more efficiently and specifying reporting requirements. Students are another main stakeholder who provide data through various acts of participation during day-to-day university dealings and business (e.g. attend classes, e-learning participation, etc.).

In relation to the data itself, asset data should be managed by the data custodian on behalf of the university. The data custodian is responsible and accountable for the quality of asset data. It is also responsible for endorsing data management and the data cleansing plan, ensuring data is 'fit for purpose', and stakeholder management. In addition, this is also crucial to ensure stewardship of data, and because of this, the function and role of data steward could be strengthened. Data stewards have detailed knowledge of the business process and data requirements. At the same time, they also have good IT knowledge to be able to translate business requirements into technical requirements. They are also responsible for training and educating data users.

University Processes

It is crucial that universities monitor the accuracy, robustness, validity and the overall quality of the data in all the university systems in order to maintain confidence with the learning analytics data. To ensure the integrity of data, the items listed under process in Table 7.1 should be understood and established before learning analytics data can be widely used and disseminated. Clear university policies and protocols with complete transparency must be set up for the data inputted and collected and how the data will be used to enhance learning experiences in order to achieve educational objectives.

When learning analytics data policies and protocols as shown in Table 7.1 are established and enacted effectively, it is easier for universities to collect meaningful data for the purposes of learning analytics with the ability to validate and the capacity to anonymise and de-anonymise data where appropriate, establish interventions to be carried out and legally discard student personal and learning data when requested while adhering to privacy, ethical and legal compliance at all times.

Relational Communications

The effective use of learning analytics data will involve active collaboration and communication between the university administrators, teaching staff and students. It is vital that universities' student guild and student representatives are consulted around the objectives, use and reporting of student demographics and learning data.

Universities should also provide clear guidelines involved in producing the analytics relating to student learning and behaviour in the unit or course. As learning analytics is an emerging strategy for universities to improve student retention and enhance student engagement and learning, it is imperative that students are advised that their learning data will be collected with a mandatory 'opt-in' approach and where appropriate intervention strategies may be recommended. This information is strategic insofar that a university has informed and sought consent from the student cohort ahead of time.

As a true enhancement to learning, students should also be able to view all the learning analytics data performed on their learning which is relevant for their decision-making. This shared responsibility will allow students to take notice of their learning behaviour, reflect on their own learning, better understand and accept any interventions and be able to take responsibility for their own learning. Shared learning may also take place between teaching staff which may ultimately lead to enhanced teaching strategies, improved learning objectives and student satisfaction. Communication and the collaboration effort to educate all key stakeholders are key in ensuring the effective and meaningful use of learning analytics data.

The undertaking of data and learning analytics governance must ensure that adverse risks are minimised and ethical consent and privacy issues must be addressed. The withdrawal of students' involvement in providing their learning data can be addressed if the university's interdependent systems follow a thorough and robust data and learning analytics governance. When such a university-wide system abides by the list of items under processes with good structures and communications in place, the data in the various interconnected systems will be easier to manage and control.

Relational communications, particularly with user groups, must accurately reflect the degree of uncertainty associated with applying learning analytics developed across students to individual students. Recent research at Curtin University (2015; Chai and Gibson, 2015) indicates that predictive algorithms improve over time as more information is added to the modelling process. This implies that decisions made at earlier stages of an individuals' educational journey should be tempered with the understanding that the inference at this point in time has a lower probability of accuracy than it will have later. A provisional stance on the inferences and interpretations can help to temper the communications and can help ensure that an openness to positive change and an orientation towards the future should be part of every communication. This could help prevent a learning analytics result from appearing to be final and immutable and can help make communications more invitational than consequential, until certainty increases over time.

Mapping Ethical Issues Within the Structures, Processes and Relational Communications Framework

The framework of structures, processes and relational communications can be applied to examining ethical issues associated with planned learning analytics activities or strategies. As a case example, we could use this framework to

Table 7.2 Matrix for examining ethical issues from the perspective of stakeholder groups

Roles	Who benefits?	Who decides, acts, redresses?	Who gives consent/is informed?	What are the risks?
Student	Student benefits from improved personalised outreach from student services	Students have choices in the options brought to their attention by the student services team. Student has the right to redress if the identification is perceived as inaccurate. There is no penalty for ignoring task force recommendations for intervention options	Actual consent for the use of information by the retention task force is needed, since intervention options are directed at the individual level	Risk of embarrassment via performance data leading to intervention options being offered. Risk of backfiring of being identified and invited to take advantage of intervention options
Instructor	(Indirect)	(None)	(None)	(None)
Head of school	(Indirect)	(None)	Head of school receives anonymous group data about retention patterns and uptake of intervention options	(None)
Executive/ admin	Retention task force team benefits from better actionable information that gives a more holistic picture of a student	Task force team members decide concerning targeted groups and individuals and acts by aligning current and optional intervention offerings	Task force analytics group receives detailed personal information that must be protected. Policies of the task force determine who should get subreports, if any, with identifying information	Risk of information security within the task force. Sanctions must be in place for any potential breach of confidentiality

explore a planned strategy: 'A retention task force team uses all available sources of student data to understand retention drivers (facilitators and barriers) in order to improve intervention and services'. Simplifying the stakeholder roles to four categories (student, instructor, head of school and executives/admin), we can consider possible ethical issues based on the questions raised in section "Ethical Considerations" of this chapter while taking into account the data and learning analytics governance shown in Table 7.1 and Marinos (2004) critical success factors with regard to data management. A matrix framework can be used to examine each ethical issue from the perspective of each of the stakeholder groups (see Table 7.2).

The matrix is designed to cover the ethical questions raised in section "Ethical Considerations" of this chapter. The first column of the matrix requires the identification of relevant stakeholders for the strategy to be examined. The second column of the matrix addresses the question 'Who benefits from learning analytics?' The third column addresses the questions 'Who makes the decisions?', 'Who is responsible for the stewardship and protection of learning analytics data?', 'Is there an obligation to act on the findings from learning analytics?' and 'What opportunities are there for redress?' The fourth column addresses the questions 'Do students need to consent to the use of their data, and if so, how?', 'How can student agency be recognised and supported?' and 'Who needs to be informed about learning analytics and what do they need to know?' The fifth and final column addresses the questions 'Who is at risk of potential harm from learning analytics?', 'Should student data be de-identified, and if so, is this sufficient to protect anonymity?', 'To what extent do privacy provisions apply?' and 'Who owns learning analytics data and what are the implications for intellectual property rights and licensing for reuse?' While a simple matrix has been provided in this chapter for illustrative purposes, it is possible (and recommended) to set up a full matrix with a column for each question and a line for each type of stakeholder. This matrix format could be applied to examine the ethical issues associated with any new or existing planned learning analytics activity or strategy.

While roles are explicitly included in the first column of the matrix, processes and relational communications need to be inferred from the remaining four columns. For example, the first row, presenting the student perspective, indicates the need for consent and privacy processes and highlights the importance of relational communication between the student services team and retention task force. That is, the points in the matrix will signal the need for action: one or more processes and/or relational communications. These processes and relational communications can then be incorporated into data governance plans.

Conclusion

With the increasing use of big data across the higher education sector, it is timely for universities to examine current governance structures, processes and relational communications guiding learning analytics. In this chapter, we have outlined key ethical considerations, highlighted the importance of developing a governance framework and guiding principles and provided a matrix that can be applied to examining ethical issues associated with current or planned learning analytics activities or strategies from the perspective of key stakeholders. Learning analytics is a rapidly growing field and universities will need to respond to new developments in the area as they arise. The matrix can be used as a tool for working through ethical considerations associated with new developments as they arise.

References

Arnold, K. E., & Pistilli, M. D. (2012). Course signals at Purdue: Using learning analytics to increase student success. *Proceedings of the 2nd International Conference on Learning Analytics and Knowledge (LAK '12)* (pp. 267–270). New York: ACM.

Beattie, S., Woodley, C., & Souter, K. (2014). Creepy analytics and learner data rights. In B. Hegarty, J. McDonald & S. -K. Loke (Eds.), *Rhetoric and reality: Critical perspectives on educational technology. Proceedings ascilite* (pp. 421–425).

Bloor Research. (2014). *Creating confidence in big data analytics*. Retrieved from http://www.bloorresearch.com/research/white-paper/creating-confidence-big-data-analytics/.

Buckingham Shum, S. (2012). *Learning analytics. UNESCO Policy Brief*. Retrieved from http://iite.unesco.org/pics/publications/en/files/3214711.pdf.

Campbell, J. P., DeBlois, P. B., & Oblinger, D. G. (2007). Academic analytics: A new tool for a new era. *EDUCAUSE Review, 42*(4), 40–52.

Chai, K. E. K., & Gibson, D. (2015). Predicting the risk of attrition for undergraduate students with time based modelling. *Proceedings of the 12th International Conference on Cognition and Exploratory Learning in the Digital Age, CELDA 2015* (pp. 109–116). Retrieved from http://www.scopus.com/inward/record.url?eid=2-s2.0-84961786619&partnerID=tZOtx3y1.

Clarke, J., & Nelson, K. (2013). Perspectives on learning analytics: Issues and challenges. Observations from Shane Dawson and Phil Long. *The International Journal of the First Year in Higher Education, 4*(1), 1–8. doi:10.5204/intjfyhe.v4i1.166.

Cohen, R. (2006). What's in a name? Data governance roles, responsibilities and results factors. *Information Management*. Retrieved from http://www.information-management.com/news/columns/-1057220-1.html.

Connolly, B. (2014). *Don't cross the 'creepy line' of data analytics. CIO Australia*. Retrieved from http://www.cio.com.au/article/538947/don_t_cross_creepy_line_data_analytics/

Corrin, L., Kennedy, G., & Mulder, R. (2013). Enhancing learning analytics by understanding the needs of teachers. *Electric dreams. Proceedings* (pp. 201–205). Ascilite.

Cumbley, R., & Church, P. (2013). Is "Big Data" creepy? *Computer Law & Security Review, 29*(5), 601–609.

Curtin University Foundation. (2015). *Annual Report 2014*. Retrieved from http://about.curtin.edu.au/files/2015/03/curtin-2014-annual-report-full-report.pdf.

de Freitas, S., Gibson, D., du Plessis, C., Halloran, P., Williams, E., Ambrose, M., et al. (2014). Foundations of dynamic learning analytics: Using university student data to increase retention. *British Journal of Educational Technology*. [Online]. doi:10.1111/bjet.12212.

De Haes, S., & Van Grembergen, W. (2004). IT governance and its mechanisms. *Information Systems Control Journal, 1*, 1–7.

Dietz-Uhler, B., & Hurn, J. E. (2013). Using learning analytics to predict (and improve) student success: A faculty perspective. *Journal of Interactive Online Learning, 12*, 17–26.

Drachsler, H., & Greller, W. (2012). The pulse of learning analytics: Understandings and expectations from stakeholders. In *Proceedings of the 2nd International Conference on Learning Analytics and Knowledge* (pp. 120–129). ACM.

Drachsler, H., Hoel, T., Scheffel, M., Kismihók, G., Berg, A., Ferguson, R., et al. (2015, March). Ethical and privacy issues in the application of learning analytics. In *Proceedings of the Fifth International Conference on Learning Analytics and Knowledge* (pp. 390–391). ACM.

Dringus, L. P. (2012). Learning analytics considered harmful. *Journal of Asynchronous Learning Networks, 16*(3), 87–100.

EDUCAUSE Center for Applied Research. (2012). *ECAR analytics maturity index for higher education*. Retrieved September 29, 2014, from http://www.educause.edu/ecar/research-publications/ecar-analytics-maturity-index-higher-education.

Fisher, J., Valenzuela, F-R., & Whale, S. (2014). *Learning analytics: A bottom-up approach to enhancing and evaluating students' online learning*. Retrieved from http://www.olt.gov.au/system/files/resources/SD12_2567_Fisher_Report_2014.pdf.

Friedman, T. (2006, March). Key issues for data management and integration, 2006, *Gartner Research*. ID number: G00138812.

Gill, M. D. (2005). *Governing for results: A director's guide to good governance*. Bloomington, IN: Trafford.

Graf, S., Ives, C., Lockyer, L., Hobson, P., & Clow, D. (2012). *Building a data governance model for learning analytics*. Panel at LAK'12, Vancouver.

Greller, W., & Drachsler, H. (2012). Translating learning into numbers: A generic framework for learning analytics. *Educational Technology & Society, 15*(3), 42–57.

Griffiths, D. (2013). The implications of analytics for teaching practice in higher education. *Cetis Analytics Series, 1*(10). Retrieved from http://publications.cetis.ac.uk/wp-content/uploads/2013/02/Analytics-for-Teaching-Practice-Vol-1-No-10.pdf.

Kay, D., Korn, N., & Oppenheim, C. (2012). Legal, risk and ethical aspects of analytics. *Cetis Analytics Series, 1*(6). Retrieved from http://publications.cetis.ac.uk/2012/500.

Long, P., & Siemens, G. (2011). Penetrating the fog: Analytics in learning and education. *EDUCAUSE Review, 46*(5). Retrieved from http://www.educause.edu/ero/article/penetrating-fog-analytics-learning-and-education.

Macfadyen, L. P., Dawson, S., Pardo, A., & Gaševic, D. (2014). Embracing big data in complex educational systems: The learning analytics imperative and the policy challenge. *Research & Practice in Assessment, 9*, 17–28.

MacNeill, S., Campbell, L. M., & Hawksey, M. (2014). Analytics for education. *Journal of Interactive Media in Education*. Retrieved from http://jime.open.ac.uk/jime/article/view-Article/2014-07/html.

Marinos, G. (2004). Data quality: The hidden assumption behind COSO. *DM Review, 14*(10), 12–15.

New Media Consortium. (2015). *NMC Horizon Report: 2015 Higher Education Edition*. Retrieved from http://www.nmc.org/publication/nmc-horizon-report-2015-higher-education-edition/.

Open University. (2014). *Policy on ethical use of student data for learning analytics*. Retrieved from http://www.open.ac.uk/students/charter/essential-documents/ethical-use-student-data-learning-analytics-policy.

Pardo, A., & Siemens, G. (2014). Ethical and privacy principles for learning analytics. *British Journal of Educational Technology, 45*(3), 438–450. doi:10.1111/bjet.12152.

Peterson, R. R. (2004a). Information strategies and tactics for information technology governance. In W. Van Grembergen (Ed.), *Strategies for information technology governance*. Hershey, PA: Idea Group.

Peterson, R. (2004b). Crafting information technology governance. *Information Systems Management, 21*(4), 7–23.

Prinsloo, P., & Slade, S. (2014). Educational triage in open distance learning: Walking a moral tightrope. *The International Review of Research in Open and Distance Learning, 15*(4), 306–331.

Prinsloo, P., & Slade, S. (2015). Student privacy self-management: implications for learning analytics. In *Proceedings of the Fifth International Conference on Learning Analytics and Knowledge* (pp. 83–92). ACM.

Rubel, A., & Jones, K. (2016). Student privacy in learning analytics: An information ethics perspective. *The Information Society., 32*(2), 143–159.

Sclater, N., & Bailey, P. (2015). *Code of practice for learning analytics 2015*. Retrieved from https://www.jisc.ac.uk/guides/code-of-practice-for-learning-analytics.

Siemens, G. (2013). Learning analytics: The emergence of a discipline. *American Behavioral Scientist, 57*, 1380–1400.

Siemens, G., Dawson, S., & Lynch, G. (2013). Improving the quality and productivity of the higher education sector: Policy and strategy for systems-level deployment of learning analytics. Retrieved from http://www.olt.gov.au/system/files/resources/SoLAR_Report_2014.pdf.

Slade, S., & Prinsloo, P. (2013). Learning analytics ethical issues and dilemmas. *American Behavioral Scientist, 57*, 1510–1529.

Swenson, J. (2014, March). Establishing an ethical literacy for learning analytics. *Proceedings of the Fourth International Conference on Learning Analytics and Knowledge* (pp. 246–250).

Thomas, G. (2006). *Alpha males and data disaster: The case for data governance.* Orlando, FL: Brass Cannon Press.

Willis, J. E., III, Campbell, J., & Pistilli, M. (2013). Ethics, big data, and analytics: A model for application. *Educause Review*. Retrieved from http://www.educause.edu/ero/article/ethics-big-data-and-analytics-model-application.

Willis, J. E., III, & Pistilli, M. D. (2014). Ethical discourse: Guiding the future of learning analytics. *EDUCAUSE Review* [Online]. Retrieved from http://www.educause.edu/ero/article/ethical-discourse-guiding-future-learning-analytics.

Chapter 8
Big Data, Higher Education and Learning Analytics: Beyond Justice, Towards an Ethics of Care

Paul Prinsloo and Sharon Slade

Abstract There is no doubt that Big Data in higher education offers huge potential. However, there is a critical need to interrogate the underlying epistemologies and paradigms which inform our understanding of the potential of learning analytics to increase student engagement, retention and success. The harvesting, analyses and application of student data are not neutral acts, and all flow from and perpetuate social, political, economic and cultural agendas. Therefore, it is crucial to explicitly recognise and engage with the complications, contradictions and conflicts inherent in Big Data and learning analytics. The context of increasing funding constraints, the impact of neoliberal and market-driven curricula and admission requirements and the proliferation of accountability and reporting regimes encourage higher education institutions to embrace the harvesting, analysis and use of student data without necessarily considering issues of justice and ethics. Considering higher education as a moral and political practice, this chapter proposes to formulate a framework for information justice based on an ethics of justice and care. The inherent tensions between an ethics of justice and an ethics of care allow for and necessitate a critical engagement with the hype surrounding Big Data in higher education.

Keywords Big Data • Ethics of care • Ethics of justice • Higher education • Information justice • Learning analytics

Introduction

The current discourses on Big Data introduce not only an "age of analytics" (Tene & Polonetsky, 2012, p. 1) but also notions of socio-material algorithmic regulation (Henman, 2004), the "algorithmic turn" (Napoli, 2013, p. 1) and increasingly a

P. Prinsloo (✉)
University of South Africa, Pretoria, Gauteng, South Africa
e-mail: prinsp@unisa.ac.za

S. Slade
The Open University, Milton Keynes, UK

B. Kei Daniel (ed.), *Big Data and Learning Analytics in Higher Education*,
DOI 10.1007/978-3-319-06520-5_8

pervasive "culture of algorithms" (Granieri, 2014). "Raw data is an oxymoron" (Gitelman, 2013) and Big Data is therefore not immune to bias (Danaher, 2014). Big Data may not be regarded as an unqualified good (Boyd & Crawford, 2013).

While many analysts may accept data at face value, and treat them as if they are neutral, objective and pre-analytic in nature, data are in fact framed technically, economically, ethically, temporally, spatially and philosophically. Data do not exist independently of the ideas, instruments, practices, contexts and knowledge used to generate, process and analyse them (Kitchin, 2014b, p. 2).

Throughout human history, technology and the use of data have been largely ideological and embedded in relations of power (Coll, 2014; Henman, 2004; Selwyn & Facer, 2013; Selwyn, 2014). "The turn to big data is a political and cultural turn, and we are just beginning to see its scope" (Crawford, 2014, par. 5).

In the context of higher education, Big Data and learning analytics promise increased efficiency and cost-effectiveness (Siemens, 2011; Siemens & Long, 2011; Hargreaves & Braun, 2013). There are claims that Big Data promises to "change everything" (Wagner & Ice, 2012), and "revolutionise learning" (Van Rijmenam, 2013). The harvesting, analysis and use of student data are asserted to be the "new black" (Booth, 2012), with student data as the "new oil" (Watters, 2013). (See Puschmann and Burgess (2014) for a discussion on the "metaphors of Big Data".)

Amidst the hype and promise of Big Data, there are a growing number of concerns regarding issues around the nature of evidence in education, issues of privacy and the scope and impact of surveillance and so forth (Biesta, 2007, 2010; Eynon, 2013; Morozov, 2013a; Prinsloo & Slade, 2013; Wagner & Ice, 2012). In the context of increasing accountability, Big Data is also seen as serving the "rhetoric and a technology of governmentality" (Suspitsyna, 2010, p. 567). Many of the current discourses may therefore be thought to resemble "techno-solutionism" (Morozov, 2013b) or "techno-romanticism" (Selwyn, 2014). It is becoming clear that Big Data potentially introduces new epistemologies and paradigm shifts and so may herald important changes in the ways in which we understand our engagement with students (Kitchin, 2014a). In the context of claims that it allows us to assume that we have access to the complete picture of individuals based on their individual data (n=all) (Mayer-Schönberger & Cukier, 2013), it is clear that Big Data heralds "a paradigm shift in the ways we understand and study our world" (Eynon, 2013, p. 237).

So, what does the rise of Big Data mean for education and the ethical use of technology in education (Eynon, 2013)? If we accept that the use of data as technology "needs to be understood as a knot of social, political, economic and cultural agendas that is riddled with complications, contradictions and conflicts" (Selwyn, 2014, p. 6), what are the implications for our understanding of the potential and challenges in the collection, analysis and use of student data? How is "data justice" defined, by whom and who does it serve?

Considering that data may inherently be biased, it follows that social privilege or marginalisation is an integral characteristic in the harvesting, analysis and use of data—"injustice in, injustice out" (Johnson, 2013, p. 2). We will argue then that data justice comprises an ethics of justice as well as an ethics of care—without meaning that an ethics of care is assimilated into an ethics of justice (Clement, 1996).

This chapter will problematise the use of Big Data and learning analytics in the context of higher education before discussing the tensions and relationship between an ethics of justice and care (Botes, 2000; Diller, 1996; Gilligan, 1982; Held, 2005; Johnson, 2014; Katz, Noddings, & Strike, 1999; Patton, 2000; Prinsloo & Slade, 2014; Ruiz, 2005; Sadowski, 2013; Stoddart, 2012; Smith, 2001). Based on the proposition that higher education is a "moral and political practice" (Giroux, 2003, p. 180), we propose an ethics of justice *and* care as an appropriate basis for revisiting and possibly reformulating the scope and limitations of information justice.

Problematising Big Data and Education in the Context of an Ethics of Justice and Care

For the sake of this chapter, we accept Kitchin's (2014a, p. 1) definition of Big Data as:

- Huge in *volume*, consisting of terabytes or petabytes of data
- High in *velocity*, being created in or near real time
- Diverse in *variety*, being structured and unstructured in nature
- *Exhaustive* in scope, striving to capture entire populations or systems
- Fine-grained *resolution*, aiming to be as detailed as possible and uniquely indexical in identification
- *Relational* in nature, containing common fields that enable the conjoining of different data sets
- *Flexible*, holding the traits of extensionality (can add new fields easily) and scalability (can expand in size rapidly)

Big Data therefore encompasses not only a wide range and variety of data sources, but increasingly real-time, exhaustive, relational data that includes academic and learning analytics resulting in what Solove (2004) describes as an "elaborate lattice of information networking" (p. 3).

While higher education institutions have access to increasingly huge date sets due to, inter alia, increased digital learning, it can be argued that these data sets and even the combination of data sources (such as data from student administration systems, learning management systems and demographic data) don't quite qualify as Big Data (see Prinsloo, Archer, Barnes, Chetty, & Van Zyl, 2015). Given the ongoing "quantification" fetish (Morozov, 2013a) within higher education and the drive to maximise effectiveness based on the utilisation of data (Prinsloo et al., 2015), we may yet see Kitchin's (2014b) characteristics of Big Data as relevant to the student data sets which higher education has access to. Engaging therefore with the notion and implications of the "elaborate lattice[s] of information networking" (Solove, 2004) from the perspectives of an ethics of justice and an ethics of care will help to prepare higher education for the issues that may arise in future.

While this "information lattice" (Solove, 2004) opens up spaces for more effective information sharing and interventions, we propose here that the ethical harvesting, analysis and use of student data should proceed from the premise that Big Data as technology is in service of "social, political, economic and cultural agendas … riddled with complications, contradictions and conflicts" (Selwyn, 2014, p. 6). As such, we should take cognisance of not only the potential but also the dangers of Big Data (e.g. Boyd & Crawford, 2013; Dormehl, 2014).

Learning analytics as a *subset* of the broader use of student data (see Siemens & Long, 2011) is therefore not neutral and becomes a structuring device "informed by current beliefs about what counts as knowledge and learning, colored by assumptions about gender/race/class/capital/literacy and in service of and perpetuating existing and new power relations" (Prinsloo, 2014). While legal international and national frameworks and guidelines provide some certainty and recourse, we agree with Haggerty and Ericson (2006) that those frameworks may not be sufficient nor current enough to "legislate away the new surveillance tools and databases" (p. 9). Accepting the relative limitations of regulatory and legal frameworks does not mean that less attention and rigour should be applied to ensure appropriate and sanctioned processes, the governance of data and access to due process or to steps which ensure data integrity and algorithmic accountability. (See, e.g. Citron and Pasquale (2014), Crawford and Schultz (2014), Lagoze (2014), Pasquale (2015), Slade and Prinsloo (2013), Tene and Polonetsky (2013), and Wigan and Clarke (2013) for mention of other issues in the discourses on the collection, analysis and use of data.) Suffice to state that while the notion and different types of "justice" provide useful legal and regulatory frameworks, in the context of higher education as moral practice, "justice" is not enough and should be combined with "care".

It falls outside the scope of this paper to discuss and explore the scope of and the distinctions between different types of justice, e.g. distributive and retributive justice and procedural and substantive justice, and the question of desert with its embedded concerns that rights are deserved and directly related to effort and fairness. Central to theories of justice is not only the question about "what is right or fair" but also "who has a right to what" (Noddings, 1999, p. 8). Throughout human history, our understanding of justice has been embedded in different classes of rights, such as the rights for citizens against those of noncitizens, the rights of the underage and, of course, the rights of the "others"—the "barbarians" and the *homines sacri*, those who are considered unhuman and not worthy even of being slaughtered for religious sacrifices (Agamben, 1998).

Data, and increasingly Big Data, also allows us to segment whole populations according to our own criteria of fairness and justice (Andrejevic, 2014; Henman, 2004). While there is no doubt that there are examples of the benefits of the benevolent use of data, the often obscure and unchecked use of data in asymmetrical power relations results in "a world in which people are sorted at important life moments according to genetic, demographic, geo-locational, and previously unanticipated types of data in ways that remain opaque and inaccessible to those who are affected" (Andrejevic, 2014, p. 1681). The threat of "algocracy" (Danaher, 2014) and its inherent "technocratic predictive logic" (Henman, 2004, p. 173) needs to be seriously considered, especially in more complex contexts where the likelihood of mistakes and misunderstandings could have long-term consequences. Subotzky and Prinsloo (2011) propose that student success is the result of mostly non-linear, multidimensional, interdependent interactions at different phases in the nexus between student, institution and broader societal factors. Harvesting, analysing and using student data should therefore take cognisance of the "combined *effects of and relationships between different predictor variables*" (Subotzky & Prinsloo, 2011, p. 182).

Higher education has always had access to student data and used this data for institutional planning and reporting cycles. Historically, most of this use was based on *aggregated* student data. With the introduction of learning management systems, the potential to monitor and impact on *individual* student performance has increased exponentially. Higher education institutions now have the ability to respond in real time to student behaviour, offering personalised, individualised and focused remedial or fast-track learning opportunities to identified students. This may result in students walking around with "with invisible triage tags attached, that only lecturers can see? Is this fair? Or is it just pragmatic? Like battlefield medical attention, lecturers' attention is finite" (Manning, 2012, quoted by Prinsloo & Slade, 2014, p. 306). How do we engage with student data in ways which are not only fair and just but in line with higher education as moral practice—and also embody an ethics of care (Prinsloo & Slade, 2014)?

1. Towards Information Justice

   "The constructed nature of data makes it quite possible for injustices to be embedded in the data itself" (Johnson, 2013, p. 2). Johnson (2013) uses the term "information justice" to address two issues. The first issue is exclusivity—where "individuals, their experiences, their values, and their interests are left out of the information system by the data collection process" (p. 13)—which includes not only the collection but also the dissemination and the whole data operation. The second problem flagged is the role that "assumptions and embedded values play in the collection and use of information" (p. 13). So, information justice not only considers the ideological nature of data, data collection and use, but also petitions for a critical stance that interrogates the collection, analysis and use of data. As Johnson (2013, p. 16) states "If contemporary societies—affluent and otherwise—are to be structured around data as many expect, we will need to know how existing social structures are perpetuated, exacerbated, and mitigated by information systems". The notion of information justice informs, and should inform, institutional responses such as found in regulatory frameworks for data governance, access, etc.

   In considering information justice as a useful heuristic for engaging with the complexities of the collection, analysis and use of student data, it is crucial to also raise (if not address) the issue of "whose justice" is served by our definition of information justice—students, faculty, the institution or society. In the context of the asymmetrical power relationship between students and the providing higher education institution, it is a real possibility that an institution's perception of information justice is determined by the reporting and compliance regimes of various regulatory and legal frameworks (Prinsloo & Slade, 2015). If we accept the notion of higher education as moral practice, and the fiduciary duty of higher education to not only provide access but also ensure an enabling environment, we must move towards a position which both protects the rights of students and their right to receive care. Whether it is our data governance policies and structures, or the issue of algorithmic accountability, this chapter proposes information justice as a counter-narrative that includes both an ethics of justice *and* an ethics of care.

2. An Ethics of Justice and an Ethics of Care

An ethics of care and an ethics of justice are often positioned as opposites (Botes, 2000)—or as ships passing in the night—with the relationship between the two described as a "duet or duel" (Jorgensen, 2006). Gilligan (1982) contends that, while they may be seen and practised as oppositional and mutually exclusionary, both care and justice have a place in ethical decision making, and "the two aspects are inextricably linked and in constant interaction" (Botes, 2000, p. 1073). If it is accepted that a justice of ethics and a justice of care *are* linked and in constant interaction, there is a resulting danger that an ethics of care is assimilated into the justice perspective (Clement, 1996). Another danger is that an ethics of care becomes subsumed into a sentimentalist position of sympathy (Slote, 2007).

In this chapter we propose that justice without care may result in gross *in*justice, while caring without justice may actually constitute *un*caring. Based on this assumed need to consider both an ethics of justice and an ethics of care in a relational understanding, it is also then necessary to consider the differences or unique emphases between them.

An ethics of justice is typically portrayed as rule-based and a reductionist (Botes, 2000; Clement, 1996; Katz et al., 1999; Slote, 2007). Approaching information justice in higher education from the perspective of an ethics of justice suggests that we may have to acknowledge that there is a point at which we have enough rules to cover all possible exceptions and emerging issues. An ethics of justice, on its own, is therefore unlikely to sufficiently address and accommodate the complexities, intersectionality and multidimensional nature of individuals and different relations in different contexts (Slade & Prinsloo, 2013). Conversely, an ethics of care is more holistic and value driven, focusing on relationships and acknowledging the impact of structural constraints on what might be considered to be "right" but not necessarily "fair" (Botes, 2000; Gilligan, 1982; Katz et al., 1999; Ruiz, 2005).

An ethics of care firstly implies a *relational* understanding in the harvesting, analysis and use of data as counter-narrative to allegations and practices of unilateral institutional surveillance processes (Epling, Timmons, & Wharrad, 2003; Knox, 2010; Kruse & Pongsajapan, 2012). An ethics of care therefore suggests to "take care" with regard to our assumptions about the role of evidence in higher education, as well as to our assumptions about the nature and use of student data, issues of governance, privacy and access to data. An ethics of care is also based on the notion of to "care for" students and to harvest, analyse and use their data to improve student retention and success, as well as ensure the sustainability of the institution in an ever-increasing resource-constrained world.

As many of the current discourses surrounding learning analytics focus on its use and potential to increase student success and issues of ethics and privacy—it is crucial to remind ourselves of the underlying assumptions regarding the use of data in higher education and then to proceed to a proposal for an ethics of justice and care as a basis for information justice. "Put bluntly, any account of technology use in education needs to be framed in explicit terms of societal conflict over the distribution of power" (Selwyn, 2014, p. 19). An ethics of care in combination with an ethics of justice allows us to provide a necessary counter-narrative to the often unquestioned assumptions that result from a "Pollyannaish" (Selwyn, 2014, p. 15) approach to Big Data, learning analytics and higher education.

A socio-critical understanding of the harvesting, analysis and use of student data to inform institutional strategies to increase student retention and success needs to take into account the relational and constrained agency of both the institution and students (Subotzky & Prinsloo, 2011). Subotzky and Prinsloo (2011) emphasise, in this first construct, that both students and the institution are situated—and as such bounded by structural and socio-material conditions. This situated-ness impacts on the scope and content of their agency, determines the scope of self-efficacy and their respective loci of controls and also points to the bounded freedom both students and the institution has "to develop, grow, and transform their attributes in pursuit of success" (p. 184).

In the following section, we explore some elements of the juxtaposition between an ethics of justice and an ethics of care and reflect on the implications for the harvesting, analysis and use of student data.

Justice Versus Care

An ethics of justice is based on the decisions of an "autonomous, objective and impartial agent" (Edwards, 1996 in Botes, 2000, p. 1072) formulating and applying universal rules and principles to "ensure the fair and equitable treatment of all people" (Botes, 2000, p. 1072). An ethics of care, on the other hand, focuses on fulfilling "the needs of others and to maintain harmonious relations" (p. 1072). Criticism against an ethics of justice in the health profession, for example, is based on the increasing depersonalisation, objectification of individuals and the "standardisation of all professional activities as part of a quality-control exercise" (Botes, 2000, p. 1072). While some might suggest that this is paralleled by the current higher education landscape, it is important to note that the parallels between higher education and health practices are critiqued by a number of authors (e.g. Biesta, 2007, 2010).

The principles and defining characteristics underlying an ethics of justice can therefore not sufficiently address and accommodate the complexities, intersectionality and multidimensional nature of individuals and different relations in different contexts. An example of this tension is the 1954 US Supreme Court decision in Brown v. Board of Education, which abolished segregation in schools based on the principle of "separate but equal" (Noddings, 1999). Noddings (1999) points to the possibility that universal rights, "handed to people whether or not they seek them, cannot compensate for losses of identity, group respect, and community feeling" (p. 12). She continues to contest the notion that *justice is necessarily achieved through sameness*. A case in point is that a standardised curriculum may not, *per se*, serve the interests or the abilities of all students. Noddings (1999) therefore suggests that "our claim to care must be based not on a one-time, virtuous decision, but rather on continuing evidence that caring relations are maintained" (p. 14). Indeed, while learning analytics holds some promise of addressing the *individual* needs of students without assuming a "one-size-fits-all" approach, it may also result in decisions to withhold support or place students on extended curricula with undesired longer-term consequences.

While it is also tempting to suggest that the end justifies the means, we cannot and should not locate and sanction procedural issues outside of the ethical considerations in a context of justice *and* care (Thomas, 1996; Wright & Wright, 2002).

Care and Equity

Noddings (1999) moots the interesting point that "when a just decision has been reached, there is still much ethical work to be done" (p. 16). In the context of providing equitable educational opportunities, caring means investigating and providing *a range* of reasonable alternatives and resources. An example of the complexities in the nexus between care and equity is the placement of special-needs students in regular classrooms—this potentially impacts not only on all students, but also on the availability and effectiveness of pedagogical strategies for educators. Noddings (1999) argues that treating everyone alike does not necessarily mean that we provide to everyone what they want, but rather meets a minimum need. An equitable and caring approach means that "instead of assuming a false universalism, it recognizes deep and perhaps irremovable differences—differences which counsel against sweeping solutions that affect people's lives directly and preclude their effective use of self-chosen strategies" (p. 19).

Considering the vast numbers of underprepared students in higher education, learning analytics may actually allow us to move beyond access and equity to care. Balanced against this is the danger that our algorithms may serve to actually increase the vulnerability of individuals through stigmatisation and "special tracks". The balancing of care and equity remains then something of a balancing act or an act of "walking a moral tightrope" (Prinsloo & Slade, 2014).

Care, Justice and Power

The understanding and practices of caring, justice and fairness should ideally be embedded in a critical understanding of the ways in which historical and present socio, cultural, economic, technological, political, and environmental power relations shape student and institutional responses (Subotzky & Prinsloo, 2011). There is ample evidence that legal frameworks have always been used to sanction dominant beliefs and societal power structures. Laws and conventions of care thus symbolise what a particular context or society values. Historically, justice and care were (and still are) gendered and informed by religious, cultural and class relations. Societal values inform societal structures which ensure that those beliefs and assumptions are sustained and perpetuated. In earlier decades, there were different dispensations with regard to, for example, education for all, racial segregation, gay rights, tolerance and respect for religious diversity and so forth. In each of these periods, we should recognise that justice and care effectively took different forms.

Within the current context of the current hegemony of neoliberalism and consumerism, it should therefore come as no surprise that our academic offerings, curricula, assessment practices and managerial practices in higher education echo market sentiments and that our definitions of status and power are driven largely by commercial and consumerist interests. Addressing student dropout and failure may then be embedded in often unquestioned assumptions and power relations where institutional rules and criteria embody the unequal power relationship between students and the institution. An ethics of care seems to more explicitly acknowledge the unequal and asymmetrical power relations and commits itself to being transparent regarding its intentions and processes, at the same time considering the often unforeseen implications of an ethics of justice and the cost and scalability.

Positive Rationality Versus an Extended Communicative Rationality

The concept of rationality proposes that findings can be justified through argumentation. An ethics of justice is founded on a positivistic or modernistic rationality that, for the sake of objectivity, reduces complexities to formulate universally applicable rules and principles. Opponents to an ethics of justice moot the notion that moral and social phenomena are complex, dynamic and multifaceted making it almost impossible to predetermine definitions of fairness and justice. A socio-critical understanding of student success or failure illustrates the relational complexity of different interdependent and often mutually constitutive variables, which almost make it impossible to formulate minutely detailed rules and regulations that encompass every possible combination and scenario. Subotzky and Prinsloo (2011) therefore point to the importance of the relationship between students and the institution and "actionable mutual knowledge" (p. 183).

Reductionist Universality Versus Holistic Contextuality

"The reductionism approach is, in all probability, the Achilles heel of the ethics of justice, as it is not plausible for the sake of objectivity to reduce ethical problems in order to relegate values and emotions" (Botes, 2000, p. 1074). An ethics of care suggests that a phenomenon to be studied in its entirety also considers the impact and causal power of structures. A case in point is acknowledging the socio-economic legacy systems and how they shaped and still shape students preparedness for higher and open distance learning. Institutional admission criteria—or criteria informing the scope and practices of educational triage—need to take cognisance of the causal historical legacies of social structures (Prinsloo & Slade, 2014). (Also see Andrejevic, 2014; Johnson, 2013; Henman, 2004.)

Most literatures on the difference between, and possibly the mutually exclusive nature of, an ethics of justice and an ethics of care refer to the foundation for an ethics of justice as an assumption that it is possible to formulate guidelines or criteria that are universally valid and applicable regardless of context. On the other hand, an ethics of care emphasises the importance of context and that contextual factors may, at times, require non-adherence to guidelines or criteria originating from an ethics of justice. (See Prinsloo and Slade (2014) for their discussion on the importance of context in an ethics of care.)

Towards a Framework for an Ethics of Justice and Caring in Higher Education

The purpose of the following propositions is to provide a tentative heuristic for engaging with the complexities of the harvesting, analysis and use of student data to inform institutional strategies to support student success and retention. The proposed propositions aim to guide us when considering the limitations of an ethics of justice and also to understand the complexities of an ethics of care. As such the propositions are anything but final or complete, but rather provide a (hopefully) generative framework for moving beyond justice in our responses to the unacceptable student dropout and failure rates in higher education.

Justice and Care Are Always Situated and Context Bound

We need rules and regulations. Particularly in massive open and distance learning contexts, it is crucial that there are broad parameters within which students, faculty and administrators function. However, it is also crucial that while rules and regulations should ensure that we are fair and just in our engagement with students, we cannot and should not forget that education is an "open and recursive system"

(Biesta, 2007, p. 8) where different variables are at play, interdependent and often mutually constitutive (Subotzky & Prinsloo, 2011). Context does not only impact on students but also on the institution and as Subotzky and Prinsloo (2011) indicate, both role players are situated and their agency constrained. Neither students nor the institution is a free agent. "Actionable mutual knowledge" (Subotzky & Prinsloo, 2011, p. 183) is therefore a precursor to an ethics of care.

An Ethics of Justice and Care as Multidimensional, Dynamic and Permeable

Agreeing with Biesta (2007) that education is an "open and recursive system" (p. 8), we should consider how our policies recognise their limitations and the need to provide a broad enabling environment for ethical and caring decisions. Noddings (1999) raises some crucial issues in considering care, equity and fairness. A framework or a set of criteria designed to be just or fair does not necessarily result in a more equitable and caring result. It is therefore crucial that institutional policies and practices aimed to address an ethics of care are transparent and involve consultation with all stakeholders, together with access for appeal and contestation (Prinsloo & Slade, 2014).

Biesta (2007, 2010) also points to the fact that, in the context of evidence-based management and education, it is important to note that effectiveness does not guarantee appropriateness. Education as moral practice entails that we cannot (and should not) separate the means from the end. Even if we know that some interventions may be more effective than others, these actions may not necessarily always be desirable. Biesta (2007) therefore rejects "the idea of education as a treatment or intervention that is a causal means to bring about particular, pre-established ends" (p. 10) and suggests that educationalists should rather make decisions regarding "the most appropriate course of action in the specific circumstances in a context of informal rules, heuristics, norms, and values" (Sanderson, 2003, in Biesta, 2007, p. 10).

The Cost and Scalability of an Ethics of Care

Any framework for an ethics of care in open distance learning contexts that does not seriously consider issues of scalability and cost will fail. While it is one thing to appeal for a consideration of context in contemplating an individual student's appeal, how does the institution ensure fairness to all students and, at the same time, ensure that the specific context of a particular case is considered when trying to apply more general rules? It is therefore important to consider the question asked by Prinsloo and Slade (2014)—"how do we make moral decisions when resources are (increasingly) limited?"

An Ethics of Care Is Different from Pity

There is a huge difference between care, compassion, empathy and pity. Zembylas (2013) provides a rich and critical exploration of the difference between care and pity pointing out that pity does not necessarily involve solidarity and can actually dehumanise the object of pity, while compassion and care require action and solidarity. Care, compassion and solidarity imply a careful weighing of the costs, scalability and appropriateness of any action to address student failure and dropout. In addition, actions arising from pity do not necessarily recognise the agency and bounded autonomy of students, while solidarity and care imply being student centred without disregarding the agency and self-efficacy of students (Subotzky & Prinsloo, 2011).

Conclusions

Much of the current discourse in higher education is dominated by issues flowing from the need to widen participation and increase opportunities for access. There is also a call for increasing effectiveness amidst technological advances, the increasing digitisation of teaching and learning and a proliferation of funding constraints. Embedded in these discourses is the need to ensure equity, transformation and to serve a particular notion of justice. In this chapter, we mooted the proposal that we cannot and should not separate our practices of ensuring justice and fairness from considering "care" as justice in action. Considering higher education as moral practice, the fiduciary duty of higher education to its students and the asymmetrical power relationship between higher education and students, we tend to agree with Noddings' (1999) proposition that "when a just decision has been reached, there is still much ethical work to be done" (p. 16).

In the context of these debates, we proposed that our collection, analyses and use of students' data should take cognisance of the need to ensure "information justice" (Johnson, 2013) that includes both justice *and* care. As we collect, analyse and use student data, we are walking a "moral tightrope" (Prinsloo & Slade, 2014), balancing seemingly contradictory interests between ensuring equitable learning experiences and realising that an approach based on a one-size-fits-all does not necessarily fit into an ethics of care. The personalisation of learning offers, on the one hand, the possibility of embodying justice and care, and on the other hand, personalisation does raise questions regarding its scalability and its long-term impacts.

In an attempt to balance the notions and practices of justice and care, we proposed a tentative framework based on four principles for implementing an ethics of care. The first principle emphasises the importance of recognising that student data (and its use) is always situated and context-bound. The second principle suggests that if education is an open and recursive ecology (Biesta, 2007, 2010), it is clear that acceptance of justice and care as multidimensional, dynamic and permeable should result in *appropriate* institutional responses to students' needs. Our data collection methods, algorithms and decision-making structures should be responsive and sensitive to student contexts as dynamic and multidimensional.

While the first two principles are, in all probability, idealistic—the third and fourth principles argue for a pragmatic approach in recognising the cost and scalability of care and in distinguishing "care" from "pity". Firstly, this is a crucial element in the collection, analysis and use of student data in as much as higher education will have access to more student data than ever before, and we should recognise that we cannot *unknow* knowing, and secondly, that much of the data we access may provide us information about students' lifeworlds over which we have no control.

Big Data "holds the promise of a data deluge—of rich, detailed, interrelated, timely and low-cost data—that can provide much more sophisticated, wider scale, finer grained understandings of societies and the world we live in" (Kitchin, 2013, p. 263). While the potential of Big Data in higher education is accepted, the harvesting, analysis and use of student data are only as good as the questions we ask (Kitchin, 2013). Data does not speak for itself—and the selection and harvesting of student data are not neutral acts but embedded in social, political, economic and cultural agendas (Selwyn, 2014).

If we accept that higher education is a "moral and political" (Giroux, 2003) practice, *information justice as praxis* can act as a powerful counter-narrative to the current hegemony of "techno-solutionism" (Morozov, 2013b) and the discourses of "techno-romanticism" (Selwyn, 2014).

Acknowledgement A related summary argument was presented at the EDEN15 Conference held in Barcelona, Spain, 9–12 June 2015. That work has not been published.

References

Agamben, G. (1998). *Homo sacer. Sovereign power and bare life* (D. Heller-Roazen, Trans.). Stanford: Stanford University Press.

Andrejevic, M. (2014). The Big Data divide. *International Journal of Communication, 8*, 1673–1689.

Biesta, G. (2007). Why "what works" won't work: Evidence-based practice and the democratic deficit in educational research. *Educational Theory, 57*(1), 1–22. doi:10.1111/j.1741-5446.2006.00241.x.

Biesta, G. (2010). Why 'what works' still won't work: From evidence-based education to value-based education. *Studies in Philosophy and Education, 29*, 491–503. doi:10.1007/s11217-010-9191-x.

Booth, M. (2012, July 18). Learning analytics: The new black. *EDUCAUSE Review*. Retrieved October 29, 2014, from http://www.educause.edu/ero/article/learning-analytics-new-black.

Botes, A. (2000). A comparison between the ethics of justice and the ethics of care. *Journal of Advanced Nursing, 32*, 1071–1075. doi:10.1046/j.1365-2648.2000.01576.x.

Boyd, D., & Crawford, K. (2013). *Six provocations for Big Data*. Retrieved October 29, 2014, from http://papers.ssrn.com/sol3/papers.cfm?abstract_id=1926431.

Citron, D. K., & Pasquale, F. A. (2014). The scored society: due process for automated predictions. *Washington Law Review, 89*, 1–33.

Clement, G. (1996). *Care, autonomy, and justice. Feminism and the ethics of care*. Boulder, CO: Westview Press.

Coll, S. (2014). Power, knowledge, and the subjects of privacy: Understanding privacy as the ally of surveillance. *Information, Communication and Society, 17*(10), 1250–1263. doi:10.1080/1369118X.2014.918636.

Crawford, K. (2014, May 30). *The anxieties of big data*. Retrieved October 29, 2014, from http://thenewinquiry.com/essays/the-anxieties-of-big-data.

Crawford, K., & Schultz, J. (2014). Big Data and due process: Toward a framework to redress predictive privacy harms, *Boston College Law Review, 55*(1). Retrieved June 15, 2015, from http://lawdigitalcommons.bc.edu/bclr/vol55/iss1/4.

Danaher, J. (2014, January 7). *Rule by algorithm? Big data and the threat of algocracy*. Retrieved October 29, 2014, from http://ieet.org/index.php/IEET/more/danaher20140107.

Diller, A. (1996). Ethics of care and education: A new paradigm, its critics, and its educational significance. In A. Diller, B. Houston, K. P. Morgan, & M. Ayim (Eds.), *The gender question in education: Theory, pedagogy and politics*. Boulder, CO: Westview Press.

Dormehl, L. (2014). *The formula. How algorithms solve all our problems and create more*. London: WH Allen.

Epling, M., Timmons, S., & Wharrad, H. (2003). An educational panopticon? New technology, nurse education and surveillance. *Nurse Education Today, 23*, 412–418.

Eynon, R. (2013). The rise of Big Data: What does it mean for education, technology, and media research? *Learning, Media and Technology, 38*(3), 237–240. doi:10.1080/17439884.2013.771783.

Gilligan, C. (1982). *In a different voice: Psychological theory and women's development*. Cambridge, MA: Harvard University Press.

Giroux, H. A. (2003). Selling out higher education. *Policy Futures in Education, 1*(1), 179–311.

Gitelman, L. (Ed.). (2013). *"Raw data" is an oxymoron*. London: MIT Press.

Granieri, G. (2014, May 17). *Algorithmic culture. "Culture now has two audiences: people and machines" A conversation with Ted Striphas*. Retrieved October 29, 2014, from https://medium.com/futurists-views/2bdaa404f643.

Haggerty, K. D., & Ericson, R. V. (Eds.). (2006). *The new politics of surveillance and visibility*. Toronto, ON: University of Toronto Press.

Hargreaves, A., & Braun, H. (2013). *Data-driven improvement and accountability*. Boulder, CO: National Education Policy Centre. Retrieved October 29, 2014, from http://co.chalkbeat.org/wp-content/uploads/sites/2/2013/10/PB-LB-DDIA-POLICY-FINAL-EMBARGOED.pdf.

Held, V. (2005). *The ethics of care: Personal, political, and global*. New York: Oxford University Press.

Henman, P. (2004). Targeted!: Population segmentation, electronic surveillance and governing the unemployed in Australia. *International Sociology, 19*, 173–191. doi:10.1177/0268580904042899.

Johnson, J. A. (2013). From open data to information justice. Paper presented at the Annual Conference of the Midwest Political Science Association, April 13, Chicago, IL. Retrieved October 29, 2014, from https://papers.ssrn.com/sol3/papers.cfm?abstract_id=2241092.

Johnson, J. A. (2014). The ethics of big data in higher education. *International Review of Information Ethics, 7*, 3–10.

Jorgensen, G. (2006). Kohlberg and Gilligan: Duet or duel? *Journal of Moral Education, 35*(2), 179–196. doi:10.1080/03057240600681710.

Katz, M. S., Noddings, N., & Strike, K. A. (Eds.). (1999). *Justice and caring. The search for common ground in education*. London: Teachers College Press.

Kitchin, R. (2013). Big data and human geography: Opportunities, challenges and risks. *Dialogues in Human Geography, 3*, 262–267. doi:10.1177/2043820613513388.

Kitchin, R. (2014a). Big data, new epistemologies and paradigm shifts. *Big Data & Society, 1*, 1–12. doi:10.1177/2053951714528481.

Kitchin, R. (2014b). *The data revolution. Big data, open data, data infrastructures & their consequences*. London: Sage.

Knox, D. (2010). Spies in the house of learning: a typology of surveillance in online learning environments. Paper delivered at EDGE, e-Learning and Beyond, Newfoundland, Canada, 12–15 October, 2010.

Kruse, A., & Pongsajapan, R. (2012). *Student-centered learning analytics*. Retrieved October 29, 2014, from https://cndls.georgetown.edu/m/documents/thoughtpaper-krusepongsajapan.pdf.

Mayer-Schönberger, V., & Cukier, K. (2013). *Big data*. London: Hachette.

Morozov, E. (2013a, October 23). The real privacy problem. *MIT Technology Review*. Retrieved October 29, 2014, from http://www.technologyreview.com/featuredstory/520426/the-real-privacy-problem/.

Morozov, E. (2013a). *To save everything, click here*. London: Penguin.

Napoli, P. (2013). The algorithm as institution: Toward a theoretical framework for automated media production and consumption. *Media in Transition Conference* (pp. 1–36). doi:10.2139/ssrn.2260923.

Noddings, N. (1999). Care, justice, and equity. In M. S. Katz, N. Noddings, & K. A. Strike (Eds.), *Justice and caring* (pp. 7–20). New York, NY: Teachers College Press.

Pasquale, F. (2015). *The black box society. The secret algorithms that control money and information*. New York: Harvard University Press.

Patton, J. W. (2000). Protecting privacy in public? Surveillance technologies and the value of public places. *Ethics and Information Technology, 2*, 181–187.

Prinsloo, P. (2014). A brave new world: student surveillance in higher education. Paper presented at the 21st Southern African Association for Institutional Research (SAAIR), Pretoria, 16–18 September. Retrieved October 29, 2014, from http://www.slideshare.net/prinsp/a-brave-new-world-student-surveillance-in-higher-education.

Prinsloo, P., Archer, E., Barnes, G., Chetty, Y., & Van Zyl, D. (2015). Big (ger) data as better data in open distance learning. *The International Review of Research in Open and Distributed Learning, 16*(1), 284–306.

Prinsloo, P., & Slade, S. (2013). An evaluation of policy frameworks for addressing ethical considerations in learning analytics. *Proceedings of the Third International Conference on Learning Analytics and Knowledge* (pp. 240–244). Retrieved September 24, 2014, from http://dl.acm.org/citation.cfm?id=2460344.

Prinsloo, P., & Slade, S. (2014). Educational triage in higher online education: Walking a moral tightrope. *International Review of Research in Open Distance Learning (IRRODL), 14*(4), 306–331. Retrieved October 29, 2014, from http://www.irrodl.org/index.php/irrodl/article/view/1881.

Prinsloo, P., & Slade, S. (2015). Student privacy self-management: Implications for learning analytics. *Proceedings of Proceedings of the Fifth International Conference on Learning Analytics and Knowledge Conference* (pp. 83–92). New York: ACM. Retrieved June 15, 2015, from http://oro.open.ac.uk/42395/.

Puschmann, C., & Burgess, J. (2014). Metaphors of Big Data. *International Journal of Communication, 8*, 1690–1709.

Ruiz, B. R. (2005). Caring discourse: The care/justice debate revisited. *Philosophy & Social Criticism, 31*(7), 773–800. doi:10.1177/0191453705057303.

Sadowski, J. (2013, June 28). The injustices of open data. *Slate Magazine*. Retrieved September 24, 2014, from http://www.slate.com/blogs/future_tense/2013/06/28/open_data_can_promote_social_injustice.html.

Selwyn, N. (2014). *Distrusting educational technology. Critical questions for changing times*. New York: Routledge.

Selwyn, N., & Facer, K. (Eds.). (2013). *The politics of education and technology. Conflicts, controversies, and connections*. New York: Palgrave Macmillan.

Siemens, G. (2011). *Learning analytics: A foundation for informed change in higher education*. Retrieved September 24, 2014, from http://www.educause.edu/library/resources/learning-analytics-foundation-informed-change-higher-education.

Siemens, G., & Long, P. (2011, September 12). Penetrating the fog: Analytics in learning and education. *EDUCAUSE Review*. Retrieved October 29, 2014, from http://www.educause.edu/ero/article/penetrating-fog-analytics-learning-and-education.

Slade, S., & Prinsloo, P. (2013). Learning analytics: Ethical issues and dilemmas. *American Behavioral Scientist, 57*(1), 1509–1528.

Slote, M. (2007). *The ethics of care and empathy*. Abingdon: Routledge.

Smith, M. (2001). Global information justice: Rights, responsibilities and caring connections. *Library Trends, 49*(3), 519–537.

Solove, D. J. (2004). *The digital person: Technology and privacy in the information age*. New York: NyU Press.

Stoddart, E. (2012). A surveillance of care: Evaluating surveillance ethically. In K. Ball, K. D. Haggerty, & D. Lyon (Eds.), *Routledge handbook of surveillance studies* (pp. 369–376). London: Routledge.

Subotzky, G., & Prinsloo, P. (2011). Turning the tide: A socio-critical model and framework for improving student success in open distance learning at the University of South Africa. *Distance Education, 32*(2), 177–193.

Suspitsyna, T. (2010). Accountability in American education as a rhetoric and a technology of governmentality. *Journal of Education Policy, 25*(5), 567–586. doi:10.1080/02680930903548411.

Tene, O., & Polonetsky, J. (2012). Big data for all: Privacy and user control in the age of analytics. *Northwestern Journal of Technology and Intellectual Property, 239*, 1–36. Retrieved October 29, 2014, from http://papers.ssrn.com/sol3/papers.cfm?abstract_id=2149364.

Tene, O., & Polonetsky, J. (2013). Judged by the tin man: Individual rights in the age of big data. *Journal of Telecommunications and High Technology Law, 11*, 351–368.

Thomas, J. (1996). Introduction: A debate about the ethics of fair practices for collecting social science data in cyberspace. *The Information Society, 12*(2), 107–118.

Van Rijmenam, M. (2013, April 30). *Big data will revolutionise learning*. Retrieved October 29, 2014, from http://smartdatacollective.com/bigdatastartups/121261/big-data-will-revolutionize-learning.

Wagner, E., & Ice, P. (2012, July 18). Data changes everything: Delivering on the promise of learning analytics in higher education. *EDUCAUSE Review*. Retrieved October 29, 2014, from http://www.educause.edu/ero/article/data-changes-everything-delivering-promise-learning-analytics-higher-education.

Watters, A. (2013, October 13). *Student data is the new oil: MOOCs, metaphor, and money*. Retrieved October 29, 2014, from http://www.hackeducation.com/2013/10/17/student-data-is-the-new-oil/.

Wigan, M. R., & Clarke, R. (2013). Big data's big unintended consequences. *Computer, 46*(6), 46–53.

Wright, T. A., & Wright, V. P. (2002). Organizational researcher values, ethical responsibility, and the committed-to-participant research perspective. *Journal of Management Inquiry, 11*(2), 173–185.

Zembylas, M. (2013). The "crisis of pity" and the radicalization of solidarity: Toward critical pedagogies of compassion. *Educational Studies, 49*(6), 504–521. doi:10.1080/00131946.2013.844148.

Chapter 9
Curricular and Learning Analytics: A Big Data Perspective

Colin Pinnell, Geetha Paulmani, Vivekanandan Kumar, and Kinshuk

Abstract Analytics is about insights. Learning Analytics is about insights on factors such as capacity of learners, learning behaviour, predictability of learning concerns, and nurturing of cognitive aspects of learners, among others. Learning Analytics systems can engage learners to detect and appreciate insights generated by others, engage learners to investigate models on learning factors, and engage learners to create new insights. This chapter offers details of this vision for learning analytics, particularly in light of the ability to collect enormous amounts of data from students' study episodes, wherever they happen to study using whatever resources they employ. Further, the chapter contends that learning analytics can also be used to make statements on the efficacy of a particular curriculum and recommend changes based on curricular insights.

The Goal of Education

Education is nominally about facilitating learning. Individuals are capable of learning without education—autodidacts can go through their own learning steps without interruption, and on a more basic level, we are all able to learn skills and facts on our own, either through explicit and conscious efforts or unconsciously in the process of living. Education is an activity which improves learning, making it easier, faster, more efficient, or more enjoyable, amongst other possibilities—anything which helps a learner to learn.

In order to facilitate learning, educational systems have a number of tricks it can use—an educator can provide games which teach during play, or they can use demonstrations, assign tasks or suggest readings and other activities a learner can go through. One of the most powerful techniques available, though, sits atop these activities. Educators can *evaluate learner outcomes and behaviours* in order to gauge learning progress. This provides a number of benefits—it provides clues

C. Pinnell • G. Paulmani • V. Kumar (✉) • Kinshuk
Athabasca University, Athabasca, AB, Canada
e-mail: vive@athabascau.ca

B. Kei Daniel (ed.), *Big Data and Learning Analytics in Higher Education*,
DOI 10.1007/978-3-319-06520-5_9

to the educator on which interventions are more or less effective, it may suggest ways in which interventions might be improved, or it may suggest deficiencies, misconceptions or areas of talent in the learners' knowledge. For the learner, the feedback that evaluation gives can help them evaluate and refocus their own efforts internally.

Bringing these techniques of evaluation and feedback into the twenty-first century is of vital importance to the continued success of formal education systems. This by necessity will involve changes to the ways that educational institutions operate. Indeed, these institutions would be wise to critically evaluate their own processes and ask themselves whether they are appropriate for the modern age. We examine the systems, processes, structures and theories behind this task, providing an introduction for the reader to the world of curricular and learning analytics with a perspective including the information-soaked big data nature of our modern world.

Learning Analytics in Traditional Learning Systems

Learning analytics is a long-standing field within education. The creation, administration and assessment of assignments and exams, the evaluation of learner activities within a classroom and the design of curricula and learning plans, all of these are established traditions within traditional learning systems. Fads in how to assess or teach topics come and go, often subject to the whims of administration and politics, but the basic structure of the evaluation of learner states and progress has been maintained as a core of practices around which learning analysis takes place.

These practices are also, by and large, wrong.

Investigations into the psychology of learning and motivation have discovered that many of the practices that make up the modern learning context are inefficient, ineffective or at times directly contrary to the goals of an educational system. This suggests that these systems, despite their long lineage, should be replaced with those that use a full, modern understanding of learning and organizational efficiency. And yet, a cursory look at the history of educational institutions will demonstrate the difficulty in bringing about significant change in any learning system, from universities and large, established institutions to rural school boards.

Fortunately, education is changing. The information revolution, beginning with the advent of the microprocessor to the modern day, has begun to change the way in which we think about evaluation and interpretation. Statistical methods that were once the domain of scientific research can be leveraged in a classroom, and the introduction of the Internet has provided a whole new platform for learning and expressing itself as modern distance education, the MOOC, MOODLE, and other digital learning platforms. Ubiquitous computing and sensing further provides us with a flood of potential data on the behaviours of learners about the process of learning itself (Boyd & Crawford, 2011).

The combination of all of these factors—sophisticated statistical techniques, high-bandwidth communication, and ubiquitous computing and sensing—has provided a foundation for a change in how we evaluate learners, educators, curricula and administrations. Further, these factors can be used to smoothly integrate these new techniques and perspectives without greatly disrupting the status quo. These factors allow the development of a *big data learning analytics system* (Almosallam & Ouertani, 2014).

Defining Learning Analytics

Learning analytics exists as a subset of general analytics which is focused specifically on the fields of education and learning. While there are properties shared between learning analytics and analytics in general, learning analytics does have its own unique characteristics which deserve special attention (Chatti, Dyckhoff, Schroeder, & Thüs, 2012).

In general analytics, it can be said that the generation of situational *awareness* is a major goal. Analytics are undertaken to understand the states within an entity. In the educational field, this awareness can be considered an awareness of the states of knowledge within a learner.

Important to learning analytics is the goal of generating growth within the learner by use of *insight*. This growth by insight can be considered using an awareness of the states of knowledge within a learner so as to generate insights such that these insights promote positive learner growth. General analytics is also concerned with encouraging growth, but learning analytics focuses on this factor more than other analytical fields. Learning analytics is interested in human educational growth, which is complex, dynamic and unpredictable.

To better describe the difference, consider a CEO using a business analytics dashboard. The primary concern of this dashboard is to give the CEO a moment-by-moment awareness of the workings of the business so that problems may be addressed, concerns may be investigated, and new ideas may be tested against real-world data. The dashboard may be used to generate new insights into how this company operates, but the primary concern is one of maintaining daily awareness.

Contrast this with the learning process of a student exposed to a new topic for the first time. Learning generally proceeds slowly and gradually, through practice, repetition and study. However, learning is also characterized by epiphany events—bursts of insight in which the student "gets it", the proverbial *eureka* moment. The periods of study and practice are in preparation of these moments of clarity.

Analytics focused on the learning process therefore concerns two phases: the slow, gradual *equilibrium* stages, punctuated by dramatic jumps in competence in *insight* stages. Like the saltation of pebbles on a riverbed, learning can be said to proceed in hops from one level to the next. Learning analytics is concerned with providing *progress awareness* during equilibrium moments with an overall goal of generating *insight* to help the learner propel themselves to higher levels of knowledge (Arnold & Pistilli, 2012).

The Flavours of Insight

Learning analytics interact with insight in three distinct ways, each of relevance to understanding learning progression. First amongst these is the *detection* of moments of learning insights already experienced and elucidated by others. This is akin to applying someone's data set on someone else's model to expose insights that have already been garnered. Understanding the moment of expression of an existing insight can be crucial information, especially if that expression occurs within a particular trace of learning episode instead of outside of that episode. Insight expression within a learning context has important implications for the successfulness of that context. By detecting such an expression, a learning system may be able to make important statements on how the learner learns, how well the curriculum handles the learning objectives related to the insight, and whether the educators' interventions are successful. This information can be further used by communicating the moment of insight to the learner directly, for their own contemplation and self-regulation.

The learning analytics system can also use this information in the construction and interpretation of models or data sets. That is, the learner may have access to a model created by someone but uses his/her own data set to arrive at insights. Alternatively, the learner may have the data set from someone else but creates his/her own model to arrive at insights. Either of these cases is the *analysis* of moments of insight. As insightful moments occur, they may imply the generation of new competencies, may indicate metacognition in the learner, or may indicate a possible new direction of successful curriculum design amongst other possibilities. A learning analytics system can use these moments of insight to make these implications, build new models, and advance a deeper understanding of the elements at work in the educational environment.

With this deeper understanding of the context in which learning is taking place, a learning analytics system can attempt to *create* moments of insight for the learner, the third point of interaction between learning analytics and insight. Here, the learner creates the data set and creates models to generate new insights.

Within the analytical store are a great number of models on how learning is occurring, both in the *precise* models of each learner and in the *aggregate* models representing the contemporary knowledge from the literature. These can be compared with theories of learning, which can suggest new directions to take and new actions to attempt to the learners, educators, and administrators using the system. The system may make these suggestions directly to each user or may simply implement changes in its own operation to provide them with the needed impetus to generate new insights.

The Levels of Learning Analytics

Learning analytics straddles a number of different practices. Beyond evaluating learner progress, learning analytics also considers things such as the efficacy of educators, usefulness of learning resources, and overall efficacy of curricula. These various analytics goals can be considered in separate groups depending on the scope of those analytics. A number of different partitions have been suggested for these groups, the simplest of which being the division between micro- and macro-scale. Micro-scale analytics concern themselves with the insights and progress regarding individual users, typically the learners of an educational system (van Harmelen, 2006). Macro-scale analytics, in contrast, are concerned with insights and processes regarding institutions, programmes, resources, teaching methods, curricular elements and other aggregates featured in an educational system.

Learning Analy*tics* vs. Learning Analy*sis*

Some confusion exists in the difference between the practice of analytics and the practice of analysis. These two words are closely related, but the difference between them is important both in the context of educational analytics and general analytics. This difference is akin to that of the different levels of learning analytics, being concerned largely with the level of focus.

Analysis, in general, is used to describe the process of using a mathematical or statistical process to convert input data into output information, with the implication that the output is useful. In going through an analysis, the researcher poses a question, conducts an investigation using a specific process, and finds an answer to that question. Notably, the process used to find the answer is specific—the process of conducting a regression test is different from a chi-square test, as an example. Rarely, a researcher may already have the data sets but then creates a new method of statistical analysis, a model, to find an answer hitherto unknown within the data sets.

Analytics exists overtop of this view of analysis towards insights. Analytics considers each analytical process available as a potential tool to find an answer, a peek into an insight, and is concerned with the appropriate selection of these processes considering the information available and questions being posed. With this understanding, the researcher conducting an analysis can also be said to be engaged in analytics, provided that the researcher has willfully chosen insights as goals of his/her investigation.

Further, analytics in the context of big data—in the context of large, loosely organized, self-similarly arriving data sets—has further implications. The data volume is very large and is constantly changing, and that the queries being asked of this data are not known in advance. It is important that any analytics or analytical process being done on this big data happens on demand because of this, instead of being performed ahead of time and curated. This sort of curation is often not possible. Analytics, therefore, implies a real-time, on-demand factor of analysis.

With these definitions in mind, we can more fully define a practical learning analytics platform as a set of interlocking parts, consisting of (1) a dynamic store of analytical processes, the *toolkit*; (2) a large store of real-time data being collected by the learning system, the *data pool*; (3) a set of processes to select and run the appropriate analytical tools for a given query, model or inference, the *analyser*; and (4) a set of models and inferences produced by the platform, the *model store*.

Types of Learning Traces

A *learning trace* is the real-time, dynamic record of all activities undertaken by a participant within a learning system. In general, a learning trace is a network of observe study activities that offer a particular measurement on learning. This tends to focus on students but also includes teachers, administrators, tutors, and anyone else connected to the system.

It would be incorrect to consider a learning trace to be the same as a transcript or record of education. These are important components of a learning trace, but are insufficiently large to consider a proper trace. Real-time data must be included in some manner for the records to be considered an appropriate learning trace, for one of the characteristics of a learning trace is fine granularity—it must capture data on a fine scale, so that not only can outcomes be recorded but also so that the behaviour leading up to those outcomes may be captured. Contrast this to a transcript of grades for a course, which contains the outcome of evaluation but keeps no record of what actions led to those outcomes. This preservation of context is the most important component of a learning trace.

Learning traces can be divided roughly into metrics which record outcomes and metrics which record behaviours which may or may not lead to outcomes. These can also be thought of as traditional vs. big data metrics, as many outcome metrics have been recorded in traditional education settings, whereas most traditional settings do not record behaviours. These are not hard and fast rules, however.

Outcome metrics may include metrics such as human-evaluated competency scores such as grades for assignments or exams, computer-evaluated competency scores for work in progress, evaluations of achievement of learning goals, educator efficacy surveys, course efficacy surveys, grades for participation, grades for attendance and other metrics. Note that not all of these are in real time, but they are all concerned with the success or failure of some aspect of the educational context.

Behavioural metrics may include such metrics as pause duration in typing, speed of typing, speed of scrolling in a webpage, eye movements, body heat or other biometric information, daily attendance, attentiveness, questions asked, language used in forums or in classroom, time and duration of stay at course websites or online resources, use of lab resources and many others. Unlike the outcome metrics, these tend to have a much larger real-time component and are less concerned with success or failure, instead being concerned with the fine-scale behaviours of the participants (del Blanco, Serrano, Freire, Martinez-Ortiz, & Fernandez-Manjon, 2013).

Learning Analytics as a Bridge

Exchanging a traditional learning platform, one that is currently being used, in a practical sense, is a very difficult job. Beyond the technical difficulties of capturing these learning traces is the much more difficult hurdle of getting sufficient support from learning institutions themselves, which can be very resistant to change. This is for a very good reason—education is a very important job, and it is important that these institutions do not chase every new technology or technique available but instead adopt only proven platforms after a series of trials (Miller, Baramidze, Sheth, & Fishwick, 2004).

This has often presented a challenge to learning platforms, which often require adoption across the board to be effective, thereby limiting their usefulness and success within an educational context. Learning analytics platforms need not be this way, however. A properly designed learning analytics system can examine both the metrics provided by a traditional system and the learning traces provided by the learning analytics platform to produce an overall competency assessment which is applicable in both domains and which provides ample learning traces to satisfy educational administrators of its veracity.

In this manner, learning analytics can be considered a bridge—a structure allowing education systems to move from one system to another, all the while maintaining a single, unified assessment of learner progress. Further, the output of these analytics systems can be carried by the learner throughout their educational career as a permanent record of what actions were actually taken and what topics were actually learned—a deep, thorough and durable lifelong educational passport. These bridges will allow learners to have more confidence in their learning and, more importantly, will allow educators to use varied, powerful new educational design systems without having to work as hard against the bureaucracy of education administration or public opinion.

A Computational Model of Learning

Educational systems have traditionally built competency models of learning for their students. These competency models are built by the manual evaluation of assignments and examinations and are aggregated into overall grades or assessment of competence. Sometimes, these models have included elements such as participation in class, attendance and other behavioural information, but in general the models in traditional systems have been simple and reductive, relying on the attention of a set of educators to interpret fine-scale behaviours within the learning context instead of using a model-based system.

Instead of relying on a single competence model of learning, a sophisticated learning analytics platform maintains sets of computable models, each with its own focus and goal. For example, in addition to a set of competency models, learners may also have models for their level of motivation, their knowledge of and use of learning strategies and self-regulation techniques, their emotional states regarding the educational material, and others (Blikstein, 2013).

An important difference between these models and the models generated by a traditional learning system is found in the automated generation of, and update of, learning models. Traditionally, models are constructed over the course of a semester by the gradual accretion of manually evaluated marks. A learning analytics platform constructs and updates its models in real time as information is made available to it and requires no manual intervention. Measurements concerning educators, tutors and other participants are included in the system as components of computable models, allowing these traditional methods to coexist as part of an analytics platform.

Just as learning analytics can be considered to have varying scopes, so too do the models within the model store of a learning analytics platform. Precise models exist at the fine scale of analytics, concerned with those models containing data pertaining to a single individual participant within the system. These could be considered to correlate with the transcript of grades for an individual student in a traditional system. Contrasting with these models are aggregate models, which consider contemporary knowledge as observed from the literature. The specific scope may vary depending on the question being asked or model required and may consider anything from learner pairs to the behaviours of entire educational institutions to anything between.

Precise models and aggregate models share many traits, holding the same superficial structure and purpose. The difference between them can be found in the type of content within the models. Data from individuals tends to be sparse, with large gaps for events outside of the educational context—mundane activities like eating or sleeping, entertainment, work and anything not related to education are outside of the purview of a learning analytics platform and may not be available. This makes individual learning traces patchy. Aggregate models, on the other hand, are constructed by merging a number of individual learning traces as reported in the literature and possibly also through merging precise models from the literature as well. This combination suggests that aggregate models ought to be more continuous and less sparse, but the mechanisms of merging will introduce their own problems as well. Just as analytics requires an attention to the analytical methods used in order to find an answer, a learning analytics platform requires an attention to the analytical methods used to merge and construct its models.

Multiple Models of Learning

Multiple models of learning can be constructed, each with its own focus and limitations (Barber & Sharkey, 2012). These models may be categorized into groups depending on the overall goal of the models.

Ontologies and Metaontologies

Ontologies are a central concept in the construction of learning models and models that represent ideas or abstracts (Prinsloo & Slade, 2015). They arrange concepts into a network of relationships and include definitions for those concepts and the relations between them. In this way, an ontology maps a concept space. This makes them useful in defining the various learning areas and objectives in an educational context and in describing knowledge itself in a structured way. For example, skill in the English language may be considered an ontological category, with skills in writing, reading, speaking and listening being subcategories contained within. These subcategories will have categories of their own. Note, too, that reading and listening have a relationship with one another in the form of the comprehension of received language, as do writing and speaking in the creation of language.

Metaontologies describe the ways in which ontologies define and describe knowledge and how ontological categories relate to one another. These models are very useful when it comes to communicating with systems outside of the learning analytics platform or for translating the models within the platform into other forms, such as human-readable reports.

Performance Models

Models of performance include those models that make statements about a learners' progress, level of skill, or some other statement regarding their competence in their learning objectives. These models most closely resemble the information generated in traditional learning systems—they show progress and measure competency. As these metrics are the arbiters of whether learning objectives are complete or not, they are important to a learning analytics platform, but they are far from the only metric. Many others are important, while performance models are not as important as most might think. Specifically, while performance models may communicate information about learning objectives, long-term learning patterns are arguably more important for a learner in the long term, and these patterns must be measured through more than simply local performance.

Metacognitive Models

While performance models describe external performance within learning domains, metacognitive models describe inferred mental states. By observing behaviours, a sophisticated learning analytics platform may be able to build models of its best guess of the cognitive states of its learners. These in turn can be analysed to see whether the learning they are doing is effective, self-regulating and focused on the required tasks. These models are difficult to assemble and verify, but their potential for providing a long-term description of how a learner conducts learning itself is a valuable goal worth pursuing.

Interactivity Models

Most learning is not done in a vacuum—it is a social exercise, conducted at the minimum between a learner and an educator in some way. Often, this is supplemented by tutors, students, friends and outsiders who are involved both formally and informally in the act of teaching.

These relationships are important. The ways in which we communicate while learning, the ways in which we reach out to one another both within and outside of the learning space, are indicative of how we learn. They are instructive in both the problems that we are facing in our learning and in the ways in which we hope to overcome. They are also instructive in identifying procrastination and counterproductive behaviours, both impediments to learning which at the same time must be respected as an expression of deeper learning issues. Interactivity models attempt to capture this complicated set of interactions between people (Ferguson & Shum, 2012; Teplovs, Fujita, & Vatrapu, 2011).

Demographic Models

Where interactivity models attempt to capture information about the complex web of relationships each person carries, demographic models are more interested in the trends around groups of people. It is the case that educational access and ability is not evenly distributed—life circumstances within communities, social groups, and ethnicities can communicate important information on learning issues that individuals may have.

Demographic models attempt to relate individuals to various demographic groups and, from these relations, determine whether these individuals are facing challenges normal to or abnormal to those groups. It is important to note that individuals belong to a number of demographics simultaneously, and membership in one may be confounded by or confused by membership in others. As with everything in analytics, demographic models are far from clear-cut.

Communication Models

People in the modern age have a large number of ways in which they can communicate. Each of these communication channels—face-to-face speech, telephone, email, Twitter, forums and others—carries a wealth of information within both the contents of the messages and the choice and use of the medium itself. Communication models are largely interested in determining the meanings of those messages and the importance of the choice of medium (Teplovs et al., 2011).

Multiple Methods of Analysis, One Way to Analyse

The first and perhaps the most important stage of analysis is *data collection*. In this stage, activities within a learning episode are assembled into a trace. The argument for this step being the most crucial one is that the robustness and accuracy of this step is a limiter on the usefulness of all other steps. Inaccuracy or incompleteness here prevents greater accuracy or completeness further down the pipe. For this reason a great deal of attention should be spent on ensuring that learning traces are assembled from as many metrics as possible, as accurately as possible, and as often as possible (Cuzzocrea & Simitsis, 2012).

Once these traces are assembled, they are used to generate *models*. Models are a simplification of the real world which can be computed or manipulated to make predictions that can be translated back into the real world with some degree of error. A great number of models exist, and more can be constructed based on the type of information desired.

With this done, the models are then used to create *inferences*, or predictions. These inferences are generated in response to user queries, either automated or by request. These queries and answers are the functional component of a learning analytics platform and are where their usefulness comes about.

The construction of models and the following inferences rely on analytical methods. There are many available to choose, each specialized to create a certain result. The role of the platform designer is to ensure that the correct analytical tools are used for each model constructed and query conducted. This is not a small task. Methods vary widely, each with its own domain, scope, tolerance for error, and other important factors. What's worse is that each requires different information and expects different levels of confidence. A learning analytics platform designer must be familiar with a wide range of analytical techniques and be confident in their use.

Implementing Learning Analytics

Modern high-volume computing, a cornerstone of big data, relies on the dynamic availability of computing power on demand, depending on the requirements at any given moment. The industry has moved to cloud computing for most of these jobs, using distributed networks of processes running on servers to handle jobs dynamically and flexibly and all while providing a high quality of service to their end users. The high-volume learning traces generated by a learning analytics platform has the same requirements, making the same solution inviting. A successful learning analytics platform therefore will be constructed to make best use of cloud resources, so that the system is not overrun or starved for resources at critical moments, such as near exams or at the beginning of semesters (Benzaken, Castagna, Nguyen, & Siméon, 2013).

Fortunately, the systems described so far have been largely compatible with a cloud-based infrastructure. Analytical processes range in scope from local, individual analyses to global analytics initiatives, with each level of scope requiring a different number of resources dedicated to the task.

Nested Levels, from Individual to Global

At the most tightly focused level, analytics can be conducted on an individual level—the modelling and prediction of a single student, educator or other learners. The requirements of these analytics tend to be smaller in terms of computational power and demands on a database, as they generally only involve referring to the learning traces of a single individual. Some models can take a lot of computational power to build, however—complex semantic networks or neural networks can demand a large amount of memory from a server. Care must be taken to ensure that not too many of these requests are made at the same time.

In contrast, some individualized models are constructed from global data, or from demographics, or from other sources not directly connected to the individual. The demands of constructing these models are generally more so than those which require only personal information, but the real demands depend heavily on the type and volume of data required.

The above models are examples of what can be referred to as precise models. These models hold information and predictions based on a single individual. They tend to be somewhat sparse, as individuals can only make a limited volume of learning traces during their time at an educational institution—their records are punctuated with large gaps for sleeping or personal time, and traces only cover those activities and behaviours which the individual can or wants to record.

Precise models are contrasted with aggregate models. These models pull together learning traces from multiple individuals—they aggregate multiple precise models—to generate larger sets representing classrooms, cohorts, grades, institutions, and other groups of learners. These data sets must draw on a larger pool of learning traces and models, requiring more database accesses in accordance with the change in scope. They may or may not require larger processing resources in order to create as well, depending on the specific kind of analysis being conducted. However, in general it can be said that aggregate models rely on larger volumes of data and tend to be much less sparse than precise models, as the gaps in any particular precise model will be filled by information in others. The trade-off is, naturally, precision, as aggregate models must naturally be made of some sort of combination of individuals.

Volume, Variety, Arrival, Veracity: The Foundations of Big Data

The field of big data is concerned with creating understanding in the modern world. Inundated with data from innumerable sources, traditional data collection and interpretation techniques have been overwhelmed—lookup times aren't fast enough, data arrives in too many differing formats and without the synchronicity that traditional analysis required, and the correctness of a given data set is forever provisional. Without new techniques of storage, aggregation and analysis, the information being collected across the world would remain unavailable to us, lost through sheer ubiquity. Modern search engines such as Google demonstrate the ability to manage these very large sets of data. And, just as Google must manage the various unique characteristics of big data, so too must any learning analytics platform (Bader-Natal & Lotze, 2011; Dobre & Xhafa, 2014).

The Challenge of Volume

One of the most obvious distinguishing characteristics of big data is its *volume*. Big data makes measurements in fine detail, with a very large number of measurements per unit of time compared to traditional data systems. An example of this can be found in a student writing a paragraph for a school assignment. Traditionally, the completed paragraph would be considered the measurement arriving into the databases of the learning management system—the ensuing analytics would be concerned with the completed written work and may include measurements of the time of submission, location the submission was sent from or other details of that event.

By contrast, measurement within a big data perspective is concerned with much finer details. Measurements are made frequently, perhaps up to individual keystrokes made by the student, thereby measuring pauses in writing, deletions, editing, and other events. While the end result is the same—a completed written paragraph—the inclusion of all of these fine details allows for a great deal more to be inferred about the students' quality of work and understanding of the subject being examined. Of course, this also creates a much larger pool of data which must be transmitted, stored, sorted, and processed for analysis. This creates a challenge that should be faced head-on.

Database technologies exist today to handle this problem. Traditional databases use a *relational* structure which can be likened to storing information in large predefined tables. This is efficient, but does not scale well—as the tables get larger, the time needed to search them to collect a subset of information increases drastically. Modern distributed databases split these tables across a network, or *cloud*, making them smaller and more easily handled. Querying the database involves sending the request to a manager which sends the query out to all members of the cloud, which conduct their own searches and return the results to the manager. The responses are merged into one large response, which is presented.

A central characteristic of this structure is that, since members of the cloud may be experiencing lag or some sort of malfunction, the reply to any given query may be incomplete depending on the condition of the network. Dealing with these inaccuracies is an important facet of big data and is a direct requirement of the large volumes of data any learning analytics platform must deal with.

The Challenge of Variety

Another key characteristic of big data is the *variety* of data found within a learning analytics platform. Continuing the example above, a traditional assignment measurement will contain the paragraph written by the student, along with perhaps the date and time of submission. These data points will be regular for all learners in the system, save those who do not complete the assignment. All of these measurements will be concerned with text processing and perhaps tracking assignment completion speed, limiting the types of analysis that can be conducted to language analysis on the paragraph and some simple time-based analyses for the timestamps.

A system collecting big data will be far more ambitious in its variety of data points per measurement, providing a much larger analytics set to the researcher and user. Such a system may collect information on the speed of typing, location and movement of the mouse cursor, browser history and scroll speed of a page and even more esoteric information such as gaze tracking or biometric information such as body heat and heart rate. These data points may or may not be available for individual learners depending on the permissions given by those learners as well as the hardware that is available to each of them.

This results in a large volume of data that has a great deal of *diversity*, allowing much more sophisticated analyses and generating much more interesting inferences. At the same time, this variety presents a problem to traditional database systems. Relational databases rely on their tables being uniform, with the same types of data being available for each entry. Highly variable data creates truly massive tables which must be modified for each new type of data presented to the system. This makes traditional databases a poor choice for dealing with the variable data needed for big data projects (Agarwal, Shroff, & Malhotra, 2013).

Fortunately, modern cloud-based database techniques are well suited for this problem. Given that the data is fragmented across the storage cloud in a modern database, each cloud may maintain its own tables and/or documents, storing data in its own way without needing to comply with a universal standard. Provided that the manager responsible for merging all of the information returning from a query is well designed, such a system can handle great varieties of data and is a good fit for the diversity problems inherent in managing a learning analytics platform.

The Challenge of Arrival

A third issue with big data systems is that of *arrival time*. Traditional systems are largely insensitive to the time of arrival, as their analytics occur once deadlines for assignments have passed—they are largely unconcerned with real-time analytics. A learning analytics platform, on the other hand, is very much concerned with providing real-time knowledge of learner states, and as such the problem of when information arrives and what state that information is in on arrival becomes very important.

A traditional assignment is submitted before a given deadline, at which point its information is stored in the learning system and analytics can then take place. Given that this system only receives a single measurement, the question of arrival is relatively moot—the information is either present or absent and is included or excluded from analysis based on this.

A learning analytics platform, in contrast, collects large volumes of diverse data in real time. The same paragraph, written in such an analytics platform, will generate partial paragraphs, sentence fragments, deletion events, eye movements, pauses, and other learning traces. Such a set of traces cannot be processed in the same way as a traditional learning trace—an incomplete paragraph, undergoing edits, cannot be analysed in the same way as a completed assignment. Evaluations of the finished product must be provisional, paying respect to the work currently being undertaken. This allows for more sophisticated analytics, but also requires more care in ensuring that proper analytical techniques are used.

Further, the structure of a cloud-based database and processing system needed for a learning analytics platform requires that the system be aware of, and attend to, the *latency problem*. Information travelling to various storage locations in the cloud will arrive at different times and therefore may not be available at the same times, both during initial storage and during recall for queries. This requires that any learning analytics platform be sensitive to these latency concerns—the output of these analytics must also be considered provisional, subject to change as latent information arrives.

The Challenge of Veracity

Another consideration—though far from the last—is the consideration of whether incoming data can be verified as authentic. Under a traditional system, incoming data are received from sources that can be trusted—educators or secured servers hosting the learning environment software. In this context there is an implicit assumption that all information coming in is valid, and this assumption is largely correct. Assignments submitted through a secure portal website can be assumed to be submitted by the learner logged in, at the time of submission.

One of the defining factors of a big data perspective, however, is that information may be entering the system from any source. Learners may be using unknown or untrusted software or computers, and the information they send may or may not be expected. Given this, the problem of verification is a real one, larger than the same issue in traditional systems. A discussion of security protocols and verification of authenticity is beyond the scope of our discussion here. However, it can be said that these concerns are valid, and any learning analytics platform dealing with big data must deal with questions of data verification.

Dealing with Uncertainty: Ensuring Validity in Learning Analytics

Learning analytics involves the creation of ordered models out of chaotic, information-rich learning traces, themselves being simplified and restricted metaphors for activities undertaken in the real world. The depth of reduction in this process must lead an honest inquirer to ask whether the results of such an analytical engine are at all valid. Surely along this process, a simplification is made which ought not to be, or an equality is assumed where no equality exists, or some other critical step is taken for granted.

This problem may seem insurmountable, and in fact in a proper sense, it is insurmountable—any model will be, by its nature, a simplification of the world and insufficient for explaining every difference. The question of whether a model is appropriate, however, doesn't require it be perfectly accurate. For a learning analytics platform, our primary concern can instead be asked in three questions:

1. Does the data entering our model accurately reflect enough of reality to shape the model?
2. Does the model sufficiently cover the areas which it needs to answer the queries it is expected to answer—is it *complete*?
3. Is the model a sufficiently accurate reflection of reality—is it *correct*?

Our first question, on the quality of data entering the learning analytics platform, is reliant on the sensors that are being used to gather it and will vary widely. The last questions, on completeness and correctness, however, are well within the scope of a learning analytics platform.

Dangerous Assumptions: Completeness and Correctness

It is inviting to think our models are correct and that they accurately reflect the reality of a situation. This is a long-standing issue with the process of quantification. When an activity can be evaluated down to a number, or set of numbers, or simple relationship, it is easy to consider the matter settled. This reduction makes complex situations simple and fools the inquirer into thinking their grasp on the situation is sure by giving them a model which can more easily fit into their mind.

This is a dangerous assumption on the part of the model designer. It is important to remember that our models are, by their nature, incomplete and that we must ensure that we have *sufficient completeness* to answer the necessary questions asked by the platform. Ensuring this sufficiency involves repeatedly testing the model in a diversity of situations to ensure that its output is accurate in all cases. Any deficiency in an area suggests that the model is incomplete and ought to examine new factors which it has not previously.

Another inviting assumption, perhaps more so, is that our models are correct—that they accurately reflect the world. This assumption grounds itself in *confirmation bias*, a very human flaw in which individuals have a harder time perceiving information which disproves their cherished beliefs. It is easy to consider information that doesn't fit our models to be somehow flawed, or outliers worthy of ignoring, and being well educated is no defence against this. A well-trained scientist has a large library of reasons at their disposal to reject something which invalidates their hypothesis. The best defence is awareness and a willingness to consider ideas that oppose our own.

It is highly unlikely that any educational models will be properly *correct* in the field of learning analytics; even physics has a difficult time achieving true precision. However, approaching as close as possible to real correctness is important to ensure that the conclusions and inferences of a learning analytics platform are reliable. These inferences will be used to evaluate real people, often minors, and to pursue less than the highest level of correctness would be unethical.

Dangerous Ground: Data Ownership

Once the models are created, an important question must be asked—who owns this information? This may be considered the defining question of the opening of the twenty-first century and critical in determining the shape and scope of privacy, anonymity and security of person in the modern age.

The information generated by a person using a learning analytics platform is unique to that person. The term *learning trace* is significant in regard to information ownership. Like a fingerprint, a learning trace is a unique identifier. In the high-density, high-granularity learning traces within a learning analytics platform, these traces are much more like a signature of personality and a very personal record of a significant portion of a person's life.

The ethics of such a situation are obvious. The models and traces generated by an individual must ethically remain their own, with full ownership and control remaining with them throughout their lives. Any less than this would surrender some portion of privacy and personal identity to an educational institution or government which may not have their permission or indeed their best interests at heart. It is the duty of any platform designer to ensure that this security is maintained.

This of course extends into to question of how can such a level of personal ownership be guaranteed? Most modern systems ignore the question entirely by assuming that the learning institution has ownership of these data. A learning analytics platform, ethically designed, does not have such luxury. Instead such a system must ensure that its information is *partible*—that each individual's data set may be joined or separated from the main database at the desire of its owner. Further, each individual must be granted full control over their data, including the requirement that each use of their data is a *willful*, *conscious* decision on the part of the user (Jensen, 2013; Prinsloo & Slade, 2015).

These two features are crucial in the development of an ethical learning analytics platform which respects the privacy and autonomy of its users. Such architecture is not without its benefits, however. In allowing learners to easily detach and move their models and traces, their learners will maintain a high-fidelity record of their learning experiences. These can be used as lifelong proof of education, as credentials for employment, or for easing admission into new learning institutions. Such an *educational passport* could change the way in which education interacts with daily life and in which individuals approach their education.

A Look at Curricular Analytics

Education is about assisting learners in the process of learning, and a well-made learning analytics will be focused on this task. Such a platform will provide suggestions, perceptions and feedback to learners and to their educators so that their overall experience is improved. It is for this reason that the models and analytics so far discussed have involved perceiving learner progress and learner behaviour.

This is not the only purpose of a learning analytics platform, however. Just as a living system includes senses that make it aware of its own state, an educational system ought to include perceptions of its successes and its flaws so that problems can be found. This allows the system to be aware of its flaws and to understand its successes, with an eye on the overall goal of improving the learning experience. This can be understood to be the field of *curricular learning analytics*, which uses the processes of learning analytics in order to understand and improve educational plans and processes.

The same models and analytical outputs of the learning analytics platform may be used to make statements on the efficacy of a particular curriculum, effectiveness of an educator or group of educators, a comparison of pedagogical techniques across different learning contexts and with different types of learners and other diverse types of information. Just as with the learning analytics platform upon which it is based, a learning analytics platform with curricular analytics will allow user queries, custom information views and other projections. Unlike the basic learning analytics platform, however, this information will be reflected on by the curriculum designers, administrators and other educators to design, critique and improve their learning materials.

A Learning Dashboard

The most crucial part of the process of learning analytics is arguably the presentation of its results. Excellent inferencing can be done on magnificently curated data, but if the results of those inferences are not understandable to the user, they are useless. Specifically, the usefulness of a query result in an analytics engine is only as good as the quality of its feedback. Even low-quality, uninteresting inferences can provide valuable information to a student or educator provided that the inferences are presented appropriately.

The presentation of a querying system, and the presentation of its replies, is normally conducted by a *dashboard*. This presents real-time feedback about the thing that the dashboard examines—in this case, real-time feedback about the learning environment. From here, users of all kinds can make inquiries and monitor changes in the learning environment, from the specifics of a particular learner working within a particular domain all the way to the effectiveness of an institution's overall curriculum (Duval et al., 2012).

Notably, though, every user of a learning analytics platform is going to have different goals depending on their role within the learning context, the learning domains they are working on, and the specifics of their lives. Presenting a single interface that will apply well to all of these variables is challenging. Two paths can be taken to address the multiple-role problem. Firstly, each role may be given a default set of data to track and a default set of useful pre-made queries. Learners, for example, might get views of the competencies that they are working on, with queries pre-made to compare themselves to others working in the same domain. The students' educator, on the other hand, might get a comparative view of all of the students' progress and comparisons of their class to other classes within the same institution.

More complex, and more useful, is the design of the query system and dashboard to allow for fully customizable tracking. Allowing users to create their own views of the data and inferences available presents a dilemma for the learning analytics platform designer. Providing customizable views is a very desirable thing, but the data and inferences in these systems are by their nature complex, making the creation of custom views difficult for the uninitiated user. At the same time, without these views, the usefulness of a learning analytics platform will not be fully tapped, and the investment needed to properly learn a complex system will be hard to come by without demonstrating that usefulness.

Solving this problem is a major challenge in presenting a learning analytics platform as a useful educational tool. The development of a query system that is both in-depth and intuitive to use is required to give the user access to the useful inferences that such a system can provide.

Conclusions

Big data analytics, the study of large volumes of loosely organized data in real time, is becoming increasingly important in our daily lives without most of us being aware of it. The incredible amount of information produced by humanity every day has the potential to be of great use in making life better for everyone. For the most part, however, much of this data goes untapped. Older systems are able to interpret data outside of a narrow range of formats, isolating data into silos. Newer systems may be able to bridge this gap, but they lack the powerful inferencing systems of an analytics engine to make more than simple statements. Proper analytics engines, however, are able to take this ocean of data and draw broad, comprehensive statements from it.

In the world of educational institutions, curricular design, and student support, these facts continue to hold true. By harnessing the methods of big data analytics, a learning analytics platform will be able to discover, investigate and create moments of insight for all members of the educational system.

References

Agarwal, P., Shroff, G., & Malhotra, P. (2013). Approximate incremental big-data harmonization. In *2013 IEEE International Congress on Big Data (BigData Congress)* (pp. 118–125).

Almosallam, E., & Ouertani, H. (2014). Learning analytics: Definitions, applications and related fields. In T. Herawan, M. M. Deris & J. Abawajy (Eds.), *Proceedings of the First International Conference on Advanced Data and Information Engineering (DaEng-2013), Vol. 285* (pp. 721–730). Singapore: Springer. (ISBN: 978-981-4585-17-0). Retrieved from http://dx.doi.org/10.1007/978-981-4585-18-7_81.

Arnold, K. E., & Pistilli, M. D. (2012). Course signals at Purdue: Using learning analytics to increase student success. In *Proceedings of the 2nd International Conference on Learning Analytics and Knowledge* (pp. 267–270). ACM. (ISBN: 978-1-4503-1111-3). Retrieved from http://doi.acm.org/10.1145/2330601.2330666.

Bader-Natal, A., & Lotze, T. (2011). Evolving a learning analytics platform. In *Proceedings of the 1st International Conference on Learning Analytics and Knowledge* (pp. 180–185). ACM. (ISBN: 978-1-4503-0944-8). Retrieved from http://doi.acm.org/10.1145/2090116.2090146.

Barber, R., & Sharkey, M. (2012). Course correction: Using analytics to predict course success. In *Proceedings of the 2nd International Conference on Learning Analytics and Knowledge* (pp. 259–262). ACM. (ISBN: 978-1-4503-1111-3). Retrieved from http://doi.acm.org/10.1145/2330601.2330664.

Benzaken, V., Castagna, G., Nguyen, K., & Siméon, J. (2013). Static and dynamic semantics of NoSQL languages. *SIGPLAN Not, 48*(1), 101–114. doi:10.1145/2480359.2429083. Retrieved from http://0-doi.acm.org.aupac.lib.athabascau.ca/10.1145/2480359.2429083.

Blikstein, P. (2013). Multimodal learning analytics. In *Proceedings of the Third International Conference on Learning Analytics and Knowledge* (pp. 102–106). ACM. (ISBN: 978-1-4503-1785-6). Retrieved from http://0-doi.acm.org.aupac.lib.athabascau.ca/10.1145/2460296.2460316.

Boyd, D., & Crawford, K. (2011). Six provocations for big data. In *A decade in Internet time: Symposium on the dynamics of the internet and society*. Retrieved from http://dx.doi.org/10.2139/ssrn.1926431.

Chatti, M. A., Dyckhoff, A. L., Schroeder, U., & Thüs, H. (2012). A reference model for learning analytics. *International Journal of Technology Enhanced Learning, 4*(5), 318–331. Retrieved from http://dl.acm.org/citation.cfm?id=2434498.

Cuzzocrea, A., & Simitsis, A. (2012). Searching semantic data warehouses: Models, issues, architectures. In *Proceedings of the 2nd International Workshop on Semantic Search over the Web* (pp. 6:1–6:5). ACM. (ISBN: 978-1-4503-2301-7). Retrieved from http://0-doi.acm.org.aupac.lib.athabascau.ca/10.1145/2494068.2494074.

del Blanco, A., Serrano, A., Freire, M., Martinez-Ortiz, I., & Fernandez-Manjon, B. (2013). E-learning standards and learning analytics. Can data collection be improved by using standard data models? In *Global Engineering Education Conference (EDUCON), 2013 IEEE* (pp. 1255–1261).

Dobre, C., & Xhafa, F. (2014). Parallel programming paradigms and frameworks in big data era. *International Journal of Parallel Programming, 42*(5), 710–738. doi:10.1007/s10766-013-0272-7.

Duval, E., Klerkx, J., Verbert, K., Nagel, T., Govaerts, S., Parra Chico, G. A., et al. (2012). Learning dashboards & learnscapes. *Educational Interfaces, Software, and Technology*, 1–5. Retrieved from https://lirias.kuleuven.be/handle/123456789/344525.

Ferguson, R., & Shum, S. B. (2012). Social learning analytics: Five approaches. In *Proceedings of the 2nd International Conference on Learning Analytics and Knowledge* (pp. 23–33). ACM. (ISBN: 978-1-4503-1111-3). Retrieved from http://doi.acm.org/10.1145/2330601.2330616.

Jensen, M. (2013). Challenges of privacy protection in big data analytics. Paper presented at the *2013 IEEE International Congress on Big Data (BigData Congress)* (pp. 235–238).

Miller, J., Baramidze, G., Sheth, A., & Fishwick, P. (2004). Investigating ontologies for simulation modeling. In *Proceedings of the 37th Annual Simulation Symposium, 2004* (pp. 55–63).

Prinsloo, P., & Slade, S. (2015). Student privacy self-management: Implications for learning analytics. In *Proceedings of the Fifth International Conference on Learning Analytics and Knowledge (LAK'15)* (pp. 83–92). New York: ACM. Retrieved from http://dl.acm.org/citation.cfm?id=2723585.

Teplovs, C., Fujita, N., & Vatrapu, R. (2011). Generating predictive models of learner community dynamics. In *Proceedings of the 1st International Conference on Learning Analytics and Knowledge* (pp. 147–152). ACM. (ISBN: 978-1-4503-0944-8). Retrieved from http://0-doi.acm.org.aupac.lib.athabascau.ca/10.1145/2090116.2090139.

van Harmelen, M. (2006). Personal learning environments. In *Proceedings of the Sixth International Conference on Advanced Learning Technologies, 2006* (pp. 815–816).

Chapter 10
Implementing a Learning Analytics Intervention and Evaluation Framework: What Works?

Bart Rienties, Simon Cross, and Zdenek Zdrahal

Abstract Substantial progress in learning analytics research has been made in recent years to predict which groups of learners are at risk. In this chapter, we argue that the largest challenge for learning analytics research and practice still lies ahead of us: using learning analytics modelling, which types of interventions have a positive impact on learners' Attitudes, Behaviour and Cognition (ABC). Two embedded case-studies in social science and science are discussed, whereby notions of evidence-based research are illustrated by scenarios (quasi-experimental, A/B--testing, RCT) to evaluate the impact of interventions. Finally, we discuss how a Learning Analytics Intervention and Evaluation Framework (LA-IEF) is currently being implemented at the Open University UK using principles of design-based research and evidence-based research.

Keywords Learning analytics • Evidence-based research • Embedded case-studies • A/B testing • Randomised control trials

Introduction

Many institutions and organisations across the globe seem to have high hopes that analytics and big data can make their organisations fit-for-purpose, flexible, and innovative. Learning analytics applications in education are expected to provide institutions with opportunities to support learner progression and to enable personalised, rich learning on a large scale (Bienkowski, Feng, & Means, 2012; Hickey, Kelley, & Shen, 2014; Siemens, Dawson, & Lynch, 2013; Tempelaar, Rienties, & Giesbers, 2015; Tobarra, Robles-Gómez, Ros, Hernández, & Caminero, 2014). With the

B. Rienties (✉) • S. Cross • Z. Zdrahal
The Open University, Milton Keynes, UK
e-mail: bart.rienties@open.ac.uk

B. Kei Daniel (ed.), *Big Data and Learning Analytics in Higher Education*,
DOI 10.1007/978-3-319-06520-5_10

increased availability of large datasets, powerful analytics engines (Tobarra et al., 2014), and skilfully designed visualisations of analytics results (González-Torres, García-Peñalvo, & Therón, 2013), institutions may be able to use the experience of the past to create supportive, insightful models of primary (and perhaps real-time) learning processes (Baker, 2010; Ferguson & Buckingham Shum, 2012; Papamitsiou & Economides, 2014; Stiles, 2012). According to Bienkowski et al. (2012, p. 5), "education is getting very close to a time when personalisation will become commonplace in learning", although several researchers (García-Peñalvo, Conde, Alier, & Casany, 2011; Greller & Drachsler, 2012; Stiles, 2012; Tempelaar et al., 2015) indicate that most institutions may not be ready to exploit the variety of available datasets for learning and teaching, or have staff with the required skills in learning design.

Nevertheless, substantial progress in learning analytics research has been made in the last 2–3 years in using a range of advanced computational techniques (e.g. predictive modelling, machine learning, Bayesian modelling, social network analysis, cluster analysis) to predict which students are going to pass a course, and which (groups of) learners are at risk (Agudo-Peregrina, Iglesias-Pradas, Conde-González, & Hernández-García, 2014; Aguiar, Chawla, Brockman, Ambrose, & Goodrich, 2014; Calvert, 2014; Gasevic, Zouaq, & Janzen, 2013; Tempelaar et al., 2015; Tobarra et al., 2014; Wolff, Zdrahal, Herrmannova, Kuzilek, & Hlosta, 2014). What these studies have in common is that by collecting (longitudinal) data from a range of sources the accuracy in predicting learning performance is increasing with every new piece of information about the learner and his/her learning.

In this chapter, we argue that the largest challenge for learning analytics research and practice still lies ahead of us: *which types of interventions have a positive impact on learners' Attitudes, Behaviour and Cognition (ABC) using learning analytics modelling?* Most of the current literature seems to be focussed on testing and applying principles of learning analytics using convenience sampling, whereby a particular context or sample of students in a course is taken to illustrate the predictive power of learning analytics approaches. However, most research seems to lack a robust *Design-Based Research* (Collins, Joseph, & Bielaczyc, 2004; Rienties & Townsend, 2012) or *evidence-based approach* (e.g. Randomised Control Trials, A/B testing, pre-post retention modelling) of testing and validating claims and arguments (e.g. Hess & Saxberg, 2013; McMillan & Schumacher, 2014; Rienties et al., 2012; Rienties, Giesbers, Lygo-Baker, Ma, & Rees, 2014; Slavin, 2008). Indeed, according to Collins et al. (2004, p. 21), design experiments should feature and "bring together two critical pieces in order to guide us to better educational refinement: a design focus and assessment of critical design elements".

Although we acknowledge that learning analytics can provide a powerful learning experience for different groups of learners and purposes, in this chapter we primarily focus on the use of learning analytics for students-at-risk. If organisations are going to adopt learning analytics approaches in order to improve learning, then the research community needs to provide evidence-based results that highlight that learning analytics approach can: (1) identify learners at risk; (2) deliver (personalised) intervention suggestions that work; (3) be cost-effective. There is an urgent need to develop an evidence-based framework of learning analytics that can help to inform students, researchers, educators, and policy makers about which types of interventions work well under which conditions, and which do not. In this chapter, we will work towards establishing principles of a *Learning Analytics Intervention and Evaluation Framework* (LA-IEF) that will be tested and validated at the largest university in Europe (in terms of enrolled learners), namely the Open University UK (Calvert, 2014; Richardson, 2012a). Firstly, we will provide a short literature review of contemporary learning analytics studies, followed by an argument in support of needing more robust evidence-based research. Secondly, we will provide two case-studies how principles of evidence-based research could be implemented in learning analytics. These two case-studies will provide stepping stones how to build an LA-IEF model, adjust, and apply the framework into their own practice.

Attitudes, Behaviour and Cognition Model and Learning Analytics

Given that learning analytics is a relatively new research field using a range of interdisciplinary perspectives that did not exist before 2010, it is not surprising that most of the research efforts have thus far focussed on identifying and raising awareness of the conceptions, boundaries, and generic approaches of learning analytics (Ferguson, 2012; Papamitsiou & Economides, 2014; Wise, 2014). Alternatively, we use a simple attitudes–behaviour–cognition (ABC) model to conceptualise the possible impacts of learning analytics on learning. *Attitudes* of learners can have positive impacts on behaviour (Giesbers, Rienties, Tempelaar, & Gijselaers, 2013; Jindal-Snape & Rienties, 2016; Pintrich & De Groot, 1990; Rienties & Alden Rivers, 2014; Rienties et al., 2012; Tempelaar et al., 2015), such as intrinsic motivation, self-efficacy, curiosity, or goal-orientation, which can trigger learners into action. In contrast, negative attitudes may hamper learners (Martin, 2007; Pekrun, Goetz, Frenzel, Barchfeld, & Perry, 2011; Rienties & Alden Rivers, 2014; Tempelaar, Niculescu, Rienties, Giesbers, & Gijselaers, 2012). A-motivation, boredom, anxiety, or stress can all lead to a restriction of action or reduction in engagement, or even withdrawal from learning. For example, in a study of 730 students Tempelaar et al. (2012) found that positive learning emotions contributed favourably to becoming an intensive online learner, while negative learning emotions, like boredom, contributed adversely to learning behaviour. Similarly, in an online community of practice of 133 instructors supporting EdD students, Nistor et al. (2014) found that self-efficacy (and expertise) of instructors predicted online contributions.

Many learning analytics applications use *behaviour* data generated from learner activities, such as the number of clicks (Siemens, 2013; Wolff, Zdrahal, Nikolov, & Pantucek, 2013), learner participation in discussion forums (Agudo-Peregrina et al., 2014; Macfadyen & Dawson, 2010), or (continuous) computer-assisted formative assessments (Papamitsiou, Terzis, & Economides, 2014; Tempelaar et al., 2012, 2015; Wolff et al., 2013). User behaviour data are frequently supplemented with background data retrieved from Virtual Learning Environment (VLE)

(Macfadyen & Dawson, 2010) and other learner admission systems, such as accounts of prior education (Arbaugh, 2014; Calvert, 2014; Richardson, 2012a). For example, in one of the first learning analytics studies focussed on 118 biology students, Macfadyen and Dawson (2010) found that some (e.g. # of discussion messages posted, # assessments finished, # mail messages sent) VLE variables but not all (e.g. time spent in the VLE) were useful predictors of learner retention and academic performance. However, a recent special issue on Learning Analytics in *Computers in Human Behaviour* (Conde & Hernández-García, 2015) indicates that simple learning analytics metrics (e.g. # of clicks, # of downloads) may actually hamper learning analytics research. For example, using a longitudinal data analysis of 120+ variables from three different VLE systems and a range of motivational, emotions and learning styles indicators, Tempelaar et al. (2015) found that most "simple" VLE learning analytics metrics provided limited insights into the complex learning dynamics over time. In contrast, learning motivations and emotions (attitudes) and activities done by learners during continuous assessments (behaviour) provided an opportunity for teachers to help at-risk learners at a relatively early stage of their learning journey. Similarly, in a more fine-grained study Giesbers et al. (2013) found that discussion forum and synchronous videoconference behaviour of 110 students, motivation of students (attitudes), and tool usage (behaviour) significantly influenced cognition.

Finally, *cognition* is conceptualised as a wide construct, such as learning a new skill, understanding and evaluating a theoretical concept, or applying something learned into practice. In Western education, cognition is often translated into performance on summative assessments (Agudo-Peregrina et al., 2014; Calvert, 2014; Macfadyen & Dawson, 2010; Tempelaar et al., 2015), such as exams, quizzes, multiple-choice tests, or open essays. However, "evidence" of cognition can also be found in more formative learning activities (Ferguson & Buckingham Shum, 2012; Knight, Buckingham Shum, & Littleton, 2013; Rienties et al., 2012), such as discussion forum postings, articulations of discourse in web-videoconferences, blog postings, or reflections. In other words, depending on the conceptualisation of cognition, learning analytics models may take a relatively narrow approach (i.e. did a learner pass a module?) or a broader approach (e.g. is there evidence of critical evaluation skills in a string of discussion forum messages on topic X?).

A Need for Evidence-Based Research in Learning Analytics

While these initial research papers have substantially contributed to forming a foundation of learning analytics as a new research field, the proof of the pudding will be whether learning analytics is able to make a fundamental, measurable impact on attitudes, behaviour, and cognition of learners, teachers, and institutions in general. To the best of our knowledge, no learning analytics studies are available that can be described as *evidence-based research* (MacNeill, Campbell, & Hawksey, 2014; Slavin, 2002, 2008). A basic approach of evidence-based research in education is to use scientific methods based upon experiments to apply the best available, significant and reliable, evidence to inform educational decision-making. While in many fields like medicine, agriculture, transportation, and technology, the process of development, rigorous evaluation, and sharing of results to practice using randomised experiments (Torgerson & Torgerson, 2008) and A/B testing (Siroker & Koomen, 2013) have provided an unprecedented innovation in the last 50 years (Slavin, 2002), educational research and learning analytics in particular has not adopted evidence-based research principles en masse (Hess & Saxberg, 2013; McMillan & Schumacher, 2014; Torgerson & Torgerson, 2008).

A major potential problem of descriptive or correlational studies is the ability to generalise the findings beyond the respective context in which particular learning analytics study has been conducted (Arbaugh, 2005, 2014; Hattie, 2009; Rienties, Toetenel, & Bryan, 2015). Especially, the issue of selection bias is a concern in early learning analytics studies. A recent meta-analysis of 35 empirical studies (Papamitsiou & Economides, 2014) indicated that most learning analytics studies have focussed on analysis of single-module or single discipline, using contexts of teachers and/or learners who are keen to share their practice for research. Although these studies provide relevant initial insights of principles of data analysis techniques, and testing the proof of concepts of data visualisation tools, without random assignment of learners (and teachers) into two or more conditions, it is rather difficult to provide evidence of impact (McMillan & Schumacher, 2014; Slavin, 2008; Torgerson & Torgerson, 2008). For example, an engaged and enthusiastic teacher who used a data visualisation tool to provide feedback to her learners might trigger a direct response from them to follow-up on the suggested feedback. However, replicating the study with a different group of learners, a different teacher, or even a different context might lead to completely different results. Similarly, attributing a positive learning effect of a particular data visualisation tool in a pre-post-test design without a clear A/B testing or RCT design to compare the data visualisation tool with another tool or approach might lead some researchers to conclude a positive effect of this tool although other elements in the learning design could have had a contribution to this positive effect.

In the second part of this chapter, we will focus on two embedded case-studies in two introductory courses in social science and science. The first case-study was selected as an example of how institutions can use learning analytics approaches to send early-warning emails to students potentially at risk (Inkelaar & Simpson, 2015). The second case-study was selected to illustrate how advanced in-house learning analytics applications can be used to identify which students are at risk when multiple sources of static and dynamic data are available. Currently, over 200,000 learners study at the Open University UK, primarily using distance education formats. An embedded case-study approach is undertaken to examine the characteristics of a single individual unit (recognising its individuality and uniqueness), namely, a learner, a group, or an organisation. Yin (2009) emphasised that a case-study investigates a phenomenon in-depth and in its natural context. Our two case-studies help us unpack and understand the challenges associated with evaluating interventions (which feeds in to the LA-IEF we developed). Using concepts of evidence-based research we will propose several scenarios how researchers could get a deeper understanding of impact of these interventions.

Case-Study 1: Sending Emails to Learners at Risk

In an introductory social science module lasting 36 weeks, 1076 learners were identified by their educational profiles (e.g. low prior education, low assessment scores on previous modules) and engagement in the course (e.g. # VLE clicks in the last 2 weeks) as potentially "at-risk". This group received an email after 4 weeks with the intention "to encourage reflection on study progress as a midmodule progress check". Learners signposted to web resources such as "back on track". Following this intervention, if learners were concerned about their progress, they could obtain further information have to move ahead, whom to contact, or signposted to the deferrals, withdrawals, and cancellation website. Another (indirect) aim of this intervention was to be able to link and measure engagements of learners through various ICT and administrative systems together to provide a more holistic perspective of the learners' journey throughout the module.

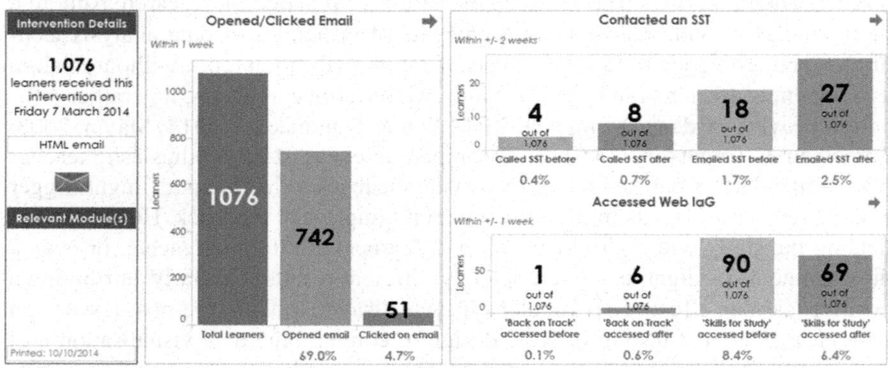

Fig. 10.1 Impact of email intervention on follow-up help-seeking behaviour

As indicated in Fig. 10.1, of the 1076 learners who received the email, 742 (69 %) learners opened the email within 1 week after receiving the email, while 51 (4.7 %) learners followed up by clicking on one or more of the various links to further information (i.e. behaviour), such as the back-on-track website, skills for study website, and a contact for the Student Support Team (SST). In terms of back-on-track website, one learner accessed this website before the intervention, and six learners accessed this website within 1 week after the intervention. Ninety learners accessed the study skills website before the intervention, and 69 learners accessed this website after the intervention. In terms of contact with SST, four learners called them before the intervention, while eight called within 2 weeks after the intervention. Similarly, 18 learners emailed SST before the intervention and 27 mailed after the intervention.

This intervention at first glance may indicate a positive impact on expected behaviour, because more learners engaged (behaviour) with one of the two support websites and/or contacted the SST team in comparison to before the intervention.

However, one has to be careful to conclude that this intervention "worked" in terms of attitudes, behaviour, and/or cognition..

First of all, the number of learners who followed up with the "expected" behaviour was relatively small (<5 %), and whether this would be statistically significant and meaningful might be questioned.

Second, it is plausible be that of the eight learners who called the SST, seven already planned to do this, or perhaps 25 learners had planned to call student support but after receiving the intervention decided that continuing with the module did not make sense and dropped out.

Third, in line with self-selection problems in non-randomised interventions, perhaps those learners with positive attitudes (e.g. intrinsically motivated) were more inclined to follow-up with the suggested action (Richardson, 2012b; Rienties et al., 2012), while those learners who actually needed help might have ignored the message. In other words, researchers need to be transparent about the relationships and fit between expected impact (i.e. planned during the intervention design) on ABC and the sensitivity of the measure(s) being used. In order to mitigate some of these issues, in an evidence-based approach we propose five possible scenarios to provide evidence of impact of case-study 1, each with its own strengths and limitations.

Scenario 1: Comparison with Previous Implementation

A natural option to compare the impact of an intervention is to contrast the ABC of learners from a previous implementation of the module. As illustrated in Fig. 10.2, the module implementation starting in February 2014 is compared to the previous implementation in October 2013. Looking only at the 2 weeks after the intervention was initiated in week 4, no substantial difference in engagement can be discerned between the two cohorts in terms of aggregate VLE engagement. Whether or not the intervention in week 4 worked (or not) depends on what kinds of relations we are looking for, and how these are measured. Furthermore, whether these two cohorts were similar at the start could be questioned as the percentage of learners visiting the VLE during the respective week was higher before the intervention for the 2014 implementation, and seemed to follow a similar trend until 4 weeks after the intervention. The substantial dip of activity in the October 2013 after 10 weeks is probably due to the Christmas break, but from week 12 onwards learners in the October 2013 presentation had substantially more engagement in the VLE than those in the 2014 implementation. Perhaps these aggregate data visualisations may under- or overestimate the complex, dynamic underlying engagements of learners with different ABC. In terms of cognition, similar passing rates were achieved in both modules. In other words, comparing the effectiveness of an intervention with a previous implementation might seem appealing, but addressing cause and effect is likely to be difficult (Hess & Saxberg, 2013; Torgerson & Torgerson, 2008).

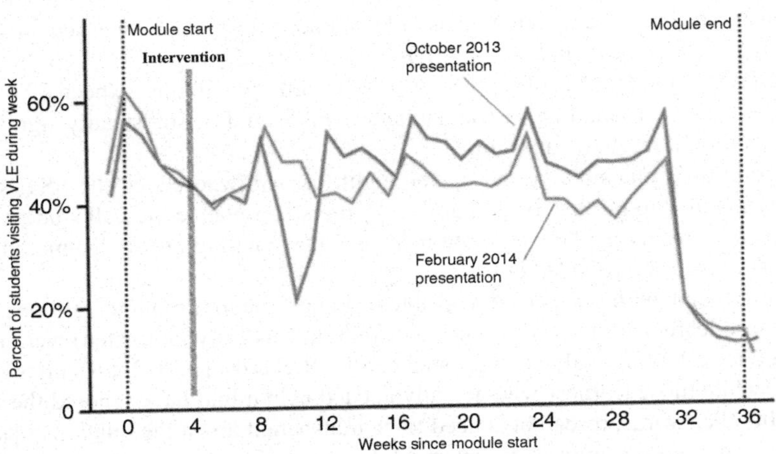

Fig. 10.2 VLE engagement before and after intervention (2013 vs. 2014 implementation)

Scenario 2: Quasi-Experimental Follow-Up

Institutions may not be able to conduct A/B testing or randomised control trials, due to potential ethical concerns (e.g. giving Group A a favourable treatment, while giving Group B a slightly less attractive treatment). When conducted well with appropriate control of confounding variables, quasi-experimental research could alleviate some of these issues as all learners in their respective cohort get the same treatment (Collins et al., 2004; Rienties et al., 2012; Torgerson & Torgerson, 2008). So in the next implementation of this module, using principles of Design-Based Research we could adjust the content of the message to encourage more learners to act upon the initial email, or change the amount and intensity of follow-up reminders. For example, we could adjust the narrative of the message (e.g. focussing more on social element of message), change the way we address the respective learner (e.g. Dear John, rather than Dear student), or provide some quotes from previous learners who struggled and found back-on-track website useful for their study to create a sense of relatedness (Bienkowski et al., 2012; Siroker & Koomen, 2013). By tracking learners' behaviour over the following 2 weeks, we can afterwards determine whether the quasi-experimental intervention was more or less successful in altering the behaviour of learners in comparison to the quasi-experimental control condition (i.e. the initial implementation). Finally, we could compare the academic performance difference between the new cohort and previous cohort in order to determine the impact on retention. However, a natural limitation of this kind of research (like in Scenario 1) is that the composition of learners in the follow-up study might be different in terms of attitudes, behaviour, and cognition, and the environment in which they study may have changed (e.g. different VLE tools, teachers, support, funding structure).

Scenario 3: A Switching Replications Design

An alternative scenario might be to conduct a specific alteration of the quasi-experimental study, namely a switching replications design, whereby first half of the cohort (Group A) will get the newly phrased intervention email in week 3, and the other half of the cohort (Group B) will receive the same email but only in week 4. In this way, Group A forms the intervention group during week 3, and can be compared and contrasted with the control Group B in terms of their behaviour, as illustrated in Fig. 10.3. For example, if 33 learners in the intervention group access the study skills modules in week 3, and only 14 learners in the control group access the skills modules, we can argue that the impact of the intervention is that 19 more learners followed up with the expected behaviour (arrow 1 in Fig. 10.3). In week 4, 45 learners in Group A accessed the skills module, and after receiving the same intervention 35 learners in Group B accessed the website (arrow 2 in Fig. 10.3). After 5 weeks, 35 learners in Group A accessed the skills module, and 44 in Group B (arrow 3 in Fig. 10.3). As all learners received the support and more or less the same number of learners engaged with the website until the end of the module, we have not disadvantaged Group B in giving them the delayed feedback. However, we are able to state that the intervention will lead to an increase in access to the skills website of approximately 30 learners in a 2-week time period (both for Group A and Group B).

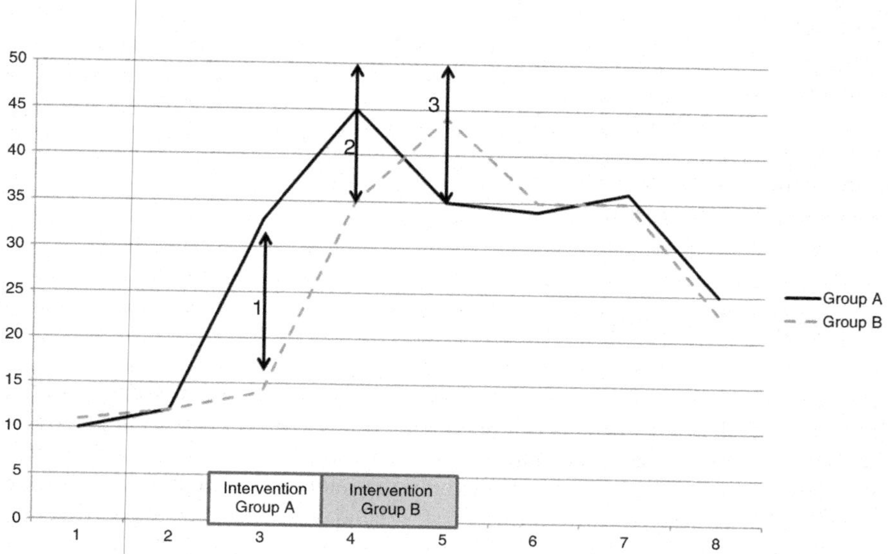

Fig. 10.3 Quasi-experimental intervention with time-delay

Scenario 4: A/B Testing Within One Study

A fourth scenario could be to implement A/B testing (Siroker & Koomen, 2013), whereby both groups get a similar treatment at the same point in time but the content/look-and-feel/navigation of the message is altered. For example, Group A gets the intervention message in week 4 primarily phrased on cognitive dimension (e.g. did you know that students who accessed the back-on-track website were 23 % more likely to pass the module?), while Group B gets an altered intervention message containing a personal example of a previous learner (e.g. did you know that 23 students looked at the back-on-track website last week, and found the website extremely useful? For example, Mary from Liverpool said "I was a bit unsure whether I was putting enough time into the course as I have a busy working life and taking care of two my two lovely, but demanding kids at the same time. The back-on-track website gave me feedback that I was well on track and gave me confidence that I am able to master this course"). Ideally, both A/B interventions should be considered as educationally valuable/progressive and not to adversely disadvantage the educational experience of the "other" group.

If in comparison to the A-group 30 more learners in week 4 clicked on the follow-up link in the B-type message, we can conclude adding a personal example could activate (some groups of) learner behaviour. A/B testing is particularly useful to unpack and understand which types of interventions are appropriate for specific groups of learners. For example, perhaps mothers with children might be more inclined to follow the link in the B-type setting due to the narrative of Mary from Liverpool, while perhaps women without children or mean might actually be less inclined to engage as they cannot really relate to the story of Mary. Again we remind readers that when planning a particular intervention researchers need to be clear about which kinds of ABC effects they are trying to impact, how they are going to measure these effects, and which kinds of statistical approaches are going to be used to verify/reject these hypotheses.

Scenario 5: Randomised Control Trial

A final scenario could be to a full randomised control trial (RCT, Rienties et al., 2014; Slavin, 2008; Torgerson & Torgerson, 2008), whereby for example we at random give 1/3 of the cohort an intervention mail with follow-up phone call 1 week after the mail is send, 1/3 of the cohort only the intervention mail, and 1/3 of the cohort a placebo (e.g. email with non-task-related message: "University cycling team is raising money for Cancer UK research, could you help?") or no specific intervention. By tracking the behaviours of learners in the two experimental conditions in comparison to the learners in the control condition, we should be able to determine the causal relations of the type and intensity of the intervention. In particular, by linking these three interventions with ABC we would be able to determine for which groups of learners the additional phone call might have a positive effect (e.g. learners with low self-efficacy, anxiety, lack of engagement with VLE) and for whom it might lead to unexpected negative effects or "mothering" (e.g. highly active learners in VLE, intrinsically motivated learners). However, a natural limitation of RCTs is that substantial time and effort needs to be invested in order to plan, design, implement, and evaluate these kinds of studies, which may not always be possible when a quick intervention is needed. This approach may be particularly useful in cases where there is no or mixed prior evidence that an intervention promises or should be expected to be beneficial (and so inclusion of a placebo can be educationally justified).

Case-Study 2: Helping Learners-At-Risk Identified by Predictive Modelling

Our second case-study is an example of highly sophisticated learning analytics system developed by the OU, which uses a range of advanced statistical and machine learning approaches to identify learners potentially at risk. In an introductory science module, data about 1730 learners were monitored using OU Analyse. The objective of the OU Analyse is to predict learners-at-risk (i.e. lack of engagement, potential to withdraw) in a course presentation as early as possible so that cost-effective interventions could be made. For this module, the accuracy of predictions grew from about 50 % at the beginning of the presentation to more than 90 % at the end of the module presentation. Recall was stable at around 50 %, but dropped to about 30 % at the very end due to the incomplete results of preceding assessments. In OU Analyse, predictions are calculated in two steps:

- Predictive models are constructed by machine learning methods from legacy data recorded in the previous presentation of the same course.
- Performance of learners is predicted from the predictive models and the learner data of the current presentation (Wolff et al., 2013, 2014).

Machine learning methods aim at constructing predictive models that capture from legacy data patterns typical for succeeding, failing, or withdrawing in formative/summative assessments and in the course. Two types of data were used for predictive modelling: demographic/static data and learner interactions with the VLE system. Demographic/static data include age, previous education, gender, geographic region, Index of Multiple Deprivation score, motivation, how many credits the learner is registered for, number of previous attempts on the course, etc. VLE data represent a learner's interaction with online study material and VLE interactions are classified into *activity types* and *actions*. Each activity type corresponds to an interaction with a specific kind of study material. For example, *resource* activity type typically refers to retrieving a segment of course text, OU *content* is used to point to the assessment, etc. (Wolff et al., 2013, 2014).

These data were collected daily, but the OU Analyse algorithms used weekly aggregates. OU Analyse applies information theoretic criteria to select 4–6 activity types most informative for the outcome of the next assessments and for the final result. These activity types were used to build predictive models. Moreover, the frequency of learners' use of activities with selected activity types indicated which study material learners visited and how many times. Activity types that were not used pointed to a potential gap in knowledge and were used by the models as an input for individualised study recommender.

OU Analyse employs three machine learning methods to develop four predictive models: Bayesian classifier; Classification and regression tree; k Nearest Neighbours with demographic/static data; and k-NN with VLE data. These four models take into account different properties of data and complement each other. Each model independently classifies each learner into classes: will/will-not submit next assessment and will fail or pass the course. The final verdict of the prediction is done by combining the outcomes and using voting techniques of all four models (Wolff et al., 2014).

A list of learners likely not to submit the next assessment is sent every week to the module team. Results of learners' prior assessments (already known at the time of prediction) and demographic/static data were included. In Fig. 10.4, a module view shows the average performance of the whole cohort and lists results of all learners with a traffic light symbols and brief justification of conclusions. Since the trajectory of each learner's activity types through presentation up to the current point of time is recorded, it can be used to recommend the best study material to successfully complete the assessment.

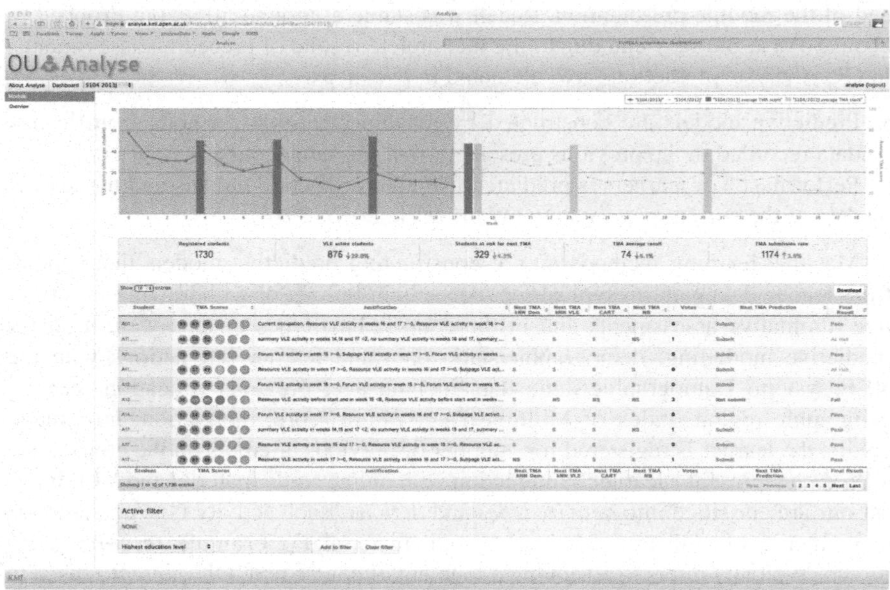

Fig. 10.4 Predicting modelling of learners at risk in OU Analyse in week 17

As indicated in Fig. 10.4, OU Analyse predicted that 329 learners were “at-risk” before the fourth summative assessment point. The first part of graph in Fig. 10.4 highlights average user engagement with the VLE and compares this to previous implementations of the same module (dashed line). This indicated that engagement in week 17 was substantially lower than the previous implementation. OU Analyse also indicates the average assessment score on the second Y-axis, whereby average scores for the fourth assessment were predicted to be lower than those of the third assessment (and in comparison to the previous implementation). The lower part of Fig. 10.4 gives a traffic light overview of each individual learner, and whether (or not) a learner is considered at risk. For example, the first learner passed the three previous summative assessments with high grades and was predicted to do well on the forthcoming assessment as well. The second learner barely passed the first assessment, did slightly better on the second and third assessment, but was still characterised at risk to pass the module as this learner had not engaged activity with the various VLE activities in week 14, 16, and 17. The sixth (and final) learner listed in Fig. 10.4 had failed the first assessment, did not submit assessment 2–3, and was predicted not to submit assessment 4 and not to pass the module. In order to allow researchers to evaluate the impact of interventions, we propose four different scenarios.

Scenario 1: Quasi-Experimental Follow-Up

Based upon the experiences of 2014 and principles of Design-Based Research, the module chair of the module could redesign some of the learning activities after the third assessment because a substantial group of learners in the previous implementation seemed to become less engaged at this point (as highlighted by lower VLE activity and lower assessment scores for fourth assessment). For example, qualitative learner evaluation feedback and input from tutors may indicate that one of the two textbooks used for this time period (weeks 13–18) was considered to be difficult and too abstract. As a result, the module chair could, for example, change this textbook with a more accessible, interactive online textbook with ample practices and real-world examples how principles of physics could be applied. In OU Analyse, we would be able to compare VLE activity of learners in weeks 13–18 with the previous implementation. More importantly, OU Analyse would be able to track each individual learner and determine whether their predictions of success will change (or not) due to this intervention.

Scenario 2: A Switching Replications Design

An alternative scenario might be to conduct a switching replications design study, whereby for example half the cohort would start in weeks 13–15 with the original textbook and its respective tasks (Group A), while the other half of the cohort

(Group B) would start with the new textbook. In week 16 the groups swap, whereby Group A would continue with the new textbook, while Group B would continue with the original textbook. In this way, both groups get the same two textbooks and related tasks, but in a different order so that the impact of the different textbooks on attitudes, behaviour, and cognition can be compared and contrasted.

Scenario 3: A/B Testing Within One Study

A third scenario could be to implement A/B testing (Siroker & Koomen, 2013), whereby both groups get a similar treatment but Group A, for example, starts in week 14 with an interactive exercise using an embedded video-quiz in the interactive textbook, followed by a theoretical part, and concluded with a short formative test, while Group B starts with the same quiz but in a text-based format. This would allow us to track whether providing embedded video-quizzes leads to more engagement with the theoretical part and cognition.

Scenario 4: Randomised Control Trial Within One Study

A final scenario could be to a full randomised control trial, whereby one-third of the cohort at randomly gets the new textbook with interactive assignments, one-third of the cohort receives the new textbook with text-based assignments, and finally one cohort gets the original textbook. In this way, we can test whether the new textbook leads to a more engaged learning behaviour and cognition, and whether the level of interactivity encourages or hampers rich learning. Given that OU Analyse incorporates a range of attitudinal and demographic data, this would also allow us to determine the impact of these three conditions for specific groups of learners.

Discussion and Learning Analytics Intervention and Evaluation Framework

Substantial progress in learning analytics research has been made in recent years to predict which groups of learners are at risk (Agudo-Peregrina et al., 2014; Calvert, 2014; Gasevic et al., 2013; Macfadyen & Dawson, 2010). However, we argue that the largest challenge for learning analytics research and practice still lies ahead of us: using learning analytics modelling, which types of interventions have a positive impact on learners' Attitudes, Behaviour and Cognition (ABC). Two embedded case-studies in social science and science were discussed to illustrate some notions of how evidence-based research approaches could be used in learning analytics, namely comparison with previous implementations, quasi-experimental research, a within-quasi-experimental research, A/B testing, and randomised control trials.

Each of these five scenarios has unique affordances and limitations. For academics familiar with educational research and who have sufficient data interpretation skills, in particular the first three scenarios are relatively straightforward to implement using principles of Design-Based Research (Collins et al., 2004; Rienties & Townsend, 2012). For academics who do not have these skills, educational psychologists, learning and teaching specialists, or data-interpreters might help them to make informed suggestions for follow-up interventions (Clow, 2014; Rienties et al., 2012). By collecting as much data as possible from a range of sources, and by triangulating quantitative and qualitative results, academics, and teachers can use data from previous and current implementations to identify bottlenecks in the learning design and how this influences ABC of learners. Afterwards, a design-based intervention (Collins et al., 2004) would allow academics and teachers to test, verify, compare, and contrast whether (or not) the expected changes in ABC of learners indeed materialised.

Implementing A/B testing or RCT testing, the "gold-standard" in research (Slavin, 2002, 2008; Torgerson & Torgerson, 2008) is partly more complex due to organisational, technical, and (potential) ethical barriers. For example, not all VLE systems allow teachers to randomly assign learners to two or three different groups and use subsequent adaptive routing to track whether learners in the experimental condition(s) behave differently than those in the control condition. Even if IT systems allow for A/B testing or adaptive routing, substantial manual labour may be needed to assign learners to the different conditions. In particular with relatively small samples (<200), even random assignment in different conditions might not guarantee an equal distribution of learner characteristics (ABC) across the conditions, so researchers may need to check appropriate sampling. Finally, obtaining ethical permission to conduct A/B testing or RCT may not always be straightforward, and at times unpractical or unethical (depending on the proposed intervention). Nonetheless, in line with Slavin (2008) we argue that often only with RCTs and A/B testing can we provide robust and reliable evidence under which conditions learning analytics can provide cost-effective, yet rich interventions to our students.

Implementing a Learning Analytics Intervention and Evaluation Framework

The Open University is currently implementing a Learning Analytics Intervention and Evaluation Framework (LA-IEF) with 15 large cohort first year modules across the various disciplines. If organisations like the OU are going to adopt and continually finance learning analytics approaches, we need to provide evidence-based results where we can identify learners at risk (e.g. using OU Analyse), deliver (personalised) intervention suggestions that work, and most importantly interventions that are cost-effective. Therefore, one pragmatic reason for choosing first year modules at the OU is that retention rates amongst these learners are traditionally lower than in follow-up years (Calvert, 2014; Richardson, 2012a). By using the power of learning analytics where it is most needed, but across a range of disciplines, we expect to be able to provide an evidence-based approach under which conditions particular interventions are successful in altering learners' ABC.

As illustrated in Fig. 10.5, using principles of Design-Based Research (Collins et al., 2004; Rienties & Townsend, 2012) extensive dialogue with key stakeholders (e.g. module chairs, tutors, librarians, multimedia designers, IT, learners) are being conducted in between September 2014–April 2015 as a baseline study to determine what is going well and what bottlenecks are (potentially) present in each of these 15 modules according to these stakeholders. At the same time, these modules will be extensively evaluated using a range of learning analytics approaches (e.g. OU Analyse, VLE monitoring) and existing evaluation practices with the OU, thereby leading to a solid baseline study.

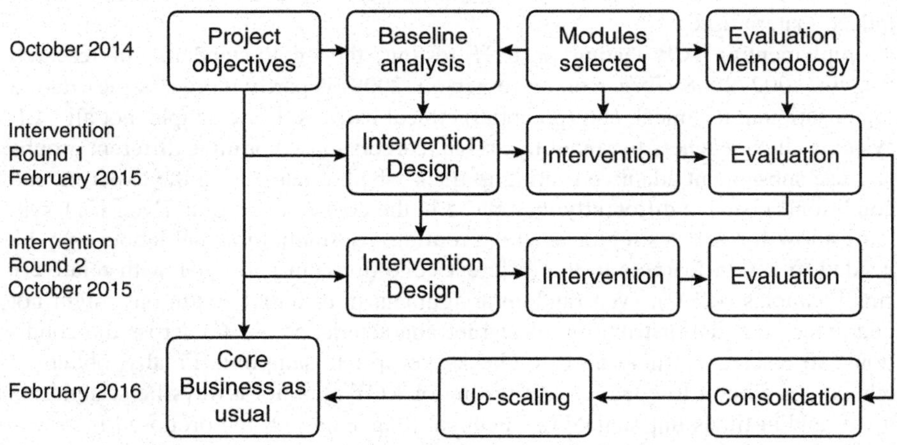

Fig. 10.5 LA-IEF framework as implemented at the OU

Follow-up discussions with module chairs and relevant stakeholders in November–December 2014 using the insights of learning analytics will determine which types of interventions will be implemented in the next implementation of the modules in February 2015 in an evidence-based manner. For some modules, a quasi-experimental design will be used, whereby based on the results of the baseline study (parts of) the module will be altered. For other modules, we aim to use A/B testing or RCT testing to be able to directly identify cause and effect of particular interventions. More importantly, by planning, implementing, and evaluating these interventions across a range of disciplines, the LA-IEF model will help to advance methodological robustness of learning analytics research, by comparing and contrasting research findings across different domains and contexts using an evidence-based approach.

A crucial element of the Learning Analytics Intervention and Evaluation Framework is the recognition that most interventions and innovations lead to unexpected, possibly even negative results. While we expect that several of the 15 interventions will lead to positive impacts on ABC of learners, several interventions will have no (measurable) impact on attitudes, behaviour, or cognition of (groups of) learner, or perhaps even lead to (in)direct negative effects. Forty years of educational research has highlighted that learning and cognition is inherently complex (Arbaugh, 2005, 2014; Hattie, 2009; Richardson, 2012a; Rienties et al., 2012; Slavin, 2008), but only with a clear evidence-based research programme will researchers be able to unpack and understand under which conditions we can help learners-at-risk in particular contexts. Given that in education there can conceivably be several different ways of teaching that may potentially be equally effective, then the question of A/B testing/randomised trials does not have to be between haves and have-nots or small variation; it could be between learning design A and learning design B, where there is some grounds to expect each to be effective (a multiplicity or range of potential designs that carry a similar risk of failure). Indeed, flipping the entire question from "how often does it work" to "how often does it fail" may lead us to see learning design as an exercise in risk minimisation.

A continuous cycle of interventions in the next 2 years are planned at the OU, which will help to replicate, fine-tune, and generalise for those interventions that had an initial positive effect. For those interventions which did not lead to a positive effect, taking the metaphor from medical science further fine-tuning the doze, level, and type of interventions will lead to a robust understanding what works and what does not. By a continuous cycle of planning, designing, implementing, and evaluating interventions across a range of modules, module chairs, and the wider organisation will be empowered to embed these intervention "recipes" into their practice. Finally, by moving towards an evidence-based research approach to learning and teaching, we aim to move towards a robust, flexible, and cost-effective university-wide implementation of learning analytics which will reduce dropout and allow learners to reach their full potential.

Acknowledgement We would like to thank Prof Belinda Tynan, Kevin Mayles, and Avinash Boroowa from the Learning and Teaching Centre at the Open University UK for their continuous support, and critical feedback to the LA-IEF framework.

References

Agudo-Peregrina, Á. F., Iglesias-Pradas, S., Conde-González, M. Á., & Hernández-García, Á. (2014). Can we predict success from log data in VLEs? Classification of interactions for learning analytics and their relation with performance in VLE-supported F2F and online learning. *Computers in Human Behavior, 31*(February), 542–550. doi:10.1016/j.chb.2013.05.031.

Aguiar, E., Chawla, N. V., Brockman, J., Ambrose, G. A., & Goodrich, V. (2014). *Engagement vs performance: Using electronic portfolios to predict first semester engineering student retention.* Paper presented at the Proceedings of the Fourth International Conference on Learning Analytics and Knowledge, Indianapolis, IN.

Arbaugh, J. B. (2005). Is there an optimal design for on-line MBA courses? *Academy of Management Learning and Education, 4*(2), 135–149. doi:10.5465/AMLE.2005.17268561.

Arbaugh, J. B. (2014). System, scholar, or students? Which most influences online MBA course effectiveness? *Journal of Computer Assisted Learning, 30*(4), 349–362. doi:10.1111/jcal.12048.

Baker, R. S. (2010). Data mining for education. *International Encyclopedia of Education, 7*, 112–118.

Bienkowski, M., Feng, M., & Means, B. (2012). Enhancing teaching and learning through educational data mining and learning analytics: An issue brief (pp. 1–57). US Department of Education, Office of Educational Technology.

Calvert, C. E. (2014). Developing a model and applications for probabilities of student success: A case study of predictive analytics. *Open Learning: The Journal of Open, Distance and E-Learning, 29*(2), 160–173. doi:10.1080/02680513.2014.931805.

Clow, D. (2014). *Data wranglers: Human interpreters to help close the feedback loop*. Paper presented at the Proceedings of the Fourth International Conference on Learning Analytics and Knowledge.

Collins, A., Joseph, D., & Bielaczyc, K. (2004). Design research: Theoretical and methodological issues. *The Journal of the Learning Sciences, 13*(1), 15–42.

Conde, M. Á., & Hernández-García, Á. (2015). Learning analytics for educational decision making. *Computers in Human Behavior, 47*, 1–3. doi:10.1016/j.chb.2014.12.034.

Ferguson, R. (2012). Learning analytics: Drivers, developments and challenges. *International Journal of Technology Enhanced Learning, 4*(5), 304–317. doi:10.1504/ijtel.2012.051816.

Ferguson, R., & Buckingham Shum, S. (2012). *Social learning analytics: Five approaches*. Paper presented at the Proceedings of the 2nd International Conference on Learning Analytics and Knowledge, Vancouver, BC.

García-Peñalvo, F. J., Conde, M. Á., Alier, M., & Casany, M. J. (2011). Opening learning management systems to personal learning environments. *Journal of Universal Computer Science, 17*(9), 1222–1240. doi:10.3217/jucs-017-09-1222.

Gasevic, D., Zouaq, A., & Janzen, R. (2013). "Choose your classmates, your GPA is at stake!": The association of cross-class social ties and academic performance. *American Behavioral Scientist, 57*(10), 1460–1479. doi:10.1177/0002764213479362.

Giesbers, B., Rienties, B., Tempelaar, D. T., & Gijselaers, W. H. (2013). Investigating the relations between motivation, tool use, participation, and performance in an e-learning course using web-videoconferencing. *Computers in Human Behavior, 29*(1), 285–292. doi:10.1016/j.chb.2012.09.005.

González-Torres, A., García-Peñalvo, F. J., & Therón, R. (2013). Human–computer interaction in evolutionary visual software analytics. *Computers in Human Behavior, 29*(2), 486–495. doi:10.1016/j.chb.2012.01.013.

Greller, W., & Drachsler, H. (2012). Translating learning into numbers: A generic framework for learning analytics. *Journal of Educational Technology & Society, 15*(3), 42–57.

Hattie, J. (2009). *Visible learning: A synthesis of over 800 meta-analyses relating to achievement*. New York: Routledge.

Hess, F. M., & Saxberg, B. (2013). *Breakthrough leadership in the digital age: Using learning science to reboot schooling*. Thousand Oaks, CA: Corwin Press.

Hickey, D. T., Kelley, T. A., & Shen, X. (2014). *Small to big before massive: Scaling up participatory learning analytics*. Paper presented at the Proceedings of the Fourth International Conference on Learning Analytics and Knowledge.

Inkelaar, T., & Simpson, O. (2015). Challenging the 'distance education deficit' through 'motivational emails'. *Open Learning: The Journal of Open, Distance and E-Learning, 30*(2), 152–163. doi:10.1080/02680513.2015.1055718.

Jindal-Snape, D., & Rienties, B. (Eds.). (2016). *Multi-dimensional transitions of international students to higher education*. London: Routledge.

Knight, S., Buckingham Shum, S., & Littleton, K. (2013). *Epistemology, pedagogy, assessment and learning analytics*. Paper presented at the Proceedings of the Third International Conference on Learning Analytics and Knowledge.

Macfadyen, L. P., & Dawson, S. (2010). Mining LMS data to develop an "early warning system" for educators: A proof of concept. *Computers & Education, 54*(2), 588–599. doi:10.1016/j.compedu.2009.09.008.

MacNeill, S., Campbell, L. M., & Hawksey, M. (2014). Analytics for education. *Journal of Interactive Media in Education, 2014*(1), 7. doi:10.5334/2014-07.

Martin, A. J. (2007). Examining a multidimensional model of student motivation and engagement using a construct validation approach. *British Journal of Educational Psychology, 77*(2), 413–440. doi:10.1348/000709906X118036.
McMillan, J. H., & Schumacher, S. (2014). *Research in education: Evidence-based inquiry*. Harlow: Pearson Higher Ed.
Nistor, N., Baltes, B., Dascălu, M., Mihăilă, D., Smeaton, G., & Trăuşan-Matu, Ş. (2014). Participation in virtual academic communities of practice under the influence of technology acceptance and community factors. A learning analytics application. *Computers in Human Behavior, 34*, 339–344. doi:10.1016/j.chb.2013.10.051.
Papamitsiou, Z., & Economides, A. (2014). Learning analytics and educational data mining in practice: A systematic literature review of empirical evidence. *Educational Technology & Society, 17*(4), 49–64.
Papamitsiou, Z., Terzis, V., & Economides, A. (2014). *Temporal learning analytics for computer based testing*. Paper presented at the Proceedings of the Fourth International Conference on Learning Analytics and Knowledge, Indianapolis, IN.
Pekrun, R., Goetz, T., Frenzel, A. C., Barchfeld, P., & Perry, R. P. (2011). Measuring emotions in students' learning and performance: The achievement emotions questionnaire (AEQ). *Contemporary Educational Psychology, 36*(1), 36–48. doi:10.1016/j.cedpsych.2010.10.002.
Pintrich, P. R., & De Groot, E. V. (1990). Motivational and self-regulated learning components of classroom academic performance. *Journal of Educational Psychology, 82*(1), 33–40.
Richardson, J. T. E. (2012a). The attainment of White and ethnic minority students in distance education. *Assessment and Evaluation in Higher Education, 37*(4), 393–408. doi:10.1080/02602938.2010.534767.
Richardson, J. T. E. (2012b). The role of response biases in the relationship between students' perceptions of their courses and their approaches to studying in higher education. *British Educational Research Journal, 38*(3), 399–418. doi:10.1080/01411926.2010.548857.
Rienties, B., & Alden Rivers, B. (2014). *Measuring and understanding learner emotions: Evidence and prospects* (LACE review papers, Vol. 1). Milton Keynes: LACE.
Rienties, B., Giesbers, S., Lygo-Baker, S., Ma, S., & Rees, R. (2014). Why some teachers easily learn to use a new virtual learning environment: A technology acceptance perspective. *Interactive Learning Environments, 24*(3), 539–552. doi:10.1080/10494820.2014.881394.
Rienties, B., Giesbers, B., Tempelaar, D. T., Lygo-Baker, S., Segers, M., & Gijselaers, W. H. (2012). The role of scaffolding and motivation in CSCL. *Computers & Education, 59*(3), 893–906. doi:10.1016/j.compedu.2012.04.010.
Rienties, B., Toetenel, L., & Bryan, A. (2015). *"Scaling up" learning design: Impact of learning design activities on LMS behavior and performance*. Paper presented at the 5th Learning Analytics Knowledge conference, New York.
Rienties, B., & Townsend, D. (2012). Integrating ICT in business education: Using TPACK to reflect on two course redesigns. In P. Van den Bossche, W. H. Gijselaers, & R. G. Milter (Eds.), *Learning at the crossroads of theory and practice* (Vol. 4, pp. 141–156). Dordrecht: Springer.
Siemens, G. (2013). Learning analytics: The emergence of a discipline. *American Behavioral Scientist, 57*(10), 1380–1400. doi:10.1177/0002764213498851.
Siemens, G., Dawson, S., & Lynch, G. (2013). Improving the quality and productivity of the higher education sector policy and strategy for systems level deployment of learning analytics. Canberra: Office of Learning and Teaching, Australian Government. Retrieved from http://solaresearch.org/Policy_Strategy_Analytics.pdf.
Siroker, D., & Koomen, P. (2013). *A/B testing: The most powerful way to turn clicks into customers*. Hoboken, NJ: Wiley.
Slavin, R. E. (2002). Evidence-based education policies: Transforming educational practice and research. *Educational Researcher, 31*(7), 15–21. doi:10.2307/3594400.
Slavin, R. E. (2008). Perspectives on evidence-based research in education—What works? Issues in synthesizing educational program evaluations. *Educational Researcher, 37*(1), 5–14. doi:10.3102/0013189X08314117.

Stiles, R. J. (2012). Understanding and managing the risks of analytics in higher education: A guide. (pp. 1–46). Educause.

Tempelaar, D. T., Niculescu, A., Rienties, B., Giesbers, B., & Gijselaers, W. H. (2012). How achievement emotions impact students' decisions for online learning, and what precedes those emotions. *Internet and Higher Education, 15*(3), 161–169. doi:10.1016/j.iheduc.2011.10.003.

Tempelaar, D. T., Rienties, B., & Giesbers, B. (2015). In search for the most informative data for feedback generation: Learning analytics in a data-rich context. *Computers in Human Behavior, 47*, 157–167. doi:10.1016/j.chb.2014.05.038.

Tobarra, L., Robles-Gómez, A., Ros, S., Hernández, R., & Caminero, A. C. (2014). Analyzing the students' behavior and relevant topics in virtual learning communities. *Computers in Human Behavior, 31*, 659–669. doi:10.1016/j.chb.2013.10.001.

Torgerson, D. J., & Torgerson, C. (2008). *Designing randomised trials in health, education and the social sciences: An introduction*. London: Palgrave Macmillan.

Wise, A. F. (2014). *Designing pedagogical interventions to support student use of learning analytics*. Paper presented at the Proceedings of the Fourth International Conference on Learning Analytics and Knowledge, Indianapolis, IN.

Wolff, A., Zdrahal, Z., Herrmannova, D., Kuzilek, J., & Hlosta, M. (2014). *Developing predictive models for early detection of at-risk students on distance learning modules*. Workshop: Machine Learning and Learning Analytics. Paper presented at the Learning Analytics and Knowledge, Indianapolis, IN.

Wolff, A., Zdrahal, Z., Nikolov, A., & Pantucek, M. (2013). *Improving retention: Predicting at-risk students by analysing clicking behaviour in a virtual learning environment.* Paper presented at the Proceedings of the Third International Conference on Learning Analytics and Knowledge.

Yin, R. K. (2009). *Case study research: Design and methods* (Vol. 5). Thousand Oaks, CA: Sage.

Chapter 11
GraphFES: A Web Service and Application for Moodle Message Board Social Graph Extraction

Ángel Hernández-García and Ignacio Suárez-Navas

Abstract This chapter introduces GraphFES, a Web service and application that processes data from forum activity in Moodle courses and transforms them into social graphs to enable social learning analytics in Gephi, a social network analysis application. The chapter gives an overview of social learning analytics in online and computer-supported collaborative learning and describes existing tools for social network analysis of educational data. The chapter also presents the main concepts associated to the data source (Moodle logs) and target (Gephi), and a more detailed explanation of GraphFES's design and operation. An example with data from two courses illustrates how GraphFES and Gephi can combine to carry out social learning analytics in Moodle courses. The final section discusses the potential of this approach for effective social learning analytics.

Keywords Learning analytics • Social network analysis • Social learning analytics • Learning management systems • Forums • Computer-supported collaborative learning • Gephi • Educational data • Visualization • Moodle log

Introduction and General Context

The main difference between face-to-face—or even blended learning—and online-only instruction is the lack of physical interaction between teachers and students, and among learners. Apart from the results of assignments and eventual tutorial support sessions, in on-site (face-to-face) and mixed-method learning (blended learning) courses, instructors often rely on real-time feedback to get an idea of students' engagement and progress, at the individual, group, and course levels (Reffay & Chanier, 2003).

Á. Hernández-García (✉) • I. Suárez-Navas
Universidad Politécnica de Madrid, Madrid, Spain
e-mail: angel.hernandez@upm.es

B. Kei Daniel (ed.), *Big Data and Learning Analytics in Higher Education*,
DOI 10.1007/978-3-319-06520-5_11

However, the distinctive lack of physical interaction in online environments makes student tracking a difficult task for instructors and course coordinators. Without any means to analyze students' progress and online participation, there is a big risk that some students may fall behind without the teacher noticing it, and this situation can ultimately lead to student failure and attrition. Furthermore, lack of timely information may also lead to an unnoticed mismatch between ideal and actual class dynamics, from a social learning perspective.

This mismatch is especially important in computer-supported collaborative learning (CSCL) settings and/or courses with high student–teacher ratios. In these scenarios, monitoring student progress may be a difficult and time-consuming task for instructors due to the great amount of raw data available in current Virtual Learning Environments (VLEs) and Learning Management Systems (LMS) (Macfadyen & Dawson, 2012). In addition, emerging new instructional methods in which students also have social interactions as part of the learning process outside the formal learning contexts—e.g., personal learning environments (PLEs), social networking sites (SNSs)—or where the number of students is very large—e.g., massive online open courses (MOOCs)—make it necessary to provide teachers with tools to analyze the social dynamics of the class in online instruction.

The results of this analysis should give teachers enough useful and meaningful information at any given moment during the course to intervene, if necessary, or make fine-tuning adjustments to improve the whole learning process. The necessity of this type of analysis has led to the emergence of learning analytics as discipline. Learning analytics focuses on the collection, analysis, and reporting of educational data to better understand and optimize learning (Long & Siemens, 2011).

Hernández-García and Conde (2014) identify three main levels of learning analytics: identification of suitable indicators; identification, understanding, and explanation of learning behaviors; and mechanisms for adaptive learning. Although they are all related to each other, the second one is, by and large, the one that has raised most interest among scholars and practitioners—probably because it is the most immediate in terms of interpretation of results, and also has good value for theory building.

Most studies following this approach try to relate a student's activity in a technology-supported educational environment (e.g., LMS), many times under the assumption that "data speak for themselves," and neglecting other situational information, such as the assessment instruments employed or the social nature of the co-construction of knowledge in networks of practice (De Laat & Prinsen, 2014).

These omissions are even more relevant in courses where the instructional method relies heavily on collaborative and teamwork-based online learning because (1) it may be very difficult for instructors to detect dysfunctional groups or lack of student's engagement—especially in courses with a large number of enrolled students— which can ultimately lead to failure or course attrition, and (2) assessment in collaborative learning must include mastering of the instructional contents and participation (Barkley, Cross, & Major, 2005). Assessment in teamwork contexts is often just based on the result—the final work—as an evidence that can be measured and compared. Nevertheless, this assessment does not take into account individual participation of group members. In addition, gathering information about participation in online settings may lead to cumbersome analysis procedures (Fidalgo-Blanco, Sein-Echaluce, García-Peñalvo, & Conde, 2015).

In online collaborative learning, most of the data about students' participation is stored in the learning platform. Therefore, the application of social network analysis (SNA) to educational data—what Buckingham-Shum and Ferguson (2012) define as inherently social learning analytics—may offer insight on participation both from an analytical and visual standpoint.

This chapter introduces GraphFES (Graph Forum Extraction Service), a Web service for data extraction and processing of forum activity in a Moodle platform, and shows how data provided by GraphFES can be used for analysis and visualization of data about participation and engagement in Gephi—an open-source SNA software—(Bastian, Heymann, & Jacomy, 2009) in order to understand, explain, and improve learning processes in online contexts. As an example, the study includes the application of GraphFES to data from two different courses: a Master's course with few students and only a group assignment, and an undergraduate course based on a team project with high number of participants.

This chapter is structured as follows: Section "Social Learning Analytics" offers an overview of prior literature on social learning analytics. Section "Social Learning Analytics: Tools" presents different tools available for social learning analytics in online and ICT-supported learning. Sections "Moodle Logs and Data Extraction and Visualization," "Gephi: A Tool for Social Network Analysis," and "GraphFES: Design and Operation" detail Moodle's log data capabilities, the Gephi software, and the design and operation of GraphFES. Section "Case Studies" explains the characteristics of the courses used for the empirical study, the main results from the SNA and some visualizations of the resulting networks. Finally, section "Conclusion" will discuss the main findings of the study, addressing the limitations and future avenues of research on this topic.

Social Learning Analytics

Online learning systems give support to individual, self-directed learning by providing tools that enable access to learning resources, and by implementing assessment instruments and tools (quizzes, essays, etc.). LMS also provide synchronous (e.g., chats) and asynchronous (e.g., message boards) communication tools to make up for the lack of physical contact between students and teachers, as well as among students, in order to make social construction of knowledge possible. As learning becomes ubiquitous—learning and interactions may happen anywhere, anytime—message boards (forums) become an essential part of social learning in online environments.

In collaborative, project-based and teamwork-based learning, social learning is at the center of the process. Social learning builds on the notions that cognitive processes take place in a social context, by reciprocal interaction between behavior and controlling conditions, both individual and environmental (Bandura, 1971), and that knowledge is created and constructed by the interactions of individuals within society (Berger & Luckman, 1967). In addition, research on CSCL and virtual communities of practice has also shown interest in knowledge creation by participation and engagement in the discourse (Hmelo-Silver & Barrows, 2008; Lave & Wenger, 1991; Zhao & Chan, 2014).

In formal online learning contexts, the interactions, participation, social exchange, and discourse-based knowledge building processes happen essentially in course forums. Therefore, it is only natural that an important stream of research has focused on describing, explaining, and understanding the social dynamics that take place in forums on online courses. One of the most novel approaches to the study of social dynamics in online courses is the application of SNA to course data, known as social learning analytics (e.g., Oshima, Oshima, & Matsuzawa, 2012).

According to Buckingham-Shum and Ferguson (2012), inherently social learning analytics has two different aspects: social network analytics and discourse analytics. The former focuses on SNA of course data in order to explain and understand the social dynamics of the course, and it will be the main focus of this chapter (i.e., we shall restrict the concept of social learning analytics to SNA of educational data); the latter explores the nature of the contents and structure of the discourse between learning agents in a course, which is out of the scope of this study. Buckingham-Shum and Ferguson state that the underlying idea behind social learning analytics is that networked learning supported by ICT consists of actors (both people and resources) and the relations between them, and that social network analysis investigates these network processes and the properties of ties, relations, roles, and network formations. Therefore, social network analysis brings together graph theory and sociology and communication to improve learning processes. The main uses of social learning analytics include detection of communities (Buckingham-Shum & Ferguson, 2012) and identification of relevant learning agents, such as at-risk students, knowledge brokers, or influential students (Hernández-García, González-González, Jiménez-Zarco, & Chaparro-Peláez, 2015).

Social learning analytics facilitates this identification in two ways: analysis and visualization. Analysis focuses on calculation of SNA parameters and metrics for each node—see Freeman (1979) for further information about centrality measures and Hernández-García (2014; p. 156) for SNA metrics and indicators for learning analytics—and network overall parameters, such as average network degree (average number of incoming, outgoing, or global links of a node in the network), network density (the number of total edges present in the network relative to the number of edges in a full-connected network), or network diameter (the largest number of nodes that must be traversed in order to travel from one node to another).

Visualization of social networks facilitates the identification, at a glance, of students who are disconnected from the network; furthermore, filtering and visual transformations of the graph, based on relevant metrics or node attributes, may help understanding the social dynamics of the course. The main advantage of the analysis is that it also provides a numerical way to characterize different aspects of the social graph (although the meaning of the different SNA parameters may be difficult to understand for instructors with no knowledge of SNA, and therefore the usefulness of the analysis is limited to the subject's ability to interpret the results). Social graph visualizations complement the analysis in a direct and eye-candy way, once the main concepts are learnt.

Regarding social learning networks, Hernández-García et al. (2015) state that teachers usually have access to one part—the visible one—of the social exchanges and participation in a course. Messages posted to the course message boards represent this visible part. More often than not, assessment in online courses rely on the final evidence from quizzes or essays that students deliver in the learning platforms, but also on evaluation of students' participation and quality of content posted to forums. Furthermore, this visible activity also allows instructors to determine whether the different concepts are actually being learnt by students and to detect lack of active engagement in the discourse. Nonetheless, Hernández-García et al. claim that there is another type of passive social exchanges where individuals interact not with teachers and other students, but with the content created by others, and that this kind of interaction that may pass unnoticed to instructors can provide additional information about student engagement. According to Wise and Hausknecht (2013), the lack of active engagement in conversations does not mean a lack of involvement or that learning is not happening, because students have different learning styles, and some students may enhance their learning with external knowledge that they do not share, or may act as learning witnesses or "invisible students" (Beaudoin, 2002), and build their learning around content created or shared by others.

Hernández-García (2014) proposes the suitability of SNA tools to perform social network analytics of both types of networks. In order to do so, he shows some examples of use of Gephi for SNA, by using data from a proprietary learning platform. Hernández-García divides forum log data into three different datasets: relations among users based on their posting behavior (the "reply network"; i.e., who replies to whom), relations among users based on message viewing behaviors (the "read network"; i.e., who reads messages posted by whom), and relations among messages (a network that relates each message to its parent in a discussion, displaying threads as message trees).

The objective of GraphFES, the Web service presented in this chapter, is to automatically build these three networks from LMS data logs (more specifically, data from Moodle logs) and show an example of the potential of social learning analytics with data from two courses with different characteristics.

Social Learning Analytics: Tools

This section offers an overview of existing tools available for social network analytics in formal learning environments (VLEs and LMS). The analysis will focus on SNA tools for Moodle, the leading open-source LMS (Edutechnica, 2015) and will detail three tools oriented toward social learning analytics (Social Networks

Adapting Pedagogical Practice (SNAPP), Forum Graph and Meerkat-ED), as well as generic SNA software for social learning analytics. Section "Case Studies" will show the different visualizations provided by each tool.

Social Networks Adapting Pedagogical Practice

SNAPP[1] is a web browser bookmarklet that extracts information about message board activity from the most widely adopted LMS (Sakai, Blackboard, Moodle, and Desire2Learn), and then builds up the resulting social network in a Java applet. The two existing versions of SNAPP (1.5 and 2.1) have similar functionalities.

SNAPP's Java applet shows different tabs, the first three of which are interactive. The first tab shows the social network graph and allows manipulating it by filtering, applying different layouts and selecting individual nodes—nodes in SNAPP represent participants in the message board. SNAPP 2.1 also displays a timeline of the messages posted in the forum. The second tab shows each user's number of posts in SNAPP 1.5 and the main social network parameters (degree, in- and out-degree, betweenness and eigenvector centrality, and network density) in SNAPP 2.1. The third tab allows exporting the graph in GraphML and VNA formats in SNAPP 1.5, or writing annotations in SNAPP 2.1 (export capabilities are included in the first tab in SNAPP 2.1., in addition to the ability to export to Gephi's GEFX format).

Lack of applet updating causes SNAPP 2.1 to not work properly in latest versions of Moodle. Neither versions of SNAPP could be tested with the courses data for comparison. Furthermore, proper installation requires configuration of security exceptions in the Java Runtime Environment and connection to an external source to perform the analysis. The process of social graph construction includes loading and rendering of all the threads and posts in a message board, and parsing and processing of the HTML content.

More information on publications covering the use of SNAPP can be found at http://www.snappvis.org/?page_id=20

Forum Graph

Forum Graph[2] is provided as a report plug-in in Moodle's repository and creates the social graph of one single forum. The visualization of the resulting social graph only displays one possible representation of data, with node sizes representing user's number of posts, and edges representing the number of times a user replies to another user. The social graph can be exported as an SVG image. Additional information includes a tooltip showing the number of discussions initiated by each user,

[1] http://www.snappvis.org

[2] https://moodle.org/plugins/view/report_forumgraph

the number of replies a user has made, different colors for teachers and students, and direct access to each user's log in Moodle's Legacy Log (see section "Moodle Logs and Data Extraction and Visualization") by clicking on them. The plug-in also shows a list with the three top contributors to the forum. Despite its ease of installation, the visualization options of Forum Graph are very limited and may not be suitable for courses with high number of students (due to display size limitations). Furthermore, Forum Graph does not include any SNA tools or information about the main SNA parameters.

Meerkat-ED

Meerkat-ED[3] is a Java application developed by Reihaneh Rabbany that loads information about forums and posts from a Moodle backup file (.xml and .mbz files, depending on the version of Moodle; its use therefore requires that the user has course backup/restore permissions and a backup of the course), extracts the information, and then constructs the social graph. Meerkat-ED includes both social network analytics and discourse analytics capabilities.

Regarding social network analytics, Meerkat-ED gives information about students' posting activity (i.e., the "reply network" in Hernández-García et al., 2015) and their degree centrality, as well as basic modularity information (weakly connected components which indicate the existence of different communities). It also shows an additional graph that represents centrality over a target, with more central users nearest to the center of the target. Meerkat-ED provides basic node manipulation (dragging and selecting nodes, dragging the network and zooming). An interesting characteristic of Meerkat-ED is that it allows dynamic analysis of interactions by selecting the timespan and dragging a timeline.

As for discourse analytics capabilities, Meerkat-ED allows filtering by forum, discussion, and posts, and builds a network with the most used terms and their relations. Graphically, it shows all thread titles in nested mode, a graph depicting the relations between terms, a table with the number of occurrences of each term, and a cloud of the different terms.

SNA Tools

The main problem with built-in plug-ins like SNAPP and Forum Graph is that they provide little information other than visualization of the network topology, and therefore they are very limited in terms of social network analytics capabilities. Meerkat-ED can be considered an intermediate step that shows how external apps can improve analysis and visualization by separating the data layer from Moodle

[3] http://webdocs.cs.ualberta.ca/~rabbanyk/MeerkatED

logs and the process and presentation layer done in the application, with the added value of basic discourse analytics capabilities.

Nevertheless, although they may be suitable to view basic information about the social interactions that take place in forums on an LMS, these tools lack the advanced SNA capabilities and advanced graph interaction and filtering that are necessary for in-depth analysis and understanding about the social learning happening in a course. Furthermore, the three tools presented in this section allow users to observe the visible networks but, despite that data being available in the LMS, none of them provides any information about the invisible network of forum reading activity.

SNA software tools, on the other hand, are specifically designed to perform these tasks. There are many proprietary and open-source solutions available for general SNA that can help carrying out social learning analytics. However, despite their suitability for SNA, these systems also have some disadvantages:

- Because they are general purpose SNA applications, they may require some adaptation for social learning analytics purposes.
- Their functionality is restricted to the domain of SNA, and therefore their use may require some training for effective analysis. Moreover, while the concepts involved in the analysis are the same, the operation of each tool may be completely different from one application to another.
- Data from LMS and formal learning systems is stored in formats that are exclusive to each platform, and generally the design of the databases is not ready for SNA. Therefore, SNA of educational data from online platforms usually requires data extraction from LMS databases, and processing and transformation of the extracted data to a format readable by SNA programs.

Some authors advocate for the use of SNA tools for social learning analytics, but they also pinpoint the need for development of plug-ins that may translate the data from LMS to SNA applications (Amo Filvà, García-Peñalvo, & Alier Forment, 2014; Hernández-García, 2014). This study aims to cover this gap in the case of the open-source LMS platform Moodle by introducing GraphFES.

The main objective of GraphFES is to provide a data extraction layer that transforms data from Moodle to Gephi—an SNA program—for social learning analytics. Understanding the process of data transformation in GraphFES requires to study the data source system (Moodle logs), the data target system (Gephi) and the design and operation of the transformation tool (GraphFES).

Moodle Logs and Data Extraction and Visualization

Moodle has a built-in logging system that stores every user interaction with the LMS. LMS logging systems are a critical source of information for the purposes of analysis, study, and visualization of interactions—and, more specifically, the social interactions that take place in online education.

Despite registering all the learning platform's activity, earlier versions of Moodle did not retrieve enough information about the learning contexts of these interactions in the system logs, and they had performance and scalability issues. Driven by the emergence of learning analytics, Moodle version 2.6 introduced an enhanced version of the logging system that facilitates different kinds of analytics.

Moodle's new logging system has many benefits when compared to the legacy log system (Moodle, 2015). It captures richer information, abstracts log reading and writing for higher scalability, monitors gathered information and facilitates storage in external systems for analysis and visualization. Therefore, from version 2.6 onward there are three logging systems in Moodle: the new version, known as Standard Log; the old version, known as Legacy Log; and the External Log, which allows connection to an external log database.

Moodle uses the Events API and the Logging API to generate and store logging information. The Events API provides a notification and a unique event collection system for the different actions that users can perform in the LMS. The Logging API consists of different plug-ins for configuration, registration, and reporting of data triggered by the different events.

When a user performs an action in any module in Moodle, the system generates an event. The log manager listens to events and, depending on system configuration, determines whether to register and log the event or not. If the event must be registered, then the log manager passes the information to the plug-ins, and they store the information in the corresponding database table.

Data extraction, reporting and visualization, on the other hand, requires reading data from the tables storing that information. For example, Moodle's built-in activity report makes a query to the log manager to verify what kind of logs it can read, including data source selection when there is more than one source available. When the activity report module is granted access, it looks up the registered events and shows them on screen.

GraphFES is a web service and application that allows external queries to Moodle's Standard and Legacy logs. GraphFES is thereby a tool for generation of social graphs with data from forum activity in Moodle. Section "GraphFES: Design and Operation" later details how the design of such a tool requires development of a Moodle local extension implementing functions for external data extraction from requests to Moodle's log systems via a web service that uses the REST protocol. GraphFES, unlike SNAPP or Forum Graph, does not allow direct visualization of data in Moodle, and uses Gephi for data analysis and visualization. The next section presents Gephi and GEXF, Gephi's data format to represent and analyze social graphs.

Gephi: A Tool for Social Network Analysis

Data Format and Dataset Characteristics

As mentioned earlier, Gephi will handle the analysis and visualization of the social networks from interactions in Moodle message boards. The reason for the choice of Gephi is that it is a widely used open-source software program, with continued

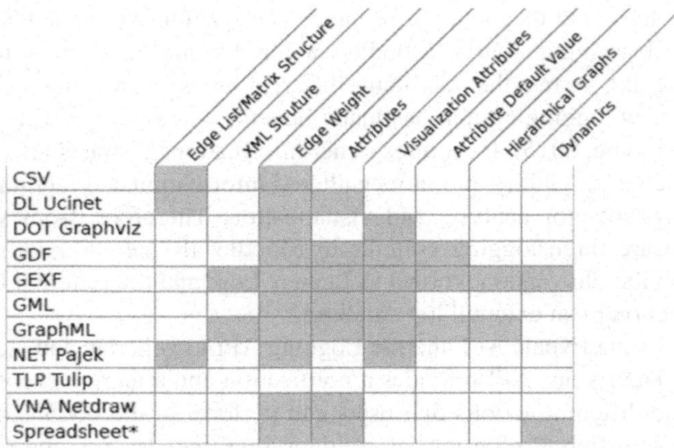

	Edge List/Matrix Structure	XML Structure	Edge Weight	Attributes	Visualization Attributes	Attribute Default Value	Hierarchical Graphs	Dynamics
CSV	■		■					
DL Ucinet	■		■	■				
DOT Graphviz			■	■				
GDF			■	■	■			
GEXF		■	■	■	■	■	■	■
GML			■	■	■			
GraphML		■	■	■	■	■		
NET Pajek	■		■					
TLP Tulip								
VNA Netdraw			■	■				
Spreadsheet*			■	■				■

Fig. 11.1 Comparison of formats supported in Gephi and their features (Gephi, 2015)

support and an active community. Furthermore, Gephi is oriented toward generic graph and social network analysis, and it can be easily extended to suit users' needs by installing NetBeans plug-ins. Gephi currently supports the following data formats (Gephi, 2015):

- GEXF (Graph Exchange XML Format)
- GUESS's GDF
- GML (Graph Modeling Language)
- GraphML (Graph Markup Language)
- Pajek's NET
- GraphViz DOT
- CSV (Comma Separated Variables)
- UCINET's DL
- Tulip's TPL
- Netdraw's VNA
- Spreadsheet (MS Excel and other programs)

The choice of the most adequate data format for GraphFES's output requires an analysis of Gephi's functionalities. Figure 11.1 shows a comparative table of the features of the different graph formats supported by Gephi. From Fig. 11.1, it is evident that GEXF has more features than the rest of formats. Furthermore, while other alternative and popular formats (UCINET DL, Pajek NET, GML, Netdraw VNA) are also compatible and supported by Gephi, their cross-compatibility is not as good (e.g., Pajek does not allow the use of attributes, and therefore it is only useful for analysis and visualization of network topologies). On the other hand, a complete analysis of the social graphs from course forums requires being able to collect additional data and incorporate them as extra information about nodes and edges. GEXF allows storing of this additional data as nodes' and edges' attributes, and therefore the choice of GEXF as data format is most likely the best fit to the characteristics of GraphFES.

Because it is XML (eXtensible Markup Language), GEXF is a consolidated, extensible, and open format. Another advantage derived from being an XML is that there are XML parsers available for all programming languages, allowing developers to process a GEXF file on practically any kind of application, regardless of the programming language or operating system it is coded in.

A GEXF definition of a graph consists of nodes, edges, and the data associated with them (GEXF Working Group, 2015). A very simple example of a graph in GEFX is the following:

Ex. 11.1 GEXF document of a simple graph

```
<?xml version="1.0" encoding="UTF-8"?>
    <gexf xmlns="http://www.gexf.net/1.2draft" version="1.2">
        <graph defaultedgetype="directed">
            <attributes class="node">
                <attribute id="0" title="username" type="string"/>
            </attributes>
            <nodes>
                <node id="0" label="NodeA">
                    <attvalues>
                        <attvalue for="0" value="John"/>
                    </attvalues>
                </node>
                <node id="1" label="NodeB">
                    <attvalues>
                        <attvalue for="0" value="Mark"/>
                    </attvalues>
                </node>
            </nodes>
            <edges>
                <edge id="0" source="0" target="1"/>
            </edges>
        </graph>
    </gexf>
```

The XML document above consists of a declaration of the document as GEXF (identified by its namespace), followed by the additional attributes for nodes and edges (in this case, only one additional attribute for nodes, with attribute id equal to 0 and attribute name equal to “username”). Then, the document lists the network

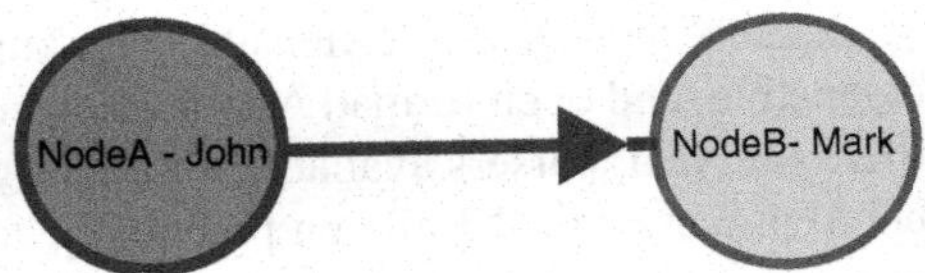

Fig. 11.2 Visual representation in Gephi of the graph from the GEXF file in Example 11.1

nodes (they include a node id and a label), including their attributes (in the example, the node with id=0 would have username="John" as attribute, and the username of the node with id=1 would be "Mark"). After all nodes have been listed, they are connected by declaring the edges, with their respective source and target nodes (the example only shows one edge connecting nodes 0 (labeled "NodeA" and with username "John") and 1 ("NodeB," "Mark"). Graphically, the visual representation of this document in Gephi would be the graph shown in Fig. 11.2.

GraphFES: Design and Operation

GraphFES as Web Service

GraphFES (Graph Forum Extraction Service) comprises two different elements: a local Moodle extension and a web application, and they serve two different purposes: data extraction and social graph building, respectively. Raw data extraction from the Moodle log tables requires the implementation of the functions that will be accessible via the web service and therefore needs to be managed by the local extension. The web application, on the other hand, serves as front-end and makes the requests to the web service in order to generate the different types of social graphs with the data it receives.

The local extension is programmed in PHP language (the same as Moodle), and its design follows the template for web service creation in Moodle. The local extension is therefore installed as a plug-in that implements two external functions (*forum_reportAllLegacy* and *forum_reportAll*). The reason to implement two functions instead of one is to ensure compatibility with both Moodle's legacy log table (*mdl_log*) and the new log table (*mdl_logstore_standard_log*). This guarantees that the web service may also be able to extract data from imported Moodle courses from versions 2.6 and lower that include log data. More specifically, the database queries made by these two functions are the following:

```
SELECT * FROM mdl_log WHERE module="forum" AND course=$courseids[0]
SELECT * FROM mdl_logstore_standard_log WHERE component="mod_
forum" AND courseid=$courseids[0]
```

The implementation of these two external functions in the internal plug-in makes the log data accessible to a web service owing to Moodle's Web services Application Program Interface (API). In order to access the data required to build the social graphs from Moodle logs, two additional operations must be performed in the

Table 11.1 Functions needed to create the web service

Function	Description
core_enrol_get_enrolled_users	Gets enrolled users by course id
core_course_get_courses	Returns course details
mod_forum_get_forums_by_courses	Returns a list of forum instances in a provided set of courses
mod_forum_get_forum_discussion_posts	Returns a list of forum posts for a discussion
local_graphfes_forum_reportAll	Full forum report
local_graphfes_forum_reportAllLegacy	Full forum report from legacy logs

Moodle platform: habilitation of the web service and activation of the REST protocol. These options appear in Moodle's administration menu, under the section "External services." In order to create the web service, it is necessary to create a new service with the functions indicated in Table 11.1.

The above operation activates the web service, but a complete setup also requires to manage access authorization. Administrators can grant authorization to individual users for using the web service in the "External services" menu, and they can then generate access tokens—if required—for authorized users in the "Manage tokens" section. In this version of GraphFES, generation of tokens is not necessary because the web application manages the authentication process after input of user login data (username and password).

The web application that serves as front-end and that builds the social graph is programmed in Node.js and the Express web framework. The combination of this programming language and the framework speeds up the development process and makes it simpler due to the high-speed of Node.js, which uses Google's JavaScript 8 engine. The use of JavaScript also allows developers to include different open-source libraries that facilitate the creation of the social graphs.

The main reason for the choice of a web application as front-end is that it facilitates the implementation of the application in any server, making it possible to access the application remotely with any browser. Additionally, it can also run locally in any computer. Besides, since the web application is programmed in Node.js, it is compatible with the most popular operating systems (Windows, Mac OS X and Linux, among others).

The structure followed by the web application follows the default generation structure of the Express framework. Apart from that, and because the role of the web application is not to store data but to request, structure, and transform them to a GEXF file in the faster and more effective way, no additional database is required.

Using GraphFES

This section details the design and operation of the web application and how it generates the different social graphs, step by step, and in a simple way. Once the application is loaded and the server is waiting for requests (users can do this locally by

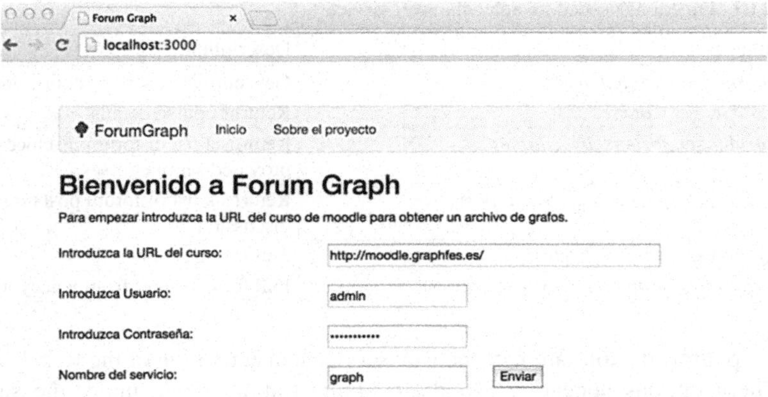

Fig. 11.3 Application main screen

running the main JavaScript file, app.js, with node from the command line), the application is accessible using any web browser (if run locally, the default access URL is http://localhost:3000). The main front-end screen asks the user to complete a form (Fig. 11.3). The different form fields are: URL of the Moodle platform, username, and password, and the name given to the web service in Moodle.

Upon introduction of the values for each field and form submission, the application sends a login request to the Moodle LMS. If successful, Moodle sends a token (the application will use this token for the different REST calls for data extraction) and the browser will redirect the user to a new screen for course selection that lists the courses to which the user has access. The data extraction process and the graphs generation start after selection of a course.

The process begins with a request to the function *core_enrol_get_enrolled_users* in order to retrieve the list of students enrolled in the course (this is important in order to also receive data from students who have no activity in the course) and another request to the function *mod_forum_get_forums_by_courses*. This function retrieves all the existing message boards in the course.

After having received this information, the application does the request for Moodle log forum data extraction. This request is done using the two functions implemented by the local extension (*local_graphfes_forum_reportAll* and *local_graphfes_forum_reportAllLegacy*) and it only retrieves log data related to forum activity. The application then differentiates between activities associated to discussion/post-creation and discussion/post-views. Additional data about users, posts, and discussions (e.g., user id, message content, timestamp) are also temporarily stored in memory in order to include richer information in the social graphs.

With all the different data, the application uses an open-source library (*element-tree*) that creates an XML document with three different social graphs, in a similar fashion to the datasets in Hernández-García (2014). The XML documents are already formatted in GEXF format and are stored in the graph folder of the application. The three different graphs correspond to the following files:

- *Views.gexf*: this graph shows the relations of messages viewed by course participants. In other words, it provides information about how many times user *a* has read a message posted by user *b*.
- *Replies.gexf*: it shows the connection between students based on who replies to whom, and how frequently.
- *Messages.gexf*: the graph shows the connection among messages (i.e., which message is a reply to another message).

In the Views and Replies graphs, each node corresponds to a course participant. Nodes in the Views graph includes information about user id and username as node attributes, while nodes in the Replies graph have additional information about user id, username, number of total posts, number of initial posts in a thread, and number of replies.

On the other hand, the Messages graph considers that each node is a message posted in one of the courses' forums. As with the two other two graphs, each node has additional information—as attributes—about:

- Name and id of the forum it was posted to.
- Post title and id.
- Message content.
- Post timestamp.
- Author's name and id.

Case Studies

In order to test the operation of GraphFES, data from two different courses were extracted from Moodle version 2.8.3. The original course data were collected from two different Moodle installations with versions lower than 2.6 and were then anonymized and restored to the Moodle 2.8.3 used to test the web service. Therefore, the original data were stored in the Legacy log, and activation of the Legacy log in the Moodle 2.8.3 was necessary. The following sections give an overview of the two courses and the results of the empirical analysis.

Context and Description of the Courses

The two courses chosen for the study were one online course from the Online Master's in Domotics and Digital Home, and an undergraduate programming course for first-year students of the Biotechnology degree at Universidad Politécnica de Madrid. There are two reasons for this choice of courses: first, there are many differences among them in terms of number of students, duration, forum use intensity, methodology, and instructional goals; the second reason is that the relatively low forum activity of the first course allowed us to easily and quickly test and compare that the output from GraphFES was correct, while the high forum activity in the second course allowed us to test the scalability of the web service (in addition, some course data was selected to check correct operation of GraphFES in this course, too). This data analysis will cover both courses, but it will focus primarily on the programming course due to the higher complexity of the resulting networks.

The online Master's course ("Socioeconomic analysis of the domotics and digital home environment," Course 1) is the first of eight mandatory courses of the Master's degree. Most of the students are architects and electrical and telecommunication engineers (i.e., there is an overall mixed background with regard to the use of information technologies). The course comprises two different modules, with 14 enrolled Spanish and South American students—in different locations—and a duration of 2 weeks. During those 2 weeks, students have access to the lectures' contents and to supplementary information and links, and they have to complete two quizzes and an individual and a group assignment based on a case study. Three different groups were formed for the group case study. There are five forums available for interaction (one debate and one teaching support forum per module, and a forum for the group assignment where students may only access and use their group's threads). Apart from the group assignment, students are expected to work individually.

The undergraduate course is "Programming Basics" (Course 2), a one-semester long mandatory course in the Biotechnology degree, with 110 students living in the Madrid area and that presumably share other in-class courses. Although there is an in-class two-hour-long introductory session, the whole course is based on project-based online teamwork, following the Comprehensive Training Model of the Teamwork Competence (CTMTC) (Leris, Fidalgo, & Sein-Echaluce, 2014).

The CTMTC has a strong focus on teamwork, and therefore students were distributed in 19 groups (with an average of six members in each team, a minimum of five members and a maximum of seven). The CTMTC determines five phases of the project, with three types of evidence for assessment along them: individual, group, and results (Fidalgo-Blanco et al., 2015). Assessment of the group and results is based on contributions to wikis and file-sharing services (e.g., Dropbox), upon which a grade is given to each group. The use of forums (there are Q&A, teaching support, and group forums) is a critical part of the instructional method because assessment of individual evidences is based on participation and contributions to the group forums. Students in this course are expected to build knowledge by working together on a project as a team.

Data Extraction

The total number of records related to forum activity is 1850 and 80185 for the first and second course, respectively. Processing times of GraphFES are almost instant for Course 1, and under 1 min for Course 2 (for comparison, Meerkat-ED cannot complete graph computation of Course 2). As expected, creation of the Views graph (the invisible or read network) takes most of this processing time because the

Fig. 11.4 Course 1: Initial resulting networks of Views (*left*), Replies (*center*), and Messages (*right*)

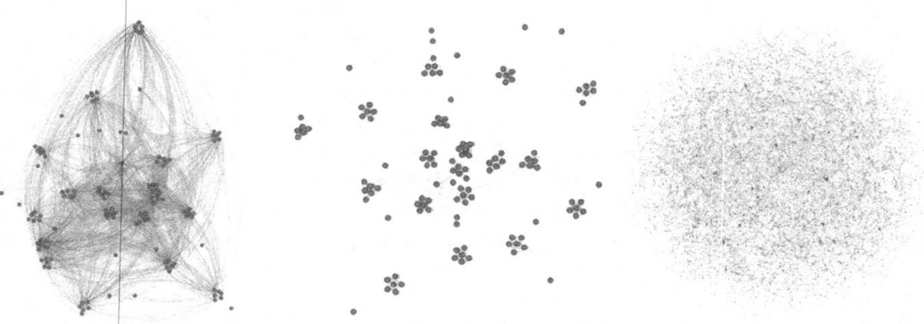

Fig. 11.5 Course 2: Initial resulting networks of Views (*left*), Replies (*center*), and Messages (*right*)

number of edges (relations) may grow exponentially as the number of posts increases—the number of edges in the Replies and Messages graphs is proportional to the number of users and messages posted, respectively.

After both sets of graphs are generated by GraphFES, data is ready for analysis in Gephi.

Initial Data Analysis

Figures 11.4 and 11.5 show the initial visualization of the resulting networks of Views, Replies, and Messages in Gephi after application of a Force Atlas 2 data transformation to Courses 1 and 2. Note that Fig. 11.4 shows a Radial Axis transformation of the Messages graph (right), as suggested by Hernández-García (2014), but in Fig. 11.5 (right) we use Force Atlas 2 due to the high number of nodes—Gephi cannot display more than 128 root nodes in the Radial Axis visualization. For comparison, Fig. 11.6 shows the Replies network of the two most active forums in courses 1 and 2 from Forum Graph, and Fig. 11.7 shows the Replies and Messages network of course 1 from Meerkat-ED.

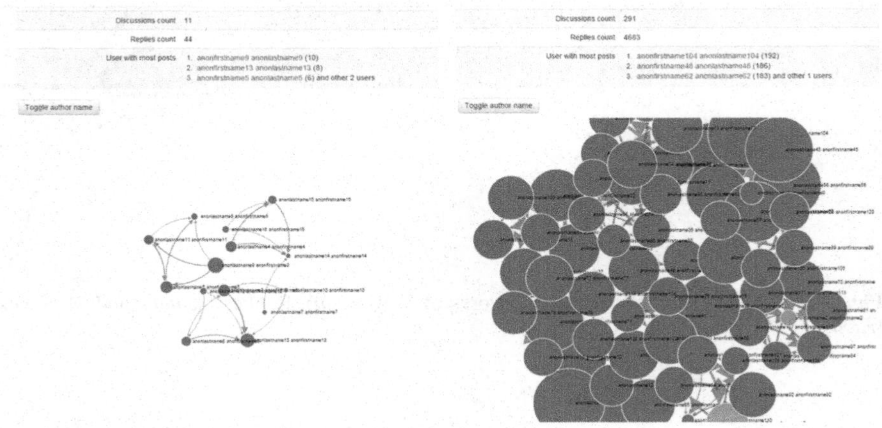

Fig. 11.6 Visualization of the Replies graph of the most active forum in courses 1 (*left*) and 2 (*right*) in Forum Graph

The visualizations depicted in Figs. 11.4 and 11.5 give some evident information about the different courses:

- As expected, the Views networks have a much higher number of connections than the Replies networks (passive versus active participation).
- The connections among students in course 2 reflect primarily intra-group communication (indicating that group members focus on the teamwork project), while course 1 shows more diverse exchanges among students (balancing individual and group-based learning).
- The Views and Replies networks in course 2 allow detection of isolated/disconnected students, who are not participating actively (Replies network) and/or passively (Views network) in the course.
- The Messages graph of course 1 shows which are the most active threads and posts within a thread, but there are simply too many messages in course 2 to perform a visual analysis.

Additionally, in the top-right part of the main window (not shown in Figs. 11.4 and 11.5), Gephi gives information about the number of nodes (users in Views and Replies networks and posts in the Messages graph) and edges (existing relations between nodes).

From Figs. 11.4, 11.5, 11.6, and 11.7, apparently Forum Graph and Meerkat-ED offer additional information when compared to Gephi, at least in course 1. However, none of the former two really provide much useful information about forum activity in course 2 (Meerkat-ED fails to load the course, and the graph nodes in Forum Graph are too cramped to extract any useful information). Furthermore, centrality values in Meerkat-ED are not weighed, and therefore it is difficult to retrieve information about which students are participating the most.

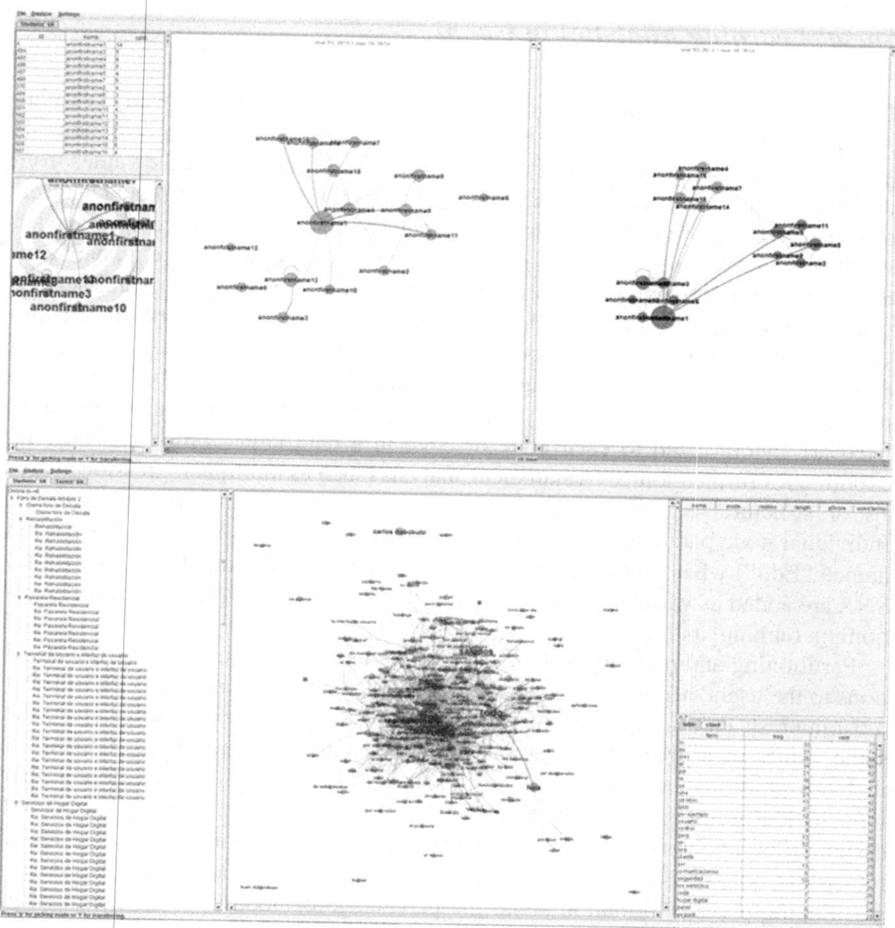

Fig. 11.7 Visualization of the Replies (*top*) and words in messages (*down*) of course 1 in Meerkat-ED

From the above, it would seem that existing tools have important limitations in order to perform successful and effective social learning analytics. However, this is where the additional features of specific SNA tools like Gephi shine and cover this gap, expanding social learning analytics capabilities. The most important features available in Gephi for these purposes, which allow creating more informative visualizations and will be covered in the following section, are:

- Calculation of SNA parameters
- Nodes' and edges' partitioning and ranking
- Filtering

Social Learning Analytics in Gephi

Calculation of SNA metrics and parameters—as in section "Social Learning Analytics," we refer to Hernández-García (2014; p. 156) for further information—is an essential part of social learning analytics for three reasons. First, the values from the analysis provide meaningful information that can be directly interpreted in terms of student participation, passive and active engagement (e.g., node centrality, edge weights in the Views and Replies networks), knowledge brokerage (e.g., betweenness centrality), leadership, authority or expertise (e.g., authority, pagerank, eigenvalue centrality), information collectors or hubs, and overall network information such as cohesion (e.g., density) or identification of communities (e.g., connected components, modularity, clustering). Second, the results of each analysis are incorporated to Gephi's data laboratory; this means that all the SNA parameters calculated are incorporated to each node or edge in a data table, which can later be exported for further non-SNA statistical analysis (such as multiple regression analysis or structural equation modeling) in other statistical software applications. Individual node parameters are also available in the information window (in a tab named "Edit") when a node is selected in the graph. Third, output variables of the SNA are added as variables to the main panel, and they become available for partitioning, ranking, and filtering.

Partitioning and ranking facilitate adaptation of the different network visualizations to the users' needs, by emphasizing aspects that the observer may consider of most interest. Partitioning assigns different colors to nodes or edges that share the same values of a given SNA parameter or node/edge attribute. Since GraphFES includes additional information about students and messages as node attributes, that information becomes already available for partition purposes, too (e.g., we could assign different colors to students with the same number of initial posts, replies or total posts, or to messages posted in the same forum or by the same user). Moreover, partitioning gives information about the percentage of nodes that are included in each partition.

Ranking is one of the most interesting features of Gephi, and it allows assigning different sizes and colors to nodes and edges, in adjustable scales, depending on the values of the chosen SNA parameter or attribute, or just to a range of them. Ranking is extremely useful because it gives a direct visual interpretation of the aspects of interest, both in absolute and relative terms. For example, ranking node size by weighed out-degree and node color by weighed in-degree on the Replies graph would provide information about who has written more (or less) posts and who has been replied most or least. Additionally, users can select whether they want to label nodes and edges with any SNA parameter and/or attribute.

Figure 11.8 shows how the selection of SNA parameters and attributes affects overall network configuration. On the left, node size ranking uses weighed out-degree, node color ranking uses weighed in-degree and nodes are labeled with the username. On the right, the only change is node size ranking criterion (betweenness centrality). The figure shows that, despite having written very few posts (small

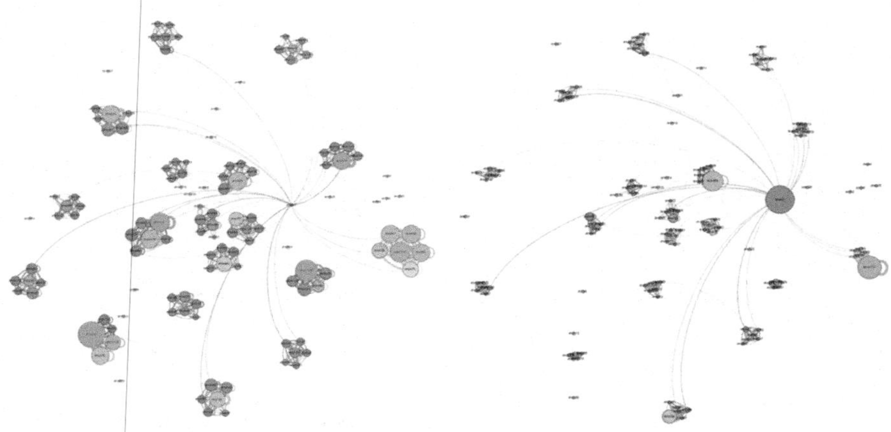

Fig. 11.8 Replies graph (course 2). Node size ranking by weighed out-degree (*left*) and betweenness centrality (*right*). Node color ranking by weighed in-degree (*grey* equals 0, higher in-degree from *red* to *green*)

size on the left) and received relatively few replies (red color on both), the teacher (user anon3) plays the main bridge or information broker in the course.

Filtering is also a powerful feature of Gephi. Filters are available as a tab in the main right panel. As said earlier, after computing the values of SNA metrics and parameters, Gephi makes them available for filtering—attributes are also initially available for filtering purposes.

The inclusion of attributes and SNA parameters for filtering vastly enhances the usefulness of SNA software programs like Gephi. By specifying different filters, users can visualize only relevant parts of the network, or analyze again the resulting networks including only the nodes or edges that fulfill the specified conditions. Depending on the type of variable, users have the option to apply many types of filters (partition, range, logical operations, dynamic processes, topology-related aspects such as levels of ego-networks, and even semantic web analysis via SPARQL queries if the attributes include semantic information). Interestingly, when a filter is applied, the data laboratory only shows information about the nodes and edges affected by the filter. Additionally, users can save simple and complex filters for later reuse.

While setting the appropriate filters for each class and instructional method may not be straightforward, some types of simple filters may provide lots of useful and actionable information. For example, in networks with high number of nodes, a partitioning filter of the Views and Replies graphs shows the students that have not read or written any messages (out-degree equal to zero, Fig. 11.9, left) or, in the Messages graph, which messages have not been answered yet (out- and in-degree equal to zero).

Filtering can be applied in successive stages. For example, after identification and selection of a potentially low-connected student, anon83 (Fig. 11.9, right), immediate node information is available in the upper left side. The student has in-

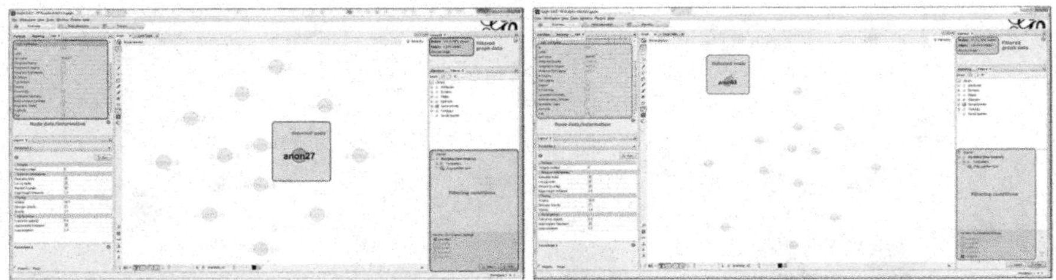

Fig. 11.9 Disconnected (*left*) and disconnected and low-connected (*right*) students in the Views graph

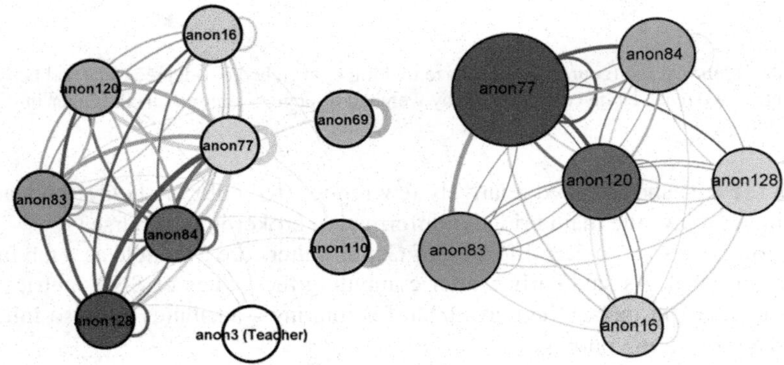

Fig. 11.10 Views (*left*) and Replies (*right*) first level ego networks of student *anon83*

degree of 7 and out-degree of 9. That means that he has only read messages from other nine people; he has read 5413 messages—above the network average—and his messages have been read 6077 times. Note that due to a limitation of Moodle logs, whenever a discussion is viewed, GraphFES considers that all the messages in the thread are viewed. Moreover, there is also information about node id; based on this information, the user can perform multiple other actions, such as further filtering to show the student's ego network, both in the Views and Replies graphs, to show whom the student is connected to (Fig. 11.10).

From Fig. 11.10, we observe that student anon83 has actually only read messages from other seven students (the other five students in his team and two students that do not belong to his team), the teacher and his own posts. Furthermore, edge thickness show that his reading has been focused on messages written by his teammates.

The above is just a simple example of how the use of SNA tools for visualization of learning networks can provide further insight and information about the dynamics of online learning. The example shows how social learning analytics and visualization of learning networks help identifying disconnected students, but also how it may offer additional information about learning agents (Figs. 11.9 and 11.10 show that student anon83, a potentially disconnected student, is just not engaged at course level but he is actively participating in the teamwork).

There are many other combinations of ranking and filtering from SNA that offer relevant information about the different social aspects of learning in online courses. For instance, we could have focused on identification of central learning agents (e.g., by making a deeper analysis of Fig. 11.8) or building of learning communities within the course (by analyzing modularity and weakly connected components of the networks, for example).

Nevertheless, and due to length limitation, the objective of this chapter is not an in-depth exploration of each of the possible uses of Gephi's features for social network analytics, but rather to show the potential of SNA tools to perform this type of analysis. Of course, the type of filters and analyses in Gephi with data from GraphFES should be tailored to the institution's and teachers' needs, taking into account that the type of course and instructional method also affect how the results may be interpreted.

This means that an institution-wide plan regarding social learning analytics strategies should be deployed in order to effectively define what ranking, partitioning, and filtering might be most useful for analysis, or what SNA parameter values might be used as learning indicators for successful learning.

Although we have already mentioned how Gephi may help extracting SNA parameters for ranking, partitioning, and filtering purposes, so far we have focused on the visual aspects of SNA tools for social learning analytics, paying little attention to the information that is directly available from SNA. The next section will give a brief outline of the SNA results for courses 1 and 2, and some possible interpretation from the values of SNA parameters.

SNA Parameters

Gephi incorporates different types of calculations of SNA metrics. Most analyses in Gephi occur in three steps: running the analysis (some additional parameters may be needed, such as specifying directed or undirected networks), HTML report of results (the reports generally include the main results and some graphics of distributions of SNA parameter values), and incorporation of the values to the data laboratory (and availability of SNA metrics for partitioning, ranking, and filtering). Both overall network and individual node SNA parameters can be calculated in the same operation (e.g., calculation of network diameter or average path length entails calculation of each node's eccentricity, and betweenness and closeness centralities). Table 11.2 gives an overview of the most relevant network parameters of Views, Replies, and Messages graphs of courses 1 and 2.

The parameters of the Views graph have useful information for instructors about the "invisible" network. In online learning, the average degree of the Views graph should ideally be as close as possible to the number of nodes in the network (this is the same as a network density of 1 or an average path length of 1). That would mean

Table 11.2 Main overall network metrics

	SNA metric	Views	Replies	Messages
Course 1	Nodes/edges	16/222	16/64	153/123
	Av. degree	13.88	4	0.8
	Av. weighed degree	348.31	7.69	0.8
	Av. path length	1.08	1.94	1.58
	Diameter	2	4	5
	Density	0.93	0.27	0.01
	Modularity	0.15	0.32	0.89
	Number of communities	2	2	32
	Weakly connected components	1	1	30
	Strongly connected components	2	1	153
Course 2	Nodes/edges	123/2854	123/662	9241/8604
	Av. degree	23.2	5.38	0.93
	Av. weighed degree	5100.43	69.95	0.93
	Av. path length	1.87	3.87	6.41
	Diameter	4	8	37
	Density	0.19	0.04	0
	Modularity	0.89	0.92	1
	Number of communities	31	33	637
	Weakly connected components	13	16	637
	Strongly connected components	15	29	9241

that every student would have read all the messages posted by his or her colleagues (including their own posts). Values lower than those indicate that: (1) there are students who have not posted any message; (2) there are students who are not reading other students' posts; or (3) there are students who are posting but their messages are not being read by their peers. Instructors may use this information to further inspect if any of these three scenarios is happening (e.g., looking for low values of node in- or out-degree). Course 1 should have both general and intra-group social interaction in forums, and the data confirms that there is high reading activity among students; in other words, most of the students are reading each other's messages, but not all. Further inspection of data shows that one student is not reading any messages and other student's posts have only been read by five of his peers. In course 2, the values are much lower. However, it must be noticed that most of the social exchanges in course 2 are focused on the group forums, and that each student has access only to the general forums and their own group forum. That is, unless a student posts a message to the general forum, his or her in-degree will not be higher than the number of group members plus the number of teachers; conversely, the maximum out-degree value will be equal to the number of group members plus the number of different students posting to the general forums. In these cases, modularity can be a more interesting parameter to observe because it gives information about how strong are the links within a given component (connected subgraph). The modularity in teamwork-intensive courses should be close to 1.

Parameters of the Replies graph show information about active interaction between students. In this graph, some of the overall network values may provide little information besides general activity. However, results of individual centrality metrics in this graph are critical for detection of relevant agents in the learning process (see, for example, Fig. 11.8). Besides this, it is also important to observe modularity values, as well as the number of communities, weakly and strong connected components to observe whether groups are cohesive and whether there may be disconnected students who are not actively engaging in the course.

Finally, parameters in the Messages graph offer relevant information about how active are the threads in a course. First, the number of nodes indicates the total number of messages, and the number of communities/weakly connected components correspond to the number of different threads—because different threads have no posts in common. Then, the average degree or weighed degree represents the number of initial posts that have been left unanswered. Interestingly, in course 1, 4 out of 5 initial posts received some answer; upon inspection in the data laboratory, most of the unanswered posts were tidbits of information left by the teacher. Course 2 had 125 (6.89 %) posts with no replies, 99 of which were posts to a forum used as an assignment repository. This information is useful for instructors to check whether there are unsolved questions in courses with high forum activity—and it can be further enhanced if they consider information about message timestamp to distinguish between older and newer posts.

Conclusion

Following higher education students' information consumption and learning habits, and in order to profit from the advantages offered by information technologies (wider audience reach, ubiquitous access or lower costs, among others), current educational trends are leaning toward ICT-based and ICT-supported learning methods and approaches.

In online learning, the use of information technologies is intensive, and the instructional methods tend to focus on empowering self-directed and social learning. As the complexity of courses and the number of students enrolled in a course increase, tracking students' progress becomes a titanic task for instructors. The data stored in formal learning environments' databases contain valuable information that can make instructor's job much easier. However, these data are available in raw format, and further processing is required in order to provide meaningful and actionable data about the courses and the social dynamics that are associated to them.

Learning analytics is a new discipline that covers the collection, analysis, and reporting of these data to improve the learning process. Within this discipline, some approaches have specifically focused on the analysis of the social interactions occurring in ICT-mediated learning using SNA techniques, in what has been named social learning analytics. While social learning analytics is a broad term that supports different perspectives, one of the main concerns of researchers and practitioners has been how to embed social learning analytics features in existing formal ICT-based learning environments.

Our approach to social learning analytics in this chapter has been different: following the idea that tools that are built to solve specific problems are more suitable to address them, we point to general purpose SNA tools as a better alternative for social learning analytics. The main problem for the use of these tools in ICT-supported educational contexts is that LMS log databases are not built with social learning relationships in mind.

Therefore, this chapter introduced GraphFES, a web service and application that extracts information about forum activity from Moodle and builds GEXF files that represent a graph of the resulting passive and active user interaction networks, as well as a graph of the relations among the messages exchanged in the course forums. These files can be later processed using general purpose SNA tools (e.g., Gephi) for social learning analytics.

Along the chapter, we described the functionality, design, and implementation of GraphFES, and we showed and illustrated with data from real courses some of the possibilities of Gephi for social learning analytics. The chapter did not aim, though, to fully explore the features and capabilities of Gephi as social learning analytics tool, but rather to show the potential of SNA tools for in-depth social learning analytics. Despite some progress in the discipline, social learning analytics is still mostly a blank canvas on which researchers are beginning to create a new type of paintings. Our effort in this chapter and the development of GraphFES would be just the equivalent of providing sketching pencils that are appropriate for these new drawing techniques.

Nonetheless, the development of such techniques will still require further research on the different topics that fall under the term social learning analytics. In our opinion, there are three main prospective lines that would contribute to radical improvement of social learning analytics.

First, the differences in course characteristics and pedagogical approaches make it very difficult to find general rules of application for successful SNA. Social learning analytics is a new discipline, and deeper investigation on relevant indicators and optimal SNA metrics' values for each type of course is encouraged. Even though the results from our case studies are not easily generalizable, throughout section "Case Studies" we have given some guidelines about how interpret the results of the analysis in Gephi of data delivered by GraphFES in two different contexts. We strongly believe that visualization of Moodle data in Gephi may help teachers to easily and rapidly detect disconnected and engaged students, especially in intensive teamwork or project-based learning, and that SNA metrics may help refine visual results with a higher degree of detail and facilitate complementary analysis for researchers. In this sense, GraphFES is just a tool that facilitates social learning analytics but, from a wider perspective, successful implementation of social network analytics across an institution requires not to consider social learning analytics as a convenient tool, but rather a part of an integral learning analytics strategy, taking into account the different learning methods and objectives.

Second, the potential of social learning analytics for the improvement of teaching and learning is enormous. However, the use of SNA tools is not simple or easy without some degree of training and understanding of the different concepts involved. There are three ways to circumvent this barrier: giving adequate training in SNA techniques to instructors and teachers, lowering entry barriers by providing teachers with basic training and a handful of useful predefined filters, and having a layer of advanced SNA users that can act as consulting advisors of teachers and help them get and understand the relevant information from the analysis of their courses. Considering the three options, the first one may be time- and cost-consuming, and thus institutions should consider a choice between the other two in their learning analytics strategy.

Third, the current initial version of GraphFES offers enough functionality for SNA of educational data, but further improvement of the tool is still possible. Future development of the tool is required to expand its capabilities, such as: collection of other information that might be of interest for researchers and practitioners, and integration of that information as node or edge attributes; transformation of temporal data—currently, only the timestamp of posted messages is collected—to build dynamic graphs that allow observation of changes in course dynamics—Gephi has the ability to build such timelines—; improved aggregation of semantic data about messages and their contexts to facilitate semantic analysis and discourse analytics; and finally, new versions of the tool should also take advantage of any new functions that may be added to Moodle's web service layer.

References

Amo Filvà, D., García-Peñalvo, F. J., & Alier Forment, M. (2014). Social network analysis approaches for social learning support. In *Proceedings of the Second International Conference on Technological Ecosystems for Enhancing Multiculturality (TEEM '14)* (pp. 269–274). New York: ACM.

Bandura, A. (1971). *Social learning theory*. New York: General Learning Press.

Barkley, E. F., Cross, K. P., & Major, C. H. (2005). *Collaborative learning techniques: A handbook for college faculty*. San Francisco, CA: Wiley.

Bastian, M., Heymann, S., & Jacomy, M. (2009). Gephi: An open source software for exploring and manipulating networks. In *Proceedings of the Third International ICWSM Conference* (pp. 361–362).

Beaudoin, M. F. (2002). Learning or lurking? Tracking the "invisible" online student. *The Internet and Higher Education, 5*(2), 147–155.

Berger, P. L., & Luckman, T. (1967). *The social construction of reality: A treatise in the sociology of knowledge*. Harmondsworth: Penguin.

Buckingham-Shum, S., & Ferguson, R. (2012). Social learning analytics. *Journal of Educational Technology & Society, 15*(3), 3–26.

De Laat, M., & Prinsen, F. (2014). Social learning analytics: Navigating the changing settings of higher education. *Research & Practice in Assessment, 9*, 51–60.

Edutechnica. (2015). *LMS Data–Spring 2015 Updates*. Retrieved from http://edutechnica.com/2015/03/08/lms-data-spring-2015-updates.

Fidalgo-Blanco, Á., Sein-Echaluce, M. L., García-Peñalvo, F. J., & Conde, M. Á. (2015). Using learning analytics to improve teamwork assessment. *Computers in Human Behavior, 47*, 149–156.

Freeman, L. C. (1979). Centrality in social networks: Conceptual clarification. *Social Networks, 1*(3), 215–239.

Gephi. (2015). *Supported Graph Formats*. Retrieved from http://gephi.github.io/users/supported-graph-formats.

GEXF Working Group. (2015). *GEXF File Format*. Retrieved from http://gexf.net/format.

Hernández-García, Á. (2014). Usare Gephi per visualizzare la partecipazione nei corsi online: Un approccio di social learning analytics. *Tecnologie Didattiche, 22*(3), 148–156.

Hernández-García, Á., & Conde, M. Á. (2014). Dealing with complexity: Educational data and tools for learning analytics. In *Proceedings of the Second International Conference on Technological Ecosystems for Enhancing Multiculturality (TEEM '14)* (pp. 263–268). New York: ACM.

Hernández-García, Á., González-González, I., Jiménez-Zarco, A. I., & Chaparro-Peláez, J. (2015). Applying social learning analytics to message boards in online distance learning: A case study. *Computers in Human Behavior, 47*, 68–80.

Hmelo-Silver, C. E., & Barrows, H. S. (2008). Facilitating collaborative knowledge building. *Cognition and Instruction, 26*, 48–94.

Lave, J., & Wenger, E. (1991). *Situated learning: Legitimate peripheral participation*. Cambridge: Cambridge University Press.

Leris, D., Fidalgo, Á., & Sein-Echaluce, M. L. (2014). A comprehensive training model of the teamwork competence. *International Journal of Learning and Intellectual Capital, 11*, 1–19.

Long, P., & Siemens, G. (2011). Penetrating the fog: Analytics in learning and education. *EDUCAUSE Review, 46*(5), 31–40.

Macfadyen, L., & Dawson, S. (2012). Numbers are not enough. Why e-learning analytics failed to inform an institutional strategic plan. *Journal of Educational Technology & Society, 15*(3), 149–163.

Moodle. (2015). *Logging 2*. Retrieved from https://docs.moodle.org/dev/Logging_2.

Oshima, J., Oshima, R., & Matsuzawa, Y. (2012). Knowledge building discourse explorer: A social network analysis application for knowledge building discourse. *Educational Technology Research and Development, 60*(5), 903–921.

Reffay, C., & Chanier, T. (2003). How Social Network Analysis can help to Measure Cohesion in Collaborative Distance-Learning. In B. Wasson, S. Ludvigsen, & U. Hoppe (Eds.), *Designing for Change in Networked Learning Environments: Proceedings of the International Conference on Computer Support for Collaborative Learning 2003* (pp. 343–352). Dordrecht: Springer Netherlands.

Wise, A. F., & Hausknecht, S. N. (2013). Learning analytics for online discussions: A pedagogical model for intervention with embedded and extracted analytics. In *Proceedings of the Third International Conference on Learning Analytics and Knowledge (LAK '13)* (pp. 48–56).

Zhao, K., & Chan, C. K. K. (2014). Fostering collective and individual learning through knowledge building. *International Journal of Computer-Supported Collaborative Learning, 9*(1), 63–95.

Chapter 12
Toward an Open Learning Analytics Ecosystem

Mohamed Amine Chatti, Arham Muslim, and Ulrik Schroeder

Abstract In the last few years, there has been a growing interest in learning analytics (LA) in technology-enhanced learning (TEL). LA approaches share a movement from data to analysis to action to learning. The TEL landscape is changing. Learning is increasingly happening in open and networked learning environments, characterized by increasing complexity and fast-paced change. This should be reflected in the conceptualization and development of innovative LA approaches in order to achieve more effective learning experiences. There is a need to provide understanding into how learners learn in these environments and how learners, educators, institutions, and researchers can best support this process. In this chapter, we discuss open learning analytics as an emerging research field that has the potential to deal with the challenges in open and networked environments and present key conceptual and technical ideas toward an open learning analytics ecosystem.

Keywords Learning analytics • Educational data mining • Open learning analytics • Ecosystem • Personalization • Learning as a network • Lifelong learning

Introduction

In recent years, learning analytics has attracted a great deal of attention in technology-enhanced learning (TEL) research as practitioners, institutions, and researchers are increasingly seeing the potential that learning analytics has to shape the future TEL landscape. Learning analytics represent the application of "big data" and analytics in education (Siemens et al., 2011). Generally, learning analytics deals with the development of methods that harness educational datasets to support the learning process.

In the past few years, the discussion about technologies for learning has moved away from only institutionally managed systems (e.g., LMS) to open and networked learning environments (e.g., PLE, MOOC) (Chatti, 2010). In fact, learning is

M.A. Chatti (✉) • A. Muslim • U. Schroeder
Informatik 9 (Learning Technologies), RWTH Aachen University, Aachen, Germany
e-mail: chatti@informatik.rwth-aachen.de

B. Kei Daniel (ed.), *Big Data and Learning Analytics in Higher Education*,
DOI 10.1007/978-3-319-06520-5_12

increasingly distributed across space, time, and media. Consequently, a large volume of data—referred to as big data—about learners and learning is being generated. This data mainly traces that learners leave as they interact with increasingly complex and fast-changing learning environments.

The abundance of educational data and the recent attention on the potentiality of efficient infrastructures for capturing and processing big data have resulted in a growing interest in big learning analytics among researchers and practitioners (Dawson, Gašević, Siemens, & Joksimovic, 2014). Big learning analytics refers to leveraging big data analytics methods to generate value in TEL environments (Chatti et al., 2014). Harnessing big data in the TEL domain has enormous potential. Learning analytics stakeholders have access to a massive volume of data from learners' activities across various learning environments which, through the use of big data analytics methods, can be used to develop a greater understanding of the learning experiences and processes in the new networked learning environments.

The research field of learning analytics is constantly developing new ways to analyze educational data. However, most of the learning analytics approaches to date are restricted to analytics tasks in a narrow context within specific research projects and centralized learning settings. Little research has been conducted so far to understand how learners learn in today's open and networked learning environments and how learners, educators, institutions, and researchers can best support this process. Operating in these environments requires a shift toward learning analytics on more challenging datasets across a variety of different sites with different standards, owners, and levels of access (Ferguson, 2012; Fournier, Kop, & Sitlia, 2011) by applying mixed-method approaches to address a wide range of participants with diverse interests, needs, and goals. Further, there is a need for a new learning analytics model as an ongoing process across time and environments, where everyone can be producer and consumer of the learning analytics exercise.

A central aspect of this discussion is the concept of open learning analytics. Siemens et al. (2011) provide an initial proposal expressing the importance of an integrated and modularized platform to integrate heterogeneous learning analytics techniques. The concept of open learning analytics represents a significant shift toward a new learning analytic model that takes "openness" into account. This leads to questions about how should "open" be interpreted in relation to learning analytics? What are the challenges in open learning analytics? What are the components of an open learning analytics ecosystem? What are the requirements for an effective open learning analytics platform? What are the technical details (i.e., architecture and modules) of an open learning analytics platform?

In this chapter, we address these questions and present the theoretical, conceptual, and technical details toward an open learning analytics ecosystem that aims at supporting learning and teaching in fragmented, diverse, and networked learning environments. Research on open learning analytics is still in the early stages of development. Our endeavor is to foster a common understanding of key conceptual and technical ideas in this research area that will support communication between researchers and practitioners as they seek to address the various challenges and opportunities in this emerging field toward sustainable practical open learning analytics.

Learning Analytics

Different definitions have been provided for the term learning analytics (LA). The most commonly cited definition of learning analytics which was adopted by the first international conference on learning analytics and knowledge (LAK11) is "the measurement, collection, analysis and reporting of data about learners and their contexts, for purposes of understanding and optimizing learning and the environments in which it occurs" (as cited in Siemens & Long, 2011, section "Learning Analytics," para. 2). Ferguson (2012) and Clow (2013) compile a list of LA definitions and provide a good overview on the evolution of LA in recent years. Although different in some details, LA definitions share an emphasis on converting educational data into useful actions to foster learning. Furthermore, it is noticeable that these definitions do not limit LA to automatically conducted data analysis. In this chapter, we view LA as a TEL research area that focuses on the development of methods for analyzing and detecting patterns within data collected from educational settings and leverages those methods to support the learning experience.

Learning analytics is not a genuine new research area. It reflects a field at the intersection of numerous academic disciplines (e.g., learning science, pedagogy, psychology, Web science, computer science) (Dawson et al., 2014). It borrows from a variety of related fields (e.g., academic analytics, action analytics, educational data mining, recommender systems, personalized adaptive learning) and synthesizes several existing techniques (e.g., machine learning, data mining, information retrieval, statistics, and visualization) (Chatti et al., 2014; Ferguson, 2012).

Chatti, Dyckhoff, Thüs, and Schroeder (2012) and Chatti et al. (2014) provide a systematic overview on LA and its key concepts through a reference model based on four dimensions. The authors further build on this model to identify a series of challenges and develop a number of insights for LA research in the future. As depicted in Fig. 12.1, the four dimensions of the proposed model are:

- **What?** What kind of *data* does the system gather, manage, and use for the analysis? This dimension refers to the data used in the LA task. It also refers to the *environments* and *contexts* in which learning occurs. Educational data comes from formal as well as informal learning channels. It can also come in different formats, distributed across space, time, and media.
- **Who?** Who is targeted by the analysis? The application of LA can be oriented toward different *stakeholders*, including students, teachers, (intelligent) tutors/mentors, educational institutions (administrators and faculty decision-makers), researchers, and system designers with different perspectives, goals, and expectations from the LA exercise.
- **Why?** Why does the system analyze the collected data? There are many *objectives* in LA according to the particular point of view of the different stakeholders. Possible objectives of LA include monitoring, analysis, prediction, intervention, tutoring/mentoring, assessment, feedback, adaptation, personalization, recommendation, awareness, and reflection.

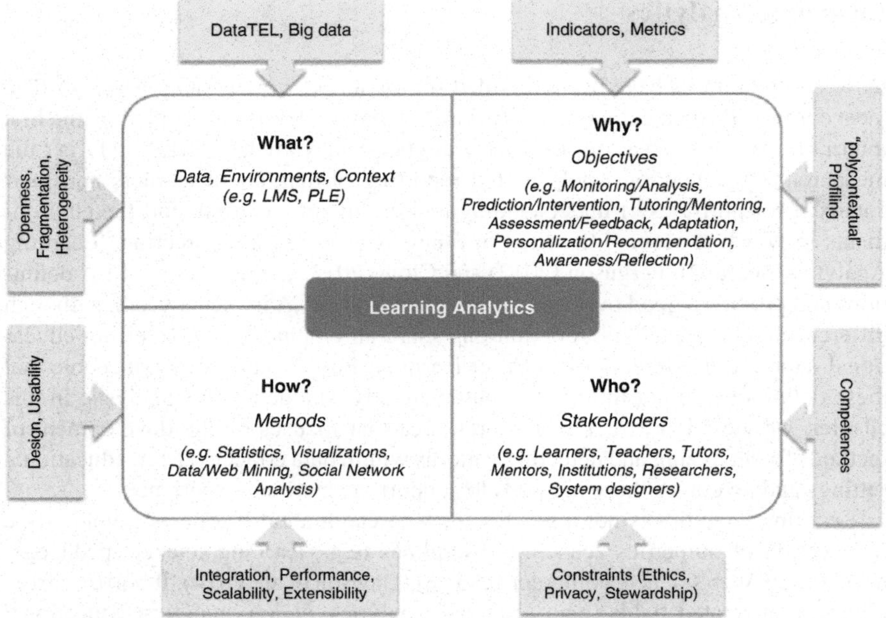

Fig. 12.1 Learning analytics reference model (Chatti et al., 2014)

- **How?** How does the system perform the analysis of the collected data? LA applies different *methods* to detect interesting patterns hidden in educational datasets. Possible methods include statistics, information visualization (IV), data mining (DM), and social network analysis (SNA).

Open Learning Analytics

A particularly rich area for future research is open learning analytics. The concept of open learning analytics was introduced in 2011 by a group of leading thinkers on LA in an initial vision paper published by the Society for Learning Analytics Research (SoLAR) (Siemens et al., 2011). A first summit was then held in Indianapolis, Indiana in March 2014 to promote networking and collaborative research and "to bring together representatives from the learning analytics and open source software development fields as a means to explore the intersection of learning analytics and open learning, open technologies, and open research" (Alexander et al., 2014). This summit initiated discussion toward the idea of open learning analytics as a conceptual and technical framework around which different stakeholders could network and share best practices. From a technical perspective, the summit focused on open system architectures and how open source communities can provide new open source learning analytics services and products. Building on the first summit, the Learning Analytics Community Exchange (LACE) project organized in December 2014 the Open Learning Analytics Network Summit Europe to develop a shared European perspective on the concept of an open learning analytics framework (Cooper, 2014a). Sclater (2014) provides a good summary of this summit. He notes that the most obvious aspect of open in the context of learning analytics is the reuse of code and predictive models.

So far, from the initial vision paper through the last summit, the development of the concept of open learning analytics was restricted to a discussion on the need for open source software, open standards, and open APIs to address the interoperability challenge in this field as well as how important tackling the ethical and privacy issues is becoming for a wide deployment of LA. The concept of open learning analytics is, however, still not well defined and concrete conceptual and development plans are still lacking. Several important questions remained unanswered. These include:

- How should "open" be interpreted in relation to learning analytics?
- How can open learning analytics be leveraged to foster personalized, networked, and lifelong learning?
- What are the challenges in open learning analytics in addition to interoperability and privacy?
- What are the components of an open learning analytics ecosystem?
- What are concrete user and system scenarios that an open learning analytics platform should support?
- What are the requirements for an effective open learning analytics platform?
- What are the technical details (i.e., architecture and components) of an open learning analytics platform?

In the next sections, we attempt to give answers to these questions. We start by providing a clarification of the term open learning analytics and then present the conceptual and technical details toward an open learning analytics ecosystem.

What is open learning analytics? The term "openness" has received a great deal of attention from TEL community, due to the growing demand for self-organized, networked, and lifelong learning opportunities. "The two most important aspects of openness have to do with free availability over the Internet and as few restrictions as possible on the use of the resource, whether technical, legal or price barriers" (OECD, 2007, p. 32). According to Wiley (2009), at its core, openness is sharing and education is a relationship of sharing. Open education has been evolving over the past century (McNamara, 2012). From the late nineteenth century and during the twentieth century, open education has been explored in the development of distance education along with other open learning initiatives, such as the open classroom, open schooling, and the open university (Peters, 2008). Open educational resources (OER) and open courseware (OCW) represent a further important advancement in the open education movement over the past decade (Downes, 2007; McNamara, 2012). With the introduction of the Massive Open Online Course (MOOC) term in 2008, MOOCs have been in the forefront of the open education movement. MOOCs have been considered as an evolution of OER and OCW (Yuan & Powell, 2013).

Driven by the different perspectives on openness as discussed in the literature on open education, OER, OCW, and MOOCs, several suggestions can be made as to how "open" should be interpreted in relation to learning analytics.

- **Open learning** by providing understanding into how learners learn in open and networked learning environments and how learners, educators, institutions, and researchers can best support this process (Chatti et al., 2014).
- **Open practice** that gives effect to a participatory culture of creating, sharing, and cooperation.
- **Open architectures, processes, modules, algorithms, tools, techniques, and methods** that can be used by following the four R's "Reuse, Redistribute, Revise, Remix" (Wiley, 2009; Hilton et al., 2010). Everyone should have the freedom to use, customize, improve, and redistribute the entities above without constraint.
- **Open access** to learning analytics platforms granted to different stakeholders without any entry requirements in order to promote self-management and creativity.
- **Open participation** in the LA process by engaging different stakeholders in the LA exercise. Daniel and Butson (2014) state that in LA, "there is still a divide between those who know how to extract data and what data is available, and those who know what data is required and how it would best be used" (p. 45). Therefore, it is necessary to bring together different stakeholders to work on common LA tasks in order to achieve useful LA results. Further, it is essential to see learners as the central part of the LA practice. This means that learners should be active collaborators, not just mere data subjects (Sclater, 2014) and recipients of interventions and services (Slade & Prinsloo, 2013). Learner and teacher involvement is the key to a wider user acceptance, which is required if LA tools are to serve the intended objective of improving learning and teaching.
- **Open standards** "to reduce market fragmentation and increase the number of viable products" (Cooper, 2014a). Open standards and specifications can help to realize the benefits of better interoperability (Cooper, 2014b).
- **Open Research** and **Open science** (Fry et al., 2009) based on **open datasets** with legal protection rules that describe how and when the dataset can be used (Verbert et al., 2012). Sclater (2014) points out that datasets "from one environment can be connected to that in another one, not only across the different systems in one institution but potentially with other institutions too." Following an open dataset approach, a group of interested researchers started an initiative around "dataTEL". The main objective was to promote exchange and interoperability of educational datasets (Duval, 2011; Verbert et al., 2011). Examples of open datasets include PSLC datashop as a public data repository that enables sharing of large learning datasets (Koedinger et al., 2010).
- **Open learner modeling** based on user interfaces that enable refection, planning, attention, and forgetting and that can be accessed by learners to control, edit, update, and manage their models (Kay & Kummerfeld, 2011). This is important to build trust and improve transparency of the LA practice.
- **Open assessment** to help lifelong learners gain recognition of their learning. Open assessment is an agile way of assessment where anyone, anytime,

anywhere, can participate toward the assessment goal. It is an ongoing process across time, locations, and devices where everyone can be assessor and assessee (Chatti et al., 2014).

The concept of open learning analytics covers all the aspects of "openness" outlined above. It refers to an ongoing analytics process that encompasses diversity at all four dimensions of the reference model introduced in section "Learning Analytics":

- What? It accommodates the considerable variety in learning data, environments, and contexts. This includes data coming from traditional education settings (e.g., LMS) and from more open-ended and less formal learning settings (e.g., PLE, MOOC, social web).
- Who? It serves different stakeholders with very diverse interests and needs.
- Why? It meets different objectives according to the particular point of view of the different stakeholders.
- How? It leverages a plethora of statistical, visual, and computational tools, methods, and methodologies to manage large datasets and process them into indicators and metrics which can be used to understand and optimize learning and the environments in which it occurs.

Open Learning Analytics Platform

The aim of open learning analytics is to improve learning efficiency and effectiveness in lifelong learning environments. In order to understand learning and improve the learning experience and teaching practice in today's networked and increasingly complex learning environments, there is a need to scale LA up which requires a shift from closed LA tools and systems to LA ecosystems and platforms where everyone can contribute and benefit.

An open learning analytics ecosystem encompasses different stakeholders associated through a common interest in LA but with diverse needs and objectives, a wide range of data coming from various learning environments and contexts, as well as multiple infrastructures and methods that enable to draw value from data in order to gain insight into learning processes.

In the following sections, we provide our vision for an open learning analytics platform through a detailed discussion of possible user scenarios, requirements, technical architecture, and components. Our goal is to form the technical foundation of an ecosystem for open learning analytics.

User Scenarios

This section presents three possible user scenarios that the open learning analytics platform will support.

Teacher Scenario

Rima is a lecturer at ABC University where she uses the university LMS to administer her courses. She uses personalized dashboard of the open learning analytics platform which gives her an overview of her courses using various indicators to augment and improve her teaching process. On the dashboard, she has various predefined indicators such as participation rate of students in lecture, students' involvement rate in discussion forum, most viewed/downloaded documents, and the progress of her students in assignments.

Recently, Rima came up with the requirement to see which learning materials are more discussed in discussion forums. She looked in the list of available indicators but did not find any indicator which can fulfill this requirement. She opened the indicator editor which helps her in generating the new indicator and defining the appropriate visualization for this indicator. The newly generated indicator is also added to the list of available indicators for future use by other users.

Student Scenario

Amir is a computer science student at ABC University. He is interested in web technologies. He uses the open learning analytics platform to collect data from his learning activities related to this subject on the university LMS, the edX MOOC platform, Khan Academy, his blog, Facebook, YouTube, Slideshare, and various discussion forums.

What Amir likes most about the open learning analytics platform is that it provides him the possibility to select which learning activities from which application can be collected in his profile. For Amir privacy is one of the big concerns. By default all the logged activity data are only available to him. He has, however, the option to specify which data will be publicly available to whom and for how long.

Amir is interested in monitoring his performance across the different platforms. He uses the indicator editor to generate a new indicator which aggregates marks from the university LMS, the peer-review feedback from the edX MOOC platform, and open badges from Kahn Academy. He specifies to visualize his marks compared to his peers as a line chart, his peer-review feedback in a textual format, and his badges as a list view. The platform then generates the visualization code that Amir can embed in the assessment module of the university LMS. Further, Amir is interested in getting recommendations related to web technologies in the form of lecture slides, videos, online articles, blog posts, and discussion forums. He generates a new indicator which recommends him learning resources from different sources. He then embeds the generated indicator in the learning materials module of the university LMS.

Developer Scenario

Hassan is a researcher at ABC University. He developed a mobile application for collaborative annotation of lecture videos. He is interested in using the open learning analytics platform to analyze the social interactions of the application's users. Based on the data model specification and guidelines provided by the open learning analytics platform, he develops a new collector to collect activity data from his mobile application and send it to the platform. Further, he uses the indicator editor to define a new indicator which should apply the Gephi social network analysis method on the collected data. Unfortunately, this method is not available in the platform yet. Therefore, he uses the platform API to register Gephi as a new analysis method. Hassan goes back to the indicator editor and selects the newly registered analysis method to be applied in his indicator.

Requirements

Open learning analytics is a highly challenging task. It introduces a set of requirements and implications for LA practitioners, developers, and researchers. In this section, we outline possible requirements which would build the foundation for an open learning analytics platform.

Data Aggregation and Integration

As pointed out in the "what?" dimension of the LA reference model in section "Learning Analytics," educational data is distributed across space, time, and media. A key requirement here is to aggregate and integrate raw data from multiple, heterogeneous sources, often available in different formats to create a useful educational dataset that reflects the distributed activities of the learner; thus leading to more precise and solid LA results.

Interoperability

The heterogeneity of data must be reduced to increase interoperability. Interoperability addresses the challenge of efficiently and reliably moving data between systems (Cooper, 2014b). A widely used definition of interoperability is the "ability of two or more systems or components to exchange information and to use the information that has been exchanged" (Benson, 2012, p. 21; Cooper, 2013). Interoperability benefits include efficiency and timeliness, independence, adaptability, innovation and market growth, durability of data, aggregation, and sharing

(Cooper, 2014b). Interoperability is needed to do comparable analyzes (Daniel & Butson, 2014) and test for broader generalizations, for instance, whether a predictive model is still reliable when used in a different context (Romero & Ventura, 2013).

Specifications and Standards

It is important to adopt widely accepted specifications and standards in order to achieve interoperability of datasets and services. LA has stimulated standardization activities in different consortia, organizations, bodies, and groups, resulting in a number of specifications and standards that could be adopted or adapted for LA (Hoel, 2014). There are numerous existing specifications and standards that contribute elements of interoperability (Cooper, 2014b). Cooper (2014c) provides a technical-level summary of the range of existing work, which may be relevant to LA system developers. The summary lists specifications and standards related to data exchange (e.g., ARFF, CSV, GraphML), models and methods (e.g., PMLL), logging (e.g., Activity Streams, CAM, xAPI), assessment (e.g., IMS QTI, Open Badges), and privacy (e.g., UMA).

As stated by Cooper (2014c) and Hoel (2014), there is no organized attempt to undertake prestandardization work in the open learning analytics domain yet. Currently, there is only preliminary work to raise awareness of existing technical specifications and standards that may be of relevance to implementations of open learning analytics. None of the available specifications are fit for use as they stand. It is expected that the focus of activity in the near future is likely to be sharing experiences in using various candidate specifications and standards, and tentatively moving toward a set of preferred specifications and standards to be used in open learning analytics practices.

Reusability

It is necessary to follow the four R's "Reuse, Redistribute, Revise, Remix" in the conceptualization and development of open learning analytics architectures. Adopting agreed upon specifications and standards would promote the reuse of data, services, and methods which is of vital practical importance in open learning analytics.

Modularity

An open learning analytics model requires new architectures that make it easy to accommodate new components developed by different collaborators in order to respond to changes over time. A modular and service-oriented approach enables a faster, cheaper, and less disruptive adaptability of the open learning analytics architecture. This is particularly relevant for LA where the methods are not yet mature (Cooper, 2014b).

Flexibility and Extensibility

Daniel and Butson (2014) note that the best platforms harnessing the power of big data are flexible. "They also blend the right technologies, tools, and features to turn data compilation into data insight" (p. 41). Thus, an open learning analytics platform should be fully flexible and extensible by enabling a smooth plug in of new modules, methods, and data after the platform has been deployed.

Performance and Scalability

Performance and scalability should be taken into consideration in order to allow for incremental extension of data volume and analytics functionality. This is a technical requirement which can be achieved by leveraging big data solutions which provide powerful platforms, techniques, and tools used for collecting, storing, distributing, managing, and analyzing large datasets with diverse structures such as Apache Hadoop, MapReduce, NoSQL databases, and Tableau Software (Daniel & Butson, 2014).

Usability

For the development of usable and useful LA tools, guidelines and design patterns should be taken into account. Appropriate visualizations could make a significant contribution to understanding the large amounts of educational data. Statistical, filtering, and mining tools should be designed in a way that can help learners, teachers, and institutions to achieve their analytics objectives without the need for having an extensive knowledge of the techniques underlying these tools. In particular, educational data mining tools should be designed for nonspecialists in data mining (Romero and Ventura, 2010).

Privacy

It is crucial to build ethics and privacy into the LA solutions right from the very beginning. As Larry Johnson, CEO of the New Media Consortium (NMC) puts it "Everybody's talking about Big Data and Learning Analytics, but if you don't solve privacy first it is going to be killed before it has really started" (as cited in Bomas, 2014).

Transparency

Data and interpretations in LA might be used in other than the intended ways. For instance, learners might fear that personal data will not be used for constructive feedback but for monitoring and grading. This could lead to the unintended effect that learners are not motivated to use LA tools and participate in analytics-based

TEL scenarios. Transparency is vital to drive forward the acceptance of LA. It provides an explicit definition of means how to achieve legitimacy in the process of learning analytics. It should be applied across the complete process, without exceptions. This means that at all times, there should be easily accessible and detailed documentation of how is the data collected, who has access to the data, which analytics methods are applied to the data, how long is the data valid and available, the purposes for which the data will be used, under which conditions, and which measures are undertaken to preserve and protect the identity of the learner (Bomas, 2014; Chatti et al., 2014; Pardo & Siemens, 2014; Sclater, 2014; Slade & Prinsloo, 2013). Further, it is important to increase institutional transparency by clearly demonstrating the changes and the added value that LA can help to achieve (Daniel & Butson, 2014; Dringus, 2012).

Personalization

It is important to follow a personalized and goal-oriented LA model that tailors the LA task to the needs and goals of multiple stakeholders. There is a need to adopt a user-in-the-loop LA approach that engages end users in a continuous inquiry-based LA process, by supporting them in setting goals, posing questions, interacting with the platform, and self-defining the indicators that help them achieve their goals.

Conceptual Approach

In the following sections, we discuss in detail the building blocks of an open learning analytics platform, as depicted in Fig. 12.2.

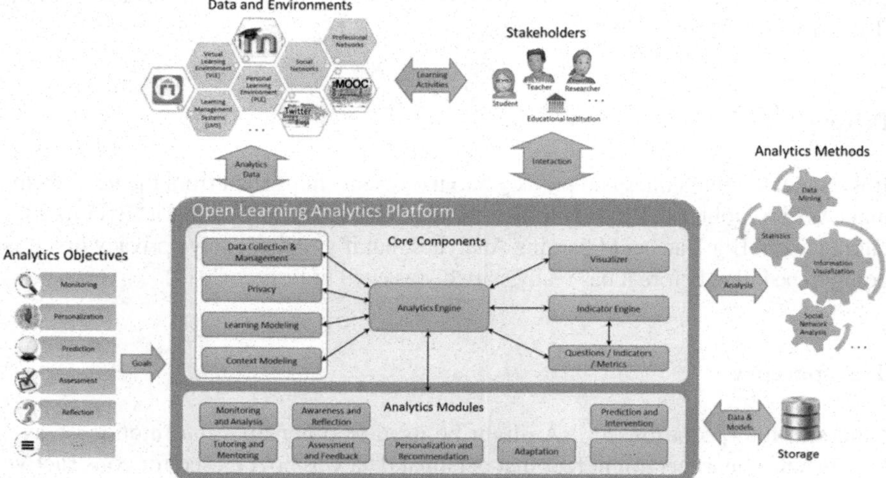

Fig. 12.2 Open learning analytics platform abstract architecture

Data Collection and Management

LA is focused on how to exploit "big data" to improve education (Siemens & Baker, 2012). The possibilities of big data continue to evolve rapidly, driven by innovation in the underlying technologies, platforms, and analytic capabilities. The McKinsey research report defines big data as "datasets whose size is beyond the ability of typical database software tools to capture, store, manage, and analyze" (Manyika et al., 2011). Gartner analyst Doug Laney uses the 3Vs model for describing big data, i.e., increasing *volume* (amount of data), *velocity* (speed of data in and out), and *variety* (range of data types and sources) (Laney, 2001). Gartner defines big data as "high volume, high velocity, and/or high variety information assets that require new forms of processing to enable enhanced decision-making, insight discovery and process optimization" (Laney, 2012). Generally, the literature presents a number of fundamental characteristics associated with the notion of big data including—in addition to volume, velocity, variety—*veracity* (biases, noise, and abnormality in data generated from various sources and questions of trust and uncertainty associated with the collection, processing, and utilization of data), *verification* (data corroboration and security), and *value* (ability of data in generating useful insights and benefits) (Daniel & Butson, 2014).

Following these characteristics, data from learning processes can be characterized as big data:

- Volume—A single online learning platform can generate thousands of transactions per student.
- Velocity—The data that is collected should be processed and analyzed in real time to, e.g., provide accurate and timely feedback.
- Variety—The data that needs to be analyzed comes from a variety of sources, such as LMS log files, assessment scores, and social web.
- Veracity and Verification—quality of data, privacy, and security issues need to be resolved in order to build trust and achieve legitimacy in the LA process.
- Value—The main aim of LA is to harness the educational data to provide insight into the learning processes.

LA is a data-driven approach. The first step in any LA effort is to collect data from various learning environments. Gathering and integrating this raw data are nontrivial tasks and require adequate data collection and management tasks (Romero & Ventura, 2013). These tasks are critical to the successful discovery of useful patterns from the data. The collected data is heterogeneous, with different formats (e.g., structured, semi-structured, unstructured documents, videos, images, HTML pages, relational databases, object repositories) and granularity levels, and may involve many irrelevant attributes, which call for data preprocessing (also referred to as data preparation) (Liu, 2006). Data preprocessing mainly allows converting the data into an appropriate format that can be used as input for a particular LA method. Several data preprocessing tasks, borrowed from the data mining field, can be used in this step. These include data cleaning, data integration, data transformation, data reduction, data modeling, user and session identification, and path completion (Han & Kamber, 2006; Liu, 2006; Romero & Ventura, 2007). After the data collection and preprocessing steps, it is necessary to carry out data integration at the appropriate level to create a complete dataset that reflects the distributed activities of the learner.

To deal with the interoperability and integration issues, the open learning analytics platform should adopt a standardized data model. Candidate data models for open learning analytics are discussed in section "Context Modeling." Moreover, the platform should provide an API that can be used by different collectors. A collector can be a component in a learning environment which gathers data and push it to the platform in the right format. It can also be an adapter as an intermediate component that enables to get data from a learning environment, map the data from the source format into the format expected by the API, and transform it into the data model used in the open learning analytics platform. In the data collection and management step, privacy issues have to be taken into consideration.

Privacy

Privacy is a big challenge in LA. This challenge is further amplified in open learning analytics practices where learner data is collected from various sources. Therefore, it is crucial to investigate mechanisms that can help develop LA solutions where ethical and privacy issues are considered. Interesting research is being done in order to understand and tackle the ethical and privacy issues that arise with practical use of LA in the student context. Pardo and Siemens (2014), for instance, provide four practical principles that researchers should consider about privacy when working on an LA tool. These practical principles are (1) transparency, (2) student control over the data, (3) security, and (4) accountability and assessment. Slade and Prinsloo (2013) propose an ethical framework with six guiding principles for privacy-aware LA implementations. These include (1) learning analytics as moral practice, (2) students as agents, (3) student identity and performance are temporal dynamic constructs, (4) student success is a complex and multidimensional phenomenon, (5) transparency, and (6) higher education cannot afford to not use data. Some of the guiding principles are overlapping or the same as the principles suggested by Pardo and Siemens (2014). Privacy by Design is another framework developed by Ann Cavoukian in the 1990s to ensure privacy and gain personal control over one's information based on seven foundational principles, namely (1) proactive not reactive; preventative not remedial, (2) privacy as the default setting, (3) privacy embedded into design, (4) full functionality—positive-sum, not zero-sum, (5) end-to-end security—full lifecycle protection, (6) visibility and transparency—keep it open, and (7) respect for user privacy—keep it user-centric (Cavoukian, 2009). It is crucial to embrace all these principles while modeling a learner and her context, as discussed in the next two sections.

Learner Modeling

Learner modeling is the cornerstone of personalized learning. The capacity to build a detailed picture of the learner across a broader learning context beyond the classroom would provide a more personalized learning experience. The challenge is to create a thorough learner model that can be used to trigger effective personalization, adaptation, intervention, feedback, or recommendation actions. This is a highly challenging task since learner activities are often distributed over networked learning environments (Chatti et al., 2014).

A big challenge to tackle here is lifelong learner modeling. Kay and Kummerfeld (2011) define a lifelong learner model as a store for the collection of learning data about an individual learner. The authors note that to be useful, a lifelong learner model should be able to hold many forms of learning data from diverse sources and to make that information available in a suitable form to support learning. Lifelong learner modeling is the continuous collection of personal data related to a learner. It is an ongoing process of creating and modifying a model of a learner, who tends to acquire new or modify his existing knowledge, skills, or preferences continuously over a longer time span. The lifelong learning modeling process may evolve by different means, e.g., by education, experience, training, or personal development. The authors further identify different roles for lifelong learner modeling. These roles bring several technical challenges and present a theoretical backbone of a general lifelong learner modeling framework. Driven by these roles, main tasks of the learning modeling module in the open learning analytics platform include:

- Collecting and aggregating learner data from different sources.
- Integrating and managing different parts of a learner model taking into consideration the semantic information.
- Providing interfaces for open learner modeling. Learners should be the ones who own the data they generate. They should have right to control, access, amend, and delete their data. This is important to build trust and confidence in the LA system.
- Sharing the learner model across applications and domains. Thereby, the learner must be able to control which parts of the model can be shared. This helps in making the LA practice more transparent.
- Promoting the reuse of the learner model by different applications by using standard data formats.

In order to achieve these tasks, several issues have to be taken into account, including questions about integration, interoperability, reusability, extensibility, and privacy. Integration and interoperability can be supported by specifications and standards. Reusability and extensibility can be achieved through open APIs that can be used by different external applications. We should always keep in hindsight the ethical and privacy challenges in the learning modeling task. This can be achieved by following the privacy principles as discussed in the previous section. Moreover, there is a need to implement mechanisms to guarantee that no unauthorized access to a learner's data model is possible and that the learner has full control over the data. Technically, this can be achieved by following specifications such as the open User Managed Access (UMA) profile of OAuth 2.0 (Hardjono, 2015). Furthermore, we can have a user interface in the open learner modeling module that enables learners to see what kind of data is being used for which purpose. Furthermore, we need to define access scopes at different granular levels to let the learner decide which data should be taken into account, which applications can collect which data, as well as which data will be publicly available to whom and for how long.

Context Modeling

The six most popular and useful features in (lifelong) learner modeling include the learner's knowledge, interests, goals, background, individual traits, and context (Brusilovsky & Millan, 2007). Context is a central topic of research in the area of learner modeling. It is important to leverage the context attribute in the learner model in order to give learners the support they need when, how, and where they need it. Harnessing context in a learning experience has a wide range of benefits including personalization, adaptation, intelligent feedback, and recommendation. A big challenge to tackle here is context capturing and modeling. A context model should reflect a complete picture of the learner's context information. The aim is that activity data gathered from different learning channels would be fed into a personal context model, which would build the base for context-aware LA solutions.

A key question here is how to model the relevant data (Duval, 2011). Different specifications for context modeling have been introduced in the LA literature. Thüs, et al. (in review) provide a systematic analysis of what is currently available in this area. They compare and contrast four of the most referenced data models in LA, namely Contextualized Attention Metadata (CAM), NSDL Paradata, Activity Streams, and the Experience API (xAPI), based on eight factors which define the general quality of a data model. These factors include correctness, completeness, integrity, simplicity, flexibility, integration, understandability, and implementability (Moody, 2003). The authors note that the studied data models are not user centered, which is required to support personalized learning experiences. Moreover, they do not preserve the semantic meaning of the stored events (e.g., the verb-ambiguity problem in xAPI), which could lead to misinterpretations and inaccurate LA results. The authors point out that the ideal data model should find a balance between completeness, flexibility, and simplicity and introduce the Learning Context Data Model (LCDM) specification as a modular, simple and easy to understand data model that holds additional semantic information about the context in which an event has been generated. LCDM can be extended by, e.g., interests of a learner, thus providing the base for a lifelong learner modeling specification. LCDM further provides a RESTful API that enables the extensibility and reusability of context models. The API encapsulates the complexity of sending context data to be sent to the server in the right format. Currently, there are libraries for the languages Java, PHP, Objective-C, and JavaScript. Most important, LCDM provides mechanisms to deal with the privacy issue through OAuth authorization and data access scopes defining what happens with the data and who may have access to it.

Analytics Modules

Each of the analytics modules corresponds to an analytics goal such as monitoring, personalization, prediction, assessment, and reflection. They represent components which can easily be added and removed from the open learning analytics platform by the analytics engine. Each analytics module is responsible for managing a list of analytics methods associated with it. Moreover, each module manages a list of user-defined indicators which are generated by the indicator generator in the form of a triad containing a reference to the indicator specification in the questions/indicators/metrics component, the associated analytics method, and the visualization technique to be used for that indicator.

Questions/Indicators/Metrics

The Questions/Indicators/Metrics component is responsible for the management of questions indicators defined by different stakeholders in the open learning analytics platform. Each question is associated with a set of indicators. For each indicator the component stores-related queries which are generated in the indicator generation phase. These queries will be used by the analytics engine to fetch the data to be analyzed.

Indicator Engine

The indicator engine is a central component in the open learning analytics platform which enables personalized and goal-oriented LA. The various objectives in LA (e.g., monitoring, analysis, prediction, intervention, tutoring, mentoring, assessment, feedback, adaptation, personalization, recommendation, awareness, reflection) need a tailored set of indicators and metrics to serve different stakeholders with very diverse questions and goals. Current implementations of LA rely on a predefined set of indicators and metrics. This is, however, not helpful in the case of open learning analytics where the set of required indicators is unpredictable. This raises questions about how to achieve personalized and goal-oriented LA in an efficient and effective way. Ideally, LA tools should support an interactive, exploratory, and real-time user experience that enables a flexible data exploration and visualization manipulation based on individual goals of users. The challenge is thus to define the right Goal/Question/Indicator (GQI) triple before starting the LA exercise. Following an inquiry-based LA approach by giving users the opportunity to interact with the platform, define their goal, pose questions, explore the data, and specify the indicator/metric to be applied is a crucial step for effective and personalized LA results. This would also make the LA process more transparent, enabling users to see what kind of data is being used and for which purpose.

The Indicator engine is responsible for the management of the Goal/Question/Indicator definition process. It can be subdivided into the following four main subcomponents.

Question/Indicator Editor

This component provides a user-friendly interactive interface to set the LA goal, formulate questions, and define indicators associated with those questions. The process starts with a user setting a goal (e.g., monitoring and analysis, awareness and reflection, personalization, and recommendation) and formulating the questions which she is interested in. A question can be "How active are my students?" While user is formulating the question, the editor will communicate with the question analyzer component to provide useful suggestions for related questions. The next step is to associate the question with a set of indicators. In our example, possible indicators can be "number of posts in discussion forums," "update rate of wiki pages," and "frequency of annotations on lecture videos." Existing indicators can be reused and new indicators can be defined with the help of the indicator generator component. To define a new indicator, the question/indicator editor can be used to specify indicator data objects, choose the analytics method to process the indicator, and select the appropriate visualization technique to render the indicator data.

Question Analyzer

The task of the question analyzer component is to analyze the question as the user is entering it and provide useful suggestions for similar questions. Thereby, information retrieval, term extraction, and NLP algorithms can be used to infer the list of closely related questions from the questions/indicators/metrics component.

Indicator Generator

This component is responsible for the generation of new indicators. To define a new indicator, the indicator generator communicates with the rule engine component to obtain the list of possible indicator rules and to the analytics engine to get possible data objects from the storage based on the data model schema used in the open learning analytics platform.

Taking the example of the indicator "number of posts in discussion forums," the user first selects the indicator rule "number of X in Y" then assigns the data object "discussion forum" to Y and the data object "post" to X from the list of possible data objects. The indicator generator further communicates with the rule engine to generate the query related to the indicator based on the selected rule and data objects. In our example, in SQL terms, the query "SELECT COUNT (post) FROM table_discussionforum"; will be associated with the indicator "number of posts in discussion forums." After defining the indicator, and based on the LA goal set by the user in the question/indicator editor, the indicator generator communicates with the respective analytics module via the analytics engine to get the list of possible analytics methods. The user can then select the analytics method to be applied on the indicator data. The indicator generator communicates with the visualizer via the analytics engine to get the list of possible visualization techniques that can be applied. After the selection of an appropriate visualization technique by the user, the indicator is processed by the analytics engine. The user can then approve the indicator which is then registered as new indicator in the questions/indicators/metrics component along with the associated query. Moreover, a triad containing the reference to this indicator, the associated analytics method, and the selected visualization technique will be stored in the respective module via the analytics engine. The indicator generator further generates the indicator data request code which can be copied and embedded in the client application (e.g., dashboard, HTML page, widget) to get the indicator visualization code to be rendered on the client.

Rule Engine

This component is responsible for managing indicator rules and their associated queries. Different rule engines can be used to support this task such as Drools, Mandarax, JRuleEngine, and InRule.

Analytics Engine

The analytics engine is the backbone of the open learning analytics platform which acts as a mediator between different components in the platform. The major task of the analytics engine is to perform analysis. The analytics engine is responsible for executing indicator queries, getting the data to be analyzed, applying the specified analytics method, and finally sending the indicator data to the visualizer. Moreover, the analytics engine supports extensibility of the platform by providing easy mechanisms to manage, add, and remove analytics modules from the platform as well as managing the repository of analytics methods which can grow as new methods are implemented.

Visualizer

A key step in LA is closing the loop by feeding back the analytics results to learners (Clow, 2012). This requires appropriate representations of the results. Statistics in the form of reports and tables of data are not always easy to interpret to the end users. Visualization techniques are very useful for showing results in a way that is easier to interpret (Romero & Ventura, 2013). Mazza (2009) stresses that thanks to our visual perception ability, a visual representation is often more effective than plain text or data. Different information visualization techniques (e.g., charts, scatterplot, 3D representations, maps) can be used to represent the information in a clear and understandable format (Romero & Ventura, 2007). The difficult part here is in defining the representation that effectively achieves the analytics objective (Mazza, 2009).

Recognizing the power of visual representations, traditional reports based on tables of data are increasingly being replaced with dashboards that graphically show different performance indicators. Dashboards "typically capture and visualize traces of learning activities, in order to promote awareness, reflection and sense-making, and to enable learners to define goals and track progress towards these goals" (Verbert et al., 2014, p. 1499). Dashboards represent a helpful medium for visual analytics widely used in the LA literature. They are, however, often not linked to the learning context and they provide more information than needed. LA is most effective when it is an integral part of the learning environment. Hence, integration of LA into the learning practice of the different stakeholders is important. Moreover, effective LA tools are those, which minimize the time frame between analysis and action, by delivering meaningful information in context and without delay, so that stakeholders have the opportunity to act on newly gained information in time. Thus, it is beneficial to view learning and analytics as intertwined processes and follow an embedded LA approach by developing visual analytics tools that (a) are smoothly integrated into the standard toolsets of learners and teachers and (b) foster prompt action in context by giving useful feedback at the right place and time.

The visualizer component in the open learning analytics platform is responsible for providing easy mechanisms to manage, add, and remove visualization techniques such as Google Charts, D3/D4, jpGraph, Dygraphs, and jqPlot along with the type of visualization (e.g., bar chart, pie chart, line chart) supported by each technique. An adapter is required for each visualization technique to transform the data format used in the analytics engine to the indicator visualization code to be rendered on the client application (e.g., dashboard, HTML page, and widget).

System Scenarios

In this section, we outline two possible system scenarios to show how the different components of the open learning analytics platform interact with each other.

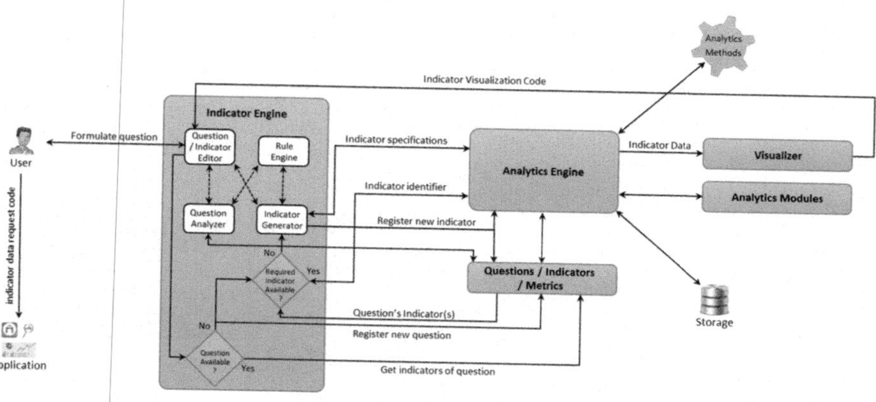

Fig. 12.3 New indicator generation flow diagram

New Indicator Generation

The new indicator generation process is depicted in Fig. 12.3. The user starts the process by selecting her goal and entering her question using the question/indicator editor. The question analyzer communicates with the question/indicators/metrics component to suggest closely related questions. The user can either select one of the suggested questions or continue to enter a new question. If the user selects one of the suggested questions, the question/indicator editor presents her with all the indicators associated with that question. If the user enters a new question, all available indicators are presented to her from which she can select which indicators to associate with the new question or generate a new indicator. If the user selects one of the available indicators, the analytics engine suggests existing instances of that indicator (i.e., related triads in the respective analytics module). The user can then select one of the instances or associate the indicator with a different analytics method and/or visualization technique using the indicator generator. The user is presented with a different interface in the question/indicator editor where she can define a new indicator using the indicator generator, as discussed in section "Indicator Engine." The analytics engine processes the indicator (see section "Analytics Engine") and sends the indicator data to the visualizer which generates the indicator visualization code to be rendered on the question/indicator editor (see section "Visualizer"). If the user is satisfied with the new indicator, she can copy the indicator data request code generated by the indicator generator and embed it in any client application.

Indicator Data Request

The indicator data request flow is shown in Fig. 12.4. To visualize the indicator on, e.g., a dashboard, an indicator data request containing the module identifier, triad identifier (see section "Analytics Modules"), and additional parameters (e.g., filters)

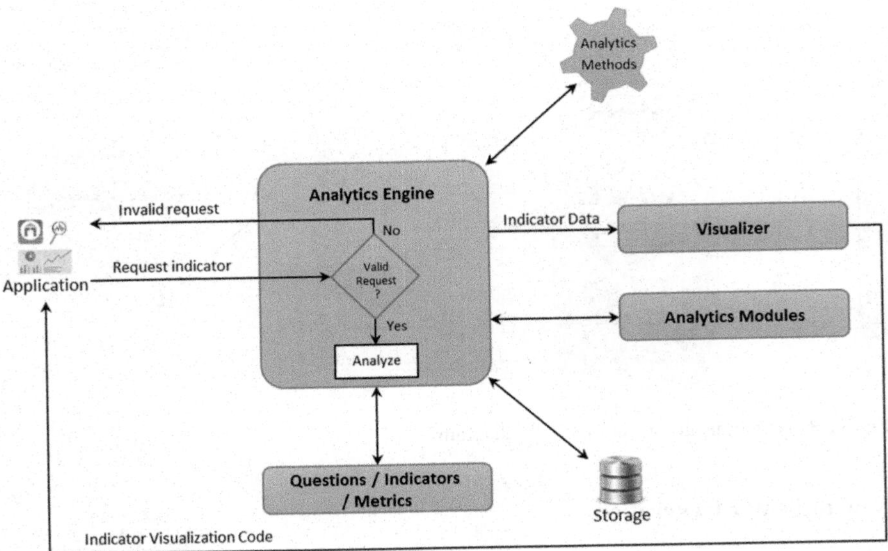

Fig. 12.4 Indicator data request flow diagram

is sent to the open learning analytics platform. The analytics engine intercepts the request and performs the following steps:

1. Check whether the request is valid or not.
2. Communicate with the respective analytics module to get the indicator reference, the associated analytics method, and the visualization technique to be used for that indicator.
3. Communicate with the questions/indicators/metrics component to get the query related to the requested indicator.
4. Execute the query and get the data.
5. Analyze the data using the associated analytics method.
6. Transform the method output data to the data format used in the analytics engine.
7. Send the indicator data to the visualizer.

The visualizer transforms the indicator data to the visualization code to be rendered on the client application (e.g., dashboard, HTML page, and widget).

Conclusion

In the last few years, there has been an increasing interest in the automatic analysis of educational data to enhance the learning experience, a research area referred to as learning analytics (LA). Significant research has been conducted in LA. However, most of the LA approaches to date are focusing on centralized learning settings.

Driven by the demands of the new networked and increasingly complex learning environments, there is a need to scale LA up which requires a shift from closed LA systems to open LA ecosystems. In this chapter, we discussed open learning analytics as an emerging research field that has the potential to improve learning efficiency and effectiveness in open and networked learning environments. We further presented a vision for an open learning analytics ecosystem through a detailed discussion of user scenarios, requirements, technical architecture, and components of an open learning analytics platform. This chapter makes a significant contribution to LA research because it provides concrete conceptual and technical ideas toward an open learning analytics ecosystem, which have been lacking until now.

References

Alexander, S., Berg, A., Clow, D., Dawson, S., Duval, E., et al.(2014), *OLA Press Release*. Retrieved from http://solaresearch.org/initiatives/ola/.

Benson, T. (2012). Why interoperability is hard. In *Principles of Health Interoperability HL7 and SNOMED, Health Information Technology Standards* (pp. 21–32). London: Springer.

Bomas, E. (2014). *How to give students control of their data.* Retrieved from http://www.laceproject.eu/blog/give-students-control-data/.

Brusilovsky, P., & Millan, E. (2007). User models for adaptive hypermedia and adaptive educational systems. In P. Brusilovsky, A. Kobsa, & W. Nejdl (Eds.), *The adaptive web, LNCS 4321* (pp. 3–53). Berlin: Springer.

Cavoukian, A. (2009). *Privacy by Design The 7 Foundational Principles.* Retrieved from https://www.privacybydesign.ca/content/uploads/2009/08/7foundationalprinciples.pdf.

Chatti, M. A. (2010). The LaaN theory. In *Personalization in technology enhanced learning: A social software perspective* (pp. 19–42). Aachen: Shaker Verlag.

Chatti, M. A., Dyckhoff, A. L., Thüs, H., & Schroeder, U. (2012). A reference model for learning analytics. *International Journal of Technology Enhanced Learning, 4*(5/6), 318–331.

Chatti, M. A., Lukarov, V., Thüs, H., Muslim, A., Yousef, A. M. F., Wahid, U., et al. (2014). Learning analytics: Challenges and future research directions. *eleed*, Iss.10. (urn:nbn:de:0009-5-40350).

Clow, D. (2012). The learning analytics cycle: closing the loop effectively. In *Proceedings of the 2nd International Conference on Learning Analytics and Knowledge* (pp. 134–138). ACM.

Clow, D. (2013). An overview of learning analytics. *Teaching in Higher Education, 18*(6), 683–695.

Cooper, A. (2013). *Learning analytics interoperability—A survey of current literature and candidate standards.* Retrieved from http://blogs.cetis.ac.uk/adam/wp-content/uploads/sites/23/2013/05/learninganalytics-interoperability-v1p1.pdf.

Cooper, A. (2014a). *Open learning analytics network—Summit Europe 2014.* Retrieved from http://www.laceproject.eu/open-learning-analytics-network-summit-europe-2014/.

Cooper, A. (2014b). Learning analytics and interoperability—The big picture in brief. *Learning Analytics Review*, March 2014, ISSN: 2057-7494.

Cooper, A. (2014c). *Standards and specifications—Quick reference guide.* Retrieved from http://www.laceproject.eu/dpc/standards-specifications-quick-reference-guide/.

Daniel, B., & Butson, R. (2014). Foundations of big data and analytics in higher education. In *International Conference on Analytics Driven Solutions: ICAS2014* (pp. 39–47). Academic Conferences.

Dawson, S., Gašević, D., Siemens, G., & Joksimovic, S. (2014). Current state and future trends: A citation network analysis of the learning analytics field. In *Proceedings of the Fourth*

International Conference on Learning Analytics & Knowledge (pp. 231–240). New York: ACM.

Downes, S. (2007). Models for sustainable open educational resources. *Interdisciplinary Journal of Knowledge and Learning Objects, 3*, 29–44.

Dringus, L. P. (2012). Learning analytics considered harmful. *Journal of Asynchronous Learning Networks, 16*(3), 87–100.

Duval, E. (2011). Attention please!: Learning analytics for visualization and recommendation. In *Proceedings of the 1st International Conference on Learning Analytics and Knowledge* (pp. 9–17). ACM.

Ferguson, R. (2012). Learning analytics: Drivers, developments and challenges. *International Journal of Technology Enhanced Learning, 4*(5/6), 304–317.

Fournier, H., Kop, R., & Sitlia, H. (2011). The value of learning analytics to networked learning on a personal learning environment. In *Proceedings of the LAK '11 Conference on Learning Analytics and Knowledge* (pp. 104–109).

Fry, J., Schroeder, R., & den Besten, M. (2009). Open science in e-science: Contingency or policy? *Journal of Documentation, 65*(1), 6–32.

Han, J., & Kamber, M. (2006). *Data mining: Concepts and techniques*. San Francisco, CA: Elsevier.

Hardjono, T. (Ed.). (2015). *User Managed Access (UMA) Profile of OAuth 2.0*. Retrieved from http://docs.kantarainitiative.org/uma/draft-uma-core.html

Hilton, J., Wiley, D., Stein, J., & Johnson, A. (2010). The four R's of openness and ALMS analysis: Frameworks for open educational resources. *Open Learning: The Journal of Open and Distance Learning, 25*(1), 37–44.

Hoel, T. (2014). *Standards and learning analytics—current activities 2014*. Retrieved from http://www.laceproject.eu/blog/standards-learning-analytics-current-activity-2014/.

Kay, J., & Kummerfeld, B. (2011). Lifelong learner modeling. In P. J. Durlach & A. M. Lesgold (Eds.), *Adaptive technologies for training and education* (pp. 140–164). Cambridge: Cambridge University Press.

Koedinger, K. R., Baker, R. S. J. D., Cunningham, K., Skogsholm, A., Leber, B., & Stamper, J. (2010). A data repository for the EDM community: The PSLC DataShop. In C. Romero, S. Ventura, M. Pechenizkiy, & R. S. J. D. Baker (Eds.), *Handbook of educational data mining* (pp. 43–56). Boca Raton, FL: CRC Press.

Laney, D. (2001). 3D data management: Controlling data volume, velocity, and variety, application delivery strategies. META Group. Retrieved March 6, 2015, from http://blogs.gartner.com/doug-laney/files/2012/01/ad949-3D-Data-Management-Controlling-DataVolume-Velocity-and-Variety.pdf

Laney, D. (2012). The importance of 'Big Data': A definition. *Gartner*. Retrieved March 6, 2015, from http://www.gartner.com/resId=2057415.

Liu, B. (2006). *Web data mining*. Berlin: Springer.

Manyika, J., Chui, M., Brown, B., Bughin, J., Dobbs, R., Roxburgh, C., & Byers, A. H., (2011). Big data: The next frontier for innovation, competition, and productivity. McKinsey Global Institute.

Mazza, R. (2009). Introduction to Information Visualization. London: Springer-Verlag.

McNamara, T. (2012). *Open Education: Emergence and Identity*. Retrieved February 5, 2015, from http://oh-institute.org/external_resources/pub/McNamara-OpenEd_Emergence_Identity-CC-by.pdf.

Moody, D. L. (2003). Measuring the quality of data models: An empirical evaluation of the use of quality metrics in practice. In *Proceedings of 11th European Conference on Information Systems*, 2003.

OECD. (2007). *Giving Knowledge for Free: The Emergence of Open Educational Resources*. Report. ISBN-978-92-64-03174-6. Retrieved February 5, 2015, from http://www.oecd.org/edu/ceri/givingknowledgeforfreetheemergenceofopeneducationalresources.htm.

Pardo, A., & Siemens, G. (2014). Ethical and privacy principles for learning analytics. *British Journal of Educational Technology, 45*(3), 438–450.

Peters, M. A. (2008). The history and emergent paradigm of open education. In *Open education and education for openness* (pp. 3–16). Rotterdam: Sense Publishers.
Romero, C., & Ventura, S. (2007). Educational data mining: A survey from 1995 to 2005. *Expert Systems with Applications, 33*(1), 135–146.
Romero, C., and S. Ventura. Educational data mining: A review of the state-of-the-art. IEEE Transaction on Systems, Man, and Cybernetics, Part C: Applications and Reviews, 40(6): 601–618, 2010.
Romero, C., & Ventura, S. (2013). Data mining in education. *Wiley Interdisciplinary Reviews: Data Mining and Knowledge Discovery, 3*(1), 12–27.
Sclater, N. (2014). Examining open learning analytics—report from the Lace Project meeting in Amsterdam. Retrieved from http://www.laceproject.eu/blog/examining-open-learning-analytics-reportlace-project-meeting-amsterdam/.
Siemens, G., & Baker, R. S. J. D. (2012). Learning analytics and educational data mining: Towards communication and collaboration. In *Proceedings of the 2nd International Conference on Learning Analytics and Knowledge* (pp. 252–254). ACM.
Siemens, G., Gasevic, D., Haythornthwaite, C., Dawson, S., Shum, S. B., Ferguson, R., et al. (2011). *Open learning analytics: An integrated & modularized platform*. Maidenhead: Open University Press.
Siemens, G.; Long, P.: Penetrating the Fog: Analytics in Learning and Education. In: EDUCAUSE Review, 46(5), September/October 2011.
Slade, S., & Prinsloo, P. (2013). Learning analytics: Ethical issues and dilemmas. *American Behavioral Scientist, 57*(10), 1509–1528.
Thüs, H., Chatti, M. A., & Schroeder, U. (in review). Context capturing and modeling in open learning environments. *International Journal of Artificial Intelligence in Education Society (IJAIED)*, IOS Press.
Verbert, K., Drachsler, H., Manouselis, N., Wolpers, M., Vuorikari, R., & Duval, E. (2011, February). Dataset-driven research for improving recommender systems for learning. In *Proceedings of the 1st International Conference on Learning Analytics and Knowledge* (pp. 44–53). ACM.
Verbert, K., Manouselis, N., Drachsler, H., & Duval, E. (2012). Dataset-driven research to support learning and knowledge analytics. *Educational Technology & Society, 15*(3), 133–148.
Verbert, K., Govaerts, S., Duval, E., Santos, J. L., Van Assche, F., Parra, G., & Klerkx, J. (2014). Learning dashboards: an overview and future research opportunities. Personal and Ubiquitous Computing, 18(6), 1499–1514.
Wiley, D. (2009). Introduction to Open Education. iTunesU. Lecture conducted from BYU, Provo.
Yuan, L., Powell, S. (2013). MOOCs and open education: Implications for higher education. A white paper. Retrieved February 5, 2015, from http://publications.cetis.ac.uk/2013/667.

Chapter 13
Predicting Four-Year Student Success from Two-Year Student Data

Denise Nadasen and Alexandra List

Abstract This chapter describes a study that evaluated the academic pathway of transfer students from two community colleges to a 4-year university. The project focused on a series of academic milestones that students must achieve prior to earning a 4-year credential. Those milestones include the first-term GPA, re-enrollment, and program completion. The purpose of this project was to develop an integrated database that contains key data on student demographics, course-taking behaviors, and performance from both the community college and the 4-year institution and to analyze the data using data mining and traditional statistical techniques to predict student success.

A series of logistic regression equations identified significant predictors of first-term GPA, re-enrollment, and graduation. For example, overall rate of successful course completion, rate of successful math completion, rate of successful English completion, completion of developmental math were found to be significant predictors of a successful first-term GPA.

Keywords Student success • Transfer student • Community college • Higher education • Predictive analytics • Logistic regression • Learner analytics • Retention • Graduation

Introduction

The landscape of higher education shows an increasingly diverse student body and an equally diverse set of institutions (Archer, Hutchings, & Ross, 2005; Cross, 1981). A common concern shared by these institutions is how to support student success, which requires the consideration of issues of access, affordability, and value

D. Nadasen, M.A. (✉)
University of Maryland University College, Upper Marlboro, MD, USA
e-mail: denise.nadasen@gmail.com

A. List, Ph.D.
Ball State University, Muncie, IN, USA

B. Kei Daniel (ed.), *Big Data and Learning Analytics in Higher Education*,
DOI 10.1007/978-3-319-06520-5_13

(return on investment) (e.g., Bamber & Tett, 2000; Miller & Lu, 2003; Bailey, 2002). Much of the research examining student achievement has centered on improving the success of first-time, full-time, degree-seeking undergraduates (e.g., Bers & Smith, 1991). While this subpopulation represented the majority of students entering 4-year institutions in past decades, the current student market has expanded to include an increasing population of nontraditional students—adult learners, with prior academic experience, attending school part-time (Bean & Metzner, 1985). Nontraditional students tend to have lower access to post-secondary education and lower success rates as compared to traditional students (Grimes, 1997; Spitzer, 2000). In part, this may be due to nontraditional students experiencing financial or family constraints that prevent them from entering post-secondary education via a traditional route (Cantwell, Archer, & Bourke, 2001; Choy, 2002; Goldrick-Rab, 2006; Keane, 2002; Paulsen & St John, 2002; Rouse, 2004) or difficulties adjusting to university culture (Lehmann, 2007; Metzner & Bean, 1987; Schuetz, 2005; Walpole, 2003). Further, nontraditional students tend to first enroll in community college, prior to attending a 4-year institution. This may signal challenges in the academic preparedness, resulting in students taking more remedial courses (Bailey, 2009; Bettinger & Long, 2005, 2009) or failing to reach key milestones, such as earning 20 credits (Calcagno, Crosta, Bailey, & Jenkins, 2007). Additionally, some researchers have argued that simply attending community college decreases students' likelihood of graduating from a 4-year institution (Alfonso, 2006; Christie & Hutcheson, 2003; Long & Kurlaender, 2009; Martin, Galentino, & Townsend, 2014).

Among the population of students who enter community college, 81 % intend to complete a bachelor's degree; however, only about 12 % of these students have been found to earn a bachelor's degree within 6 years of transferring to a 4-year institution (Community College Research Center, 2014). In part, this may be because nontraditional students are more likely to attend college part-time and to balance academic commitments with work or family obligations (Bamber & Tett, 2000; Matus-Grossman & Gooden, 2002; Moreau & Leathwood, 2006). Due to the discrepancy between student ambition and achievement, community college transfer students enrolled at a 4-year university are the target population for this project.

The impetus for this project was to define and evaluate the academic pathways of community college transfer students earning a 4-year credential. Through a grant from the Kresge Foundation, a 4-year institution partnered with two highly diverse community colleges to identify factors associated with community college transfer student success. While current literature has focused primarily on graduation as a success outcome, this project focused on examining a series of academic milestones that students must achieve prior to earning a credential. Examining such milestones provided a more nuanced and process-based understanding of students' transition from community college and progress through a 4-year university. Defining such milestones (e.g., re-enrollment, retention) presented challenges, as the 4-year institution is an online university, serving primarily nontraditional learners, who have been found to be more likely to have discontinuous enrollment pathways in higher education (Goldrick-Rab, 2006). Tracking nontraditional students' persistence in an online university required addressing issues associated with data management, the reliability and validity of data elements, standardized variable definitions, and model complexity (Park & Choi, 2009).

The purpose of this project was four-fold:

1. To develop a collaborative relationship between two community colleges and one four-year, online institution,
2. To develop an integrated database that includes key information on student demographics, course-taking behaviors, and performance,
3. To analyze data using traditional statistical techniques and data mining to predict student success, and
4. To develop, implement, and evaluate interventions designed to improve student success.

This project was guided by a cross-institutional, collaborative workgroup that included external evaluators who validated the integrity and relevance of the research.

Methods

Population

In defining the population of interest, the 4-year institution identified all undergraduate students enrolled between Spring 2005 and Spring 2012. From this list of students, each of the two partner community colleges identified students who previously attended their institutions. All students, including those who had attended community college more than 5 years prior to enrollment at the 4-year institution were included in the total dataset. Across both community colleges, over 32,000 students were identified as transfer students.

The analyses presented in this chapter focused on students who transferred from one of these two partner community colleges and who first enrolled at the 4-year institution between Spring 2005 and Spring 2012. This dataset included 8058 students, with 59 % ($n=4724$) transferring from one community college and 40 % ($n=3220$) from the other community college.

Data

The three partner institutions developed a Memorandum of Understanding (MOU) that guided the collection, security, and use of data. Each institution provided student-level records with demographic and performance data. An Oracle database was developed to store the data. All student records were securely stored, with restricted access. The database contained over 300 natural and derived variables that were collected or generated. A data dictionary consolidated and integrated the research variables for the project.

Outcome Variables

Based on a review of the literature, institutions worked collaboratively to align data definitions, to define student success, to identify key milestones in students' academic pathways, and to determine which factors were most important to consider in predicting each milestone. Success has been defined in a variety of ways in the research literature, including as degree completion and as the various benchmarks leading up to completion (Park & Choi, 2009). For this project, four indicators of student success were identified: successful first-term GPA, re-enrollment, retention, and graduation. Each of these success metrics is defined:

- *Successful First-Term GPA*—Average of all course grades received in the first term of enrolment at the 4-year institution that was 2.0 or above, on a four-point scale
- *Re-enrollment*—Enrolment in the immediate next semester after initial enrolment at the 4-year institution
- *Retention*—Re-enrolment at the 4-year institution in any term within 12 months after initial enrolment
- *Graduation/Degree Completion*—Earning a bachelor's degree from the 4-year institution within 8 years of transfer from the community college

These definitions were developed by reviewing a number of sources including: (1) the literature on retention and online learning (e.g., Cabrera, Nora, & Castaneda, 1993; Lau, 2003; Seidman, 2005; Tinto, 2006); (2) institutional publications, such as reports to the regional accrediting body, studies on retention or course success, and course catalogues, and (3) common definitions used within the institutional research community.

Model of Academic Trajectories

Based on institutional models of student progression and success, supported by the literature, a theoretical model of students' academic trajectories from community college to graduation from a 4-year institution was developed (Fig. 13.1). This model included key milestones in students' progress including earning a successful first-term GPA, re-enrolling in the immediate next semester after transfer, and being retained within a 12-month period. The academic trajectory model developed reflects both findings in the empirical literature on student success (e.g., Bean & Metzner, 1985; Cabrera et al., 1993; Chemers, Hu, & Garcia, 2001; DeBerard, Spielmans, & Julka, 2004; Hagedorn, 2005; Kuh, Cruce, Shoup, Kinzie, & Gonyea, 2008; Ronco & Cahill, 2004) and partner institutions' policies and practices for keeping students on track to completion.

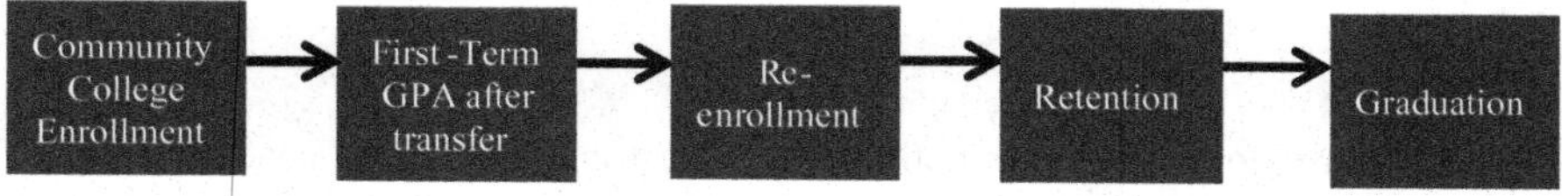

Fig. 13.1 Model of academic trajectory

Analyses

Two data analytic approaches were adopted to examine factors predictive of each key milestone. First, logistic regression models were run examining factors predicting students' likelihood of attaining each milestone. Second, data mining algorithms, including neural networks, association rules, decision trees, naïve bayes, and boosted random forests were used to corroborate findings from logistic regression and to determine which factors were associated with achieving each milestone.

Exploratory data mining techniques, including cluster analyses, were additionally used in the initial stages of data development to identify meaningful derivations and combinations of variables associated with milestones indicative of student success. The final dataset used in both logistic regression and data mining analyses included over 30 variables. These variables were examined both independently and in combination as potential predictors of each success milestone.

This project employed both predictive modelling and data analytics to enhance the validity and scope of findings. Drawing on the research literature, factors previously associated with student success (e.g., age, prior achievement) were used in predicting students' achievement of each target milestone using logistic regression. Data mining techniques were used to capitalize on the volume and variety of data amassed as a part of the data-sharing initiative undertaken by partner institutions through this project. Additionally, given the unique population of interest (i.e., community college transfer students enrolled in an online university), exploratory data mining techniques (e.g., cluster analyses) were warranted in exploring factors associated with student success.

Analyses were carried out in-sequence, predicting each target milestone, in turn. First, students' demographic characteristics and community college academic data were used to predict first-term GPA at the 4-year institution. Next, demographic characteristics and community college data were used alongside 4-year institution first-semester variables to predict re-enrollment and graduation.

In this study, first-term GPA was both a target outcome and a predictor of later persistence. The dual role of earning a successful first-term GPA reflects both the need for students to perform well in their first term of transfer and the role the first term plays in leading students to later achievement and persistence

Results

Logistic regression models predicting each milestone in students' academic trajectories are presented. The re-enrollment and retention models were highly similar. For this reason and for brevity, only the re-enrollment model is presented in this chapter. All models were validated with data mining algorithms. Models are presented predicting:

1. Successful first-term GPA
2. Re-enrollment
3. Graduation

Additionally, this chapter presents a brief overview of interventions carried out at the community colleges and at the 4-year institution, aimed at improving student success and targeting identified milestone in students' academic trajectories.

Predictive Modelling

Predicting Successful First-Term GPA

The logistic regression model predicting students earning a successful first-term GPA was significant, $X^2(21)=756.43$, $p<0.001$, correctly classifying 76.8 % of students as earning a successful first-term GPA or not. Cox and Snell's R^2 suggests that the model explained 9.1 % of variance in earning a first-term GPA, while Nagelkerke's R^2 indicates that 13.7 % of variance was explained (see Table 13.1).

Table 13.1 Predicting successful first-term GPA using demographic characteristics, community college course-taking behaviors, and summative measures of CC Background

		β	SE(β)	Significance	β*
Demographic characteristics					
Gender*		0.12	0.06	0.043	1.13
Age**		0.01	0	0.001	1.01
Race/ethnicity: compared to White students	Black***	–0.36	0.08	0	0.7
Hispanic/Latino Asian		–0.1	0.11	0.367	0.91
		–0.06	0.11	0.57	0.94
American Indian		–0.28	0.27	0.3	0.76
Race not specified*		–0.23	0.1	0.021	0.79
Marital status**		0.25	0.08	0.001	1.29
PELL grant recipient***		–0.3	0.07	0	0.74
Community college course-taking variables					
Successful course completion overall***		1.63	0.21	0	5.08
Successful Math completion**		0.2	0.06	0.004	1.22

(continued)

Table 13.1 (continued)

	β	SE(β)	Significance	β*
Successful English completion**	0.18	0.06	1	1.2
Developmental Math completion**	0.27	0.08	0.001	1.31
developmental writing completion	−0.08	0.1	0.38	0.92
Developmental reading completion	−0.07	0.11	0.48	0.93
Developmental Math exempt	−0.03	0.08	0.747	0.97
Developmental English exempt	−0.11	0.05	0.07	0.89
Repeated courses	−0.27	0.07	0	0.76
Summative measures of CC background				
GPA***	0.22	0.05	0	1.25
Credits earned	−0.001	0.002	0.62	1
Associates received***	0.39	0.08	0	1.47

Note: *sig. at 0.05 level, **sig. at 0.01 level, ***sig. at 0.001 level

Among demographic characteristics, gender, age, and marital status were all significant predictors in the model. Specifically, students who were female, older, and married were significantly more likely to earn a successful first-term GPA at the 4-year institution. At the same time, students reporting their race/ethnicity as African American or not designating a race/ethnicity were less likely to earn a successful first-term GPA. Further, receiving a Pell grant at the community college, as an indicator of financial need, decreased the likelihood of students earning a successful first-term GPA at the 4-year institution.

In examining indicators associated with students' community college course-taking behaviors, students' overall rate of successful course completion (i.e., ratio of the number of courses passed with a grade of D or above to the total number of courses attempted), rate of successful math completion, and rate of successful English completion were all significant predictors in the model. Further, students' completion of developmental math was a significant predictor in the model.

Cumulative GPA and earning an Associates degree, summative measures of community college performance, were both significant predictors of earning a successful first-year GPA. Examining the standardized betas determined that, holding all else constant in the model, students' overall rates of successful course completion carried the most impact in increasing students' probability of earning a successful first-term GPA at the 4-year institution.

Predicting Re-enrolment

The overall logistic regression model for predicting re-enrolment was significant, $X^2(19)=1063.24$, $p<.001$. The model was able to correctly classify 71.6 % of students as re-enrolling or not. Pseudo R^2 measures of effect size ranged from an estimated 12.5 % of variance in re-enrolment (Cox & Snell's R^2) to 17.4 % of variance (Nagelkerke's R^2) explained (see Table 13.2).

Table 13.2 Predicting re-enrolment using demographic characteristics, community college course-taking behaviors, summative measures of CC backgrounds, and first-term indicators

		β	SE(β)	Significance	β*
Demographic characteristics					
Gender***		0.20	0.05	0.000	1.22
Age		0.00	0.00	0.638	1.00
Race/ethnicity: compared to White students	Black*	0.17	0.07	0.013	1.19
	Hispanic/Latino	−0.02	0.10	0.83	0.98
	Asian	0.07	0.10	0.492	1.07
	American Indian	0.19	0.27	0.469	1.21
	Race not specified*	0.05	0.09	0.60	1.05
Marital status**		0.24	0.07	0.001	1.28
PELL grant recipient		0.13	0.07	0.065	1.14
Community college course-taking variables					
Repeated a course**		0.17	0.06	0.005	1.19
Enrolled in a developmental course***		0.21	0.06	0.001	1.23
Exempt from developmental Math**		0.22	0.08	0.004	1.25
Summative measures of community college backgrounds					
Community college GPA**		−0.11	0.04	0.005	0.89
Cumulative credits earned at CC		−0.00	0.00	0.208	1.00
Earned an associate's degree		−0.13	0.07	0.059	0.88
First-term at the four-year institution					
First-term GPA***		0.26	0.02	0.000	1.30
First-term credits earned***		0.14	0.01	0.000	1.14
Enrolled full time		−0.16	0.08	0.054	0.86
Cumulative credits transferred***		0.01	0.00	0.000	1.01

Note: *sig. at 0.05 level, **sig. at 0.01 level, ***sig. at 0.001 level

An examination of demographic characteristics found that gender and marital status were both significant predictors in the model. Specifically, being female and married increased students' probability of re-enrolling in a subsequent term at the 4-year institution. Further, unlike with first-term GPA, race/ethnicity designated as African American or unspecified were significant positive predictors of re-enrolment.

In considering students' community college course-taking behaviors, different predictors were found to be significant in predicting re-enrolment than those found to be significant in predicting performance. Specifically, students' likelihood of re-enrolment at the 4-year institution increased if they either enrolled in a developmental course or were exempt from having to take developmental math. Repeating a course at the community college was also found to be a significant, positive predictor of re-enrolment; in other words, retaking a course in community college increased the likelihood that a student would reenroll again (or persist) at the 4-year institution.

Among summative measures of students' community college performance, only community college GPA was a significant predictor in the model. Further, despite being a positive predictor of first-term GPA, community college GPA was a negative predictor of persistence (i.e., re-enrolment). More work is needed to understand why this may be the case.

At the 4-year transfer institution, first-term GPA and total number of credits earned were significant predictors of re-enrolment. Further, the cumulative number of credits transferred was a significant positive predictor in the model.

Predicting Graduation

The dataset used for predicting graduation was reduced to include only those students who had been enrolled at the 4-year institution for at least 8 years (i.e., had 8 years in which to complete a degree). Over 2000 of the original 8058 students were used for this part of predictive modelling. The logistic regression model predicting 8-year graduation was found to be significant, $X^2(17)=1271.59$, with 69.6 % of cases correctly classified as graduating or not. Effect size measures suggest that between 20.0 %, according to Cox and Snell's R^2, and 26.7 %, according to Nagelkerke's R^2, of variance in graduation was explained by the model (See Table 13.3). The variables used as predictors of graduation included demographic characteristics, community college course-taking behavior, summative community college measures, and first-term performance at the 4-year institution.

Table 13.3 Predicting graduation using demographic characteristics, community college course-taking behaviors, summative measures of CC backgrounds, and first-term indicators

	β	SE(β)	Significance	β*
Demographic characteristics				
Gender	.029	.106	.785	1.029
First-term age***	−.023	.007	.000	.977
Minority status	−.169	.104	.104	.845
Receiving PELL at CC	−.262	.167	.116	.770
Community college course-taking variables				
Math enrolment at CC*	.329	.135	.015	1.390
Percent W's at CC	−.670	.381	.079	.512
Summative community college measures				
Receiving AA at CC	.127	.129	.325	1.135
CC CUM GPA*	.168	.081	.038	1.184
CC Credits earned	.005	.003	.059	1.005
First-term indicators				
First-term GPA***	.482	.044	.000	1.619
First-term credits earned***	.021	.002	.000	1.022

Note: *sig. at 0.05 level, **sig. at 0.01 level, ***sig. at 0.001 level

Among demographic characteristics examined, only age in the first-term age at the time of transfer to the 4-year institution was found to be a significant predictor; being younger increased students' likelihood of graduating.

Examining course work at the community college, enrolling in a math course was found to be a significant predictor of graduation. In terms of summative community college course-taking indicators, community college cumulative GPA was a significant positive predictor. Students' GPA and the number of credits earned in their first-term at the 4-year institution were significant positive predictors of graduation.

Interventions

In addition to predictive modelling using integrated community college and 4-year data, this project included the development, implementation, and evaluation of interventions designed to improve community college transfer student success at the 4-year, online university. These interventions were adopted at both the community college level and at the 4-year institution. Three areas of student success, aligned with the Academic Trajectory Model, were targeted for intervention:

(a) Academic achievement—associated with earning a successful GPA
(b) Social and institutional integration—considered to support persistence and retention
(c) Goal setting and academic planning—in support of students' progress toward graduation

Following are brief descriptions of the interventions undertaken along with intervention results.

Supporting Academic Achievement

Online Tutoring for Accounting Students

In collaboration with the Predictive Analytics Reporting Framework (PAR), an independent nonprofit organization providing support for learner analytics in higher education, two courses, Accounting 220 and 221, were identified as having a low course completion rate as compared to other courses at the 4-year institution. The PAR team found that introductory Accounting courses at other institutions likewise had high failure rates. The faculty teaching Accounting 220 and Accounting 221 developed and implemented an online tutoring intervention for accounting students. The effectiveness of the online tutoring intervention was evaluated. Independent sample t-tests were used to determine if students who participated in the online tutoring sessions performed better than students who did not. Students participating in online tutoring (Test group) had a significantly higher term GPA and a significantly higher rate of successful course completion, when compared to students not participating in online tutoring (Control group); however, the two groups did not significantly differ in their rates of re-enrolment (See Table 13.4). However, limited conclusions can be drawn as students self-selected to participate in online tutoring. More work is needed to understand the relation between students' background factors and election to take advantage of supplemental academic support such as participating in tutoring.

Table 13.4 Outcomes for online tutoring test and control groups

	Test	Control
	Participating in online tutoring	Not participating in online tutoring
Term GPA	2.52	2.10
Successful course completion	72 %	58 %
Re-enrolment	78 %	72 %

Nonetheless, results from this evaluation suggest that course performance data can be analyzed to identify risk points (i.e., courses with high failure rates) that influence student success. When risk points are identified, appropriate and relevant interventions can promote student success. As a result of project findings emphasizing students' performance particularly in introductory courses, the online tutoring program was expanded to support all students in accounting.

Supporting Social and Institutional Integration

New Student Orientation Checklist

A New Student Orientation Checklist was developed to assist community college students transferring to the 4-year, online institution in navigating support resources available in-person and online. For example, students were asked to find their advisor's contact information and to identify the time and location that math and statistics tutoring was available. Students were randomly assigned to Test and Control groups to evaluate term-based outcomes for students who participated in the Checklist intervention. Although no significant differences were found on the selected outcome measures (see Table 13.5), students responding to a survey found the checklist to be a useful tool. One student reported: "It helped me compile information and learn how to use [the institution]'s website." The 4-year institution has developed and launched a broader checklist to help all students prepare for their academic careers and for graduation.

Table 13.5 Outcomes for checklist test and control groups

	Test		Control
	Received the checklist	Completed the checklist	Did not receive the checklist
Term GPA	2.87	3.00	2.91
Successful course completion	73 %	77 %	77 %
Re-enrolment	67 %	72 %	67 %

College Success Mentoring Program

For the College Success Mentoring Program, a random group of students were assigned to receive a mentor (i.e., Test group) or not (i.e., Control group). Those students receiving a mentor participated in an 8-week structured mentoring program in which community colleges transfer students were paired with a peer mentor—a successful student at the 4-year institution who had also transferred from the same community college. Each week, mentors contacted mentees to provide academic and social support and to help with mentees' adjustment to the 4-year, online institution. Although no statistically significant improvements in semester performance were found for mentees, unexpectedly, students serving as mentors had a significantly higher cumulative GPA and a significantly higher rate of successful course completion when compared to a control group of students who were invited to be mentors and elected not to serve (see Table 13.6).

Goal Setting and Academic Planning

JumpStart

JumpStart was developed as a 4-week on boarding course for students new to the 4-year institution and designed to support students' academic planning. JumpStart was first offered to students in Fall 2013 and found to improve successful course completion. In Summer 2014, the 4-year institution ran a pilot to assess the effectiveness of jointly offering the JumpStart course and mentoring to community college transfer students. Students participating in JumpStart and in the mentoring program were compared to a control group and to students participating in only one of the programs (i.e., only in JumpStart or only mentoring). No significant differences in performance were found; however, development of JumpStart continues at the 4-year institution based on previous evidence of its success (see Table 13.7).

Table 13.6 Outcomes for mentees and mentors

Mentees		
	Test	Control
GPA	2.70	2.66
Successful course completion	78 %	69 %
Re-enrolment	74 %	75 %
Mentors		
	Test	Control
	Served as mentors	Invited but did not serve as mentors
GPA	3.56	3.34
Successful course completion	95 %	89 %

Table 13.7 Outcomes for JumpStart Summer 2014

	Test		Control
	Enrolled in JumpStart	Completed JumpStart	Did not enroll in JumpStart
Term GPA	2.42	3.06	2.69
Successful course completion	61 %	89 %	74 %
Re-enrolment	76 %	91 %	75 %

Women's Mentoring, Boys to Men, TRiO

The Women's Mentoring, Boys to Men, and TRiO mentoring programs, developed by one of the community colleges, provided minority students with comprehensive academic and social support throughout their transfer pathways from high school to community college and ultimately to a 4-year institution. Going forward, the partner institutions will work together to identify students participating in these programs at the community college and transferring to the 4-year institution in order to track students' progress, performance, and completion.

Diverse Male Student Initiative

The Diverse Male Student Initiative (DMSI) is a 2-year program at the other community college that provides minority male students with role models and academic and career mentoring. DMSI held a 2-day summer institute that featured keynote speakers and awarded book and tuition vouchers for early course registration to participants with the aim of improving academic planning and community college persistence. The two partner institutions will track and evaluate the success and persistence of students who participated in this program and who transferred to the 4-year institution.

Conclusions and Implications

Based on work completed as part of this collaborative project, a number of conclusions may be drawn.

1. Demographic Factors: Gender and marital status were associated with both performance (i.e., earning a successful first-term GPA) and persistence (e.g., re-enrolment). These characteristics may indicate students' maturity and commitment to pursuing academic goals. Interestingly, minority status behaved in unexpected ways in some of the analyses. Specifically, while African American status was negatively associated with earning a successful first-term GPA, it was positively associated with persistence metrics. This suggests that, while not always successful in terms of first-term performance, African American students may nonetheless be particularly committed to their educational goals. Further, such findings point to the importance of considering both performance and persistence as independent factors contributing to students' success.
2. Math at the Community College: In the literature, math has been identified as a key course in helping students' prepare for transfer to a 4-year institution. Taking math at the community college, in addition to reflecting academic abilities, may also reflect students' commitment to meeting the requirements in part for transfer and graduation. In examining both persistence and performance, the models

developed for this study found variables associated with taking math at the community college to be significant predictors. This suggests that taking courses with added difficulty may contribute to later academic success.
3. First-Term Performance: Students' performance in the first term at the 4-year institution remains crucial in predicting their re-enrolment, retention, and graduation. In fact, across models, it was the strongest individual predictor of persistence. First-term GPA may be an indicator of factors contributing to students' success beyond academic abilities. Specifically, students who are better in acclimating to an online university and to the demands associated with a 4-year institution may have a higher first-term GPA. Earning a successful GPA in-and-of itself may in turn encourage students to persist in their educational goals.
4. Instructor Driven Interventions: Looking across interventions, programs that were efficacious in promoting students' success were those that were instructor driven. Specifically, Accounting 220 and 221 and JumpStart were both effective in promoting students' success, in part, because they were led by engaged instructors who encouraged and worked closely with their students. Further, these interventions were academic in nature and closely tied to course content. It may be the case that for online, nontraditional learners, social and institutional integration (targeted through the New Student Checklist and the Mentor Program) is a secondary concern. These students may be more driven by academic goals and motivated to complete their course work as quickly as possible. As such, they may derive more benefits from course-specific, instructor-driven interventions.
5. Collaboration is Key: Across both research initiatives and interventions undertaken, collaboration between the 4-year institution and the community colleges proved to be a valuable aspect of gathering and analyzing cross-institutional data and informing policies and practices. Particularly in addressing the needs of nontraditional students enrolled in an online institution, combining expertise across institutions was crucial. Community colleges have distinct knowledge of their students' backgrounds but often lack insight into how their students' perform once they transfer to a 4-year institution. That knowledge guided research and intervention development for this project. Pragmatically, data sharing enabled the 4-year institution to gain understanding and to develop insight by examining students' transfer records from the community colleges that were more accurate than information available via the 4-year institutions' student information system. This type of data sharing not only enabled research using predictive modeling to take into account students' community college backgrounds but also ensured this research was based on valid data.

Data mining has been around for more than 20 years; however, educational data mining is a developing field. This study contributes modestly to the field of educational data mining by applying data mining techniques to a unique population of community college transfer students at a 4-year online university and to analyze an innovative dataset, linking student records across institutions. Through this project, data mining techniques were used in an exploratory fashion to both identify and derive indicators of student success (e.g., successful course completion) and for confirmatory analyses to validate results from logistic regression. This project has the potential to serve as a model of how data mining techniques can be used alongside traditional statistical methods to inform educational researchers, instructors, and administrators about student progress and performance.

While these findings begin to explore factors that are associated with transfer student success, additional research is needed for three primary reasons. First, the results need to be validated across other institutions and students to be able generalize to a broader population. Second, the link between factors identified in predictive modeling and interventions implemented needs to be further examined. Third, differences in faculty-driven, versus institutional-level, interventions need to be explored further in order to determine the models of intervention design that are most effective. With a growing number of nontraditional, transfer students attending 4-year institutions, research and interventions targeting this population have the potential to yield great value for higher education institutions and for communities benefitting from an increasingly educated workforce.

References

Alfonso, M. (2006). The impact of community college attendance on baccalaureate attainment. *Research in Higher Education, 47*(8), 873–903.

Archer, L., Hutchings, M., & Ross, A. (2005). *Higher education and social class: Issues of exclusion and inclusion*. London: Routledge.

Bailey, T. (2002). Community colleges in the 21st century: Challenges and opportunities. In P. A. Graham & N. G. Stacey (Eds.), The knowledge economy and postsecondary education: Report of a workshop (pp. 59-75). Washington, D.C.: National Academy Press.

Bailey, T. (2009). Challenge and opportunity: Rethinking the role and function of developmental education in community college. *New Directions for Community Colleges, 2009*(145), 11–30.

Bamber, J., & Tett, L. (2000). Transforming the learning experiences of non-traditional students: A perspective from higher education. *Studies in Continuing Education, 22*(1), 57–75.

Bean, J. P., & Metzner, B. S. (1985). A conceptual model of nontraditional undergraduate student attrition. *Review of Educational Research, 55*(4), 485–540.

Bers, T. H., & Smith, K. E. (1991). Persistence of community college students: The influence of student intent and academic and social integration. *Research in Higher Education, 32*(5), 539–556.

Bettinger, E. P., & Long, B. T. (2005). Remediation at the community college: Student participation and outcomes. *New Directions for Community Colleges, 129*, 17–26.

Bettinger, E. P., & Long, B. T. (2009). Addressing the needs of underprepared students in higher education does college remediation work? *Journal of Human Resources, 44*(3), 736–771.

Cabrera, A. F., Nora, A., & Castaneda, M. B. (1993). College persistence: Structural equations modeling test of an integrated model of student retention. *Journal of Higher Education, 64*(2), 123–139.

Calcagno, J. C., Crosta, P., Bailey, T., & Jenkins, D. (2007). Stepping stones to a degree: The impact of enrolment pathways and milestones on community college student outcomes. *Research in Higher Education, 48*(7), 775–801.

Cantwell, R., Archer, J., & Bourke, S. (2001). A comparison of the academic experiences and achievement of university students entering by traditional and non-traditional means. *Assessment &Evaluation in Higher Education, 26*(3), 221–234.

Chemers, M. M., Hu, L. T., & Garcia, B. F. (2001). Academic self-efficacy and first year college student performance and adjustment. *Journal of Educational Psychology, 93*(1), 55–64.

Choy, S. (2002). *Access and persistence: Findings from 10 years of longitudinal research on students*. Washington, DC: American Council on Education.

Christie, R. L., & Hutcheson, P. (2003). Net effects of institutional type on baccalaureate degree attainment of" traditional" students. *Community College Review, 31*(2), 1–20.
Cross, K. P. (1981). *Adults as learners. Increasing participation and facilitating learning*. San Francisco, CA: Jossey-Bass.
DeBerard, M. S., Spielmans, G., & Julka, D. (2004). Predictors of academic achievement and retention among college freshmen: A longitudinal study. *College Student Journal, 38*(1), 66–80.
Goldrick-Rab, S. (2006). Following their every move: An investigation of social-class differences in college pathways. *Sociology of Education, 79*(1), 67–79.
Grimes, S. K. (1997). Underprepared community college students: Characteristics, persistence, and academic success. *Community College Journal of Research and Practice, 21*(1), 47–56.
Hagedorn, L. S. (2005). How to define retention: A new look at an old problem. In A. Seidman (Ed.), *College student retention* (pp. 89–105). Westport: Praeger Publishers.
Keane, M. P. (2002). Financial aid, borrowing constraints, and college attendance: Evidence from structural estimates. *American Economic Review, 92*(2), 293–297.
Kuh, G. D., Cruce, T. M., Shoup, R., Kinzie, J., & Gonyea, R. M. (2008). Unmasking the effects of student engagement on first-year college grades and persistence. *Journal of Higher Education, 79*(5), 540–563.
Lau, L. K. (2003). Institutional factors affecting student retention. *Education, 124*(1), 126–136.
Lehmann, W. (2007). "I just didn't feel like I fit in": The role of habitus in university dropout decisions1. *Canadian Journal of Higher Education, 37*(2), 89–110.
Long, B. T., & Kurlaender, M. (2009). Do community colleges provide a viable pathway to a baccalaureate degree? *Educational Evaluation and Policy Analysis, 31*(1), 30–53.
Martin, K., Galentino, R., & Townsend, L. (2014). Community college student success: The role of motivation and self-empowerment. *Community College Review, 42*(3), 221.
Matus-Grossman, L., & Gooden, S. (2002). *Opening doors: Students' perspectives on juggling work, family, and college*. New York: MDRC.
Metzner, B. S., & Bean, J. P. (1987). The estimation of a conceptual model of nontraditional undergraduate student attrition. *Research in Higher Education, 27*(1), 15–38.
Miller, M., & Lu, M. Y. (2003). Serving non-traditional students in e-learning environments: Building successful communities in the virtual campus. *Educational Media International, 40*(1-2), 163–169.
Moreau, M. P., & Leathwood, C. (2006). Balancing paid work and studies: Working (class) students in higher education. *Studies in Higher Education, 31*(1), 23–42.
Park, J.-H., & Choi, H.-J. (2009). Factors influencing adult learners' decision to drop out or persist in online learning. *Educational Technology & Society, 12*(4), 207–217.
Paulsen, M. B., & St John, E. P. (2002). Social class and college costs: Examining the financial nexus between college choice and persistence. *Journal of Higher Education, 73*(2), 189–236.
Ronco, S. L., & Cahill, J. (2004). *Does it matter who's in the classroom? Effect of instructor type on student retention, achievement and satisfaction*. Paper presented at the 44th Annual Forum of the Association for Institutional Research, Boston.
Rouse, C. E. (2004). Low-income students and college attendance: An exploration of income expectations. *Social Science Quarterly, 85*(5), 1299–1317.
Schuetz, P. (2005). UCLA community college review: Campus environment: A missing link in studies of community college attrition. *Community College Review, 32*(4), 60–80.
Seidman, A. (Ed.). (2005). *College student retention: Formula for student success*. Westport, CT: ACE/Praeger.
Shapiro, D., Dundar, A., Wakhungu, P.K., Yuan, X., Nathan, A. & Hwang, Y. (2015). Completing college: a national view of student attainment rates – Fall 2009 cohort (Signature report no. 10). Herndon, VA: National Student Clearinghouse Research Center.
Spitzer, T. M. (2000). Predictors of college success: A comparison of traditional and nontraditional age students. *Journal of Student Affairs Research and Practice, 38*(1), 99–115.
Tinto, V. (2006). Research and practice of student retention: What next? *Journal of College Student Retention: Research, Theory & Practice, 8*(1), 1–19.
Walpole, M. (2003). Socioeconomic status and college: How SES affects college experiences and outcomes. *The Review of Higher Education, 27*(1), 45–73.

Chapter 14
Assessing Science Inquiry Skills in an Immersive, Conversation-Based Scenario

Diego Zapata-Rivera, Lei Liu, Lei Chen, Jiangang Hao, and Alina A. von Davier

Abstract Innovative, interactive tasks that include conversations among humans and virtual (pedagogical) agents can be used to assess relevant cognitive skills (e.g., scientific inquiry skills). These new assessment systems aid the collection of additional information (e.g., timing data, information about conversation path sequences, and amount of help used) that provide the context for assessment and can inform assessment claims in these specific environments. In order to assess science skills, we have implemented and evaluated a game-like assessment with embedded conversations called the Volcano Scenario. This chapter describes the Volcano Scenario and highlights the techniques used to collect and analyze the data generated by the system. A hybrid approach to analyzing data from interactive, assessment environments that makes use of traditional psychometric analysis and several big data-related processes is described and illustrated through the analyses of data from 500 participants who have at least a year of college experience.

Keywords Hybrid approach • Conversation-based assessments • Science inquiry skills

Introduction

New types of assessments usually involve the use of computer technologies in the collection of evidence of students' skills, knowledge, and other attributes from a variety of sources. Some of these new types of interactive, assessment environments (IAEs) include computer simulations (Bennett, Persky, Weiss, & Jenkins 2007; Clarke-Midura, Code, Dede, Mayrath, & Zap, 2011; Quellmalz et al., 2011) and

D. Zapata-Rivera (✉) • L. Liu • L. Chen • J. Hao • A.A. von Davier
Research and Development. Educational Testing Service,
660 Rosedale Road, Princeton, NJ 08541, USA
e-mail: dzapata@ets.org

B. Kei Daniel (ed.), *Big Data and Learning Analytics in Higher Education*,
DOI 10.1007/978-3-319-06520-5_14

games (Mislevy et al., 2014; Shute, Ventura, Bauer, & Zapata-Rivera, 2009). The use of these technologies for assessment affords collecting rich data of students' complex problem-solving process by logging students' interactions within the IAEs.

Assessment design frameworks such as Evidence-Centered Design (ECD; Mislevy, Steinberg, & Almond, 2003) have been used to design many of these IAEs. However, these rich IAEs also lend themselves to a variety of interactions such as unpredictable actions or emerging behavior that may not be expected when the assessment was first designed. DiCerbo and Behrens (2012) describe the concept of "an assessment ecosystem" as an environment in which information is accumulated from a variety of natural digital experiences to form a cohesive view of students' knowledge, skills, and attributes (KSAs).

Big Data or Educational Data Mining (EDM) processes and techniques can be used to analyze large and diverse sources of data gathered by these assessment systems in order to discover interesting patterns of user interactions that can help us better understand student performance (Baker & Yacef, 2009; White, 2012). By using top-down (ECD) and bottom-up (Big Data) approaches, it is possible to draw inferences about students' KSAs based on both their interactions in the game (process data) as well as their responses to predefined tasks.

Conversations with artificial characters can be used to gather additional evidence that may be difficult to obtain using traditional assessment approaches (e.g., evidence of science inquiry skills), provide multiple opportunities for students to elaborate about particular issues (target constructs), and elicit explanations about decisions that students make in the scenario. These conversations can be embedded in a variety of assessment tasks including simulations, scenario-based, game-based assessments.

In this chapter, we illustrate a hybrid approach that involves applying data mining and psychometric approaches in order to interpret data collected as students interact with an IAE designed to assess science inquiry skills. The Volcano Scenario is an immersive, conversation-based IAE of scientific inquiry in the context of collecting seismic data from a volcano to determine an alert level for a possible eruption. After describing the main components of the Volcano Scenario, we elaborate on the nature of the data it collects during students' interaction with the system, including both more traditional "responses to questions" as well as log files that capture the processes by which students interact with the IAE. We describe the hybrid analysis process and illustrate its use in a case study dataset of 500 adults who interacted with the Volcano Scenario.

The Volcano Scenario

The design of the Volcano Scenario draws on social constructivist literature (Lave & Wenger, 1991; Pear & Crone-Todd, 2002; Vygotsky, 1978), taking the approach of using conversations with virtual agents as a means to collect evidence about students' KSAs. Our research leverages advances made in the area of dialogue systems

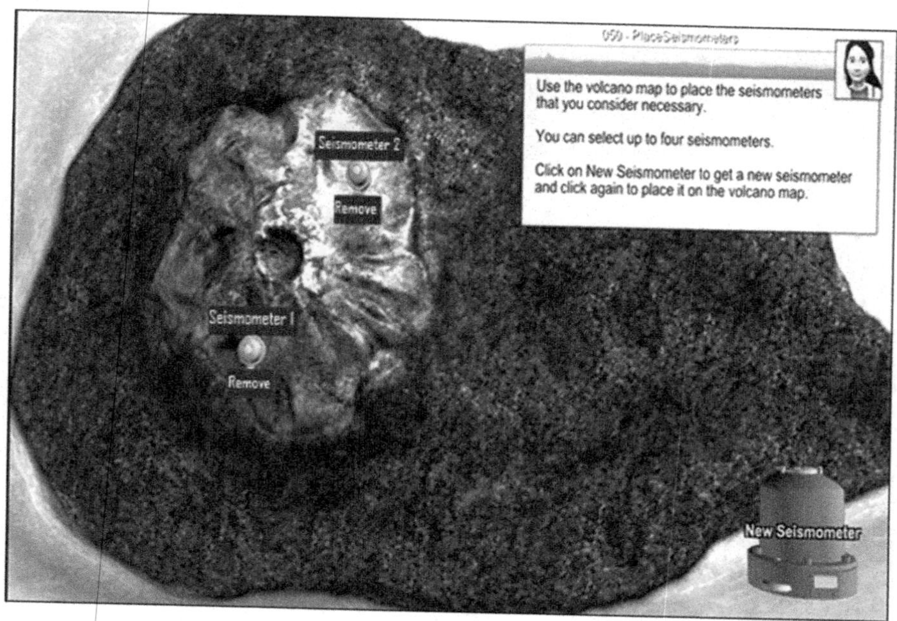

Fig. 14.1 Collecting data using seismometers

(Adamson, Dyke, Jang, & Rosé, 2014; Graesser et al., 2004; Graesser, Person, & Harter, 2001; Millis et al., 2011).

The Volcano Scenario aims to measure students' earth science knowledge and science inquiry skills (e.g., collecting and analyzing data, making data-based predictions). In this scenario, students interact with two artificial characters: Dr. Garcia, a virtual scientist and Art, a virtual student. These characters introduce themselves and provide information about earth science content knowledge (i.e., knowledge about volcanoes, seismometers, seismic events, and alert levels) through a video simulation and other materials. Students have the opportunity to place seismometers for data collection, collect data, identify data patterns, and make predictions. Figure 14.1 shows how a student places seismometers around a volcano in order to collect data that is sent to the virtual laboratory to be analyzed.

Students have conversations with the artificial characters about the quality of data collected and the predictions that can be drawn from that data. These conversations are used to gather information about students' science inquiry skills. For example, after making notes about the data collected using seismometers, the student is asked to review and compare one of his/her own notes with one of Art's notes. Art's note is created based on the student's notes and is used to gather additional evidence of the student's data collection skills. Figure 14.2 depicts a conversation among the student, Dr. Garcia and Art on the quality of the collected notes. These conversations include two or three cycles of turn taking where the student receives limited feedback and has multiple opportunities to elaborate on the reasons for choosing a particular note.

Fig. 14.2 A screenshot of a conversation on the quality of the notes

Table 14.1 Sample conversation

Agent	Utterance
Dr. Garcia:	Art, can you please show us one of your notes?
Art:	Here is one of my notes
Dr. Garcia:	Tim. Can you compare these two notes? Which one do you think we should keep for making predictions later?
Test Taker:	I don't understand what you mean
Dr. Garcia:	Tim. Can you compare these two notes and tell us which one you think we should keep?
Test Taker:	Art's note has two more seismometers than mine
Dr. Garcia:	Do you want to use Art's note instead?
Test Taker:	Yes
Art:	Why?
Test Taker:	Because it has more data
Dr. Garcia:	Ok. Let's continue

Table 14.1 shows a sample conversation. As illustrated in this example, the test taker was provided multiple opportunities to respond meaningfully to the main question. For example, when the test taker was unsure about the question, the virtual agent (Dr. Garcia) rephrased the question. In addition, the test taker's response was diagnosed whether it was complete or not. If diagnosed as incomplete, the virtual agent followed up with additional questions so that the test taker received additional opportunities to elaborate his/her thinking.

The Volcano Scenario also includes seven multiple-choice questions designed to assess students' earth science knowledge, a volcano simulation where students can place seismometers and select the data collection time, a virtual lab where students annotate the data collected and two conversations with virtual agents.

Multiple-choice items are used to assess student understanding of the information about volcanoes provided at the beginning of the scenario. Each multiple-choice item is mapped to a particular earth science concept/skill. There are seven multiple-choice items. Items 1, 2, 3, and 4 deal with understanding earth science concepts (*E1*) such as the parts of a volcano, volcanic seismic events, and alert levels. Items 5, 6, and 7 are about applying earth science concepts (*E2*). In general, E1 items measure student factual knowledge of seismic events and E2 items measure student skills of matching certain seismic data patterns with appropriate seismic events.

Conversations are designed to measure one or more of the following science inquiry constructs: *C1: Data Collection; C2: Making Predictions based on Data; C3: Evidence-based reasoning; and C4: Communication*. The construct of *Data Collection (C1)* refers to student skills of collecting relevant data and using appropriate sampling procedures for a particular situation. The construct of *Making Predictions based on Data (C2)* relates to student skill of making accurate and appropriated predications based on available data. The construct of *Evidence-based Reasoning (C3)* is to determine whether students can clearly explain and demonstrate how evidence is related to the accuracy of claims. The construct of *Communication (C4)* refers to student skills of provide relevant and desired information when communicating with others. Conversation 1 was designed to assess C1, C3, and C4. Conversation 2 assesses C2, C3, and C4. The scoring process of these conversations has two components: (1) path-based scoring (automatically assigned partial credit scores per each relevant construct based on expert judgment); and (2) revised scores based on additional evidence from human raters or other automated scoring engines.

We applied the principles of ECD (Mislevy et al., 2003) to develop these conversation-based assessments through iterative cycles of developing, testing, and revising. ECD provides a systematic approach to assessment design, beginning with the construct to the measured, explicating the observable student behaviors that provide evidence of these constructs, and designing the scenario and the overall environment to collect this evidence. All elements of the Volcano Scenario—the questions asked, the conversations scripted, and the scoring approach taken—were derived through the systematic process of design outlined by ECD. For example, the different conversation "paths" (alternative conversations that different students might have) were designed through a combination of expert judgment and use of theories of how students learn scientific inquiry skills (Liu, Rogat, & Bertling, 2013; Zapata-Rivera, 2013; Zapata-Rivera et al., 2014). The ECD process provides a top-down, theory-driven approach to assessment. However, students' interactions with the system might reveal patterns of behavior that provide more information about students' learning than was originally designed into the assessment scenario. In the next section, we illustrate a hybrid approach to analyzing both responses and process data collected using the Volcano Scenario.

A Hybrid Approach to Analyzing IAE Data

The essence of data analysis of IAE data is to reveal the insights that teachers and schools need in order to pinpoint teaching and learning problems and identify the best ways to solve them. Current data analysis research is not sufficient to analyze the data from complex IAEs because many of these tools are focused on outcome data. We describe a process that makes use of traditional psychometric analyses done on student responses and analyses on process data that usually fall under "Big Data" or EDM analytics.

Although a top-down scoring approach can be used to score multiple-choice items and conversations tasks, more evidence is required to understand the process by which people arrive to those responses (e.g., path followed, scaffold received, use of help, and time spent on particular tasks). Results from both traditional psychometric and EDM analysis inform each other.

The hybrid process to analyzing IAE data starts by determining how current tasks measure the intended construct(s). A variety of traditional psychometric analyses can be used to examine the psychometric properties of each effective item. This process may result in actions such as: the removal of particular items (e.g., items that are too hard or too difficult), the need for additional items to achieve target reliability levels, and the generation of a single score or several scores based on results of dimensionality analyses. Similarly, understanding how process features relate to the target construct(s) facilitates the process of selecting and evaluating these process features. By focusing on construct-relevant features, the EDM process may result on features that can be potentially used for scoring purposes, refine/expand the construct or provide insights on the underlying cognitive processes students' experience before arriving to an answer.

The following sections outline the data analysis procedures used in this study. These procedures include: log file design, traditional psychometric analysis (e.g., item analysis, dimensionality of the construct supported by multiple-choice items, and correlation analyses with an external general measure of science knowledge; and data mining processes including feature identification, feature extraction, and feature evaluation.

Log File Design

The log file is an important source of information for both traditional psychometric and EDM analysis. The types of analyses that can be done depend on what data was captured and how the data was structured. Scoring rubrics are usually developed to map observed data (e.g., student actions or responses) with the constructs (e.g., students' inquiry skills).

Students' process and response data is time-stamped and recorded in a single log file following certain XML conventions, which includes rich information about sequences of student problem-solving processes. To make the log system scalable, we adopted a distributed log file uploading system. That is, the log file from each student is uploaded to a designated data server directly from the student's session. Such a mechanism allows us to distribute both the workload of the game-like task itself, and provide a scalable way to store the log files by assigning (or randomly assigning) data servers for each session to upload to. In terms of the data processing, each log file is parsed separately and then the results are aggregated, which mimics processes such as the map-reduce scheme when dealing with large datasets. In addition, the log system allows us to apply new analytics tools that transform a bunch of numbers (e.g., frequencies of using available tools and resources, responding time) into actionable facts and/or visualizations about students' KSAs, which in turn, provides insights that can be used to change the instruction, if needed.

The log file plays an important role in reconstructing the information about the performance of a student in conversation tasks. Therefore, it is essential to structure the log system appropriately. We designed a well-structured data model for the log files to facilitate the analysis (Hao, Liu, von Davier, & Kyllonen, 2015). In our log system, all events in the Volcano Scenario are categorized into two classes in XML format: system state events and student activities. Both of them are treated as "generalized actions" that can be characterized by certain attributes and values. In our log system, there are five general attributes. The first attribute is the name of the action (ActionName), which records the nature of the action (e.g., filling in a multiple-choice question, placing seismometers, making notes). The second attribute records the time of the action (ActionTime). The third attribute records who committed the action (ActionBy). The fourth attribute records to which event the action is applied (ActionTo). Finally, the fifth attribute records the results of the action (ActionResult), which includes students' actual responses or interactions. With these five attributes, we were able to reconstruct each student's interactions in the Volcano Scenario.

Traditional Psychometric Analysis

We conducted basic item analysis to investigate the task quality and fairness before we evaluate student performance. These analyses include: (1) item difficulty, (2) item discrimination, (3) clustering of items based on the responses, and (4) analysis of student performance on various types of items by conducting correlation analyses with an external general measure of science knowledge.

Data Mining Techniques

Feature identification involves determining process features that can provide additional information about students' cognitive processes, information that can explain their actions/responses and possible connections with the target construct(s).

These features can be extracted from the log files and analysis can be done to investigate how they correlate with target skills. Sample possible features, may include: the time students spent on particular areas of the IAE (e.g., time spent watching a tutorial video or annotating data), and frequencies of checking different available resources (e.g., the notes, video on seismic events, alert table).

Once students' input data is captured, we can apply feature extraction methods to transform the input data into sets of features. The feature identification and extraction highly depends on the research questions to be answered. For example, if the research question is to explore the relationship between the amount of time that the students spent on viewing a simulation about volcanic eruption and their performance on making a prediction about the likelihood of a volcanic eruption in their field trip, we could extract the feature of total time that each student used to watch/revisit the video and calculate. Similarly, if the research question is to investigate how long the students spent to plan their data collection may impact their correctness of their prediction, we could extract a feature of the total time of the data collection from the raw log data. By extracting the relevant information from the log data, we can help reduce the amount of log data required to perform the desired data analyses.

The next sections showcase the hybrid data analysis approach in the context of a study using the Volcano Scenario.

Use Case Study

Our data collection strategy was crowdsourcing through Amazon Mechanical Turk, which has become popular for data-driven research in cognitive and social science (Kraut et al., 2004). We carried out our data collection using Amazon Mechanical Turk in December 2013. In 2 weeks, we collected data from 500 from college level Turkers who completed the Volcano Scenario online (Hao, Smith, Mislevy, von Davier, & Bauer, 2016; Liu, Hao, von Davier, Kyllonen, & Zapata-Rivera, 2016). Data mining techniques and psychometric approaches were applied to these data.

An external general science measure (GS) composed of 37 multiple-choice science questions was used as a common instrument to compare students' scores on multiple-choice items, conversations, and performance on features. This instrument was produced by adapting two existing science instruments: 12 items from the SLiM instrument (Rundgren, Rundgren, Tseng, Lin, & Chang, 2012) and 25 items from an ETS in-house science instrument; both sources focus on the application of core science knowledge and have been validated as a measure of general science literacy. Each multiple-choice question has four alternatives. The selected items provide a context of daily life-related science questions.

Table 14.2 Item difficulty (proportion of correct response) and point-biserial correlation values for seven multiple-choice items

Item	Item difficulty	Point-biserial correlation to the total
Item 1	0.640	0.688
Item 2	0.615	0.701
Item 3	0.677	0.651
Item 4	0.582	0.670
Item 5	0.938	0.312
Item 6	0.856	0.471
Item 7	0.973	0.347

Results

Item Analysis

Item analysis was performed for the seven multiple-choice items linked to E1 and E2. This analysis was performed using the R psychometric package. The Cronbach's alpha for the first seven items is 0.65. The item analysis results are presented in Table 14.2.

From the table, one can see that item 4 is the most difficult item while item 5 to item 7 are too easy. Item 4 requires students to order the sequence of seismic events as typical patterns before a volcanic eruption. In other words, students need to recall multiple seismic events knowledge to answer this question; therefore, the cognitive load is heavier than other items which typically only require recalling one or two seismic events knowledge.

Point-biserial correlation values seem good (positive values greater than 0.25) showing that students who receive a high total score tend to answer the item correctly and those who receive low scores tend to answer the item incorrectly.

When we design the task, the item 1–4 and item 5–7 belong to different dimensions of the construct (see The Valcano Scenario). We would like to check whether our data support this. In Fig. 14.3, we show the clustering of the items based on the responses.

Figure 14.3 shows the results of a hierarchical clustering analysis based on the scores of the first seven items. In the clustering process, we used the Euclidean distance with complete linkage. The results show that item 1, 2, 3, and 4 are clustered together while item 5, 6, and 7 are clustered together. These two clusters seem to correspond with the definitions of E1 and E2 that we described above.

Correlations Among Skill Scores

Correlations among scores on the external general science measure (GS), earth science knowledge items (E1), earth science application items (E2), and science inquiry skills (C1–C4) were calculated (see Table 14.3). Due to missing data, this analysis is based on results from 470 of the participants.

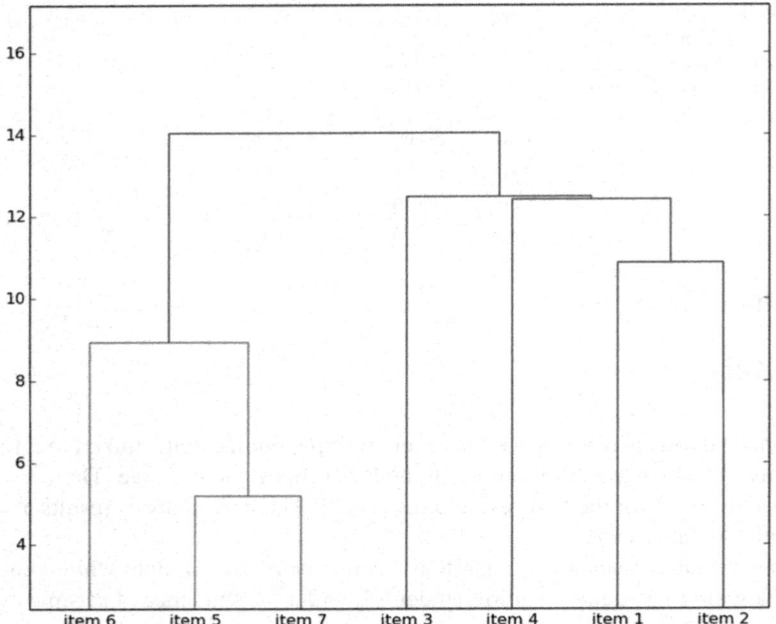

Fig. 14.3 Hierarchical clustering of multiple-choice items

Comparing scores on multiple-choice items (E1 and E2) to conversation scores (C1–C4): C2 (Making Predictions based on Data) and C3 (Evidence-based reasoning) scores have a very strong, positive relationship (r=0.764). This is consistent with the nature of these skills. Both of these skills relate science reasoning processes. C3 (Evidence-based reasoning) and C4 (Communication) scores have a strong, positive relationship (r=0.65); this can be explained by noticing that usually students who provided complete evidence-based explanations received higher communication scores. C2 (Making Predictions based on Data) and C4 (Communication) have a weak positive relationship. This may be explained by the fact that selecting the correct alert level and supporting evidence did not require students to provide longer and detailed explanations. The relationship between C1 (Data Collection) and (C2–C4) is negligible (r values less than 0.2). This seems to indicate that knowing about appropriate data collection procedures do not seem to tap on the science reasoning skills (C2–C4). This also suggests that C1 seems to provide additional information not measured by C2–C4.

Comparing scores on multiple-choice items (E1 and E2) and conversation scores (C1–C4) to an external measure (GS): In order to validate the scores obtained in the Volcano Scenario using multiple-choice and conversation tasks, we compared these scores with scores on the external, general science measure. GS scores have a strong positive relationship with E1 (r=397) and a moderate, positive relationship E2 (r=0.333), C2 (r=0.333), and C3 (r=0.309) scores and a negligible, positive

Table 14.3 Pearson correlation coefficients among an external general science measure (GS), earth science knowledge items (E1), earth science application items (E2), and science inquiry skills (C1–C4). r values greater than 0.3 appear in bold

Skill	GS	E1	E2	C1	C2	C3	C4
GS	1.00	**0.397****	**0.333****	0.188**	**0.333****	**0.309****	0.187**
E1	**0.397****	1.00	0.271**	0.136*	0.186**	0.210**	0.132*
E2	**0.333****	0.271**	1.00	0.216**	0.240**	0.216**	0.160**
C1	0.188**	0.136*	0.216**	1.00	0.072	0.058	0.115*
C2	**0.333****	0.186**	0.240**	0.072	1.00	**0.764****	0.287**
C3	**0.309****	0.210**	0.216**	0.058	**0.764****	1.00	**0.650****
C4	0.187**	0.132*	0.160**	0.115*	0.287**	**0.650****	1.00

**$p<0.01$; *$p<0.05$

relationship with C1 and C4 (*r* values less than 0.2). In the context of the volcano task, this result indicates that to collect sufficient data and to conduct inquiry-related communication was not necessarily related to the amount of scientific content knowledge that students mastered. In science, researchers identified some domain-general inquiry practices, which may not require specific content knowledge (Zimmerman, 2000). Designing experiments, which includes data collection (C1) is one of such practices. However, for other practices such as reasoning and argumentation, recent research argues that a variety of content knowledge is important for successful engagement in inquiry tasks that requires students to provide evidence to support certain claims (Gotwals & Songer, 2006).

These results seem to indicate that conversations are assessing other constructs that are not being measured by the multiple-choice questions. So far we have shown how some of the traditional psychometric analysis can be used to investigate how existing tasks are measuring the target construct(s). The next section focuses on EDM processes.

Feature Identification

The XML log files were converted into flattened CSV files with multiple columns. As described above (see A Hybrid Approach to Analyzing IAE Data), there are various ways to extract informative features about students' learning behaviors from this CSV file.

In our game-based scenario, there are several key features that provide evidence about students' science inquiry skills, including collecting and analyzing data, and making data-based predictions. Experts identified a list of potential features to be extracted based on the definition of the construct. To analyze students' inquiry skill of collecting data, the following features would be useful for making a claim: the number of seismometers that the student placed on the volcano map when planning for data collection, location of each seismometer, and the total time that the student

Table 14.4 Construct relevant features

Science inquiry skills	Relevant features
Collecting data	**Number of seismometers**
	Location of each seismometer placed on the volcano map
	Total time of data collection
Analyzing data	Number of notes
	Number of data patterns identified in the notes
	Total number of words in data pattern description
	Total time of making notes
Making data-based predictions	Time of learning about the scientific knowledge
	Frequency of checking the seismic event video when making a prediction
	Total time of checking the seismic event video when making a prediction
	Frequency of checking the alert level table
	Total time of checking the alert level table

spent on planning and conducting data collection. To make a claim about students' inquiry skill of analyzing data, the following features would be necessary including the number of notes that the student made, the number of data patterns identified, the total number of words in the note description, and the total time spent on making notes. For the inquiry skill of making data-based predictions, the following features are relevant: total time of learning about the seismic events, frequency of checking available resources (e.g., seismic events videos, alert level table). Table 14.4 summarizes a list of potential features that can be extracted for data analyses.

Due to time limitations, only a subset of these features were extracted and analyzed for this study. These features include (see features in bold font, Table 14.4): number of seismometers, total time of data collection (sec.), frequency of checking the alert level table, and total time of checking the alert level table.

Feature Extraction

During their learning processes, students can choose the number of the sensors used in exploring virtual volcanos. First, it is possible that the *number of seismometers* being used can be used as evidence of data collection skills. Therefore, we extracted this feature from this CSV file containing many actions from each student and each time stamp. To efficiently extract the needed feature and also create data analysis truly understood by human users, we utilized the *dplyr* package, a very powerful data frame manipulation package and *pipeline* function available in the R language (R Core Team, 2013). Using these two techniques, the feature extraction became a very simple solution (see Table 14.5).

Table 14.5 Feature extraction—code snippet

```
# 2. Number Seismometers Dropped
sensors<- df %>%
group_by(playerID) %>%
filter(actionName=="Number
Seismometers Dropped") %>%
summarize(sensor=actionResult)
```

Note here %>% is the pipeline operator, quite similar to the "|" operator widely used in Unix systems to link a series of data manipulation procedures. The df is the data frame after loading the massive CSV file containing all of process details. The above code piece shows the data process including (a) grouping each students' entries, (b) only checking the entries whose actionName is related to number of "seismometers dropped," and summarize the numbers of sensors used.

We hypothesized that the time each student spends on collecting evidence (*total time of data collection*) may be related to their data collection skills. This time can be computed from the time stamp gap between the time the student starts placing seismometers and the time the student finishes annotating the data.

The *frequency and the time spent on checking the alert level table* were identified as useful features, since understanding the evidence needed for each of these alert levels was important to support the prediction. Therefore, we also extracted them from the CSV file.

In summary, using the dplyr package and R's pipeline functionality, we extracted a set of process-related features from students' actions. These features are compared to the science inquiry scores (C1–C4) obtained through conversations 1 and 2.

Feature Evaluation

Correlation coefficients among these four process features and the scores on each of the skills and the external measure were computed. The results only showed a weak, positive relationship (r=0.21) between *frequency of alert level table views* and *C3* scores. This seem to be associated to the need for double checking the contents of the alert table to be able to make good arguments connecting evidence to prediction of volcanic eruption. All the other correlations were negligible (r values less than 0.2).

Although these features did not show a high predictive value, there are more features that need to be explored. Information about how potential features can be connected to the construct will guide future EDM analyses. In addition aggregation of several features may provide useful information. Some of the features that seem promising to explore next include: the location of seismometers on the map, the time taken watching the instructional videos and the time annotating the data.

Discussion

Although scores from the multiple-choice questions and conversation-based tasks seem to provide good evidence to assess students' science knowledge and science inquiry skills, these rich, complex scenarios also provide a variety of data/features that can potentially contribute to (1) better understand the cognitive processes that student experience during their interaction with these tasks, (2) refine/expand the construct that is being measured, and (3) inform extended reporting. Finding interesting features with instructional relevance can improve the type of information that teachers, students, and parents currently receive as part of the score reports. An extended reporting framework not only produces scores but also provides stakeholders with information on how particular features relate to student performance. This information can be relevant for formative purposes. For example, it is possible to provide information on the feature profile of students who perform at a particular level.

The hybrid process described in this chapter is iterative and makes use of process data and product data. Using the definition of the construct(s) as a guiding mechanism for identifying potential features can facilitate the process of analyzing and interpreting process data in IAEs. This process can be made more efficient by creating tools to facilitate data identification, data extraction, and analysis processes. Other relevant analyses that were not explored in this study include: principle component analysis, reliability analysis, other clustering/classification algorithms, and visualization techniques. These additional analyses can reveal interesting patterns or sets of features that can have potential uses as mentioned above.

Summary and Future Work

In this chapter, we described a game-like scenario task that was designed to collect evidence about students' science inquiry, described a hybrid approach to analyze IAE data and illustrated the approach by applying traditional psychometric and EDM analyses the data collected using the Volcano Scenario. These analyses were used to understand students' responses and actions in a complex task. This hybrid approach can inform science educators and assessment developers about making meaning from various types of data including responses to multiple-choice items, conversation tasks, and process data. These data can inform the analysis of students' underlying cognitive processes that, in turn, helps us measure complex, higher order thinking skills. Future research includes extracting and analyzing other potential features and conducting additional studies to validate the identified features.

References

Adamson, D., Dyke, G., Jang, H. J., & Rosé, C. P. (2014). Towards an agile approach to adapting dynamic collaboration support to student needs. *International Journal of Artificial Intelligence in Education, 24*(1), 91–121.

Assunção, M., Calheiros, R., Bianchi, S., Netto, M., & Buyya, R. (2014). Big data computing and clouds: Trends and future directions. *Journal of Parallel and Distributed Computing, 75*(13), 156–175.

Baker, R., & Yacef, K. (2009). The state of educational data mining in 2009: A review and future visions. *Journal of Educational Data Mining, 1*, 3–17.

Bennett, R. E., Persky, H., Weiss, A. R., & Jenkins, F. (2007). *Problem solving in technology-rich environments: A report from the NAEP technology based assessment project* (NCES 2007–466). Washington, DC: National Center for Education Statistics, U.S. Department of Education

Clarke-Midura, J., Code, J., Dede, C., Mayrath, M., & Zap, N. (2011). Thinking outside the bubble: Virtual performance assessments for measuring complex learning. In M. C. Mayrath, J. Clarke-Midura, & D. Robinson (Eds.), *Technology-based assessments for 21st century skills: Theoretical and practical implications from modern research* (pp. 125–147). Charlotte, NC: Information Age.

R Core Team (2013). *R: A language and environment for statistical computing. R Foundation for statistical Computing*, Vienna, Austria. Retrieved October 5, 2014, from http://www.R-project.org/

DiCerbo, K., & Behrens, J. (2012). *From technology-enhanced assessment to assessment-enhanced technology*. Paper presented at the annual meeting of the National Council on Measurement in Education (NCME), Vancouver, BC. Canada, 12–16 April 2012.

Gotwals, A. W., & Songer, N. B. (2006). Measuring students' scientific content and inquiry reasoning. In S. Barab, K. Hay, & D. Hickey (Eds.), *Proceedings of the 7th international conference of the learning sciences* (pp. 196–202). Mahwah, NJ: Lawrence Erlbaum.

Graesser, A. C., Lu, S. L., Jackson, G., Mitchell, H., Ventura, M., Olney, A., et al. (2004). AutoTutor: A tutor with dialogue in natural language. *Behavioral Research Methods, Instruments & Computers, 36*, 180–193.

Graesser, A. C., Person, N. K., & Harter, D. (2001). The tutoring research group: Teaching tactics and dialogue in AutoTutor. *International Journal of Artificial Intelligence in Education, 12*, 257–279.

Hao, J., Liu, L., von Davier, A., & Kyllonen, P. (2015). Assessing collaborative problem solving with simulation based task. In *Proceedings of the 11th international conference on computer supported collaborative learning*, Gothenburg, Sweden, 7–11 June.

Hao, J., Smith, L., Mislevy, R., von Davier, A., & Bauer, M. (2016). Taming log files from game and simulation based assessments: Data models and data analysis tools. doi:10.1002/ets2.12096

Kraut, R., Olson, J., Banaji, M., Bruckman, A., Cohen, J., & Couper, M. (2004). Psychological research online: Report of board of scientific affairs' advisory group on the conduct of research on the internet. *American Psychologist, 59*, 105–117.

Lave, J., & Wenger, E. (1991). *Situated learning: Legitimate peripheral participation*. Cambridge: Cambridge University Press.

Liu, L., Hao, J., von Davier, A., Kyllonen, P., & Zapata-Rivera, D. (2016). A tough nut to crack: Measuring collaborative problem solving. In Y. Rosen, S. Ferrara, & M. Mosharraf (Eds.), *Handbook of research on computational tools for real-world skill development*. Hershey, PA: IGI-Global.

Liu, L., Rogat, A., & Bertling, M. (2013). *A CBAL™ science model of cognition: Developing a competency model and learning progressions to support assessment development* (ETS Research Report Series. 2:1–54). Princeton, NJ: Educational Testing Service.

Millis, K., Forsyth, C., Butler, H., Wallace, P., Graesser, A. C., & Halpern, D. (2011). Operation ARIES! a serious game for teaching scientific inquiry. In J. Lakhmi & M. M. Oikonomou (Eds.), *Serious games and edutainment applications* (pp. 169–196). London: Springer.

Mislevy, R., Oranje, A., Bauer, M., von Davier, A., Hao, J., Corrigan, S., et al. (2014). Psychometric considerations in game-based assessment. Retrieved October 9, 2014, from http://www.instituteofplay.org/wp-content/uploads/2014/02/GlassLab_GBA1_WhitePaperFull.pdf.

Mislevy, R. J., Steinberg, L. S., & Almond, R. G. (2003). On the structure of educational assessments. *Measurement: Interdisciplinary Research and Perspectives , 1*, 3–62.

Pear, J. J., & Crone-Todd, D. E. (2002). A social constructivist approach to computer-mediated instruction. *Computers & Education, 38*, 221–231.

Quellmalz, E. S., Timms, M. J., Buckley, B. C., Davenport, J., Loveland, M., & Silberglitt, M. D. (2011). 21st century dynamic assessment. In M. C. Mayrath, J. Clarke-Midura, & D. Robinson (Eds.), *Technology-based assessments for 21st century skills: Theoretical and practical implications from modern research* (pp. 55–90). Charlotte, NC: Information Age.

Rundgren, C. J., Rundgren, S. N. C., Tseng, Y. H., Lin, P. L., & Chang, C. Y. (2012). Are you SLiM? Developing an instrument for civic scientific literacy measurement (SLiM) based on media coverage. *Public Understanding of Science, 21*(6), 759–773.

Shute, V. J., Ventura, M., Bauer, M. I., & Zapata-Rivera, D. (2009). Melding the power of serious games and embedded assessment to monitor and foster learning: Flow and grow. In U. Ritterfeld, M. J. Cody, & P. Vorderer (Eds.), *Serious games: Mechanisms and effects* (pp. 295–321). Philadelphia, PA: Routledge.

Vygotsky, L. (1978). *Mind in society*. London: Harvard University Press.

White, T. (2012). *Hadoop: The definitive guide* (3rd ed.). Sebastopol, CA: O'Reilly Media.

Zapata-Rivera, D. (2013). *Exploring the use of trialogues in assessment*. Paper presented at the Cognition and Assessment SIG Symposium. Annual meeting of the American Educational Research Association (AERA), San Francisco, CA, April 27–May 1.

Zapata-Rivera, D., Jackson, T., Liu, L., Bertling, M., Vezzu, M., & Katz, I. R. (2014). Science inquiry skills using trialogues. In S. Trausan-Matu, K. Boyer, M. Crosby, & K. Panourgia (Eds.), *Proceedings of the 12th International Conference on Intelligence Tutoring Systems. Honolulu, HI, June 2014: Vol. 8474: Lecture notes in computer science* (pp. 625–626). Switzerland: Springer International.

Zimmerman, C. (2000). The development of scientific reasoning skills. *Developmental Review, 20*, 99–149.

Chapter 15
Learning Analytics of Clinical Anatomy e-Cases

Vivek Perumal, Ben Daniel, and Russell Butson

Abstract Interactive online resources to support the learning of clinical anatomy are limited. While there is an assumption that such resources are useful, it is not known whether or not these resources support students learning. A new online problem-based supplementary learning resource named clinical anatomy e-cases was developed using Moodle and piloted on undergraduate medical students ($n = 282$). We examined users and usage analytics within the online learning management system. This chapter presents results of a study undertaken to explore students' experiences in utilizing the e-cases in an informal learning environment. 80.85 % of the students accessed the resource with 14.5 % repetitions. We also report on a number of indicators that can be used to assess learning outcomes in nonformal learning environment. The construction of the e-cases ensured student interaction and engagement, even during weekends and after hours. Regular usage promoted increased scores within the environment and their formative examinations. The use of such simple, tailor made online clinical resources might promote student engagement and augment student learning outside classroom setting.

Keywords Anatomy • e-Cases • e-Learning • Moodle • Learning analytics

Introduction

Anatomy is central to biomedical sciences; it is the basis for understanding human architecture and core to other subjects including medicine and surgery. Students spend a significant amount of time in mastering this subject. While this requires a problem-solving approach in addition to traditional lectures and dissections (Ganguly, 2010), the amount of classroom teaching time allotted to anatomy is being drastically reduced recently (Bergman, Prince, Drukker, Vleuten, &

V. Perumal (✉)
Department of Anatomy, University of Otago, Dunedin, New Zealand
e-mail: vivek.perumal@anatomy.otago.ac.nz

B. Daniel • R. Butson
Higher Education Development Centre, University of Otago, Dunedin, New Zealand

B. Kei Daniel (ed.), *Big Data and Learning Analytics in Higher Education*,
DOI 10.1007/978-3-319-06520-5_15

Scherpbier, 2008; Drake, Lowrie, & Prewitt, 2002; Ganguly, 2010; Nayak, Ramnarayan, & Somayaji, 2005; Turney, 2007).

Faced with lack of resources to support students' growing divergent needs, university teachers have to explore new ways of providing learning outside the traditional classroom setting, thus expecting the students to be independent learners. Some of these attempts include the exploration of online learning environments (McNulty, Halama, & Espiritu, 2004)—including nonformal learning environments (Selman, Cooke, Selman, & Dampier, 1998), where learners exercise various degrees of self-directedness and where interactions might not be mediated by a teacher (Schwier & Seaton, 2013)

In the University of Otago, basic anatomy for medical students is introduced from their first year, but detailed clinical anatomy is taught in the third year. Based on the wider application of information technology among the present student population and limited availability of online materials in clinical anatomy, we developed a tailor made web-based clinical anatomy learning resource for the third year medical students. We named it the clinical anatomy e-cases, evaluated the resource usage and extracted analytics to explore if the series of interactive supplementary material can engage the students' attention and maintain interest beyond the classroom setting. We also analysed if the resource contributed to their learning, promoting their understanding of the subject.

Development of the Clinical Anatomy e-Case

The "clinical anatomy e-cases" was developed using initially the freeware CourseLab v2.7 (Websoft, Moscow, Russia) and later within Moodle2.7.2+ (Moodle HQ, Perth, Australia). Since 2011, 22 e-cases have been developed and introduced into the anatomy course. The instructional design of the e-cases was driven by a needs analysis, including reviewing the lab manual to identify potential topics that required attention. These included: relevance of clinical application in general practice at an undergraduate level; utilization of audio-visual resources (angiography, ultrasound) and sectional anatomy tools (e-12 slices, MRI) to enhance interaction and clinical application; introduction to the embryological basis of related anomalies; emphasis on surface landmarks and radiological anatomy topics that are important in physical examination and emergency procedures. Paper-based quizzes from the lab manual were removed and included into the e-cases, allowing more time for the students to get hands on experience during the laboratory sessions.

Pedagogical Sequencing of the Clinical Anatomy e-Case

A typical e-case starts with a clinical presentation and explores the gross, surface and radiological anatomy and the anatomical basis of clinical procedures related to a particular disease condition. Each case was presented as progressive exposure of multiple interactive questions, demanding a right or wrong response or short answer. A hint, reference or brief explanation followed and a formative answer was also provided immediately at the end of each question (Fig. 15.1).

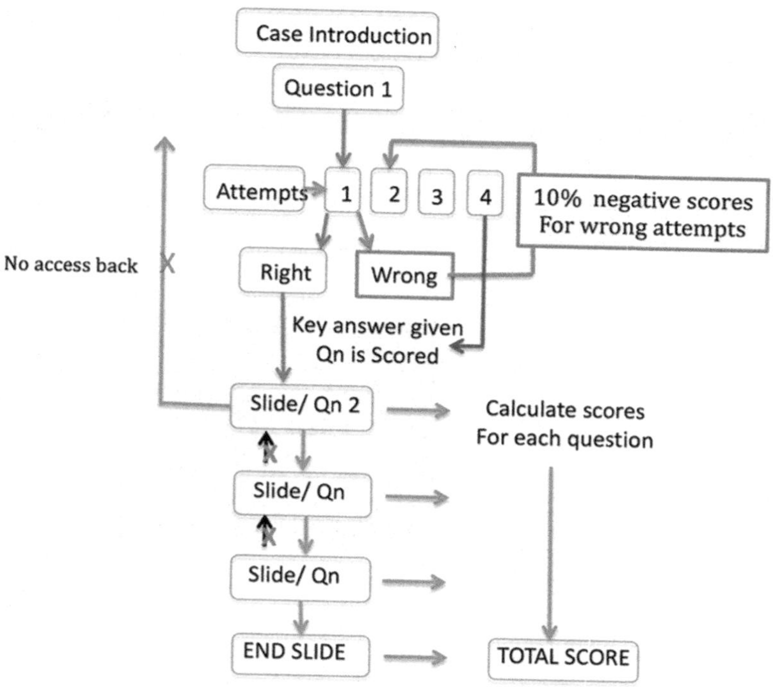

Fig. 15.1 Clinical anatomy e-case design showing the workflow process

Care was taken not to overload each slide with text or questions (Fig. 15.2).

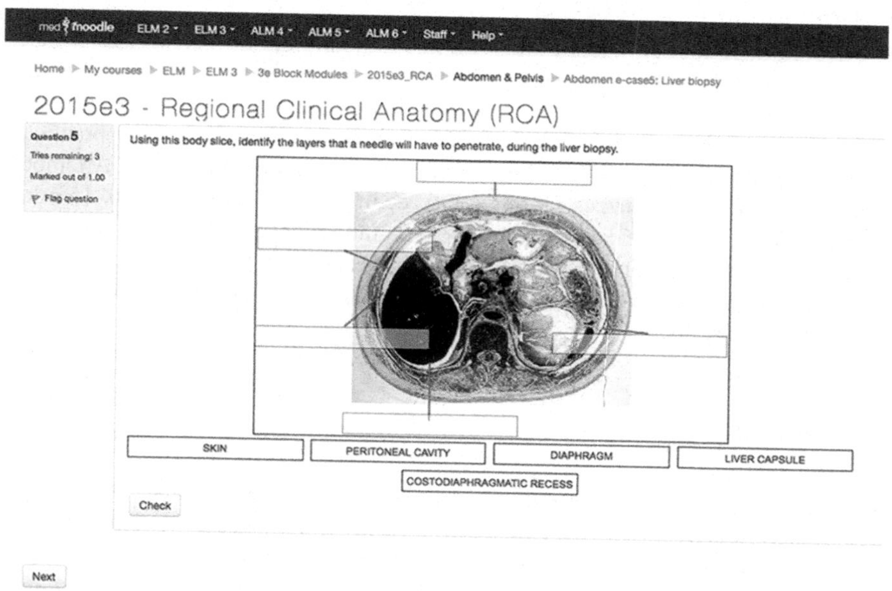

Fig. 15.2 Screen shot from an "abdomen" e-case showing the labelling task on an e-12 plastinated slice, a practice to understand cross sectional anatomy

As anatomy is more visually dependent, animations, movie clips and links to external resources were provided (Fig. 15.3).

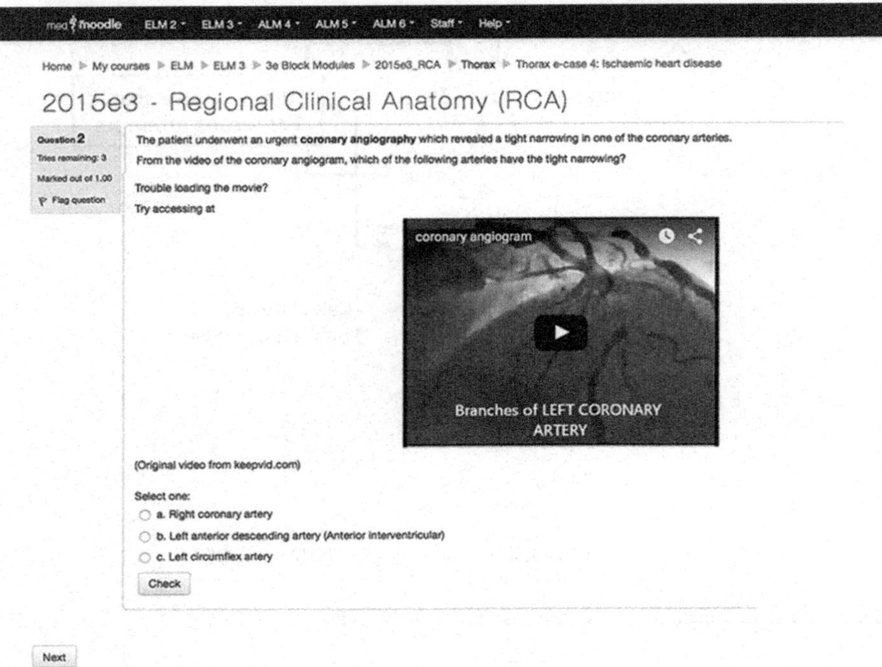

Fig. 15.3 Screen shot from a "Thorax" e-case showing the use of video clips and interactive questions

The number of attempts to answer the questions was limited, but there was no time limit to complete each e-case, which could be accessed any number of times. In the first module head and neck, two such e-cases were distributed per practical session and one e-case in all the other modules (thorax, abdomen, pelvis). Attempts were made to keep the quizzes short—not exceeding a working time of 10–15 min.

Students' performance data and time spent on individual questions was obtained, which helped to understand the difficulty level of each case. Students' participation was optional but students were encouraged to access each case in their own time outside class sessions.

Participants

The project was approved by the University of Otago ethics committee. The e-cases were made available to all third year medical students ($n=282$) as a supplementary resource. Informed consent was sought online from all participants to enable us use their performance data. A small group of students were chosen anonymously, and their formative exam scores were analysed against their e-case usage data.

Datasets and Analytics

Learning analytics based on students' access and performance was extracted from the Moodle LMS at the end of every week's task from 2011 to 2014. The analytics presented here are mainly 2013 data but a comparison with other years is also included (Fig. 15.4). The datasets generated from the activity analytics were:

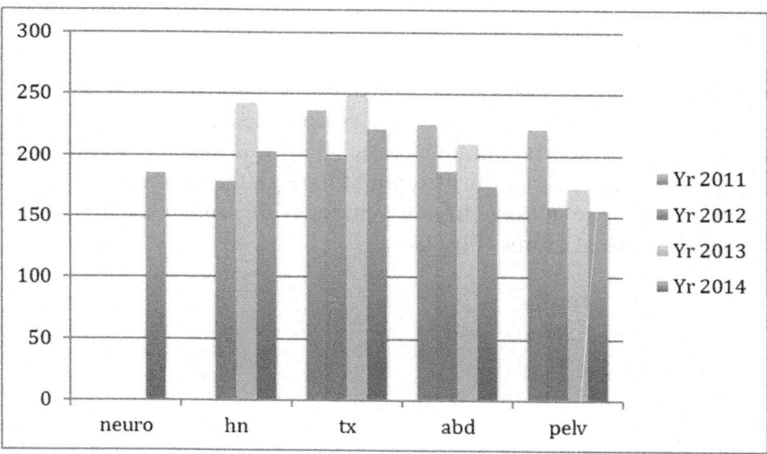

Fig. 15.4 Comparison of students' access to the e-cases at the end of semester across a 4-year period (2011–2014). *X*-axis: e-case modules, *Y*-axis- number of accesses. Note that the "hn" was developed only from 2012 and "neuro" module from 2014

- *Resource access analytics*: number of visits by individual students
- *Repetition analytics*: number and frequency of repeated accesses
- *Duration analytics*: time taken to complete each case (in minutes)
- *Timeline analytics*: access time of the day (across 24 h period) and period of the week (across semester)
- *Score analytics*: a formative score to assess the performance and to compare them with their formative exams.

In addition to the above mentioned, the impact of lectures, exams, holidays, etc. on the rate of resource access is also summarized here.

Results

Variables analysing the core utility of the resource were studied (Table 15.1). The formative scores obtained for individual questions were noted but not analysed in detail.

Table 15.1 Quantitative variables analysed across each module

Module name	Mean no. of accesses ($n=282$)	% of students completed each case	% of students repeated each case	Mean formative scores
Head and Neck	242	88.67	18.81	86.01
Thorax	250	84.70	17.33	84.73
Abdomen	209	86.42	10.01	83.32
Pelvis	173	83.79	6.68	83.70
Mean	228	86.6	14.56	84.72

Resource access analytics (*Fig.* 15.5): 91.5 % of the class group consented to take part in the study. They started using the e-cases from the day of distribution, with an overall 86.8 % completion rate (Table 15.1). There was a steady but insignificant decline in the number of e-case hits from first through the last case of the module, but showed a drastic rise in usage from two to four times in the last few days of the course, towards the final exams (Fig. 15.6).

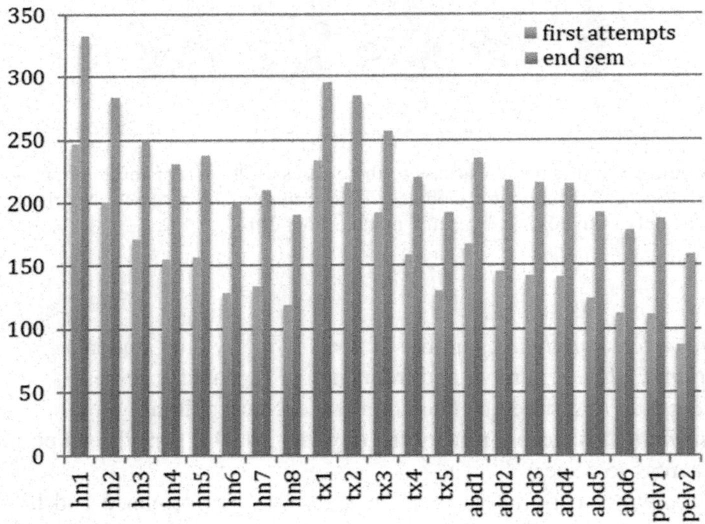

Fig. 15.5 Total number of e-case accesses by Med 3 students ($n=282$). Both single attempts (*blue*) and overall attempts including repetitions at the end of semester (end sem—*red*) are shown. (*hn* head and neck, *tx* thorax, *abd* abdomen, *pelv* pelvis modules). (*X*-axis: e-cases, *Y*-axis: number of students)

Repetition analytics: 14.6 % of students repeated accessing the cases up to five times, some in spite of scoring 100 % in earlier attempts. 78.4 % of repetitions showed statistically significant scores and students completed at shorter time duration than earlier attempts. The number of repetitions did not follow a specific pattern and was not related to the number of questions in the case or their formative scores. The e-cases on the head and neck module were repeated in more numbers than the other modules (Fig. 15.5). Though this seems to reveal interesting patterns, participants were not interviewed to understand underlying repeats on particular content.

Duration of access analytics: Although there were individual variations, the mean time taken to complete the cases was 14 min, which was within the expected time range (10–15 min). There was no significant correlation between the time taken to complete the e-case and students' scores ($R^2=0.08$) or the number of questions in the cases ($R^2=0.003$).

Timeline across semesters: The e-cases were accessed most days of the academic year, exceptions being formative exam days, community events and long vacations (Fig. 15.7). Online visits were found throughout the day, with more visits made after college hours (Fig. 15.8). The resource usage increased steadily towards their final examination (Fig. 15.8).

Formative scores: The average scores obtained in the e-cases were 84.7 % with the maximum being 100 %. There was no statistical relation between the average scores and the completion status or number of times the e-cases was accessed ($R^2=0.007$). Higher than average scores were observed in the head and neck module, which also had more repetitions.

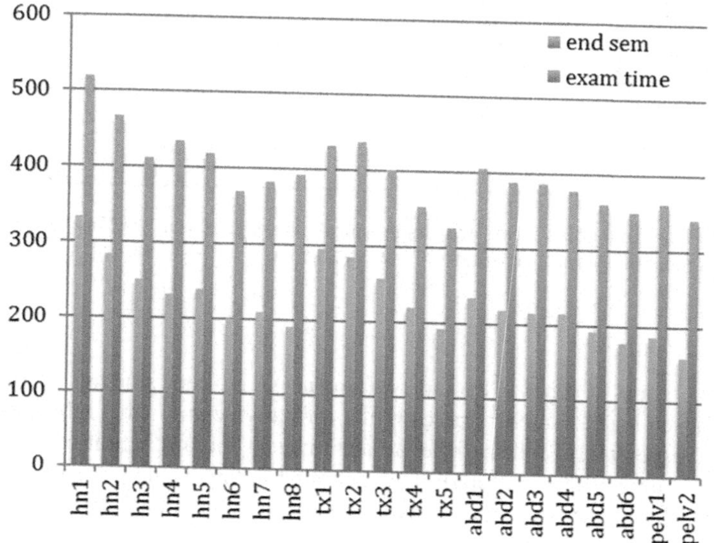

Fig. 15.6 Increased utilization of the resource during examination period (*red*) compared to end of teaching period (*blue*). (*X*-axis: e-cases, *Y*-axis: number of students)

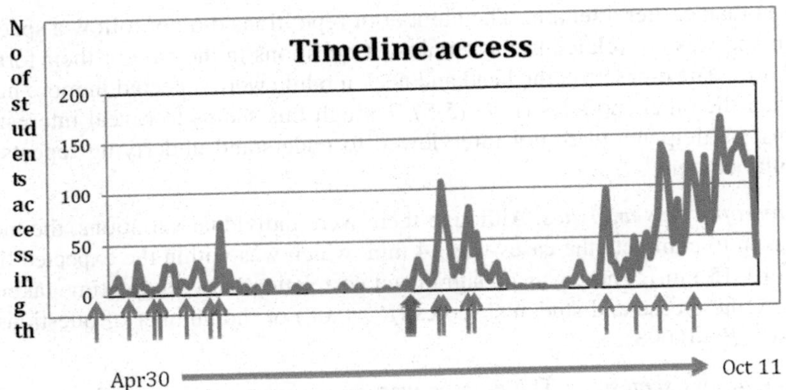

Fig. 15.7 A calendar timeline curve showing the variation in student access to all cases across Aug–Oct 2013. *Y*- axis—number of hits. *X*-axis—calendar (*Blue arrows*—An increase is noticed every time a new e-case is uploaded online.) *Green arrow*—Beginning of semester 2

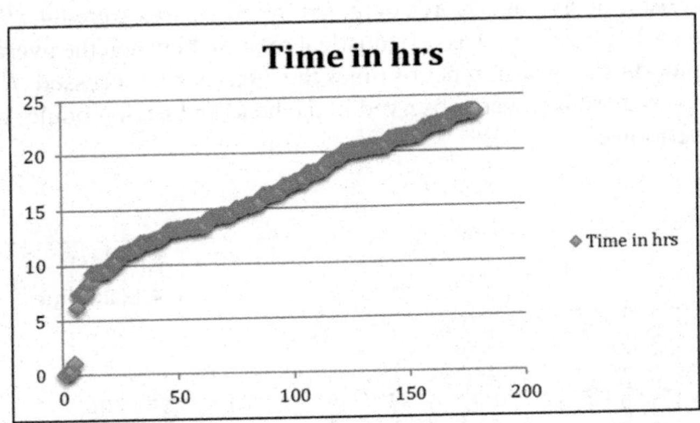

Fig. 15.8 Twenty-four hours access of a single typical e-case (data from head/neck module e-case 1) *X*-axis: number of access, *Y*-axis: time of the day in hours

A small group of top ($n=8$) and bottom ($n=9$) ranking students were anonymously chosen based on their grades in the formative exam, where they scored 98 and 36 %, respectively, and their behaviour towards the utilization of this supplementary resource was monitored. The bottom ranking students from the group showed interest in accessing the e-cases, only towards the final exams, where as the top scorers utilized them regularly. There was also a significant correlation ($p=0.001$) between their formative exam scores and the rate of e-case utilization across modules.

Discussion

Each e-case was developed using similar question types and numbers. Thus, the progressive reduction in number of hits per e-case is due to lack of involvement of some students, not the standards of the resource. Re-accessing the cases irrespective of having a 100 % in their previous attempts shows that the students were interested in using the resource purely for learning. Even during exams, students recognize the importance of accessing these supplementary material, provided the content stimulates interest and absolutely related to their existing curriculum.

In the larger module on head and neck (nine e-cases), the number of completed e-cases reduced steeply (Fig. 15.5), when compared to the abdomen module (six e-cases). This would reflect back to the number of cases distributed per practical session, which was more in head and neck module only. This data prompts us to deliver not more than one case per practical session in the prospective modules.

As students' interest might drop after 15–30 min (Miller & Wolf, 1996) and the social media or procrastination might interfere the online engagement (Kirschner & Karpinski, 2010), we made the e-cases short, with a work time not more than 10–15 min. No attempt was made to provide a time limit and learning strictly at the students' pace was encouraged. The cases that rendered incomplete did not depend on any time of the day or night, which shows that supplementary material usage does not fit into any specific time of the day or day of the year, making them accessible 24/7 (Figs. 15.7 and 15.8).

The quantitative data collected from the students on the case completion status clearly showed that the cases did not overload their regular tasks because of its good integration into study material (Perumal et al., 2012). Comparing the different platforms trialled in our 4-year analysis, Moodle-based clinical anatomy quizzes remain the better choice to learn online clinical anatomy, which overcomes most of the technical issues associated in resource distribution.

The clinical anatomy e-cases were intended to support the current teaching programme, augmenting the already existing standard of anatomy education. This project aimed to examine the overall resource utility, instead of the academic status of students. Impact of the e-case scores on the related topics in main exam was not analysed. As Walsh and Bohn (1990) reports, an increase in test performance could be a positive trait of any educational tool, but it should not be viewed as the sole factor in determining the success or failure of an educational approach. These resources might be effective when combined with conventional class teaching (Petersson, Sinkvist, Wang, & Smedby, 2009; Stanford et al., 1994).

While the study clearly shows students' engagement in interactive online resources, we did not conduct any focus group interviews to confirm the strengths and weaknesses of the resource. Another limitation is that the study did not compare the user analytics to their final exam scores. We also found that the academically good students utilized the resource consistently but the weaker students accessed them only during the examination period. This prompts us to design more strategic educational methods to increase the engagement to those students who arguably need the resources most, which is beyond the scope of this current study.

Conclusion

The reduction in teaching time and an inequality in the teacher–student ratio can be overcome by the use of supplementary resources provided they are tailor made for individual courses focussing on the existing curriculum. The attention meta-data (Wolpers, Najjar, Verbert, & Erik, 2007) collected online revealed that the students spent equal time on all modules of the supplementary resource.

The analysis of students' access pattern showed their great interest in the supplementary material when it remains short, self-paced and not compulsory. Supplementary resources would become beneficial if introduced in the beginning of the semesters when students' engagement appears to be maximal. These factors, coupled with ease of access of the online resource and short duration needed for completion, would make the supplementary learning a 24/7 task. Our future research will focus on the analysis of a large-scale data being collected.

References

Bergman, E. M., Prince, J. K., Drukker, J., Vleuten, C., & Scherpbier, A. (2008). How much anatomy is enough? *Anatomical Sciences Education, 1*, 184–188.

Choi, A., Tamblyn, R., & Stringer, M. (2008). Electronic resources for surgical anatomy. *ANZ Journal of Surgery, 78*, 1082–1091.

Drake, R., Lowrie, D. J., & Prewitt, C. (2002). Survey of gross anatomy, microscopic anatomy, neuroscience and embryology courses in medical school curricula in the United States. *Anatomical Record, 269*, 118–122.

Ganguly, P. (2010). Teaching and learning of anatomy in the 21st century: Direction and the strategies. *The Open Medical Education Journal, 3*, 5–10.

Heylings, D. F. A. (2002). Anatomy 1999-2000: the curriculum, who teaches it and how? *Medical Education, 36*, 702–710.

Johnson, I. P., Palmer, E., Burton, J., & Brockhouse, M. (2013). Online learning resources in Anatomy: What do students think? *Clinical Anatomy, 26*, 556–563.

Jones, D. G. (1997). Reassessing the importance of dissection: A critique and elaboration. *Clinical Anatomy, 10*, 123–127.

Kirschner, P., & Karpinski, A. (2010). Facebook and academic performance. *Computers in Human Behavior, 26*(6), 1237–1245.

Mahmud, W., Hyder, O., Butt, J., & Aftab, A. (2011). Dissection videos do not improve anatomy examination scores. *Anatomical Sciences Education, 4*, 16–21.

McNulty, J. A., Halama, J., & Espiritu, B. (2004). Evaluation of computer- aided instruction in the medical gross anatomy curriculum. *Clinical Anatomy, 17*, 73–78.

Miller, W., & Wolf, F. (1996). Strategies for integrating computer based activities into your educational environment. A practical guide. *Journal of the American Medical Informatics Association, 3*(2), 112–119.

Nayak, S., Ramnarayan, K., & Somayaji, S. N. (2005). Anatomy that must be taught to a medical undergraduate: An interview based survey in an Indian medical school. *Anatomical Record, 285B*, 16–18.

Perumal, V., & Stringer, M. (2012). Clinical anatomy e-cases: A useful supplement to learning. *Clinical Anatomy, 25*(4), 539.

Petersson, H., Sinkvist, D., Wang, C., & Smedby, O. (2009). Web based interactive 3D visualization as a tool for improved anatomy learning. *Anatomical Sciences Education, 2*, 61–68.

Schwier, R., & Seaton, J. (2013). A comparison of participation patterns in selected formal, non-formal, and informal online learning environments. *Canadian Journal of Learning and Technology, 39*(1).

Selman, G., Cooke, M., Selman, M., & Dampier, P. (1998). *The foundations of adult education in Canada* (2nd ed.). Toronto: Thompson Educational.

Smith, C., & Mathias, H. (2010). Medical students' approaches to learning anatomy: Students' experiences and relations to the learning environment. *Clinical Anatomy, 23*, 106–114.

Stanford, W., Erkonen, W. E., Cassell, M. D., Moran, B. D., Easley, G., Carris, R. L., et al. (1994). Evaluation of a computer-based program for teaching cardiac anatomy. *Investigative Radiology, 29*, 248–252.

Turmezei, T. D., Tam, M. D. B. S., & Loughna, S. (2009). A survey of medical students on the impact of a new digital imaging library in the dissection room. *Clinical Anatomy, 22*, 761–769.

Turney, B. W. (2007). Anatomy in a modern medical curriculum. *Annals of the Royal College of Surgeons of England, 89*, 104–107.

Walsh, R. J., & Bohn, R. C. (1990). Computer-assisted instructions: A role in teaching human gross anatomy. *Medical Education, 24*, 499–506.

Wolpers, M., Najjar, J., Verbert, K., & Erik, D. (2007). Tracking actual usage: The attention metadata approach. *Educational Technology & Society, 10*(3), 106–121.

Author Index

B. Kei Daniel (ed.), *Big Data and Learning Analytics in Higher Education*,
DOI 10.1007/978-3-319-06520-5

Subject Index

B. Kei Daniel (ed.), *Big Data and Learning Analytics in Higher Education*,
DOI 10.1007/978-3-319-06520-5